SIR ARTHUR BRYANT was knighted by Queen Elizabeth II in recognition of his outstanding work in the field of English history. In addition to his many books in this area, including *The Turn of the Tide* and *Triumph in the West* with Lord Alanbrooke, Sir Arthur has written celebrated biographies of Samuel Pepys and Charles II. *Makers of England* is the first volume of a proposed trilogy entitled *Atlantic Saga*. The second volume, *The Age of Chivalry*, is also available in a Plume edition.

Sir Arthur Bryant

MAKERS
OF ENGLAND

Formerly titled

THE STORY OF ENGLAND
Makers of the Realm

A PLUME BOOK from
NEW AMERICAN LIBRARY
TIMES MIRROR
New York, Toronto and London

PLUME TRADEMARK REG. U.S. PAT. OFF. AND FOREIGN COUNTRIES
REGISTERED TRADEMARK—MARCA REGISTRADA
HECHO EN CLINTON, MASS., U.S.A.

SIGNET, SIGNET CLASSICS, MENTOR AND PLUME BOOKS
are published *in the United States* by
The New American Library, Inc.,
1301 Avenue of the Americas, New York, New York 10019,
in Canada by The New American Library of Canada Limited,
295 King Street East, Toronto 2, Ontario,
in the United Kingdom by The New English Library Limited,
Barnard's Inn, Holborn, London, E.C. 1, England

First Printing, March, 1970

PRINTED IN THE UNITED STATES OF AMERICA

For
Pierre and Billy Collins
with affection

Dear Country, O how dearly dear
Ought thy remembrance and perpetual band
Be to thy foster child, that from thy hand
Did common breath and nouriture receive?
How brutish is it not to understand
How much to her we owe that all us gave,
That gave unto us all whatever good we have.

Spenser

ACKNOWLEDGMENTS

The author would like to thank Mrs. George Bambridge, the owner of the copyright, and Messrs. Macmillan for permission to quote passages from "Puck's Song" from *Puck of Pook's Hill*, "The King's Task" from *Traffics and Discoveries* and "The Reeds of Runnymede" from *Rudyard Kipling's Verse, Definitive Edition;* also the Oxford University Press for their permission to quote a passage from *Medieval England* by Sir Maurice Powicke, Mrs. Robin Flower for her permission to quote "Pangur Ban," which was published by Messrs. Constable in *Poems and Translations,* by Robin Flower, The Society of Authors as literary representatives of A. E. Housman for their permission to quote from "The Welsh Marches" which was published by Jonathan Cape in *The Collected Poems* of A. E. Housman, Messrs. Eyre & Spottiswoode for quotations from *English Historical Documents, Vol. II* edited by Professor David Douglas, and Messrs. Longmans Green & Co. for quotations from *England Under Henry III* by M. Hennings.

CONTENTS

MAKERS
OF ENGLAND

Trackway and Camp and City lost,
Salt Marsh where now is corn;
Old wars, old peace, old arts that cease
And so was England born!
Kipling

ISLAND HERITAGE

Of the world's three thousand million inhabitants more than a quarter live either in the United States or in the multi-racial group of nations known as the Commonwealth. Both at one time formed part of the ocean empire which grew out of the little island kingdom of England which three and a half centuries ago, through a union of the English and Scottish crowns, became Great Britain.

For this reason the history of England is important. Throughout a third of the earth's habitable surface the forms of government and law which men practise are based on forms of government and law evolved in England before the discovery of the ocean trade routes and the colonisation of North America. This is true not only of English-speaking countries like the United States, Canada, and Australia, partly or principally inhabited by men of British blood, but of Asian and African countries like India, Pakistan, Ceylon, and Nigeria whose peoples are of different colour, race, social habits, and religion to those of the small Atlantic island whose governing institutions they have adopted.

All these peoples—as well as others still in process of acquiring their unity and sovereign independence—are members not only of their own separate nations but of a world-wide union which English political ideals created. Those which have reached full nationhood enjoy a form of government to which England first introduced the modern world. It is one in which every man and woman, regardless of race, has the right to help in electing the parliament that makes his laws and controls his government. In every one of these countries there is a growing, if still incomplete, belief that every man should be allowed to worship God as he pleases, to express his views on his rulers without fear, and be free from imprisonment unless he has been condemned by its courts for breaking laws passed or sanctioned by its parliament.

In all, men feel that violence is wrong and that disputes should be settled by peaceful debate and process of law.

Nor does the living influence of English history end with the Commonwealth. Even the French Revolution, with all its immeasurable consequences for mankind, stemmed, not from France's history alone, but also from England's. The great Gallic philosophers who prepared the way for it drew their inspiration, not from the authoritarian monarchy of Louis XIV and XV, but from the libertarian and parliamentary kingdom of Locke and Hampden. The richest and most powerful nation in the world today is the United States of America. Though probably not more than half its people have British blood, it began its existence as a union of English colonies, whose people, being English, insisted on governing themselves in their own way instead of being ruled by a far-away king and parliament over whom they had no control. They founded, after fighting England for their freedom, a new nation based on English ideas of liberty, justice, and self-government, and dedicated to the belief "that all men are created equal; that they are endowed by their Creator with certain inalienable rights; that among these are life, liberty and the pursuit of happiness; that to secure these rights governments are instituted among men, deriving their just powers from the consent of the governed."

The man who wrote these words—among the most important ever written—was an English colonist of English descent who took his life in his hands, because, having English beliefs, he held that freedom was more important even than loyalty to England's rulers. That, as this book may show, was a very English thing to have done. The people of the nation he helped to found, though drawn from every European land, speak the English language, use forms of law and self-government that are English in origin, and honour the same ideals of justice, truth, and gentleness as Englishmen.

The geographical centre of this world-wide grouping of mankind, based on political and legal ideas and forms derived from England is the Atlantic. The English-speaking nations living on either side of that ocean and at the end of the global sea terminals that radiate from it are its heart. On their unity and readiness to defend the libertarian ideals, the existence of free institutions in the world mainly depends. Because of this I have

called the trilogy of which this book is the start *Atlantic Saga*
and the present volume, *Makers of England*. For though Scotsmen and Irishmen played almost as great a part as Englishmen
in founding the second British Empire that became the Commonwealth, those who in the seventeenth century founded the
first that became the United States were "mere English." The
men who created in the transatlantic wilderness the hard core
of earth's greatest nation named their chief settlement New
England. It was only later, when New England had grown into
New World and Scotsmen and Irishmen were pouring through
the door Englishmen had opened, that another settlement beyond the oceans was named New Britain.

It was in the England of Elizabeth that the earliest colonisers
of North America were born. They called their first colony Vir-
ginia after her. The great queen—the last English sovereign to
reign before the union of the crowns of England and Scotland—
belongs as much to American history as Britain. Without her
there would have been neither a United States nor a British
Empire. Her reign prepared the way, not only for Cook and
Wilberforce, but for Washington and Lincoln. She was queen,
not of Britain, but of England, and, like her subjects, Shakespeare and Cecil, Drake and Raleigh, was the product of English
history. And the two mighty Anglo-Saxon communities which
stem from her inheritance—one governed from Washington, the
other centered on Westminster and ruled from London, Ot-
tawa, Canberra, Wellington, and Salisbury—are not British-
speaking, but English-speaking communities. Indeed, of the
two, the United States is the more exclusively English-speaking.

Yet my story would be as incomplete without the history of
the three indomitable little nations—Scotland, Wales, and Ireland—which once fought against England and later became
joined with her under the name of Great Britain. Theirs was
the challenge that helped to make England, just as England's
was the challenge that helped to make them. And I have sought
to show how her history and theirs—and that of the vaster
ocean nations that sprang from it—grew itself out of the Christian heritage of western Europe. For the secret of England's
history is that she has never for long been self-contained. She
has received ideas and men, or sent them out to others. She
has been invaded or been the invader.

That story—of an island alchemy that has changed human

history—began eight thousand years ago when the ocean broke through the isthmus joining an Atlantic peninsula to the world's main land-space. To the flood of salt water that created the Straits of Dover has been due the destiny of England—the kingdom which grew up in the richest part of the island so formed. It explains why her people, secure behind their sea-defences, were able to develop a form of government in which the last word rested, not with centralised authority, but with public opinion. It explains too why later, whenever a conqueror overran Europe, Britain was able, first to defy him and then, by closing the sea-ways round him, to rally the forces of human freedom against him. Philip of Spain, Louis XIV, Napoleon, Kaiser William, and Hitler all met in England the rock on which their hopes foundered.

Yet the moat of stormy, dangerous, tidal water dividing Britain from the mainland is only twenty miles wide at its narrowest and so shallow that, if St. Paul's cathedral were sunk at the deepest point, its golden cross and ball would still rise above the waves. Of the three land-linked continents to which she is all but joined, Europe is twenty-four times her size, and Asia and Africa each more than a hundred times. Only the Royal Navy's ceaseless vigilance and the fierceness of the Channel tides and gales kept that ditch inviolable throughout modern historical times.

Yet England's immunity from invasion, immense though its consequences, is comparatively recent. It is only nine centuries since a foreign army last conquered her. And in the scale of history nine hundred years is not long. In the century before that in which Winston Churchill was born Richard Cromwell, who governed England for a short time in the mid-seventeenth century, was still alive. A century before his birth men were living who had been born during the Hundred Years War. And when that conflict began old men could remember Henry III, who was the great-grandson of Matilda, the granddaughter of William the Conqueror.

Though Britain has been an island geographically for eight thousand years, she has been one strategically for less than a thousand. She was made the first by Providence; she only became the second through her people's efforts. No island of comparable wealth was so easy to invade; none more tempting to invaders. The longest part of her history was of repeated inva-

sion. The Iberian and Windmill Hill neolithic men, the Bronze
Age pastoral warriors, the Celts and Romans, the Jutes, Angles
and Saxons, the Danes, Norwegians and Normans, all in turn
invaded her, bringing death, enslavement and destruction. A
short voyage up her rivers could carry their war-boats to her
heart. Her four-thousand-mile coastline was indefensible by a
small population fighting on land. It could only be defended
by sea. It took the British people thousands of years to discover
this truth, and even longer to apply it.

It was not the island's first inhabitants—solitary, shambling,
unaspiring, sheltering among the rocks of the Cheddar Gorge
or Gower peninsula—who set the course of her history. It was
those who, reaching the ocean's shores, put out in frail boats
across uncharted seas. The trend of history was for the world's
growing population to move in search of food from the steppes
of central Asia—the "heartland" of the human race—towards
the ocean. The ancestors of the British peoples, as later of those
who crossed the oceans from Britain to found new nations, were
seamen and pioneers: bearers of new ideals and new tech-
niques. Halted by the vast ocean beyond her, they made the
island their home. And, as her southern and eastern lowlands
were the easiest to conquer and cultivate, each invader tended
to settle there, driving earlier comers into the mountains, bogs,
and mists of the West, where—since these offered little to tempt
conquerors—they survived.

The colonisers of Britain were confronted by a wet, wind-
swept northern island. Even when they had won the land,
they had to win a tougher and longer battle against Nature.
They had to fell dense forests, covering at first the entire lowlands, clear and drain swampy river valleys and break up
thick cold clays with implements the making of which called
for all their skill and ingenuity. Theirs was not a land where
men could be both comfortable and idle. They could only survive with stoutly built houses, warm clothing and good food
and drink.

For these they had to work in an ocean climate. Its constant
changes forced them to farm as sailors navigate, with eyes for
ever cocked at the sky, ready to adapt themselves to its unpredictable vagaries. The national distrust for long-term plan-
ning and the capacity for adaptation may have arisen from
this. In war—an activity in which the expected rarely happens

—the English, though unprepared for conflicts planned by others, have usually emerged victorious.

Yet though it offered them much to master, their island climate was never too harsh to endure. It did not, like that of Labrador or Greenland, break men's hearts. It steeled, not ossified, stamina and character. To the challenge of environment was added the blessing of the "golden mean." The age-long struggle with wind, rain, and changing temperature made the English not only workers but optimists; their weather at its worst changes soon for the better, and its harshest wind blows someone good. Gusty and invigorating, it is tempered by a warm ocean stream from the southwest that spares the island continental winters. The soil, when cultivated with regard to local conditions, is more productive than almost any in the world. Infinitely varied, it is nearly all fertile. It bred vigorous, hardy and adaptable plants, beasts and men. Britain's domestic animals—Angus and Ayrshire, Shorthorn and Hereford, Hampshire and Ryeland—became household words wherever men farm. They have been sent, generation after generation, to restock other lands.

Equally beneficial was the survival of racial minorities, defying and intermarrying with the predominant majority. Long skull and broad, short build and tall, dark pigmentation and blonde, did persistently mingle; so have the instincts and memories of a score of races. Such intermixture in so small an island made its people many-sided and versatile. Left to themselves the Anglo-Saxons of a thousand years ago—florid, large-limbed, blue-eyed, phlegmatic—might have settled down into a sluggish complacency. But they were harried by Danes and Norsemen and later conquered by the clear-minded, ruthless Normans. In face of these powerful minorities they had to struggle for centuries to retain their customs, institutions and language. And beyond their well-ploughed shires, and even in the hills, marshes and woodlands in their midst, lurked the pre-Saxon inhabitants of the island—fierce red-haired Celts and the little dark Neolithic and Bronze Age peoples with their rugged irregular features, loose mouths and deep-set eyes. They, too, constituted a perpetual challenge to the dominant majority, their Highland and Cymric raids and the alluring, alien ways of their young men and maidens bringing deeper and more mysterious strains into the blood of the honest, ox-like Saxons.

The island was full of unexpected influences—Wendish customs among the sandy Surrey gravels beside the Thames at Wandsworth, Scandinavian usages in the Chilterns, ancient pre-Roman and even pre-Celtic settlements in hollows on the lonely Wiltshire and Dorset downs. And all along the Marches of the Celtic West and North ran the incessant, challenging warfare of the races:

> When Severn down to Buildwas ran
> Coloured with the death of man,
> Couched upon her brother's grave
> The Saxon got me on the slave . . .
> In my heart it has not died,
> The war that sleeps on Severn side;
> They cease not fighting, east and west,
> On the marches of my breast.[1]

It is probably this that has accounted for the intermixture in the British blood of the matter-of-fact with the poetic; of love of home with the itch to adventure; of business aptitude with fantasy, speculation and idealism. English literature is full of examples of this conflict in the national make-up; of books like *Alice in Wonderland* written by a professor of mathematics, or *Songs of a Shropshire Lad* by a clerk in the Patent Office who became a master of Latin philology. "Lord," prayed the commander of the royalist foot at Edgehill, "Thou knowest how busy I shall be this day; if I forget Thee, do not Thou forget me. March on, boys!" So too Cromwell, on the other side, bade his men trust in God and keep their powder dry. The British—and more particularly the English in whom the mingling of the races was most marked—have often been charged with hypocrisy, with serving both God and Mammon, with trying to eat their cake and have it. Since they have so many sides to their nature, there has been truth in the charge; yet, in a world in which spirit and matter are inextricably mingled, it has not served them badly. Their greatest poet wrote that men were such stuff as dreams are made on, yet contrived by sound business methods to make a competence in real property.

This clash of racial characteristics and cultures may have accounted, too, for the extraordinary range of English genius:

[1] A. E. Housman, *A Shropshire Lad*. Grant Richards, 42.

in politics, agriculture and commerce, in literature and the arts, in craftsmanship, war, adventure, and colonisation. So much diversity among neighbours was a constant stimulus and education. "No nation," wrote Emerson, "was ever so rich in able men." Shakespeare and Milton, Elizabeth and Cromwell, Chatham and Churchill, Drake, Nelson, Marlborough and Wellington, Wren and Purcell, Newton and Darwin, the inventor of the steam-engine, and the discoverers of the anaesthetic, electricity and the atom, were a remarkable harvest for one small island. And Washington, Jefferson, Lee and Lincoln were of the same argumentative versatile stock.

Yet England was fortunate, too, in that the invasions which gave her so mixed and challenging an ancestry were separated by long periods. This enabled each new influence to be digested and saved the island from anarchy. The sea-barrier, even before the islanders learnt to hold it, proved a better protection than a land frontier. And after the Norman Conquest the growing use by her kings of the sea for defence gave her almost complete freedom from armed invasion. They made the waters around her a moat "against infection and the hand of war." The only invaders who settled in Britain thereafter were refugees flying to her shores from persecution: Flemings in the fourteenth and sixteenth centuries, Huguenots in the seventeenth century, Jews in the eighteenth, nineteenth, and twentieth centuries. The racial challenge became a purely internal one: of Norman, Saxon and Celt, Englishman, Scotsman, Welshman and Irishman, contending and competing with one another.

This, and the strong rule of her kings—Norman, Plantagenet and Tudor—gave England, for all its diversity, an inherent unity. Beneath immense differences of speech, outlook and custom there grew up, under protection of the Common Law within and the patrolled seas without, first an English, and later a British identity. This cohesion existed side by side with the most strongly held and freely expressed differences of opinion. But it never failed to unite the islanders when any major threat arose from outside.

Even more striking than England's unity has been the freedom of individual choice on which it has been based. Because the Channel lay between her and the Continent, her people were able to develop a form of government in which power, instead of being centralised in a few hands, was distributed in many. Not being threatened across a land frontier, they had no need to entrust their rulers with standing military forces or despotic rights over private liberties. Authority normally was exercised only after those subject to it had had an opportunity to make their views known. From the Saxon Witenagemot to the nineteenth-century Parliament, from the village hustings and manor court to the trade union lodge and parish council, there was nearly always some working machinery in England by which those in authority could test the opinion of those over whom authority had to be exercised. Government was conducted subject to the right of the governed to criticise and, within lawful limits, to oppose. "His Majesty's Opposition" is the most characteristic and certainly the most original of English contributions to politics; the Leader of the Opposition is today even paid by the State. However inefficient in the short run, such a system proved efficient in the long, because, by delegating responsibility, it trained men for it. It is liberty alone, wrote Gladstone, that fits men for liberty.

For, like the Americans after them, the English regarded the person—even if at first only the privileged person—as more important than any abstract ideal. The State, they felt, existed more for the individual than the individual for the State. Their history was a struggle for the freedom of individuals. It was fought for at every stage of their developing consciousness, from the barons' stand for Magna Carta to the Tolpuddle martyrs paying with transportation for the rural worker's right to combine against his employer.

England's rulers often contended against this national distaste for authority. King John tried to repress his barons, Mary Tudor the Protestants, King Charles his unruly parliaments. The eighteenth-century landowners sought to extinguish the independent cultivators of the common-field village and were themselves later overthrown by the yeomen who turned to industry. They denied, too, to the colonists of North America the right of self-determination and, by doing so, created a more powerful champion of that principle than themselves. And the nineteenth-century manufacturers tried to repress the trade unions of their rough, liberty-loving factory-hands. Dr. Johnson expressed the eternal English answer to all such attempts. "From this neglect of subordination I do not deny that some inconveniences may from time to time proceed . . . But good and evil will grow up in this world together; and they who complain, in peace, of the insolence of the populace, must remember that their insolence in peace is bravery in war."

Loving private liberty, yet finding that it could not exist without public order, the English devoted themselves to making the two compatible. Freedom within a framework of discipline became their ideal. They achieved it through the sovereignty of law. "All our struggles for liberty," wrote Disraeli, "smack of law." And by law the English meant an enforceable compact between themselves and their rulers, deriving not from unilaterally imposed force, but from assent freely given. Both they and their American descendants constituted such law, rather than the Executive, their ultimate sovereign.

This respect for law gradually made the English people, who would otherwise have been one of the most difficult to govern, one of the easiest: easy, that is, so long as they were governed lawfully. It became habitual to them to obey the law and see it enforced. Their inter-racial experience in a small island left them with a profound distrust of violence. "Force is not a remedy," declared John Bright: "All force," wrote the seventeenth-century Lord Halifax, "is a kind of foul play." From this sprang the curious tolerance of a fighting people with strong convictions for minority opinions, non-conformity and eccentricity. No other community has ever so richly rewarded its critics or been so indulgent to those whom it terms conscientious objectors.

Compromise, give-and-take, live-and-let-live became a national habit. The freedom of the Press—a forbearance unnatural in any Government—was an English invention; so was the secret ballot which enabled a man to record an unpopular vote without danger to himself. The English, as self-opinionated as any people in the world, mastered the lesson that they could only possess liberty by allowing it to others, enjoy the propagation of their own views by listening patiently to their neighbours'. "Opinion in good men," wrote one of their poets, "is but knowledge in the making." "I beseech you, in the bowels of Christ," Cromwell implored the religious dogmatists of his time, "think it possible you may be mistaken!"

This hard-learnt toleration, and all the tolerated eccentricity that sprang from it, rested in the last resort on the Christian belief in the sanctity of the individual. It stemmed from the creed of personal responsibility to which first the Celts of Wales, Ireland and Scotland, and then the Anglo-Saxons of England, were won by the great Celtic and Latin missionaries of the fifth, sixth, and seventh centuries. Without that creed neither England's history nor her influence on the world can be understood. At its core lay the thesis that every man, being free to choose between good and evil, was a soul of equal value in the eyes of God. It was this that gave rise to an Englishman's saying in the English revolution of the seventeenth century that "the poorest he in England hath a life to live as the greatest he."

From Sidney passing the cup to the dying soldier to Oates walking into the blizzard to save his friends, from Coeur-de-Lion forgiving the archer who shot him to the soldiers of the Line standing motionless on the deck of the sinking *Birkenhead* while the women and children were lowered to the boats, the common denominator of the nation's idealism remained constant. It was expressed in the fourteenth-century *Piers Plowman,* in the seventeenth-century *Pilgrim's Progress,* and in the nineteenth-century *Christmas Carol.* Langland, Bunyan, and Dickens spoke with the same voice. Whenever England was false to that voice she was false to herself. The English, Disraeli said, have not committed fewer blunders than others, but, being free to criticise their rulers according to individual conscience, have shown themselves as a people more sensible of their errors. In the end it has usually been the English themselves who have made amends for their injuries to others and reformed the abuses they had perpetrated. "I choose the people under whom we suffered forty years ago," declared General Smuts in 1940, "but who, when we were at their mercy, treated us as a Christian people!"

"By this sacredness of individuals," wrote Emerson, "the English have in seven hundred years evolved the principles of freedom." In this volume, which carries their story to Edward I's reign, I have tried to show how they began to do so. It relates how the nation was first made, how its peoples—the descendants of England's many invaders and the ancestors of so many Americans, Canadians, Australians, New Zealanders, South Africans, and Rhodesians—were blended into one, and how its basic institutions were created. The Monarchy, Church and Common Law, the Shire, Hundred and Parish, the Gentry, Yeomanry and the Great Council that became Parliament, were all formed in this period. My second volume, *The Island Kingdoms,* will open with the winning of Scotland's Independence and end with the union of the English and Scottish crowns. Its theme is how the islanders, having vainly attempted to found an empire in Europe, turned outwards to the ocean and found the key to a new destiny for themselves and others. In my final volume, *The Ocean Nations,* I shall be tracing the evolution of English ideas and practice, not only in Britain, but in the ocean nations that sprang from it.

I have written for both young and old, for those who know a little of England's past and for those who know scarcely anything at all. My aim has been to set down in a small compass the essential things a man or boy should know who wants to understand her history. I have taken as little for granted as possible, but have told the story, so far as my scale admits, as it unfolded itself to the men and women of the time. Throughout I have tried to picture the outward form of their lives; to show how they lived and what their country looked like: to recall the warmth and actuality of an existence once as real as ours. Private lives have been as much grist to my mill as public, and the hearth as the throne. Chaucer's Canterbury pilgrims and Christian setting out with his burden have been seen as part of the same pilgrimage as Drake circumnavigating the globe or Gladstone touring Midlothian.

I am very conscious of my presumption. The writing of history is now so specialised and the volume of study available for every period so vast, that to tell the story of England adequately in a single volume, or even in three short ones, has become a task beyond the powers of even the boldest historian. No life is long enough to compass all the reading required for its foundation, let alone to distil and reduce to literary form such an immense and often conflicting volume of learning. Yet "the best is the enemy of the good"; and, in an age in which society depends on the knowledge and opinion of the many, historians must try to present their country's past in a form capable of reaching those who have to shape its present. My book makes no claim to originality; it merely tells a familiar tale in a new way. It is not a work of scholarship, but only a collation of the scholarship of others, to whom my debt is incalculable.

Every generation needs its popular history written in a way it can understand. The great classic historians of the eighteenth and nineteenth centuries wrote the history of England for their time. J. R. Green wrote it for our grandfathers', and G. M. Trevelyan for our fathers'. Trying to write it for mine, I have presented it in a new form: not one that equals theirs, for that would be far beyond me, but a different one. My history contains fewer names, battles, political events, and Acts of Parliament, but dwells longer on certain deeds and words that stirred the hearts of Englishmen and awoke their imagination. For history, as a great living Anglo-American poet has written,

> "is a pattern
> of timeless moments."

Paulinus and Aidan preaching to the Northumbrians; the Saxon thanes dying to the last man at Maldon and the house-carls in the stricken ring at Senlac; Becket towering above his murderers in the darkened cathedral, and the jingling Canterbury pilgrims riding through the Kentish fields "the holy blissful martyr for to seek"; Robin Hood in the greenwood, and the "grey goose feather" falling like hail at Crécy and Agincourt; the staplers with their wool-packs, and the church towers among the limestone wolds and dales; such were the stuff out of which England's banner in time was woven.

Chapter One

THE FIRST INVADERS

Grey recumbent tombs of the dead in desert places,
  Standing stones on the vacant, wine-red moor,
Hills of sheep and the howes of the silent vanished races,
  And winds, austere and pure.
                    R. L. Stevenson

In his "Stones of Venice," John Ruskin pictured Europe seen by a swallow flying from the south. He painted the Mediterranean, a blue lake with ancient promontories and islands lying like pieces of golden pavement in the sun. Then gradually the orient colours changed to a belt of rainy green, where the poplar valleys of France, the pastures of Switzerland, and the dark forests of the Danube and Carpathians stretched from the Loire to the Volga, "seen through clefts in grey . . . swirls of rain-cloud and flaky veils of the mist of the brooks, spreading low along the pasture lands. And then, farther north, to see the earth heave into mighty masses of leaden rock and heathy moor, bordering with a broad waste of gloomy purple that belt of field and wood, and splintering into irregular and grisly islands amidst the northern seas, beaten by storm, and chilled by ice-drift, and tormented by furious pulses of contending tide, until the roots of the last forests fail from among the hill ravines, and the hunger of the north wind bites their peaks into barrenness; and, at last, the wall of ice, durable like iron, sets, death-like, its white teeth against us out of the polar twilight."

It is in these northern seas that Britain's history has been made. Her isles lie in the centre of a vast semi-circle of ocean coast stretching from the North Cape of Norway to Finisterre in Spain. The largest—that nearest Europe—is only six hundred miles long and from three hundred to a hundred miles broad. Its southern part is called England, its mountainous northern and western projections Scotland and Wales. Another island, Ireland, less than half its size, lies fifty miles to the west, verdant, windswept and drenched by perpetual Atlantic clouds.

On the world's map these islands are only a pin-point off the unbroken land-space of Europe, Asia and Africa. They look at first as though they belong to it. And before they became islands eight or nine thousand years ago, they did. At that time the present English and Irish Channels were the mouths of continental rivers emptying into the Atlantic, while the Thames was a tributary of the Rhine, flowing northwards to the Arctic across plains now covered by the North Sea.

Yet historical time only began about five thousand years ago when Britain was already an island. It had no reality until man began to measure it, and, by ploughing and sowing, to plan in one season for another. Before that he was only a hunting and hunted animal, living from hour to hour on what he could gather or snare. He knew no clock, map or calendar. All he inherited from yesterday were his instincts; all he contributed to tomorrow were children like himself to re-live the life of the cave, the chase and the kill. For over half a million years, as we measure them, man has lived on the earth and competed with its other creatures for existence. His earliest traces in Britain are some bones found in a Sussex gravel-pit at Piltdown which archaeologists now think to be about forty thousand years old, and some others at Swanscombe in Kent which they date back a further hundred-and-fifty thousand years. In warmer regions like Africa there is evidence of his existence much earlier.

Yet even this vast stretch of time is insignificant beside the age of the world itself. If an ordinary human lifetime of seventy years is taken as the measure of the latter, mankind has come into being only in the last two or three weeks, and historical man—from Abraham to Eisenhower—in the last few hours. Scientists, studying the rocks, believe that the earliest of them were made at least two thousand million, and possibly four thousand million years ago.

"In the beginning," the Bible tells us, "God created the

heaven and the earth. And the earth was without form, and void. . . . And God said, Let the waters under the heaven be gathered into one place and let the dry land appear." This is the language of poetry, a glimpse of a vast landscape revealed by a flash of lightning. The shape of our home on the globe's circumference has been created during unmeasured immensities of time by the gradual rise and fall of its crust which a modern scholar has likened to breathing.[1] Ancient sea-floors, land-surfaces and lake bottoms, and the lavas of long-extinct volcanoes, lie under our feet in layers left by convulsions divided from one another by hundreds of millions of years.

The rocks of Britain have a different past from those of Europe. They were made by the ocean that stretches to the west of her and today surrounds her. Long before she was joined to Europe she belonged to another continent called by archaeologists Atlantis which embraced North America and the North Atlantic. Her western mountains are all that remain of the eastern peaks of the poets' drowned land of "Lyonesse." She and her isles were formed in the Atlantic bed. She arose, as the song has it, "at Heaven's command from out the azure main."

No other land of the same size is so rich in geological experience and, as a result, in variety of scenery, soils and mineral deposits. At one time—indeed many times—part of Britain's surface was the ocean's floor, at another a burning desert of rock, at another an enormous lake surrounded by forests haunted by vast, predatory monsters and, later, by elephants and hippopotami. The white chalk downs which gave her first recorded name, Albion, were made by the seas of the Cretaceous Age a hundred million years ago; the coloured limestones of her loveliest buildings by those of the Jurassic Age before it. The veins of tin and copper which drew her earliest invaders were formed by molten magma from submarine volcanoes. The slates which roof her industrial towns were made out of alluvial mud lying on the ocean's bed; the coals, which provide her manufacturing power, out of decomposing tropical jungle. From their seams, it has been said, we draw the heat and energy of the primeval sun.

[1] Jacquetta Hawkes, *A Land*, 22.
"The bosom of the landscape lifts and falls
With its own leaden tide."

It is the age of her rocks—once mountain ranges long crumbled
away to form the loams of her cornfields—that makes Britain
such a gentle, well-covered and domesticated-looking land. Her
history is largely the story of how men learnt to turn that
geological wealth into human wealth: to till her soil, tame her
beasts, control her rivers and tides, shape her rocks, minerals
and timber into useful and beautiful forms, and, in doing so,
live with one another in justice, peace and mutual profit. It
has been a slow, gradual process with many setbacks and
difficulties. The earliest was to survive in such a land at all.
During the comparatively recent period during which man has
existed, Britain has four times been wholly or partly enveloped
in ice. Each of these arctic visitations lasted for an immense age
and either drove man out of Britain altogether or forced him to
live in caves like those in the Cheddar Gorge or Creswell in
Derbyshire. It was only as the ice retreated for the last time
between ten and twenty thousand years ago that, first plants
and trees, then reindeer and grazing animals, and then men,
following and hunting them, were able to make a permanent
home on our soil.

Even then it must have been a hard country to live in. It was
still bitterly cold and, as the ice receded, it left behind a
gloomy landscape of bogs, meres and barren moors, which later
became covered with pines. We know little of the men who
braved it except that they survived and handed down the torch
of life. They cannot have been many—probably only a few
hundred families in the whole island. Their sole food was roots
and berries and such wild creatures as they could trap or har-
poon. Yet from the sites of their camping-places and the relics
in their caves we can tell that they fashioned minute tools and
weapons of flint and bone, that they trained dogs to aid them
in hunting, and that sometimes, following an instinct that distinguished them from other creatures, they drew on the walls
of their caves the likenesses of men and animals. In all other
ways man's life in the Stone Age must have been that of the
beasts. His days were spent in hunting and being hunted, with
fear of hunger and destruction never far from his mind. Some of
his fears still haunt us in dreams: of dark, terrifying forests, of
pursuit by monsters, of snakes and reptiles writhing in the night.
Some of his joys, too, have come down to us; the thrill of the
chase, of being alive on a sunny morning, of plunging into

cold water, of running, climbing and wrestling. He left us two of the great stand-bys of human existence: fire, with which he learnt to cook and warm himself, and the art of communicating with his fellows by sound that we call speech.

Let us recapture Ruskin's aerial vision and see Britain, set in her frame of wide, stormy ocean, as she would have appeared about five thousand years ago—three or four thousand years, that is, after she became an island. From a distance her shape would seem much as today, though as we approached nearer we should notice differences. Along her eastern coast are stretches of cliff and low-lying land which have since vanished under the sea; other areas like the Fens and Romney Marsh, which now are farming land, still lie under the water. Yet the main coast-line, the cliffs, the winding course of the rivers, the hills and mountains are those we know. Equally familiar seem the passing sea-clouds and mists.

There the resemblance ends. The appearance of the country-side is so different as to be unrecognisable. Looking down we can discover no towns, villages, buildings, fields or roads. In-stead, the entire lowland is covered by forest—mostly of gloomy conifers which have spread over the country after the retreat of the ice; though, with the milder oceanic winters since Britain's separation from the continent, these are giving place in the south to the deciduous green of oak, elm, hazel, ash, lime and alder. The valleys are flooded on either side of the rivers, the sides of the hills thick with impenetrable vegetation. As we come nearer still we can see that the damp woods are alive with game, like the jungles of the east today: wild boars and oxen, elk and deer, and in the hills wolves, lynx and bears, eagles and ravens. Everywhere nature is untrammelled. Only man seems missing.

Yet, if we look closely, we shall find him. Here and there, sleeping like beasts on the earthen floors of caves and pits in the hills, and in huts and wind-breaks made of sods and branches, are little family-groups of upright, two-legged creatures with half-naked, skin-clad bodies. They still exist, as their an-cestors have done for thousands of years, by seeking roots, berries, eggs and shell-fish, and by trapping and slaying wild animals with flint hand-axes and bone and flint-tipped spears and harpoons. Such men, like the beasts, live for the hour, their one end today's meal, their unsleeping instinct survival. Each generation repeats the pattern of that before; there seems no progress, for there is no change.

Yet change is on its way: change of immense significance. And, as we look south-eastwards beyond the Alps and into the Mediterranean sunlight, we can see at the other side of that sea, and in bright islands in its eastern half, communities of men living lives very different from those of the sparse, animal-like families dotted about the downs and rocks of misty Britain. In Mesopotamia and Syria, in Anatolia and on the Persian uplands, and in the green Nile valley, and, still further away, in India and China, men are grouped, not merely in families, but in tribes, cities and even nations. For here, in the sunshine, man has made the greatest step in his history. He has mastered the arts of digging, tilling and planting the soil—of sowing in winter and reaping in summer. These, by assuring him of tomorrow's food, have secured him the blessing we name home. They have given him a place he can call his own, make better and hand down to his children, and time in which to fashion tools, clothes and houses. He has leisure, too, to think beyond the span of his own brief life: to make laws for societies outlasting individuals and to raise memorials to the dead and altars to the gods whom he imagines control his existence. He has learnt to write and keep records. History has begun.

Presently, as we watch across the centuries, we see similar societies growing up in the Mediterranean islands and along the shores of southern Europe—in Crete and Cyprus, in the Greek archipelago and later in Sicily, Malta, Sardinia, Italy and Spain. Little by little, the seeds of that fuller life are blown towards the remote islands of Britain amid their clouds and waves. They are carried by traders of copper, tin and gold adventuring into the Atlantic through the Pillars of Hercules—today the Straits of Gibraltar—or by families and small tribes of husbandmen, wandering in search of fresh soil. These pioneers move up the eastern coast of Spain and the south-western plains of France until they reach the shores of Brittany and the Channel. Presently, after a sojourn there, they put out into the ocean in frail coracles. Some, striking across the Soundings at the mouth of the Channel, reach Cornwall, Pembrokeshire, Anglesey, Ireland and the islands to the west of Scotland. Others, of different race, coming from the east by a more northerly route, take a shorter crossing and enter Britain at its south-eastern corner, where its white cliffs can be seen on clear days from the European coast. The newcomers bring with them the knowledge of agriculture; of grain and domestic animals, of the hoe, the spade and the grinding-stone; of weaving clothes and fashioning pots of clay. They bring, too, another art: of making boats and navigating by oar and paddle. The society they create in Britain is grouped round its western seas, along whose coasts —from Brittany to the Hebrides—they move in small, skin-covered vessels of wicker and woodwork.

The settlements of these Iberian or Mediterranean colonisers —little, dark, slender men—are at first few and far between. Their mattocks and hoes allow them to break only the lightest soils: those on the hill-tops out of reach of the all-pervading forest, on the drier gravel-terraces above the rivers, and on rocky shores and islands along the coast. Yet during the first five hundred years of their occupation—a period of time as long as that which divides us from the Wars of the Roses—the appearance of the country begins to change. For the first time in Britain's history man is imposing his ideas on his environment. Settlements of bee-hive shaped huts, covered with branches and surrounded by little fields, hewn or burnt out of the forests, appear here and there on higher ground. Earthenwork entrenchments are dug at intervals along the chalk and limestone hills for protection and the seasonal round-up of flocks and cattle: the tangled downland bushes and scrub are slowly nibbled away by generations of horned sheep, goats and swine. And in chalk galleries beneath the ground—like those of Grimes' Graves at Brandon—men are quarrying with antler-picks for flint to grind into axes and shape a wild land to their needs. The foundations of settled life, tillage and pasturage are being laid: a basis on which a nation can one day be built.

Great stones or "dolmens," and mysterious hollow mounds and barrows with tunnelled chambers are raised, too, on the western coasts and on the high, inhabited uplands. They are symbols and tribal tombs, where the spirits of the dead are believed to await, like seeds, a day of resurrection and rebirth. For these primitive farmers, having raised themselves above animal existence and learnt to contemplate past and future, are much concerned with the mystery of life and death. They know that man's body dies, yet believe that his spirit survives.

Like the river valley-folk of the East, they worship the dead
and the powers of fertility which recreate life in each generation and spring. To propitiate them and secure their help for
the tribe, their priests or magic men perform mysterious rites
and at special times offer up human and animal sacrifices in
sacred places. And when their leaders die, hopeful of rebirth,
they are buried with their belongings around them. To this we
owe much of our knowledge of their ways. Standing at nightfall at the entrance to such burial mounds as Hetty Pegler's
Tump or Belas Knap in the Cotswolds, one can feel something of their terrors, hopes and fears.

The first invaders are followed by others. There is nothing
to stop them but the waves and tides. Some continue to come
from the south in search of Ireland's gold and of the tin and
copper which the wandering smiths of that land and Cornwall
are learning to smelt into a hard and durable alloy called
bronze. Others come from the east across the shallow straits and
North Sea. Among them are men of a fairer, stronger race,
moving from eastern Europe through dense forests and the
plains of the Low Countries. These Beaker Folk, as archaeologists
call them from their buried drinking-vessels, are nomads from
the steppes of western Asia who have learnt a new technique of
living—breeding and pasturing flocks which they drive from one
grazing-ground to another. They have mastered, too, another
technique, that of war, which they wage with bows and arrows
and sharp axes, first of polished stone and later of bronze. These
lordly shepherds have some affinity with the nomadic warrior
peoples who overran the ancient city civilisations of the Middle
East: the Semitic tribes who founded Babylon, and the Shepherd kings who ruled Egypt in the days of Joseph and his
brethren. Toughened by their wandering and possessing stronger
weapons through their bronze-smiths' skill in metal-work, they are
able to impose their will on their lighter-armed, smaller predecessors. They do not annihilate them—for there is still plenty
of room for all even in a little island covered by forest and
marsh. But they make them work for them. And they breed
from their womenfolk. After a time intermarriage brings a blending of the types; in their burial grounds we find the bones of
the races mingled.

These newcomers are also concerned with the causes of life and with what happens after death. But, like their fellow pastoralists in the East, they worship, not the patient cultivator's earth-mother, but the sun which, as they watch their flocks on the heights, they conceive to be the source of life. At the axis of their radiating sheep-tracks along the bare chalk-downs of the south-west, we see them and their slaves laboriously dragging and erecting huge stones in mysterious clusters, where they sacrifice men and beasts to their flaming god. The stone circles at Avebury and Stonehenge are among the greatest monuments of early man; they seem to have enshrined the religious beliefs and ritual both of the new Beaker and old Iberian folk. Here, a modern writer has suggested, as awed tribes waited in the darkness of midsummer night for dawn, the sun "would smite down through the gloom and the long alley of temple pillars and light up the god above the altar and irradiate him with glory."[2] The men who brought these vast rocks—some like the blue Pembrokeshire stones of Stonehenge from hundreds of miles away—and placed them in elaborate patterns based on the movements of the sun and stars must have learnt much, including the practice of subordination to authority. They created something which has lasted for more than thirty centuries and may still stand on the Wiltshire uplands when we and our works are forgotten.

For more than a thousand years the men of the Bronze Age dominated southern Britain. The earthen ditch in the chalk or oolite, the lonely dewpond on the height, the hill-turf nibbled close and enriched by countless generations of sheep are their legacy. Theirs was a society built on the flocks that gave them food and raiment. Their priests tended the sun-temples, their craftsmen made vessels and weapons of bronze from the tin and copper mines of the south-west, their princes wore splendid helmets and rings and bracelets of gold brought by Irish smiths from Wicklow streams. Their traders, travelling the green hill-roads—Icknield Way, Whiteway, Ridgeway—that linked their priestly capital on Salisbury Plain with the uplands of the east and south-west carried from earthwork fort to fort the bronze weapons, tools and ornaments that were their wealth. Others, more daring, trafficked tin and copper across the Channel or

[2] H. G. Wells, *Outline of History*, I, 240.

with Carthaginian merchants from North Africa. Irish gold objects of this period have been found as far away as Denmark and the Mediterranean and Aegean cities, where this remote, half-fabulous country at the world's end was known as the Tin Islands.

The Bronze Age men had their hour, giving place in the fullness of time to others. New races were on the march, moving westwards from the great heartland of the human family on the Asian plains. It is doubtful if at any time during the two thousand years that followed the first Neolithic colonisation of Britain such infiltration ever ceased. There was no central government and, save in a few settled places along the coast, no-one to oppose a landing. The numbers involved in each invasion must have been very small, for boats were few and minute.

Most of the invaders brought to the island something new, in husbandry, craftsmanship or ways of living. The most important of all was a language which had originated in western Asia and spread, with the movements of the nomadic peoples who spoke it, into India, Persia, the Aegean, Italy and most parts of western Europe. From the basic sounds of this so-called Aryan speech—"outlines . . . drawn only in sound, in the air, as elusive almost as the call of birds"—[3] are derived certain words, used with variations by successive invaders, which still constitute the foundation of our language and are to be found, in not dissimilar forms, in other countries colonised by tribes of Aryan stock. Among these are *father, mother, daughter, sister, brother, son* and *widow:* the first ten numerals; and some of the more important parts of the body, like *knee, foot* and *tooth.* So are *night, wind* and *star,* and the names of domestic animals, *cow, ox, steer,* with their plurality, *herd; hound, goat, sow* and *goose; ewe* and *wether* and their product, *wool.* The words *wheel, axle* and *yoke* show the nomadic character of these Aryan ancestors; our modern *wain* or *waggon* is derived from another of their basic sounds. Other words, whose derivations are not to be found in the speech of the Asiatic descendants of the race but are known to its European descendants—*beech, elm* and *hazel, throstle, finch* and *starling*—must have been added

[3] Jacquetta Hawkes, *A Land,* 174.

in the centuries when the latter were dwelling, in the course of their westward march, among the forests of central Europe. Similar words were added, too, before the western branch split into Greek, Latin, Celt and Teuton, that reveal the substitution of agricultural for nomadic life—*corn* and *ear, furrow, bean* and *meal.*

It was between three thousand and two thousand-five-hundred years ago—between 1000 B.C. and 500 B.C., as we call it—that an Aryan-speaking race, the Celts or Gaels, first appeared in Britain. They were a tall, blue-eyed, flame-haired folk who had crossed Europe from the east and settled in the country which is now called France and which took their name of Gaul. For as long a time as that which divides us from the Crusades Celts were moving into Britain and Ireland, first in small bands and families and later in tribal armies, until they had become the dominant racial strain in both islands. The earlier peoples survived, but were mostly driven into the western moors and hills. They figure in Celtic legends as the faeries or little people—the *Tylwyth teg*—elusive, mysterious and dangerous, who sometimes stole their neighbours' children or provided a bride, dark, shy and inscrutable, for some giant, clumsy, good-humoured Celtic farmer. In such tales a recurrent feature is their dread of iron—the metal whose use the Celtic smiths introduced from the steppes and which, forged into swords and chariots, gave their warriors their long ascendancy. Smelted in charcoal furnaces in the demon-haunted and till now uninhabited lowland forests, it was made also into rotary-lathes to make wheels, and into ploughs which, drawn by oxen, could break virgin soil too stiff for the hand hoes and small wooden ploughs of the past. This brought about a gradual increase in population which, it is estimated, rose during the Celtic occupation to around a quarter of a million—say about a two-hundredth part of its present size. These iron-users were probably the first of Britain's invaders to create permanent fields and villages, mostly on the greensands and light clays of the south-east and in the south-west. At their zenith they may have occupied a sixth of the country. The rest of it, including the thick forest clays of the Midlands, remained uninhabited.

The island still had no unity; it had not even a name. To visualise it we must think of it as divided into loosely defined and warring tribal areas, rather like South Africa in the days of the Zulu and Kaffir wars. In the south-east were the latest comers, the warlike Belgae, whose territory stretched as far west as Salisbury Plain and the Dorset coast, with their fine blacksmiths and iron chariots and plough-coulters. Their name survives only on the far side of the Channel in the country from which they came, though one of their tribes, the Cantii, gave theirs to Kent and Canterbury. Another tribe, whose name has endured on the continent, were the Parisii—a warlike people from the Seine and Marne valleys, who, landing in the Humber, conquered the plain between what is now Yorkshire and Lincolnshire. Others, like the Brigantes of the Pennine dales and the Iceni of Norfolk, dispersed by later invasions, have left little memorial of their sojourn. But in the south-west, where Celtic and pre-Celtic stock has always been predominant, the Dumnonii and the Durotriges have transmitted their names to the Devonians and men of Dorset. And for no very clear reason one group of invaders—the Prythons or Brythons—later gave their name to the whole island.

The hereditary chieftains of these tribes seem to have had a love for beautiful things. They employed craftsmen whose graceful designs surpassed anything yet seen in the barbaric West. When they died their treasures were buried with them— bronze armour and helmets; embossed shields decorated with vivid enamels, like the one found in the Thames at Battersea; golden torques, bracelets and brooches with which to fasten their tartan plaids; amber cups and hand-mirrors engraved with exquisite circular designs like the Birdlip mirror in the Gloucester Museum. Vanity was a characteristic of the Celts; a Greek traveller of the time describes them as smearing their fair hair with chalk-wash to make it still brighter and then drawing it tightly back from the foreheads till they looked like hobgoblins. "Their nobles let their moustaches grow so long that they hide their mouths and, when they eat, get entangled in their food. . . . They use amazing colours, brightly dyed shirts with flowing patterns, and trousers called breeches. . . . Their appearance is amazing, with voices deep sounding and very harsh." They were boastful, threatening and braggarts, he added, but their intellects were keen, and they were quick to acquire knowledge. "When they have killed their foes, they cut off their

heads. . . . They nail them up on their walls as trophies and
preserve those of their chief enemies in boxes."

These head-hunting tribesmen cannot have been comfortable
neighbours. At Salmonsby in Gloucestershire they were still eating their womenfolk about two thousand years ago. Their
religion reeked of blood, and travellers from the civilised South,
whose own ideas about sacrifice were far from squeamish, brought
back horrifying tales of ritual massacres in dark sacred groves
by their magicians or druids. And they were incorrigible fighters.
They crowned Britain's hill-tops, not with burial-barrows and
sun-temples, but with vast earthwork castles with concentric
ditches and ramparts, like Mai Dun or Maiden Castle in Dorset,
Chanctonbury Ring in Sussex, Almondbury in Yorkshire, and
the great Dun of Downpatrick in Ireland. In the ancient Celtic
ballads of Ireland, Wales and the Scottish Highlands—the parts
of Britain least affected by later invasions—pride of battle takes
precedence of every other emotion. For centuries these fierce,
passionate, braggart, though sometimes touchingly noble, tribesmen constantly raided one another's land for heads, slaves and
cattle, but observed the rules and rites of their savage code of
honour. The wars of the early Greeks, fought in the Aegean
sunlight and sung by Homer, were matched by wars fought
under the misty skies and dripping hills of western Britain by
men of the same remote ancestry. In Celtic Ireland, as well as
in Wales and the Scottish Highlands, this "heroic" age continued long after it had ceased in Greece and the British lowlands. The flashing swords and flails of the Fianna, and Finn
Mac Cool and Gull Mac Morna setting targe to targe, were
the counterparts of "godlike Achilles and his squire Automedon
and Alkimas in battle upgrown." And the story of how Graínne,
daughter of King Cormac, eloped with Diarmuid, echoes the
tale of Helen of Troy.

But by now a conqueror of a different kind was approaching
Britain. A few centuries earlier a Celtic tribe had plundered
its way down the Italian peninsula as far as the little hill town
of Rome. But the Romans, a vigorous peasant folk, had defeated
and driven them back. Henceforward the Romans themselves
expanded, first into the neighbouring lands of Italy and later
across the Mediterranean into North Africa, Spain, Greece and
the Levant. With their breast-plated, helmeted, disciplined in-

fantry and their fleets of triple-banked war-ships, they proved
the greatest conquerors the world had known. They were a people
of high courage and patriotism, with an instinctive feeling for
order. Led by aristocrats of strong practical bent, they quickly
absorbed the advanced ideas of the conquered city civilisations
of Greece and the Near East. Just over two thousand years ago
they crossed the Alps and invaded Gaul. In three years their
great general, Julius Caesar, conquering by dividing, subdued
the warring tribes of that land and carried the rule of Rome
to the Channel shore. Behind his legions came the metalled
roads, the stone cities, the laws and administration which the
Romans took with them wherever they went.

From their camps on the Channel Caesar and his veterans saw
the white cliffs of Britain. Some of the Gallic tribesmen had
taken refuge there with their Celtic kinsmen, and to teach them
a lesson he made a reconnaissance across the straits. In August
55 B.C., two thousand years ago, he landed in Kent with two
legions. He did not stay long, for the Britons with their scythed
chariots opposed him fiercely, and his ships, equipped only for
the milder waters of the Mediterranean, were badly damaged
by storms. But he returned in the next summer with a larger
force, and this time advanced, though with difficulty, across the
Thames and burnt the Chiltern kraal of the Belgic chieftain,
Cassivelaunus—king of the Catuvellauni and bearer of the first
recorded personal name in British history. Then, having made
the power of Rome felt, he withdrew.

Julius Caesar never came back to Britain, though his memory
is enshrined in the name of one of our summer months. So is
that of his nephew, Augustus, who became the first Roman
emperor, ruling over a dominion from the Euphrates to the
Atlantic and from the Sahara to the mouth of the Rhine. For
ninety years after Caesar's two invasions Britain remained outside the great union of races welded together by Roman discipline
and good sense—a misty, unexplored forest land of squabbling
tribesmen on the world's fringe. Yet the example of the new
order beyond the Channel affected it profoundly. Its princes
aped the pomp and power of the Empire and bought, with
slaves captured in their wars,[4] the luxuries its traders proffered.

---

[4] "Chained neck to neck in iron collars . . . sometimes at the pitiless rate of
one slave per jar of wine."—Ian Richmond, *Roman Britain*, 8.

The leading king of the south-east, Cunobelin—great-grandson of Cassivelaunus and the Cymbeline of Shakespeare's play—had the same kind of relationship with the imperial province of Gaul as the rulers of Afghanistan with British India in the nineteenth century. In imitation of a Roman emperor he issued gold and silver coins with Latin lettering and built himself a capital on the banks of the Colne named after the Celtic god of war, *Camulodonum*—today Colchester. This, though probably only a cluster of rude thatched huts guarded by a stockade, was the first town in Britain. When children in their nurseries sing about "old King Cole," they are unconsciously commemorating this far-away British king and his savage capital.

It was the chaos of tribal war and the interruption of trade after his death that caused the Roman authorities in A.D. 43 to annex Britain. Ninety years after Caesar's expedition four legions crossed the Channel. This time it was a full-scale invasion. The Medway and Thames were forced after heavy fighting and *Camulodonum* besieged. Before it fell the Emperor Claudius himself arrived from Rome with the Praetorian guard, batteries of catapults, and an elephant corps to share in the triumph. The invaders' left wing, under another future emperor, Vespasian, moved westwards through the territory of the friendly Regni of what today is Sussex towards Mai Dun, the great hill-fortress of the Belgic tribes of the south-west. Skeletons of the vanquished defenders were found centuries later buried under the eastern gateway, one of them with the head of a catapult-arrow in his spine.

Yet the scattered peoples of Britain put up a long, stubborn fight. The legions fanned out across the country—the Ninth to *Ratae*, the modern Leicester, and later to *Lindum*, Lincoln; the Second to *Glevum* or Gloucester; the Fourteenth and Twentieth to *Corinium* or Cirencester in the Cotswolds. The core of the resistance was beyond the Severn where Cunobelin's son, Caradoc or Caractacus, rallied the wild Silures and Ordovices of Wales. Behind them lay the mountains and the great Druid stronghold, the sacred isle of Mona.[5] While the Second Legion moved forward to *Isca*, now Caerleon-on-Usk, and the Fourteenth and Twentieth to *Uriconium* in Shropshire and *Deva*, the modern Chester, the Brigantes of the Pennine dales harried

[5] Later called Anglesey.

the latter's flank. For eight years the Britons of Wales held out until their leader was finally brought to bay and defeated near the hill-camp between the Teme and Clun which is still called by his name, Caer Caradoc. Afterwards he fled to the north, but was betrayed by the queen of the Brigantes and handed over in chains to the invaders. Taken to Rome and led in triumph through its streets, his dignity so impressed his captors[6] that in the end they released him and restored him to his family and country.

Yet there was still a long, bloody chapter before Britain was finally at peace under her new rulers. The price of conquest and civilisation was heavy: forced labour-gangs to build roads, fortifications and cities, crushing tributes to pay for garrisons, and hordes of corrupt and arrogant officials. In A.D. 61, while Nero was ruling in Rome and the main imperial forces in Britain were attacking the Druids in the dense groves of Mona, there was a terrible rising in the south-east. Maddened by tax-exactions and by the outrages done to their queen and her daughters by the Roman soldiery, the Iceni of what today is Norfolk and their southern neighbours, the Trinobantes, overwhelmed the garrison and Roman colony of the capital, Colchester. Repeating their massacre at *Verulamium* on the edge of the Chilterns, they swept down on the new trading-port of *Londinium* in the Thames estuary—named, it is believed, from the Celtic ford, *Lyn Dyn,* the hill by the pool. Skulls from that dreadful day of slaughter were found centuries later in the Wall-brook. A desperate struggle followed in which the disciplined forces of the Empire gradually gained the ascendancy, and at the end of which the British queen, Boadicea, took poison. Later, during the reign of the great soldier-emperor, Vespasian, the legions reduced the Brigantes of the north, besieging their vast 800-acre earthworks at Stanwick near Barnard Castle and establishing a permanent garrison city at *Eboracum,* the York of later ages. The Legate Agricola—the historian, Tacitus's, father-in-law—completed the pacification of the southern half of the island. With the help of a fleet, which circumnavigated Britain, he drove the Celtic tribesmen who still resisted as far north as the Grampians.

Thereafter for three and a half centuries—a period as long as

[6] "Why," he is said to have asked them, "when you had all this, did you covet our poor huts?"

from the death of Elizabeth I to that of George VI—southern Britain was a Roman province. During the greater part of that time the entire lowlands, comprising what today is southern and midland England, enjoyed almost unbroken peace. It was the policy of Agricola and his successors to tame the tribal chieftains by making them citizens. The city was the instrument with which Rome, having conquered barbarians, shaped them to its ends. They were encouraged to transform the old tribal camps and cattle-kraals into towns on the universal Roman model; to vie with one another in raising temples, colonnades, pillars, and arches, and to build themselves houses and gardens where, garbed like Roman patricians, they could live out their lives in luxury under the eyes of authority. Their sons were educated in Roman schools and taught Latin, and their tribal warriors conscripted into the legions or auxiliary regiments and turned into Roman soldiers.

Behind the legions rose the cities on which Roman civilisation depended: rustic miniatures of Rome, even in this remote frontier land, with neat chess-board-pattern streets, forums and temples, porticoed town-halls and amphitheatres, public baths, aqueducts and drains. The capital of the Catuvellauni became *Verulamium,* or, in modern English, St. Albans; that of the Atrebates of the Thames valley *Calleva Atrebatum* or Silchester; that of the Iceni *Venta Icenorum* or Caistor-next Norwich; that of the Dumnonii *Isca Dumnoniorum* or Exeter. Even the wild Silures of Wales built *Venta Silurum* or Caerwent and boasted of the little garrison-town of Caerleon with its golden roofs and towers. In these minute but elegant tribal capitals traders built shops, and tribesmen brought their crops and cattle to market and assembled at sacred seasons to sacrifice to their local gods. Yet though Rome, true to her universal policy, encouraged the worship of the older native deities, she subordinated it, as she had done that of her own gods, to that of the all-embracing State. For its head, the Emperor, sacrifice and tribute were asked of all. It was to express and enforce that authority that the cities arose. More even than markets and dwelling places, they were temples to Caesar and the imperial bureaucracy.

At the height of the Roman occupation there were more than fifty cities in southern Britain. Most of them were very small by continental standards, with between two and five thousand inhabitants. The largest, *Londinium,* the hub of the country's road and trading system, may have had four or five times as many.[7] Though all these cities later perished, at Bath or *Aquae Sulis,* the fashionable watering-place in the southern Cotswolds, the old Roman bath and its tutelary god can still be seen, much as they were when the rich provincials of eighteen centuries ago flocked there for health and amusement. Beyond the tribal capitals and close to the untamed northern and western moors lay the garrison cities of York, Chester, Uriconium, and Caerleon, and in their rear Lincoln, Colchester and Gloucester —the *coloniae* where soldiers' families were settled on retirement with land and houses to breed more soldiers. There were also the Channel ports of Richborough, Porchester, and Chichester, and naval Dover with its lighthouse or *pharos,* guarding the island's communications with the Mediterranean empire of which it was the farthest province.

Linking the towns and camps ran straight Roman roads, paved and cambered on stone causeways, with milestones marking the distances to the imperial capital on the Tiber. Along them passed, not only the marching legionaries who were the guardians of all this order and prosperity, but the native corn, minerals, slaves and hunting-dogs which were exchanged for jewels, statues, wine and oil in jars, perfumes, marbles, mosaics, glass and pottery from the continent. Britain in those years was called the granary of the north. Though the oak forests of the Midland clays still remained untouched and uninhabited, her population, as a result of agricultural improvements, seems to have risen to between a million and half a million. The chief grain exporters were the Celto-Roman landowners, living in *villas* or country-houses on sheltered and sunny slopes in the southern half of the island. Here, amid mosaics and tessellated pavements, glazed windows, baths and central heating, statues and terraces, they aped the life of the Mediterranean and tried to ignore the northern mists and forests around them. Drawing their culture from a wider civilisation, these aristocrats, with their stately Roman manners and Latin speech, introduced into Britain the poultry and geese of her farmyards, the pheasants of her woods, the pears, cherries, figs and mulberries that, planted in their gardens, survived when their gardens and civilisation were

[7] It covered about 350 acres along the north bank of the Thames. The site of its *basilica* or town hall is now occupied by Leadenhall Market.

no more. They worked their great farms with slave labour which they housed in barracks at their gates.

As we look down on the island in this long, peaceful interlude we can see the stone cities, with their forums and market places, the roads running straight as arrows across the still thickly wooded land, the terraced villas amid the corn-farms of the south, and, centuries behind them in civilisation, the squalid hill-villages and little fields of the aboriginal peasants who alone remained untouched by all this luxury, education and prosperity. Within the frontiers of the vast empire of which Britain was part, there were no foreigners, no barriers of race or colour. Italians, Gauls, Africans, Spaniards, Syrians, Greeks, Jews, Egyptians, Britons, all thought of themselves, in those years of peace and unity, as citizens of imperial Rome. Her language, Latin—*nostra lingua*—was the universal tongue of educated men. All could serve in the armies, earn the privilege of Roman citizenship and rise to the highest positions in the State, even the Emperor's purple. And far off, amid northern rocks and heather, the legionaries kept guard on a Wall that stretched from coast to coast. Beyond it lay the mountains of Caledonia and the wild, unconquerable Picts of the North with their spears and painted bodies.

For, true to the unchanging pattern of her history, only part of Britain accepted the new order. The poorer West and North retained their customs and habits, including a passionate belief in tribal freedom. Mountain Wales was never more than superficially civilised, though its peace was ensured by a network of roads and forts, while the Scottish Highlands and Ireland were never subdued at all. The whole northern half of the island remained in a state of permanent unrest, not unlike the north-west frontier of nineteenth-century British India. At some shifting point, which varied from time to time, the Pennine moors ceased to be a tribal area controlled by forts and governed by Roman officials and became a no-man's land visited only by military patrols and marauding bands.

In early days Agricola carried the Roman eagles as far as the Tay and Highland passes, which he tried to block with forts. But the demand for troops to hold barbarian raids elsewhere—particularly on the Danube—made such an advanced line untenable, and the Emperor Hadrian, when he visited Britain eighty years after the conquest, built a seventy-three mile wall from the mouth of the Tyne to the Solway to seal off the North. In the next generation a shorter turf wall farther north was dug between the Clyde and Forth. But about halfway through the Roman occupation, following a disaster when the Picts bore fire and sword as far south as the Dee, this wall was abandoned. Henceforward everything was based on the defence of Hadrian's Wall. Twenty feet high and of stone, running over hill and dale, with twenty-three camps and with watch-towers every mile, it became the strongest defensive line in Europe.

Yet every now and then the barbarians broke through the Wall and swept beyond it, leaving its garrisons isolated and rousing the tribesmen in its rear. This was liable to occur whenever, as increasingly happened, some ambitious general crossed the Channel and, stripping Britain of troops, joined in one of the recurrent struggles for the imperial purple. For there was a fatal defect in the Roman political system. Everything was centralised in the State's officials, yet the succession to the supreme office of all was uncertain. Again and again the Emperor's death was followed by a scramble for power. Sometimes he was assassinated by rivals or his own Praetorian guards, who became the arbiters of the Empire. The Roman world worshipped a ruler who was the guarantor of its peace, and that ruler turned out more often than not a parade-ground bully or a crude political intriguer who stopped at nothing to achieve his ambition.

By treating its possessors as divine Rome deified despotic power. Those in authority were not responsible to the moral feeling and wishes of those they governed; their sway, while it lasted, was uncontrolled. An all-pervading bureaucracy, increasingly wasteful and petty-minded, represented omnipotence at every level. The cost of that immense army of officials plunged society into ever deeper debt and taxation, and, a millstone round the neck of production and trade, destroyed all private independence and sense of initiative. Little by little it reduced the population of every city in the Empire to a mob.

Rome had grown out of greatness of individual character. It became a community in which individual character counted for nothing compared with an abstraction which proved, in the hour of testing, capable of nothing. By sacrificing the individual to the State the rulers of the Roman world undermined the real virtues which sustained it. They turned active and self-respecting citizens into inert and selfish ones. They discouraged the capitalist from thrift and foresight, the trader from enterprise, the craftsman from his hereditary skill, the husbandman from pride in the soil, the mother from maternity, and the soldier from courage and self-sacrifice. They made the moral shell that protected society so soft that it could protect it no longer. A creeping inertia paralysed everyone and everything. Even before the barbarians broke in, the elegant cities had begun to crumble, trade to die for want of purchasers, learning, art and even bureaucratic efficiency to disappear for lack of men of ability. The middle-class was exterminated. Civilisation slowly gave place to barbarism at the Empire's heart.

There was a further reason for Rome's decay. At its root lay a lack of faith and hope. The citizens and rulers of the Empire came in the end to see no purpose either in society or their own lives. The religion of their remote predecessors—a little pastoral Italian State—had been a simple nature worship based on love of home and country. But the Mediterranean peasant's adoration of grove, stream and hill, and of the imaginary gods who personified them, could not satisfy the sophisticated citizens of an international empire. For, though Rome accepted every local god as her own and promoted to her pantheon, under names half-Roman and half-British, the Celtic deities of river and spring, earth and sky—Apollo-Maponus, Sol-Minerva, Mars-Nodens, Victoria-Brigantia—no educated person any longer believed in them. The only thing that Rome really worshipped now was herself—the all-embracing State—and, as its power began to disintegrate in a murderous welter of ambitious generals contending for the throne, it became impossible any longer even to believe in that.

While the strains and stresses of the Empire grew and disasters multiplied, men and women sought feverishly for some answer to the tragic conundrum of existence. Despite the noble creeds of small philosophical minorities like the Stoics, neither pagan deities nor a meaningless succession of divine Caesars offered an ideal strong enough to inspire the masses to perform public duty or sacrifice themselves for the community. The gods in the old Mediterranean myths had behaved without regard to morality or justice. So did the rival emperors who fought one another for the purple. It was natural that their worshippers should come to despise and despair of them. And when men despise and despair of their gods, they presently despise and despair of one another.

Chapter Two

THE COMING OF THE ENGLISH

Stubborn were all his people from cottar to overlord,
Not to be cowed by the cudgel, scarce to be schooled by the
    sword,
Quick to turn at their pleasure, cruel to cross in their mood,
And set on the paths of their choosing as the hogs of Andread's
    Wood. . . .

Kipling

Once more let us take our station above Europe, some sixteen hundred years ago—three centuries, that is, after the first Roman occupation of Britain. All along the northern frontiers, from the Caucasus to the Solway, the barbarians whom Rome has never touched are on the march. Behind them move other hordes, pressing out of the Asian steppes with horses and camels. For Rome, the invincible, is dying, and the richest prize the world has known awaits the bold.

Already the Empire has broken in two. The eastern half is governed from a Greek city on the Bosphorus, called, after the Emperor who built it, Constantinople. The western half is rent by wars between the garrisons of Italy, Gaul, Spain and Britain. Even these are splitting into fragments; Britain has become four administrative provinces instead of one. And all the while the armed ranks on the frontiers are dwindling. They are drawn now almost entirely from the half-civilised tribesmen of the frontier regions, for the decadent Roman townsmen, with their falling birth-rate, are no longer prepared to perform the duties of citizenship and despise soldiering as a trade fit only for barbarians. The thin line of steel that guards the rich cities round the Mediterranean is beginning to bend and break. Though few can yet believe it, the inconceivable is about to happen.

In Britain, at one end of the three thousand-mile ribbon of river and towered wall that divides civilisation from barbarism, we see the first signs of disaster. In the year A.D. 367 the island's northern defences snap. The Picts, swarming out of the heather hills, break through the wall and destroy the legion based on York. Simultaneously pirate war-bands from beyond the North Sea descend on the east coast and overwhelm the second of the three legions guarding the province, while sea-pirates from Ireland raid its western coasts. Then, joined by slaves from the gutted villas and burning, plundering and slaying, they sweep across a defenceless land.

Next year, after Picts have penetrated as far as Kent, reinforcements from Europe drive them back. For forty more years —the span of a lifetime—the legions resume their watch on the threatened coasts and moors. But the ravaged province never recovers its prosperity. Their villas burnt and their slaves dispersed, the rich landowners, already ruined by taxation, are unable to maintain their farms and former standards of living. The poor in the towns suffer even more, for there is no-one to employ them. The cities, saved during the invasion by their walls, perish without trade. The pillars crumble, the tessellated pavements are no longer patched, the homes that once bred good citizens become hovels and pigsties. The researches of archaeologists reveal a dying civilisation.

Meanwhile the barbarian pressure grows. Other branches of the Nordic race, the fierce Teutons from the forests of central Europe, are moving in along the frontiers. Whole nations— Vandals, Ostrogoths, Lombards, Visigoths, Franks, Burgundians —are on the march. Through the degenerate citizens' habit of hiring barbarians to defend them, many of these savages are already serving in the legions, ready to betray their soft masters to their kinsmen without. On the last night of A.D. 406 a great army of Germans, swarming across the frozen Rhine, pours into Gaul. Soon every city north of the Alps is in flames. The last regular troops in Britain, drained by the wars of rival generals, are recalled to defend Italy. All is in vain. In 410 a Visigoth host sacks Rome itself.

Thus, fifteen hundred years ago, the British people were cut off from the civilisation to which they had belonged for nearly four centuries. Their appeals for help were unanswered and they were left to defend themselves. At first, freed from the restrictions of an over-centralised bureaucracy, they seem to have organised themselves under local generals or tribal princes, particularly in the north-west, where the old Celtic organisation had survived and resistance to the Picts had kept men hardy and self-reliant. The province's only land-frontier was short, and the barbarians of Caledonia, though fierce, were few in number, with no new races on the march behind them. For perhaps fifty years, British-Roman civilisation, though fast disintegrating, appears to have survived.

Yet the threat of barbarism came not only from the land. The fishermen and whalers of the desolate marshes along the eastern shores of the North Sea—the "Saxons" or men of the long knives, as the British called them—had also felt the pressure of Asiatic hordes moving westward through the forests behind them. Even before Rome fell, spurred on by hunger and hope of loot, they had taken to their boats to prey on the rich Roman island beyond the sunset. For a time Britain's shores and her cross-Channel trade had been guarded against them by a Roman fleet, the *classis Britannica*, based on Richborough and Boulogne. But the imperial authorities had found that its ships could make a rebellious general independent of Rome. They found too that patrols of Mediterranean inshore galleys rowed by slaves and manned by soldiers, however cunningly camouflaged, were no match for pirates who were as much a part of the sea as the whales they hunted. During the last century of the occupation they had relied increasingly on a cordon of coastal and estuary forts, stretching from the Solent to Brancaster on the Wash and supported by an army under an official called the Count of the Saxon shore.[1] This used up a great many troops, and left the pirates free to concentrate against any point on the coast they chose. The Count—some stern Roman or dark Iberian or African—must have cursed them for flaxen, pestilent barbarians as he marched and countermarched his dusty cohorts to repel first one, then another, of their unpredictable raids.

After the withdrawal of the last Roman troops the Anglo-Saxons, who were to become the dominant strain in our long, mixed ancestry, made their first lodgment on the land that now bears their name. From Frisia and the mouths of the Rhine,

---

[1] Ruins of these can still be seen at Pevensey, Richborough and near Yarmouth.

Ems and Weser, from Schleswig and Angle in what is now Holstein and Denmark, the curved boats of the barbarians, growing bolder every year, poured up the estuaries and rivers of southern Britain, landing their crews to plunder and slay. The island became a magnet for the boldest of all the barbarians—the men of the sea.

For a time the British leaders and Celtic tribal chieftains, like Roman provincials elsewhere, seem to have tried the expedient of hiring half-tamed Teuton war-bands from the continent to defend them. The ruler of the south-eastern corner of the country settled in Thanet an army of Jutish mercenaries who had served with the legions on the Rhine. But finding that their employers could not protect themselves, the newcomers presently raised their demands for food and pay. When they were not met, they turned their swords against them. Under their chieftains, Hengist and Horsa, they threw in their lot with the sea-raiders, and began to plunder, burn and massacre.

Of the events that followed—so important for the making of our history—we know almost nothing, the records having been lost amid so much destruction. All we know is that the little cities of Roman Britain were gutted, that the flame of invasion, to quote the hysterical and no doubt exaggerated account of the Welsh monk, Gildas, "blazed from sea to sea" until, "having burned nearly the whole island, it licked the western ocean with its red and savage tongue." "The barbarians drive us into the sea," cried the Britons in a last despairing appeal to Rome, "and the sea drives us back to the barbarians!" In the wake of invasion came famine and pestilence.

Looking down on Europe during that troubled century—the fifth after the great days of Augustus—we can see the German war-bands pouring over the civilised but sparsely inhabited lands of the old western Empire. On the continent the cities which had been the glory of Roman civilisation escaped complete destruction, for the barbarian chieftains, fancying themselves heirs of the mighty emperors before whom they had so long trembled, made them their own. But in Britain the invaders came from remote shores and mud-flats where the fame of Rome had scarcely penetrated. They despised, not only the effete, luxurious owners of the wealth they seized, but the wealth itself. They took the land, the crops and flocks, the slaves

and treasures of gold and silver, but destroyed or shunned the
cities—the camps or *chesters*, as they called them—leaving only
their charred, lonely, ghost-haunted ruins. For they were countrymen who hated towns and regarded their refinements as vices.

During this confused and savage age, which only the most
exquisite scholarship has been able to rescue from oblivion,
the island, with its dense forests and undrained valleys, was inhabited by three separate peoples. There were the Teuton invaders, with their boar-crested helmets, woollen cloaks and long
ash-shafted spears, moving up the rivers in their shallow war
boats or tramping the disused Roman roads—rechristened now
with Saxon names like Watling Street and Fosse Way—in search
of plunder and land. Behind them came their sturdy women-
folk and children, brought across stormy seas in open boats
from the Saxon and Angle settlements in Europe. Opposed to
them, fighting also in small divided bands and driven ever
farther into the west—into what today are Devon, Cornwall,
Wales, the Lake District, and the south-western corner of Scotland then called Strathclyde—were the descendants of the British or Celtic-Roman provincials. But though their petty tyrants
or princes, for ever squabbling with one another, might still
wear Roman armour and flowing togas—or plaids, as they later
became called[2]—and boast high-sounding Latin names, the few
towns left had become little more than squatters' settlements,
bereft of trade and the arts of civilised living, and their inhabitants almost as savage as the barbarians who had driven
them from their former homes. And left behind by the receding
British tide in squalid, remote villages as the victors' slaves, were
the primitive, pre-Celtic peasants who continued to live much as
before. They survived in the impenetrable scrub of the Chiltern
hills, on the Pennine and northern moors, in the marshy islands
of the Fens—now reverting to inland sea with the decay of the
Roman dykes—and in the ancient chalk uplands of the south-
west. They were not exterminated but surrounded and absorbed. And their women-folk, and those of the Celts, bore children to the conquerors.

Nor, for all the bloody battles and massacres of that terrible
time, did the British tribes of the West perish. They merely

2 T. C. Lethbridge, *Merlin's Island*, 50.

ceased to be civilised and Roman, and became pastoral and Welsh. Like their remote ancestors of the Age of Bronze, they reverted to the hills and sheep. For a time, rendered desperate by suffering and schooled by hardship, they fought back so fiercely that the Saxon advance was halted. And they were sustained, like many others in that calamitous age of falling civilisation, by a Faith called Christianity which had spread across the Empire during its decline and which, hailing from the East, taught men that happiness could be achieved only by sacrifice. Under two successive leaders with Roman names, Ambrosius Aurelianus and Arturius or "King" Arthur—heroes of whom little is known save the legends handed down by un-lettered folk and later enshrined by poets—they won a series of battles culminating in the victory of Arthur and his cavalry at Mount Badon which ensured the survival in Britain of the Celtic tribes and the Christian Faith. The Celtic names of streams, rivers and hills, which, outlasting the Teuton flood, mark our maps, and the scattered farms and hamlets of the West Country, are, as much as the Arthurian tales, a memorial to this heroic king and the breathing-space he gained for his people. For fifty more years the invaders were confined to the eastern half of the island, the two races—speaking different tongues and holding different beliefs—facing one another in an uneasy, bitter truce across an uncertain frontier.

But in the middle of the sixth century the Saxons and Angles, first in the south and then in the north, resumed their advance. By the end of it the Britons of the south-west, driven into the Devonian-Cornish peninsula, were cut off from their Celtic kinsfolk of the little, quarrelling principalities of Wales—Gwent, Dyfor, Powys, Gwynedd. In the north the creation of an English kingdom called Northumbria, stretching from coast to coast across the Pennine moors, soon afterwards separated the Welsh from their fellow Celts of the Cumbrian mountains and Strathclyde. In 603 the Northumbrian king defeated the Britons of Strathclyde and their northern Christian neighbours, the Scots of Dalriada or Argyllshire, in a great battle in Liddesdale. "From that day," a Saxon boasted, "no king of the Scots dared to meet the English nation in battle." From the North Sea to the Severn and Dee, from the Channel to the Forth, the conquest of Britain was complete. Except for the rocky, rainswept west, it was Britain no longer. It had become England.

What manner of people were these Anglo-Saxons? They were great seamen, fighters and colonisers. Coming from desolate coasts and windswept mud-flats, gale and storm were in their blood. "The blast of the tempest," sang one of their poets, "aids our oars, the bellowing of the heaven, the howling of the thunder hurt us not; the hurricane is our servant and drives us where we wish to go." They crossed the seas in undecked, mast-less, clinker-built boats—"foam-cresters" seventy or eighty feet long and scarcely a dozen wide, with a paddle in the stern for steering and fourteen or sixteen oars a side. If they were with-out mercy to their foes, they looked for none at the hands of a Nature very different from that of the sunny Mediterranean of Roman civilisation. They viewed even shipwreck as a form of practice. Theirs was a world in which there was no place for the weak or craven. One thinks of them, in those days before they found a permanent home, as wild geese, tense on their solitary flight over the waste of waters as they followed the whale, the herring and the seal.

They loved fighting. Their poetry, chanted in the mead-halls of their chieftains as they sat feasting at the long benches, is full of the clash of "the hammered blades," "the serried bucklers," "the shields of linden wood," of "arrows sleeting like hail." They loved the symbols of death and carnage: the raven who followed the host with his beak dripping blood, the hungry hawks hovering over the battlefield, the funeral pyre hung with shields and helmets—"the beacon of the man mighty in battle" —round which the companions of the fallen sang the joys of war and the warrior's virtues.

Yet they had another side. Though to the defeated Britons, to whose homes they had brought fire and sword, they seemed only cruel, boorish savages, they were great farmers: by far the best the island had known. Their first settlements were on the lighter soils, but presently, with their iron axes and deep four or eight-ox ploughs, they embarked on the titanic task of clearing the forests and heavier clay soils of the eastern midlands: rich land that Neolithic and Bronze Age men, Celts and Romans alike had left untouched. For, barbarians though they were, they were more patient, industrious and methodical than any of the peoples they had conquered. And, on the lowest and working social level, they had more genius for co-operation. They worked together, just as they had rowed and fought together. Wherever they settled they waged their battle against nature shoulder to shoulder. They shared the same ploughs, helped to cultivate one another's land, and followed common rules of tillage and forestry. In this way they were able to make far steadier progress against the cold, stubborn clay and oaken wilderness around them than any of their predecessors. In their homesteads or "tuns" of thatched, tent-shaped huts, sited by streams in the forest clearings, and in their closely-knit communities whose names—Barkings of Barking, Hastings of Hastings, Gellingas of Ealing—still mark our maps, these sturdy colonists, with their fine smiths, carpenters and wrights, cleared virgin ground to support growing numbers of their folk. In doing so they created in the course of time the English countryside, turning marshy valley bottoms into water-meadows, terracing fields on the slopes, and eating ever farther into the forests. As each village became established, the younger and bolder spirits, for whom the cleared land was insufficient, "swarmed off" to found, still deeper in the woods, new settlements which they distinguished from the old by the addition of prefixes like Upper and Lower, East, West, South and North, and or of suffixes like Bottom and End, Bere and Den—pig-pasture—Ley and Hurst.

For these people loved the soil and the tending of it and its beasts. They loved it as much as their fathers had loved fighting and the sea. They left their memorial, not like the Romans in stone or the Bronze Age men in burial-grounds, but in the imperishable shape of the earth they tilled; it is writ large across our shires, with their villages, meadows, farms, and ploughlands. And in the work of their artists that has come down to us, in their carvings in wood and stone of leaves, trees and animals, we can see their deep feeling for nature. "His coat," runs the old song, "is of Saxon green," and it is of a green-clad folk in a green land that we must think of them, swinging their axes and driving their ploughs through mysterious forest and dark earth to make the land we love.

Their main settlements were at first near the coast—the East Saxons of what became Essex, their big-nosed Jutish neighbours across the Thames in Kent and the Isle of Wight; the flaxen-haired, blue-eyed, heavy-limbed South Saxons of Sussex; the West Saxons who, coming from the Wash or up the Thames, settled on Salisbury Plain or, in smaller numbers, landed near

Southampton Water and followed the Avon to the Plain; the Angles of East Anglia—the North-folk and South-folk—and their kinsmen who, pushing up the Midland rivers, established the tribal communities that by the beginning of the seventh century had merged to form the kingdom of Mercia. Farther north other Angles, overrunning and intermarrying with the British tribes of Deira and Bernicia between Humber and Forth, founded the still greater kingdom of Northumbria in what today is northern England and south-eastern Scotland. All brought from their diverse starting-points in Europe different customs and ways of life, which they continued to follow in their new homes. And all were separated from one another by trackless expanses of oak forest, thorn, scrub and swamp, like the dense Epping and Chiltern woods that hemmed in London from the north, the eighty-mile wide Andredsweald between the North and South Downs, Selwood in the west, the Midland forests of Bernwood, Arden and Wyre, Cannock Chase, Sherwood and Hatfield.

The population of these pioneer communities in the backwoods was at first very small. In the whole of Mercia—an area today comprising a dozen crowded counties—there were only 12,000 households a century and a half after the first invasion. Other Anglo-Saxon settlements, though these were presently swallowed up by their larger neighbours, were even smaller: the Hicce around what today is Hitchin numbered only three hundred households. Except when they had to combine against the Welsh or Scots, the chieftains of these little States perpetually fought one another, either for their crowns or for wider territories.

Their form of government, though aristocratic, was far simpler and freer than that of Rome. There were no officials, no central administration, and every village community kept its own peace and justice. The ranks were those of chieftain's kin or atheling, lord, freeman, and slave. Every freeman carried his scaex or knife to defend his home and family. No-one could write or keep records, and the only checks on a man's conduct were the customary vengeance of his kin and neighbours, or of his lord or the more distant king for breaches of their simple laws. These primitive farmers and lumbermen lived on family holdings or "hides" in the little isolated "tuns," "hams," "steads" and "leas" their ancestors had conquered and cleared in the forests. Such holdings consisted of long unfenced strips, scattered for fairness about the two great communal fields—sown one year with seed and the next lying fallow—that surrounded each stockaded village. Beyond lay the common pasture where they kept their cattle and sheep, and the encircling forest where they gathered fuel, pastured swine, and hunted wolf, elk, fox and wild boar.

The pioneer farmer, or ceorl as he was called, was the core both of the local community and of the petty kingdom or "kindred" to which he belonged. He was a freeman, responsible only to his neighbours and to his fighting leader—king or lord: a man, to use the old English phrase, "moot-worthy, fold-worthy and fyrd-worthy," worthy, that is, of a place in the justice-court, the sheep-fold and the tribal fyrd or militia that turned out at the king's summons in time of war. He was wont to speak his mind out freely in the court of the village or tun, for among this simple people the man who spoke truth fearlessly was as honoured as the man who fought bravely. Though ready to enslave others, the English were great lovers of their own freedom. Their homes, rude and rough though they were, were their castles.

The tribal king was chosen for life by the kinsfolk and chief warriors from the descendants of the hero who had led the war-band or folk during the invasion. He lived in a little earthwork, palisaded fortress called a burgh with his thanes or gesiths —war-companions—and their servants and slaves. Even such a royal burgh would only have a few hundred inhabitants. We must not picture a Saxon king in a palace like his modern counterpart, with a clearly defined succession and rights and duties laid down by law. He was merely the chosen head of a family of rough tribal nobles whose duty it was to lead the folk in war. As there was no civil service, no police force, no posts or means of communication except a few grassy tracks, he could hold his throne only so long as he was acceptable to those he governed, and, most of all, to the kinsmen and retainers who formed his body guard or "hearth-horde." If they ceased to respect him, he lost both throne and life.

Such kings, some of them ruling kingdoms smaller than a modern county, were little richer than their subjects. They might wear a few ornaments and jewels in their rough, homespun clothes, and own gold or silver-mounted cups, armour of chainmail and finely made swords, daggers and shields, like those found in the seventh century royal ship buried in the sands of Sutton Hoo in East Anglia. Yet a king's or lord's hall was merely a gabled log-barn, with stag-horns and rude arms on its unplastered walls, a sunk open hearth on the centre of a rush-strewn earthen floor, and a hole in the roof to let out the smoke. Here on great occasions he and his companions would gorge themselves on meat and hot spiced ale and mead—a fermented spirit of honey and herbs—and, while the harp passed from hand to hand and the minstrels sang their sagas, shout with drunken joy at the remembrance of their forefathers' heroic deeds and battles.

For the gods of these simple forest folk—seamen and warriors turned farmers—were the spirits of Battle, Storm and Nature common to all the Nordic peoples. They honoured only the brave and warlike. It was because of this that, despite their love of independence, they gave such loyalty to their kings and lords, heirs of the warriors who had led them to conquest and who, perhaps, boasted descent from Woden, god of victory and plunder, or Thunor, god of the mountain-thunder, deities whose names, like those of Tiw and Freya, spirits of war and fertility, survive in the days of our week.[3] The greater the king's prowess, the larger his following of thanes and companions. They felt for him as dogs for their hunting masters: "happy days," sang one, "when I laid head and hands on my lord's knee." From him they received the meat, bread and salt, the ale and mead on which they feasted in the winter, the bracelets and buckles of gold and silver, the gems and embroidery with which they loved to adorn their shabby persons, the crested helmets, ringed mail and runed swords, said to be made by Wayland the smith-giant, which they used in battle.

Such men, though they might slaughter man, woman and child in anger or to placate their cruel gods, were not without rough virtues. They were brave, loyal and true to their kin and leaders; there was no shame in their eyes like that of the man who turned his back in fight or betrayed lord or comrade. Those who had eaten a man's salt must die by his side. "Never shall the steadfast men round Stourmere," cried the Essex thane as his eorl fell, "reproach me that I journey lordless home."

In this lay the nobility of these far-off ancestors of ours. There was no weak comfort in their harsh creed. They believed that the end of all was death: that no triumph or happiness, however

[3] Also in the names of towns and villages like Wednesbury (Woden's burgh or borough) and Tewesley (Tiw's lea).

great, could last. "Now," sang their bards, "is the flower of thy strength lasting awhile, yet soon sickness or the sword, fire or flood, the arrow's flight or blinding age shall take away thy might." They saw in the mystery of life a riddle beyond man's explaining. "Where," they asked, "is the steed? where the rider? where the giver of treasure? The bulwarks are dismantled, the banqueting-hall in ruins, the lords lie bereft of joy, and all their proud chivalry is fallen by the wall!" It was not in man's power to control his lot; his virtue lay in his capacity for suffering and endurance. Even the gods, feasting in their paradise of Waelhaell or Valhalla, must fall in the end to the hateful hags, Hel and Weird—the Fates to whose inexorable decree all things bowed. There was no escape, no mercy or tenderness on icy earth or in storm-riven sky.

In the eyes of this brave people there was only one rule: to accept without flinching whatever the Fates had in store. The craven whined; the valiant kept his grief locked in his heart. The worse fortune treated him, the truer he must be to creed and comrade; the craven and traitor could gain only shame by their baseness. The hero at least lived on in his comrades' memory; the coward drowned in the mud beneath the feet of those he had betrayed.

It was a rough, masculine creed, without much subtlety or refinement. It judged men, not by what they said or thought, but by their deeds. Yet it bred a sense of duty and responsibility without which no nation can be great or endure. It taught the rank and file to be loyal, and their leaders to sacrifice themselves for the led. "I have bought with my death a hoard of treasures," cried Beowulf after his fight with the dragon, "I give thanks that before my dying day I have won it for my people." So long afterwards on the battlefield of Maldon the outnumbered English fought on without hope of victory:

"Thought shall be the harder, heart the keener,
Mood shall be the more as our might lessens."

In the hour of adversity and danger they closed their ranks and were true to one another.

Yet at the root of their fierce pagan myths was the same hopelessness that had underlain the creed of Rome. Behind their cold, inexorable heavens lay only terror and disaster. They feared death and the unpredictable forces of nature and the mysterious powers—demon and monster, giant and ghoul—with which they identified them. They feared the wild passions of human nature that unloosed so many disasters on the world. And, though they faced their fears manfully, they did not believe that man in the end could master his fate or that anything could save him from his terrible dilemma and the annihilation that awaited him.

Chapter Three

THE FAITH

I saw them march from Dover, long ago,
With a silver cross before them, singing low,
Monks of Rome from their home where the blue
                              seas break in foam,
Augustine with his feet of snow
                    Flecker

More than two hundred years after the last legions left Britain, and soon after the completion of the English conquest, a tall, dark stranger stood before the king and chieftains of Northumbria. His "hair was black, his face thin, his nose slender and aquiline, his aspect venerable and awe-inspiring." His name was Paulinus, and, like the men who had once governed Britain, he was a Roman. But he bore no arms and stood there at the mercy of the rough warriors around him.

He had come to Northumbria—the wild northern kingdom that stretched from the Humber to the Forth—with a Kentish bride for its king. Thirty years earlier her father, the Jutish ruler of Kent, had welcomed to his capital a band of Roman monks to minister to his own queen, a Christian princess from Gaul. Their leader, Augustine, had been so persuasive that he had converted the Kentish king and his nobles to Christianity—the mysterious religion that had survived the Roman collapse on the continent, and, though rooted out of southern Britain, had lingered on in the mountains and islands of the Celtic west.

The Northumbrians around Paulinus were no friends to this creed. Fourteen years before, they had slaughtered hundreds of its priests after a great victory over the Britons of north Wales. The very word, *church*, that they used for its houses of worship was associated in their minds with plunder.[1] They listened, therefore, to the eloquent Italian with suspicion. Yet what he told caused them to do so in silence. For it was a tale of heroism and devotion. Its purport was that behind the forces of fate was a God who had made men in his own image and, loving them, had given them freedom to choose between good and evil. He had made them, not helpless actors, but partners in the drama of creation. And because men had misused that freedom and God still loved them, He had sent them His son as leader and saviour to show them, by revealing His nature, how to live and, by sharing theirs, how to overcome sin and death.

For by a miracle beyond human comprehension God had made his love for man incarnate. Six centuries before, when Rome was establishing her empire of force, there had been born to a poor peasant woman in an oppressed eastern land a child named Jesus. With the flawless and compassionate nature of God, whose true son he was, he had taken upon his shoulders all the sorrows and burdens of mankind and voluntarily chosen pain and death. Rejected and misunderstood by those he had come to save, he had fought his last battle on earth alone and deserted. Yet, even in agony on a criminal's cross, his love for men had never faltered, and he had died forgiving those who had betrayed and slain him.

Then the English were told how in death Jesus had triumphed as no victor in battle had ever done; how his body had vanished from the tomb in which it had been stoned up, and how he had appeared to those who loved him, risen from the grave. Poor, unarmed, abandoned, this gentle, heroic leader was now worshipped as Lord and Saviour in almost every land over which the Roman oppressors of his country had ruled. And he had opened the doors of God's kingdom to all with faith and courage to follow him.

Paulinus' tale cannot have seemed wholly strange to his hearers. He had spoken of a leader who had been brave and true, who offered his followers a freeman's choice between good and evil and a hero's reward for those who were faithful. But in two respects his message was revolutionary. For the virtues

[1] Derived, through the German mercenaries serving in the Eastern provinces of the Empire, from the Greek word, *kuriakon*—the Lord's house. L. P. Smith, *The English Language*, 98.

Jesus had shown were not merely those the English honoured, but others they had never regarded as virtues at all. Love not hate, gentleness not force, mercy not vengeance had been the armour of this great captain. The Northumbrians' own valour in battle was small compared to the cold courage of facing death with only these meek virtues.[2] And, as proof of it, here was this solitary stranger standing unarmed in their midst.

Most startling of all, Paulinus' message offered the English hope beyond the grave. Here was the reply to a problem deep in the human heart which their priests had never answered. When he ended, an old counsellor spoke. "The life of man, O king," he said, "is like a sparrow's flight through a bright hall when one sits at meat in winter with the fire alight on the hearth, and the icy rain-storm without. The sparrow flies in at one door and stays for a moment in the light and heat, and then, flying out of the other, vanishes into the wintry darkness. So stays for a moment the life of man, but what it is before and what after, we know not. If this new teaching can tell us, let us follow it!"

For these northern heathens, who held that a man should stand up to his fate but believed he could never master it, responded eagerly to the hope that there might be a purpose behind it. It made sense of life, and all its pain and suffering, in a way that the tales of their own dark gods had never done. The very simplicity of the Christian story and the courage of the man who told it disarmed a people themselves simple and brave. Living in a world of terrors and wonders they could not explain, they were used to taking things on faith. As they crowded round the man who had brought them such tidings, their own high priest was the first to cast his spear at the idols

---

[2] "Then I beheld the Master of mankind
Approach with lordly courage as if He
Would mount upon me, and I dared not bow
Nor break, opposing the command of God,
Although I saw earth tremble; all my foes
I might have beaten down, yet I stood fast.
    Then the young Hero laid His garments by,
He that was God almighty, strong and brave,
And boldly in the sight of all He mounted
The lofty cross, for He would free mankind."
    The Dream of the Rood (transl. La Motte Iddings)
    Select Translations from Old English Poetry (ed.
    A. S. Cook and C. B. Tinker). Boston 1902.

their fathers had worshipped. Afterwards they were baptised in thousands, pressing into the Yorkshire streams to receive from Paulinus' hands the cross of water which enrolled a man as Christ's follower and offered him deliverance from the grave.

Six centuries had passed since Jesus had been born in Bethlehem. His life had been spent in poverty and obscurity among a poor, obscure and conquered people. Yet its impact on history had been greater than that of the Caesars. He had based his teaching on the religious experience of his countrymen, the Jews, who, alone among peoples, had learnt to believe in a single, righteous and everlasting God. Like their prophets of old, he had stressed the importance of unchanging moral laws. But he made men see them in a new light. At a time when the Jews were expecting a Messiah to end their subjection to foreigners and establish the kingdom of heaven on earth, Jesus proclaimed that it lay in their own souls. "The Kingdom of Heaven," he said, "is within you." The fight between good and evil could only be won through the surrender of the individual soul to the love and will of God. In that alone lay eternal life.

God was love, and the way to God, on earth as in Heaven, was through loving and serving others. "The first commandment," Jesus preached, "is, 'Thou shalt love the Lord thy God with all thy heart and all thy soul and all thy mind.' The second is, 'Thou shalt love thy neighbour as thyself.'" The kingdom of Heaven was made out of love expressed in service. There was no other kingdom, no other enduring joy or dominion, and everything else was an illusion of a world which had no permanence.

Speaking in parables that the humblest could understand, Jesus restated man's values in those of God. He bade men love their enemies, do good to them that hated them, forgive trespasses. Self-denial not self-righteousness, giving not taking, pity for others not pity for self were the gates of salvation. Whoever sought his life should lose it; whoever lost it should save it. When Jesus' disciples, who, for all their love for him, could never wholly understand him, asked which of them should be first in God's kingdom, he replied that the first should be last and the last first. The only precedence was that of love and service.

Seeing God's love in everything and at the root of man's

being, Jesus taught that no-one, however abandoned, who truly repented, need despair of forgiveness and grace. He insisted on uncompromising righteousness, and yet was the friend—and redeemer—of publicans and sinners. It was this that aroused the fury of the Jewish religious leaders. Unable to comprehend his meaning or his claim to speak for God, they sentenced him to be crucified as a blasphemer. He accepted the agony of the cross with the same faith in the divine goodness as he accepted life itself. "Not as I will," he prayed, "but as Thou wilt." He pursued his course to the bitter end. "Take up thy cross," he had told his disciples, "and follow me." They were now shown what he meant.

For in nailing Jesus' body to the cross, his foes nailed his memory and teaching there. His life in time had only begun. By sacrificing it he had given it to mankind for ever. Death was swallowed up in victory. A poor, obscure provincial, who had revealed God's nature to a few men as poor and obscure as himself, henceforth became a living, personal presence to unborn millions. Convinced that he had risen from the dead and was the Christ and Son of God for whom Israel had been waiting, his disciples became a band of inspired heroes. In the teeth of peril and persecution, they communicated a conviction of what he was, so intense that it seemed to their hearers the most important thing that had ever happened; so important that, not only did they try to base their lives on his teaching and to live, however unsuccessfully, as he had lived, but in many cases deliberately chose to die like him in order to testify to his divinity. "I am persuaded," declared the great apostle, Paul, "that neither death nor life, nor angels, nor principalities nor powers, nor things present nor things to come, nor height nor depth, nor any other creature, shall be able to separate us from the love of God which is in Christ Jesus our Lord."

Through the agency of the Christian congregations that sprang up, first in the scattered Jewish communities of Asia Minor and later among the Greeks and other peoples of the Empire, this burning faith in Christ was carried into every corner of the Roman world. During the centuries when Britain was an imperial province Christianity was winning adherents from every pagan cult and religion. Its defiance of military despotism and the mass-brutality of the amphitheatre proved a turning-point in history. The brave men and women who were burnt alive or torn to pieces by wild beasts in the public arenas for refusing to worship Caesar showed that a spiritual ideal could be stronger than force.[3] And just as it was the conviction of Christ's presence that gave ordinary men the power of behaving like heroes, so the sight of their constancy won thousands to a Faith that could arm men with such virtue. Three centuries after Christ's death the Emperor Constantine—builder of Constantinople and divider of the Roman world—himself became a Christian.

Though Christianity's influence was too late to save the old Mediterranean civilisation from corruption and decay, the collapse of the Roman West revealed its full power. Amid massacre, destruction and the blaze of ancient cities, the guardianship of civilisation passed from the defeated legions to the Christians. They alone refused to despair. Instead of despising and fearing their terrible enemies, they sought by faith and love to redeem them. While panic-stricken imperial bureaucrats abandoned frontier province after province, the Christian missionaries, resuming the mission that the Caesars had abandoned, carried the ideals of law and human brotherhood into the forest stockades and nomad camps of the barbarians.

Stirred by their courage and awed by the majesty of the fallen empire they represented, the chieftains who overran western Europe accepted one after another the Christian faith for themselves and their peoples. And rough champions of the Cross though they were, they fought under its banners to defend the West from new invaders. When Saxon and Jutish pirates were conquering Britain, a Christian Vandal and a Visigoth king had defeated the Mongolian savage, Attila, and his Huns on the plains of Chalons in a battle that saved Christendom—the name by which the Roman West now became known.

Yet the gulf between the passions of ignorant Gothic and Frankish tribesmen and Christ's religion of love and humility was not easily bridged. In becoming the creed of barbaric nations Christianity absorbed many of the beliefs and practices of those it converted. To some extent its churches took the place of the secular institutions their converts overthrew. In that cha-

[3] Among those who died for their faith were the future patron saint of England, the Roman soldier, St. George of Cappadocia, and the first British martyr, St. Alban of Verulamium.

otic age they represented the only remaining law and administration outside the Greek or Byzantine empire. Their bishops
became officials as well as teachers, their beliefs legal dogmas
enforced by prison and excommunication. Only by unquestion-
ing acceptance of their discipline, doctrine and ritual, it was
held, could the individual approach God and share in Christ's
legacy of redemption. An intolerant orthodoxy, intolerantly enforced, provoked struggles with heresies equally vehemently asserted. Jesus' precepts of love and mercy were forgotten, and
war and misery unloosed on thousands by the passions of Christian leaders.

Yet Christianity's fundamental truth, that love and sacrifice
could unlock the gates of Heaven, was somehow preserved. Nor
without the Churches, for all their imperfections, could it have
been. If they partly perverted Christ's creed, they guarded it
and transmitted it to posterity. But for them Europe would
have sunk into the same tyranny of the few, and squalid, fatalistic misery of the many as Asia and Africa. By insisting on the
worth of the individual soul, they reminded the conqueror and
tyrant of their responsibility to their fellowmen. In an era of
warring tribes and races they recalled the Roman ideals of
unity, order and reason. When man could see nothing but the
insecurities and disasters of the present, they preserved some
memory of his past achievements. Their self-governing congregations survived when the brittle centralised bureaucracy of
the Roman provinces broke. To their missionaries, saints and
martyrs, as well as to their administrators, the world, in those
first terrible centuries after Rome's fall, owes the survival of
almost everything that today makes life worth living.

It was through them that, when it most needed it, Europe
enjoyed a brief respite from disaster. A century after Alaric's
sack of Rome there was a breathing-space: when Theodoric,
the Christian Ostrogoth, ruled Italy; when the convert, Clovis,
was founding a Frankish kingdom in Gaul; when Arthur, victorious at Mount Badon, guarded western Britain; and when, a
little later, the Greek emperor, Justinian, restoring the imperial
rule in the eastern Mediterranean, built in his capital beside the
Bosphorus the cathedral of St. Sophia and enshrined the ancient justice of Rome in the Codes that bear his name. For
that short-lived pause mankind has cause to be grateful.

Yet the lull was only a trough between waves of destruction.

The insatiable ambition that drove Justinian to embark on the reconquest of Italy from its Ostrogoth rulers, and a flood of new barbaric invasions plunged the dying Roman world into further wars and disasters. In 539 the entire male population of Milan was massacred. A generation later, when the Anglo-Saxon tribes were resuming their advance in Britain, the Lombards crossed the Alps and established a new barbarian kingdom in the Italian plains. The peninsula which for centuries had led the world in civilisation became a wilderness of ruined estates and burnt-out cities. Meanwhile Clovis' Frankish kingdom disintegrated, and plague spread across Europe, slaying the survivors of war and famine.

It was through the lives of two great Christians that the darkness of the sixth century—the second after Rome's fall—was redeemed. The first was Benedict of Nursia who in 529 established at Monte Cassino in the hills of southern Italy the Rule which for centuries was to govern the monasteries of western Christendom. Into the fervent but chaotic communities of religious enthusiasts pursuing lives of prayer and self-denial that had sprung up on remote mountains and islands out of reach of barbarous armies, Benedict, with his Roman passion for order, introduced discipline and continuity. Regarding enthusiasm as an uncertain guide, he established at Monte Cassino what he termed "a little rule for beginners." Avoiding extremes of asceticism, which he saw usually ended in backsliding, he insisted only on vows of obedience, poverty and chastity. He laid down times for prayer and work, ordering every hour by the monastery bell until regularity of devotion became second nature. Above all, he insisted on the importance of manual labour. Idleness he denounced as the enemy of the soul. "The brethren must work with their hands, and at other times must study holy books. . . . Let them serve in turn and let none be excused the work of cook. If possible let the monastery be so that all necessary work, in mill, garden and bakehouse, can be done within it. . . . Let no-one have any property—not a pencil, nor a pocket book, nothing whatsoever—for these are they whose bodies and wills even are not their own. In a monastery none follows the will of his own heart."

The Benedictine monasteries became islands of example in a confused, ignorant world. Their black-gowned monks built churches and granaries, converted and taught the heathen, farmed and made gardens and vineyards, practised the seemingly dying arts of music, painting, carving and sculpture, and laboriously, with loving and beautiful skill, copied books and manuscripts. With their Latin speech and learning they kept alive the means of communicating cultured ideas between one country and another and between successive generations. And, by their habit of keeping written records, they made it possible for the barbaric chieftains they converted to establish the beginnings of regular administration and justice.

It was from a Benedictine monastery that Augustine and his monks brought back the Faith to southern Britain. The man who sent them was one of the greatest in human annals—a Roman magistrate who had given up wealth and position to become a monk. Raised during the plague of 590 to the office of pope or bishop of Rome, it was Gregory's fate to live when his native city had been laid waste by wars between the barbarian conquerors of Italy and a Greek emperor trying to regain the former dominion of the Caesars. Still, despite sack and ruin, the noblest monument to human achievement on earth, it was conceived by Gregory as the capital of a new and spiritual empire. A student of the great theologian, St. Augustine, whose book, the "City of God," had rallied Christendom in the hour of Rome's fall, he made it his mission to give to that earlier conception a terrestial habitation and name. A Roman living among Rome's fallen glories, he made it Rome.

Gregory sought for his bishopric, not merely its former primacy as the see of the imperial capital, but a sovereignty over all the Christian Churches. "*Servus servorum Dei,*" he styled himself, "servant of the servants of God." Yet by servant he also meant master. "I know of no bishop," he wrote, "who is not subject to the Apostolic See." Relying on an unproved tradition that the first bishop of Rome had been the apostle, Simon Peter, to whom Christ had entrusted the foundation of his Church,[4] he contended that, as his successor, he was keeper of the keys of Heaven. The effect of this tremendous claim on simple barbarians can hardly be overestimated. For with it was linked the Nordic belief in an eternal Hell for all who failed to obtain entry to Heaven. Behind this terrifying assumption lay another;

---

[4] "Thou art Peter, and upon this rock I will build my church; and the gates of hell shall not prevail against it."—*St. Matthew xvi. 18.*

that the universal cruelty, greed, lust and treachery of the time could be redeemed only by the intercession of the Church.

The Patriarchates of the Greek Empire—Constantinople, Antioch, Jerusalem, Alexandria—never, except under duress, admitted Rome's right to such authority. But to the Churches of the West, isolated and threatened by ever fresh barbarian invasions, Gregory's super-national organisation offered a lifeline. It was not a resurrection of the Roman empire; that, as Justinian's tragic failure had proved, though the dream of every educated man, had become an impossibility. Like Augustine's City of God, it was an alternative world, aloof from and at first indifferent to the changing policies of earthly princes. It bound men and nations together, not by arms, but by a common faith and doctrine.

To establish his ecclesiastical empire Gregory had first to extend the borders of western Christendom. Italy and southern Gaul were devastated by war, and the best hope for the future, he saw, lay with the vigorous barbarians of the north. Especially he fixed his gaze on England, the land of the Anglo-Saxons whom Christianity had never touched. Ever since he had first seen English boys, with their fair hair and blue eyes, in the slave-market at Rome, he had dreamed of recovering their remote island for the Church. "Of what race are they?" he had asked. *"Non Angli sed angeli,"* he had replied when told; "not Angles but angels!"

To win them he chose his friend, Augustine, prior of the monastery he had founded in his former palace at Rome. Since the barbarians had swept over it a century and a half before, Britain had seemed to the peoples of the Mediterranean a lost land, where Nordic demons dwelt in mist and storm and where, some supposed, the souls of the dead were ferried by night in phantom ships. So formidable did the dangers of the mission appear that Augustine's thirty monks, "seized with a sudden fear of going to a barbarous, fierce and unbelieving nation to whose very language they were strangers," hesitated for nearly a year before they could bring themselves to cross the Channel. But in the spring of 597 they landed in Caint or Kent, the most populous and civilised of the English kingdoms, and with a silver cross and banners, and chanting litanies,[5]

[5] "Having a silver cross carried before them for a banner, the image of our Saviour painted on a table, and singing the Litany in the way as they went." —Thomas Fuller.

made their way over the downs. It was the most important invasion England had ever known, and the most peaceful. The mysterious, unarmed visitors were received by King Ethelbert sitting at his tent door lest they should cast spells on him. He listened to what they had to say, gave them a ruined Roman church for their work in his capital, Canterbury, and resolved to embrace their faith. After he was baptised thousands of his chieftains and nobles followed his example.

The mission's success, and that of Paulinus to the Northumbrians thirty years later, were largely due to the wisdom of Gregory's instructions. He bade the monks tell their tidings of hope and salvation simply, to insist only on the essentials of faith and baptism, and to avoid anything that might needlessly offend the traditions of the people they had come to save. "It is impossible," he wrote, "to cut off everything at once from their rude natures; he who tries to ascend to the highest places rises by steps, not bounds." They were to merge the old heathen feasts in the festivals of the Christian year; to destroy the idols but keep the temples. "That the people may not have to change their places of worship, where they used to sacrifice cattle to demons, let them continue to come on the saint's day to whom the church is dedicated and slay their beasts, no longer as a sacrifice but as a feast in honour of Him they now worship." Heathendom must be destroyed, not by violence, but by Christ's way: by love, compassion and understanding.

Such a conversion did not involve too great a leap for simple heathens. Christianity was presented as the correction rather than the denial of their beliefs. They were used to thinking of gods as controlling their fate, though gods of terror. They were now told there was one God—of justice, peace and love. They were used to offering sacrifices to appease the wrath of Heaven; they were told of a new form of sacrifice, self-sacrifice. They believed in magic, and learnt of a heavenly king who was born in a manger, gave his life for man on the "healer's tree," and rose from the grave to sit on God's right hand. They were wont to celebrate the seed sown in winter darkness and the renewal of life in the spring; they were given a midwinter feast to celebrate Christ's birth and a spring one for his resurrection. Their fertility festival to Eastra, a Teuton goddess, purged of its grossness became Easter; their Yuletide junketings around the December log-fires the Christ Mass or Christmas.

Such a conversion was necessarily incomplete. It made heathens Christian, yet it also made Christianity a little heathen. And it suffered from the disadvantage—the reverse of its bloodless character—that it was a conversion from the top. It rested too much on the Germanic principle of lordship. It depended on the changing policies of a Court rather than on the hearts of a people.

When Ethelbert died in 616 it seemed doubtful whether English Christianity would survive even in Kent. Both Essex and East Anglia, where one of Ethelbert's under-kings set up a Christian altar in a temple where sacrifices were still offered to a heathen God, reverted to the old creed. Even after Paulinus' successful mission to the Northumbrian court in 625 the greater part of England, including the deep-wooded, savage hinterland, remained stubbornly pagan. Only six years after the conversion of Northumbria the heathens struck back. They were aided by the Britons of North Wales who, though they prided themselves on their retention of Christianity, regarded it as a religion too good for hated Saxons; a generation earlier they had rejected with scorn the overtures of Augustine's Kentish mission. In 632, at a great battle in Hatfield Chase, Penda, the heathen king of Mercia, and Cadwallon, a Christian prince of North Wales, routed and slew Paulinus' royal patron, Edwin. Paulinus himself fled to Kent, and Christianity was driven from Northumbria with fire and sword. In Rome it was believed that the mission to England had failed.

Yet it was not only from the south that the Faith was brought to England. Two centuries earlier, when the Saxons had overrun the lowlands, the Roman-Celts among the mountains and moors of Strathclyde, Wales and Cornwall had fallen back on the one creed of a dissolving civilisation that gave them courage and hope to endure. And though, in their harsh life of struggle and poverty, they grew almost as barbarous and illiterate, and quite as fierce, as their foes, the light of Christ's teaching still shone through the war-clouds that overhung their rugged lands. Chapels of wood and wattle with beehive vaulting, and monasteries with tiny enclosed grass lawns or "llans,"[6] appeared in Welsh valleys, and granite wheelhead crosses flowered beside the Atlantic among the Cornish rocks. All round the western

[6] The prefixes Capel and Llan still mark them on our maps.

seas, from Brittany to the Isle of Man and Clyde, the names of Celtic saints are still commemorated where once, in tiny cells and oratories, they lived their lives of faith and self-denial— Ninian who converted the Picts of Galloway; Dyfrig, Illtyd, Govan, Teilo, Padarn and David, the apostles of Wales; Samson of Dol who crossed the seas from stony Caldey to preach to the Bretons; Morwenna, Cleder, Endellion and a score of others who made the name of Christ loved by the lonely fishermen and herdsmen of Cornwall.

The distinguishing trait of all these early evangelists was their selflessness in the love of God and their sublime faith that, with Christ's aid, there was nothing they could not dare and do in their Master's name. St. Patrick's mission to the Irish in the fifth century is one of the great stories of mankind. A Roman-British landowner's son, who in youth had been carried into slavery by the Scots pirates of northern Ireland,[7] he insisted, after his escape, on returning to the island where he had suffered so much in order to save the souls and soften the harsh existence of its poor peasants. Braving the wrath of its slave-raiding princes, he faced the High King himself and his magicians in the hall of Tara. "I have cast myself," he said, "into the hands of Almighty God . . . and he shall sustain me." Wherever he went on his constant journeyings he baptised the people in river and well, impressing on them the memory of his simple, unpretending, heroic personality. When he died he left behind him the beginnings of a Christian nation.

The impact of his work was felt far beyond Ireland. The pirate raids on the British coasts ceased; instead of slavers, with their dreaded war-horns, the western isle exported saints and missionaries to convert others. During the dark centuries after Rome's fall Ireland was a Christian haven in a world of storm. Secure in her ocean remoteness from Teutonic barbarism, she became a training ground for scholars, visionaries and artists. Little more than a hundred years after Patrick's death the poet saint, Columbanus, and his disciple, St. Gall, planted the seeds of her austere learning in the monasteries of the Vosges and Switzerland. Others even braver crossed the Atlantic in open curraghs to the Faroes, Iceland and Greenland, where their relics are still found.

[7] Traditionally supposed to have been led by the famous High King, Niall of the Nine Hostages. T. C. Lethbridge, *Merlin's Island*, 149.

The most famous of all Patrick's disciples was the evangelist who, a generation before Augustine's landing in Kent, founded a monastery off the coast of Dalriada—today Argyllshire. Here he ministered to the Scots settlers from Ulster who had conquered south-western Caledonia. Tall, with brilliant eyes, a descendant of the Irish pirate kings, St. Columba was as eager and fearless in saving men as his forbears in enslaving them. On the island of Iona, clad in coarse cassock and hood of homespun, he set up a monastery church and chain of stone and wattle cells that became a camp for the conversion of a nation. Up and down the northern moors and islands where even the Roman legions had never penetrated, Columba's monks made their way, preaching, healing, and winning men's hearts. And when in 597 the proud, gentle, humble, impulsive old saint died, blessing with his last breath his monastery and island, the winnowed corn and the old white horse that worked the dairy, he left behind him apostles to carry his work, not only into the mountains of Caledonia, but southwards into England.

It was one of them who, after the flight of Paulinus, brought back the faith to Northumbria. In 635—two years after its king's defeat and death—his heir, Oswald, by his victory at Heavenfield, drove out the Welsh and Mercian invaders. The new king had been an exile at Iona and had become a fervent Christian. He appealed to its monks to help him restore Christianity in his ravaged realm. The first who was sent failed to make much impression on the Angles—the hereditary foes of his race. "What did you teach them?" asked his successor when he returned to Iona: "the love of God or only his anger? Did you forget God's word to give them the milk first and then the meat?" It was in this spirit that Aidan—the Celtic apostle of northern England—travelled up and down Northumbria for seven years, carrying the Christian message to every lonely hut and hovel. Once his royal master, who sometimes went with him as an interpreter, gave him a horse, but true to Christ's precept of sharing all things in common, Aidan gave it to the first beggar he met. With Oswald's help this barefoot saint planted Christianity so deep in the hearts of the Northumbrians that nothing could afterwards root it out. And when the king fell in battle against the Mercians, he and his disciples continued their work from the holy island of Lindisfarne, which they made an English Iona.

These Celtic evangelists surpassed even Augustine's and Paulinus' achievement. Drawing their faith, not from Peter's throne in Rome but from the saints of wind-swept Atlantic islands, their contribution to England's conversion lay not in doctrine but in example. It was this that won the simple English to Christ. For if the preachers' arguments were sometimes a travesty of their Master's, their lives were touchingly like his. Like him they took no thought for the morrow, of what they should eat or wear; they put their faith wholly in his spirit and, giving themselves to his selfless gospel, lived it. With those among whom they went, purseless and on foot, they left an image of the Good Shepherd giving his life for his sheep that was to run like a silver thread through the English tradition.

So it came about that during the seventh century after Christ England became a Christian land. From Canterbury and Rome Latin monks carried their missions into Wessex, making Christians of the warrior-farmers who had driven the Britons beyond Exe and Severn. From Northumbria the disciples of Aidan took their simple message of faith and goodness to the peoples of Mercia, converting them in thousands until even the children of its fierce old king, Penda, were baptised. These northern evangelists also regained for the Cross the kingdom of Essex, from which Augustine's Roman monks had been driven fifty years before. By 664 "all the rude nation of the English," save the South Saxons of the Andredsweald forest and the Jutes of the Isle of Wight, had accepted the creed that was beginning to re-unite and re-civilise the lands which Rome had once ruled.

This great victory for the Cross was won when a new threat to Christendom was growing in the south. Shortly before the conversion of Kent there had been born in the Arabian desert a tribesman called Mahomet. When he died in 632—the year of Edwin's defeat by Penda—the whole Arab world was ablaze with a new crusading religion. The creed of Islam or "surrender," and its devotees, the Moslems or "self-surrenderers," united the East, long subject to the Greek and Roman West, in a Holy War against the Christians. Founded like Jewry on the belief there was but one God, it proclaimed that his rule, unlike Christ's, could be established by force. When Aidan was making his missionary journeys through Northumbria, the Caliph

Omar, Mahomet's successor, captured Jerusalem—the most sacred city of Christendom. All round the eastern and southern shores of the Mediterranean the Byzantine empire crumbled at the approach of the fierce fanatics of the desert, and Christ's cross gave place to Mahomet's star and crescent. From south and east the Saracen horsemen and camel-men who overran Syria, Egypt and Carthage laid siege to the western peninsula which Paul and Peter, Patrick and Columba had won for Christ. The missionaries to England, though they knew little of what was happening elsewhere, had done their work just in time. They had redressed the balance of Christendom with a new Christian people.

To that people Christianity brought the beginnings of far-reaching change. To its teaching the English responded with great enthusiasm. They were an earnest folk, with a strong vein of emotion and poetry running through their gloomy legends; their new land, with its mists and half-lights, had intensified it. Though they only partly comprehended Christ's revolutionary creed, it came to them as a wonderful revelation. It took the darkness out of their sad, fatalistic beliefs and offered them hope and purpose. By proclaiming the equality of every soul before God, it even gave some meaning to the life of common men. It offered those with no prospect on earth—the poor toiling in the fields, the weak and sick, the slaves and prisoners—the hope of a spiritual and everlasting kingdom open to all. For the first time men were made to feel, however dimly, that it was wrong to maltreat those who were in their power but who in Christ's universal family were their brothers.

The growth of this feeling was, however, only very gradual. So, too, after the first enthusiasm roused by the barefoot Celtic saints of the north, was the spread of Christianity among the pagan peasant masses. For centuries, in England as on the continent, it remained a religion mostly of the upper classes, drawing its monks, saints and bishops from the well-born. Even for them it was often only a new and superior kind of magic: a means of buying, by prayers, incantations and pious bene-factions, protection from misfortune or foes and, still more important, from the ancient equaliser, death. It was the promise of eternal life that drew most men to Christ's creed. The hope of everlasting Heaven and the fear of its dreadful opposite, everlasting Hell, proved a rival force to the hope of plunder and the lust for pleasure and power.

Yet despite the extreme slowness of Christianity's humanising work and the immense obstacles it had to overcome, its survival and continued mission in such a rude and bloody age is one of the miracles of history. And in that miracle England now shared. Into a world inherently unequal, where the strong and fortunate had always ruled without pity, Christianity introduced the conception of the ultimate worthlessness of earthly distinctions in the light of the everlasting and far more dreadful distinction between Heaven and Hell. By its doctrine that every man had to save his soul during his life on earth, and its insistence that all were sinful and the winning of salvation no easier for king or lord than for beggar or slave, it began to modify social assumptions in a thousand subtle ways. It did not, for instance, abolish slavery—the degrading institution on which every society had hitherto rested. Yet by reminding the slave-owner that in God's eyes his soul and that of his slave were equally precious—and precarious—it created between them a bond that had never existed before. It made the denial of the rights of humanity to a fellow-being harder to justify.

To women too—though the English warrior nobility had always honoured women of its own class—Christianity brought a slow but perceptible improvement of status. For the Church taught that, if their bodies were weaker than men's, their souls were of equal importance. It was a woman who had brought Christ into the world and guarded his infancy; it was women who had stood by his cross when all mankind deserted him. The Church recognised their moral stature by the responsibilities with which it entrusted them. It stressed the sanctity of marriage and the home. It offered to women who, renouncing the joys of family life, dedicated themselves to Christ's universal family, a career as leaders of religious society. In these early centuries queens and princesses took vows of chastity and poverty, and embraced the conventual life. It was a woman, St. Hilda—a Northumbrian princess and head of the great abbey of Streoneshalh[8]—who trained many of the earliest English bishops and set the first Christian poet in England—the poor herdsman Caedmon—to sing the wonders of creation.

[8] Re-named Whitby after the Scandinavian invasions.

Christianity, too, taught men to base their social relationships on something wider than tribe or kindred. It preached the virtues of mercy and forgiveness, and of charity towards strangers. It presented peace, however hard to attain, as a virtue. It brought the warlike tribes and nations of England into the same communion as the other western European tribes and nations, and into closer contact with one another. At the time of the conversion there were seven English kingdoms—Northumbria, Mercia, Kent, Wessex, East Anglia, Essex and Sussex. Their princes were almost constantly at war, with their own kinsmen for their crowns and with their neighbours for new territories, and, at times, for the title of *Bretwalda* or overlord of England. Yet such a title had never been more than nominal, for the unity of the island under a single ruler had become only a memory. There was no sense of nationhood; a man thought of himself as a Kentish man or a Northumbrian, not as an Englishman. Without communications or regular administrations, no king's authority could reach far. Even that of the strongest died with him.

But with the coming of Christianity kings gained an instrument for governance more potent in the long run than any army. In its quiet monasteries the Church began to teach men the forgotten arts of writing and keeping records. In Jarrow and Wearmouth which the Northumbrian thane, Benedict Biscop, had founded in the north, at Melrose and Whitby, in Glastonbury, Malmesbury and Pershore in the west, in Canterbury and Minster in the south, it trained, not only the missionaries who converted the English tribes, but the men who showed their barbarian rulers how to govern justly. It gave them clerics or clerks to reduce their chaotic affairs to order, draft laws, and reckon accounts and taxes.

For the way of life the Church preached called for a lawabiding world: one, like ancient Rome, in which men made and kept promises instead of perpetually resorting to force. The king's peace was a better basis for Christian relationships than violence and anarchy. So long as the rulers of society were faithful Christians, the Church, therefore, supported their authority. It bade men, while rendering unto God the things that were God's, render unto Caesar the things that were Caesar's. It transformed the military institution of Teutonic kingship into a sacred office. In place of the traditional raising of the chosen leader on the warrior's shield by the armed host, the Church crowned him with a sacred diadem and anointed him with holy oil, praying that God would give him the armour of justice to preserve peace and do righteousness. In return the king—sanctified as the Lord's anointed—guarded the Church's property, made gifts of land and treasure to its monasteries, and conferred high office on its clerics, the only men in his realm who could read or write.

And to England itself the Church offered the first ideal of unity that transcended tribal frontiers. Though independent bishoprics were founded in every English kingdom, the Church of Rome established at Canterbury what became a metropolitan see for the whole country. In 669, five years after a great plague had carried off many of the leading English missionaries, the pope sent to fill it a sixty-six-year-old Greek monk from Tarsus in Asia Minor named Theodore, who in his twenty-one years of office did more to unite the island than any man before. A few years earlier a Northumbrian abbot named Wilfred —afterwards bishop of York and the evangelist of Sussex[9]—had persuaded the rulers and churchmen of the north at a synod held at Streoneshalh or Whitby to accept the authority and ritual of Rome—an important step, for the Celtic churches practised their own separate rites and even celebrated Easter on a different day from the rest of Christendom. The king of Northumbria himself had presided at it, giving his vote in favour of St. Peter's see, lest, he said, smilingly, when he came to the gates of Heaven there should be none to open them. It was a bitter blow to the Celtic missionaries, who liked to work by the light of their unaided consciences without organisation. But it enabled Archbishop Theodore, ceaselessly travelling the country, to carry the unifying ideas and discipline of the Roman Church "wherever the English inhabited."

Theodore was wise and tolerant. He had lived in the border land between eastern and western Christianity and had much wider views than was usual among contemporary clerics. He allowed for divorce and remarriage in certain cases, and adopted the Celtic practice of permitting the confession of sins to be made in private instead of in front of the congregation—a procedure afterwards adopted throughout the western world.

[9] He is said to have converted its people by teaching them to catch fish in nets.

He was a statesman who applied practical means to achieve
his ends, and knew how to humour men into working together.
In his monastic school at Canterbury he had law, music, arith-
metic and astronomy taught, as well as the scriptures and
Latin, the language which alone opened the doors of learning.
And he strengthened the organisation of the Church in England, not only by persuading its kings to appoint able men as
bishops of their rustic dioceses, but by summoning the latter at
regular intervals to synods where the ecclesiastical affairs of all
England were discussed. Unity in religious matters prepared the
way for unity in political.

In the century that followed the Conversion the national
genius flowered for the first time. During it the earliest English
churches were built, like Brixworth in Northamptonshire and
Escombe by the Wear, and the tall, beautiful sculptured Celtic
crosses, with their runic inscriptions and Gospel figures of men
and beasts,[10] before which the Angles of the north worshipped
in the open air. No sculpture in western Europe at that time
approached theirs in skill and beauty. It was the age in which
the first English books and manuscripts, with their exquisitely
interlaced illuminations of birds and dogs, were copied and
painted by monks in their cells; in which the stately Wilfred
taught Northumbrian choirs to sing double chants; in which
Aldhelm, a prince of the West Saxons—the reputed builder of
the little cruciform church at Bradford-on-Avon, who became
abbot of Malmesbury and first bishop of Sherborne—blended
Celtic with Roman rule, and, setting himself to master the
learning of the ancient world, offered its wisdom to all comers.
As a young monk he used to stand on Malmesbury bridge
singing the songs of his native land until he had gathered a
crowd of listeners, and then preach the gospel story and the
wonders of God's universe.

In that dawn of childlike faith Caedmon, the Streoneshalh
herdsman, too shy to sing before his fellow monks, was inspired
in a vision to write the first Christian poem in English. "Sing
to me," an angel bade him, "sing the beginning of Creation."

10 "They were wont to have, not a church, but the standard of Holy Cross
lifted up on high." Fuller, *Church History*. Some of these beautiful northern
crosses, as at Bewcastle in Cumberland and Ruthwell in Dumfriesshire, still
stand.

"Now must we praise the guardian of the realm of heaven,
The Creator's might and His mind's wisdom,
And the works of the glorious Father."

The same faith gave Cuthbert, the Tweedside shepherd who became prior of Melrose and bishop of Lindisfarne, a wonderful power over his own body and the hearts of his fellow men. On his island rock, where during his meditations he walled himself in so that he could see nothing but the sky, he lived for days without food. To be stern to himself and loving and gentle to others became part of his nature; as he walked across his wide diocese, the northern peasants would come running to confess their sins and beg his intercession. The very eider-duck, it was said, nestled against his garments. His inspiration can still be seen in the wonderful Lindisfarne Gospels in the British Museum, written on Holy Island "for God and St. Cuthbert," and in the great cathedral shrine that long afterwards rose on the rocks above the river at Durham to house his body.

Perhaps the most wonderful of all the achievements of the time was that of the Venerable Bede, the greatest scholar in Christendom. From his monastery cell at Jarrow he poured out a never-ceasing stream of books: history, theology, poetry, grammar and natural science. To him England owes the practice of dating years from the birth of Christ and the first prose written in Latin by an Englishman. His vision of Hell—"where there is no voice but of weeping, no face but of the tormentors" —expresses the very soul of the dark ages he helped to illumine.[11] The most famous of his works was the Ecclesiastical History of the English nation—the story of the Conversion. Lucid, just, immensely learned, it is a monument to his age, his Faith and his country. That life of scholarship and labour, with the tireless hand writing amid the intervals of prayer and teaching, sometimes so frozen that it could hardly grip the pen, is one of the proud memories of England. "Write quickly, I know not how long I shall hold out," the old saint cried as he lay

[11] So does his picture of Heaven:
" Nor any night
To snatch the splendour of the gracious light,
Nor sorrow comes, nor tears, nor tired old age."
Helen Waddell, *Wandering Scholars*, 39.

dying on the floor of his cell, dictating the last sentences of his translation of St. John. He left his countrymen the earliest version of the gospel in their own tongue and a tradition, rare in that age, of gentleness, love of truth, and scrupulous fairness.

In their zeal for saving souls the English, who had inherited the missionary tradition of the Celtic Church, carried their new-found Faith to the lands of their forbears overseas. During the first half of the eighth century a succession of great Englishmen, at the risk of their lives, took the Gospel to the heathen tribesmen of Germany and Frisia. Just as St. Patrick two hundred years earlier had converted the Irish, so Wilfred and Willibrod of Northumbria and Boniface of Wessex brought Christ to the Teutons. By doing so they went farther than the legions in the high noon of Rome and planted the seeds of civilisation in the forests of central Europe. At one time there were seven English bishops working there. To the greatest of them all, Boniface of Crediton, a West-Saxon landowner's son who became spiritual adviser to the king of the Franks and first archbishop of Mainz, the West owes the conversion of Germany. "Have pity on them," he wrote of its people, "for they themselves are wont to say, 'We are of one blood and bone.'" No Englishman's work has had a greater influence on the world. The German Gothic cathedrals, the testimony of Luther, the Christian music of Schültz and Bach all sprang from the seed this west-country saint sowed.

After a life of tireless endeavour—baptising the heathen, founding monasteries, teaching the arts of church-building, music, book-making and illumination—Boniface died a martyr's death in Frisia. He wrote the first chapter in the history of the expansion of English ideals beyond the seas. One thinks of him, like St. Patrick, standing unarmed, with sandalled feet and tonsured head, among the barbarians, confronting them with the words of Christian Rome: *"Hi in curribus, et hi in equis, nos autem in nomine Domini nostri ambulabimus. . . ."* "Some in chariots and some on horseback, but journey we in the name of the Lord!"

Chapter Four

ALFRED

So long as I have lived I have striven to live worthily. I desire to leave the men who come after me a remembrance in good works.

Alfred

If we could look down on Europe at the end of the eighth century, two hundred years after Augustine's landing, we should see a continent in whose western half, from the Mediterranean to Scotland, Christianity had become the principal faith of man. This vast tract of land was divided into many little kingdoms, whose uncertain frontiers changed constantly with the wars and family quarrels of their rulers. Yet one institution crossed all frontiers and outlasted all earthly rulers—the Christian Church. In a landscape of peasants' huts and rude wooden hunting-lodges, its monasteries were everywhere the largest buildings to be seen, save for the marble temples and palaces of the Roman past which still stood in the walled cities of Italy and southern Gaul. And winding past squalid villages and little wooden castles, through forests, fords and mountain passes, ran the grassy tracks, trodden by horsehooves and the feet of monks and pilgrims, that led to Rome, the "eternal city" and capital of western Christendom.

Only in the remote Celtic islands of Ireland and western Scotland, and in the south-east, beyond the Balkan mountains, where the Greek emperors still maintained the ancient pomp of the Caesars and the Byzantine Patriarch ignored the pope's claim to be Christ's vice-regent, were there Christian communi-

ties that refused to acknowledge the spiritual supremacy of
Rome. But Christendom was only a world within a world. Europe itself was half heathen. Its eastern plains and forests and
northern mountains were still peopled by savages who had
never heard of Christ. And all along the eastern and southern
shores of the Mediterranean—the earliest cradle of the Faith—
the patriarchates of Alexandria, Jerusalem and Antioch had
been overrun by fanatic tribesmen from the Arabian deserts. A
Christian sea, given over to peaceful trade, had become a pirate-
ridden frontier between Christendom and Islam, swept by Arab
fleets. Constantinople only escaped capture through its superb
strategic position. In the east, emulating Alexander a thousand
years before, Moslem armies passed the Oxus and reached
the frontiers of India. And early in the eighth century, while
Bede was still working in his cell at Jarrow, the Moors had
crossed from Africa into Spain and, over-running the peninsula,
planted the Crescent on the Pyrenees. Thence they had poured
through the passes into the land of the Franks.

In that dreadful hour it had seemed as though Christendom
was broken. Then in 732 the Franks under Charles Martel, the
Hammer—mayor of the palace and chief minister to their
titular king—saved the West at Poitiers. Having secured its
southern frontier, this great soldier, with his tall Frankish
swordsmen, turned eastward against the heathens of central Europe. It was with his help that Archbishop Boniface converted
the Saxons and advanced Christendom's outposts to the Elbe.
Later the great English evangelist, with the pope's blessing,
anointed Charles's son, Pepin, king of the Franks in place of
the last feeble Merovingian monarch. This alliance with the
Papacy conferred the leadership of western Christendom on the
new dynasty.

Pepin's son, Charlemagne, had even wider ambitions. Like
all the great men of his age he was haunted by memories of the
imperial unity of the past. Though four centuries had elapsed
since the western Empire had fallen, every attempt to revive
civilisation led men back to Rome. Charlemagne, though he
could scarcely read and was framed by nature for the saddle
and the battlefield, had a passionate admiration for learning.
This blond, barbarian giant, who slept with a slate under his
pillow, and made the English scholar, Alcuin of York, his chief
counsellor and head of his palace school, conceived the tre-

mendous ambition of reuniting the West in a new Roman empire in place of the remote and now almost entirely oriental
empire of Byzantium. He tried, though in vain, to reconquer
Spain from the Moors—the heroic death of his general, Roland,
in the Roncesvalles pass inspired Frankish poetry for centuries.
And he sought, with greater success, to embody in his empire
all his fellow Teutons beyond the Ems and Weser. For thirty
years he warred against them, repeatedly defeating them and
striving to break their stubborn savagery by enforced mass bap-
tisms.

Yet more than to the eastern forests from which his forbears
had come, Charlemagne's spirit was drawn to the Roman south.
He saw himself as the head of Christendom and its guardian.
Like his father, Pepin, he led a Frankish army across the Alps
against the Lombard conquerors of north Italy. And on Christmas day 800, as he knelt at mass in St. Peter's, Rome, his ally
the pope crowned him with traditional imperial rites as Augustus and emperor of the Romans. To dreamers it appeared as if
the hand of time had been set back and the Roman Empire
was restored. And it was now, it seemed, a Holy Roman Empire.

In Britain, too, attempts were made to restore the Roman
past. Under the inspiration of Christianity the Anglo-Saxon
kings were groping towards some wider union of society than
the tribal gathering and pioneer settlement. Ine, king of the
West Saxons—a contemporary of Charles Martel—published a
code of written law for his people and made a pilgrimage to
Rome. Half a century later Offa, king of Mercia, established an
overlordship over the whole island south of the Humber and
assumed the Roman title of *Rex Anglorum*, king of the English.
He encouraged trade with the continent, made a commercial
treaty with Charlemagne—with whom he corresponded on
friendly terms—and minted gold coins, some of which, bearing
his name, circulated as far as the Moslem caliphate of Bagdad.
And at home he built an earthen dyke to keep out Welsh
raiders which, running from Dee to Wye, still marks the border
between England proper and Wales and Monmouthshire.

Yet neither Charlemagne's vast empire, stretching from the
Ebro to the Carpathians, nor Offa's smaller English kingdom
endured. Barbarian kings, however lofty their aspirations,
could not govern large areas. They lacked roads and bridges,

trained servants, regular administration and justice. They
could not give their peoples the security from which patriotism
and the habit of subordinating self to the public interest arise.
They thought of their dominions as family possessions which
they were free to treat as they pleased. Even when they ruled,
as Charlemagne, with a sense of vocation, they could not transmit it to their sons, who by tribal custom had the right to divide
their patrimony. Charlemagne's empire quickly dissolved after
his death. Under his grandchildren and their heirs—a succession
of phantom royalties with names like Lewis the German, Lewis
the Blind, Charles the Bald, Charles the Simple—it was broken
up into even smaller kingdoms.

Nor were the methods by which the rulers of that age sought
to widen their realms calculated to preserve them. Their Christianity, though strongly felt, was only skin-deep. Enraged by
the resistance of the Saxon tribesmen, Charlemagne massacred
his prisoners in thousands; Offa, founder and patron of monasteries, put out the eyes of a Kentish rival. Such actions created,
not love and loyalty, but bitter hatred. When the strong hand
of their perpetrators was removed, civil war and vengeance over-
took the realms they had created. On Offa's death in 796 his
English empire fell to pieces. So did the kingdom of Northumbria, whose rulers had tried to unite the northern half of the
island by similar means. In less than a century five of its kings
were murdered or slain in battle, five more deposed and four
forced to abdicate.

The recurring problem of what historians call the Dark Ages
—the long blood-stained centuries after the fall of Rome—was
that of preventing society from disintegrating because its
stronger members could not be subjected to any law but their
own passions. The Church had familiarised Christians with
ideals of what just government should be. It offered, through
its clerics and scribes, a means of applying them. What was
lacking was a profession of dedicated kingship, pursued by
hereditary princes with the power to preserve peace, social continuity and order.

And just as the Northumbrian attempt to conquer Caledonia
aroused in the Picts and Scots a resistance so strong as to break
up the conquerors' realm, so Charlemagne's campaigns to enlarge his frontiers provoked a response from the northern heathens that all but destroyed Christendom. During the ninth

century there fell on western Europe a sudden and dreadful terror.

It came from the northern seas. The chief power in these desolate waters had been the Frisians—the heathen fisher-folk among whom Boniface had met his death. Their absorption in the Frankish empire—a land-power uninterested in the sea— had left their rivals, the piratical Danes and the Norsemen of Scandinavia, in control of the German ocean. By his Saxon conquests Charlemagne had destroyed the buffer between his dominions and heathen Denmark, where many of his foes had taken refuge. The Danes viewed their new neighbours with deep suspicion. Even while Charlemagne was still alive they began to ravage the Frisian coast.

It was a portent of what was to come. Already its shadow had fallen on the Christian North. In the summer of 793 there had appeared off St. Cuthbert's Holy Island of Lindisfarne a pirate fleet. Its crews seized the gold and silver from the monastery church, slew the monks and carried off the novices as slaves. Then, setting fire to the buildings, they vanished into the summer seas.

A year later others like them appeared off Bede's old monastery at Jarrow, fifty miles down the coast. This time Northumbrian fighting men arrived before they had finished plundering and captured one of their chiefs, whom they threw into a pit filled with adders. But the seas were wide. The English had no fleet, and the pirates could come and go as they pleased. They soon reappeared, hundreds of miles to the south in Weymouth bay—"three ships of the Northmen out of Haerethaland." When the reeve of Dorchester rode down to stop them, they slew him and sailed away with their treasure. "For almost 350 years," wrote Alcuin on hearing the news, "we and our fathers have dwelt in this fair land and never have such times appeared in Britain like these we now endure from a pagan people." To him it seemed a scourge from God to punish the vices of the age.

But if to earnest-minded contemporaries such visitations were a judgment on moral laxity—on drunkenness, gluttony and other Anglo-Saxon failings—to us they seem even more the result of neglect to defend the seas and forgetfulness of what lay beyond. The ancestors of the English had also harried Britain from the sea. Now their successors bore down from the same savage shores to plunder the wealth they had created. The island's coast had ceased to be a quiet retreat for saints and scholars and become what it was four centuries before, a place of terror.

From the fiords of Norway to the Jutland flats, the Scandinavian peoples were on the move. The soil they tilled could not any longer sustain their rising population, nor a pastoral life satisfy their more turbulent members who were in revolt against their rulers. They were vigorous, picturesque, flamboyant rascals, younger sons of petty fiord jarls for whom there was no place at home, with long, flaxen hair, bright burnished spears and two-handed battle-axes. They delighted in silver-bound swords and jewels, golden bracelets and scarlet cloaks with brilliant borders. And, like all their race, they had a passionate love of independence and self-help. Around them they gathered bands of bloodthirsty followers, who feasted and drank in their halls in winter, sallying forth each spring "to play the game of Freyr." Berserks and wolf-coats they called themselves; wherever they went, they boasted, the ravens followed.

Accustomed to using the sea as a highway—the only communication between their scattered settlements—these adventurers were now offered a wonderful prize. For though the land-frontiers of Charlemagne's ill-knit empire were still guarded by numerous warlike levies, its backdoor to the ocean was almost undefended. It took them a generation to grasp the extent of their opportunity. While Charlemagne lived, their attacks were confined almost wholly to coasts outside his control. Even southern Britain was left unmolested as too dangerous to be profitable. But the northern half of the island suffered a dreadful martyrdom. Every spring the young pirate seamen of Norway and Denmark—Vikings as they were called from the *viks* or creeks they haunted—set out in fleets of long, narrow, open-decked war-boats, with carved dragon-heads, raven banners and bright, striped sails. The very word sail in English derives from their *seil*. Following the mountainous island fringe of the Atlantic southwards from Norway, they plundered in turn the Shetlands, Orkneys, Sutherland and the Hebrides. In 802—two years after Charlemagne's coronation in Rome—they sacked the monastery of Iona. Then they fell on Ireland.

During the three centuries since Patrick's mission the Irish had achieved great things. Their monasteries and monastic schools were among the best and most learned in Europe; their illuminated manuscripts, like the lovely Book of Kells, still preserved at Trinity College, Dublin, the flower of western art. In the monk, John Scotus, they produced the first philosopher of the age, while their wandering scholars and poets fashioned verses more subtle than any to be found in that barbarous time.[1] But politically they had changed little. Their titular High King still reigned with his fellow kings over their five sovereign and equal provinces, while a host of tribal chieftains kept their petty state and raided one another for cattle and hostages. Of unity, or capacity to combine against an external foe, there was none.

Thus, the raiders' impact was calamitous. No-one could make any effective resistance. With their shallow-draft boats they swept up the estuaries and rivers, sacking every monastery, farm and building, and carrying off the younger men and women as slaves. Every spring the north-east wind brought more of them; "there came," a despairing chronicler wrote, "great sea-cast floods of foreigners into Erin." Soon they took to wintering on her coasts, making permanent forts on island and promontory. The round-towers whose ruins can still be seen were built as shelters from their ravages. Ireland's "Golden Age" of art and

---

[1] A delightful example occurs in the commonplace book of a ninth century Irish monk at Reichenau.

"I and Pangur Ban my cat,
'Tis a like task we are at;
Hunting mice is his delight,
Hunting words I sit all night.

'Tis a merry thing to see
At our tasks how glad are we,
When at home we sit and find
Entertainment to our mind.

'Gainst the wall he sets his eye,
Full and fierce and sharp and sly;
'Gainst the wall of knowledge I
All my little wisdom try.

So in peace our task we ply,
Pangur Ban, my cat, and I;
In our arts we find our bliss,
I have mine and he has his."
　　　　Robin Flower, *Poems and Translations.*

learning faded into the Atlantic mists at the whip of a few
thousand arrogant Norsemen who knew how to combine. The
brutal pirate, Turgeis, ruled Ulster from Patrick's holy Armagh,
while his wife, a bloodthirsty witch, profaned the high altar at
Conmacnoise with human sacrifices.

During the generation that followed Charlemagne's death
the Norwegians, extending their circle round the British isles,
reached the coasts of Brittany and western France. And the
Danes, sailing westwards along the southern shores of the North
Sea and Channel, began to encircle Britain from the other direction and to appear in Ireland, too. Often there were fights
between the two branches of the Scandinavian race—the "white
strangers" and "black strangers." By this time both were out, not
merely for plunder—of which there was little left—but for land
for permanent settlement. From the ports they established at
Dublin, Waterford, Wexford and Limerick, they sought to turn
the western isle into a new and, for them, freer Scandinavia, as
they had done—or were doing—to Iceland, the Faroes, Shetlands and the Orkneys.

But, with the disintegration of Charlemagne's empire under
his squabbling heirs, richer prey was now ripe for plucking.
Between 834 and 845 the Danes sacked Utrecht and Dorestad
at the mouth of the Rhine, Rouen on the Seine, and finally Paris,
the island stronghold a hundred miles up the river which Clovis,
first king of the Franks, had built three centuries before. They
even reached Aix-la-Chapelle, the former imperial capital, and,
harrying the Moorish conquerors of Spain, sailed up the Gua-
dalquivir to Cordova. The wonderful mobility given by unchallenged sea-power in that roadless age enabled a few thousand
swordsmen to terrorise half a continent. Able to concentrate
against any point on an enemy's coast, they could nearly always
surprise and outnumber their victims. When they failed, they
could take to their boats and descend on some other point.

In 859 these sea-kings rounded the Pillars of Hercules and
entered the Mediterranean, terrorising both Moors and Christians. In clinker-built ships of forty or fifty tons, steering by
sun and stars without compass, chart or sextant, they crossed
the Atlantic and discovered the "long beaches" of North America.
Their kinsfolk from Sweden, sailing up the rivers of eastern
Europe, reached the Black Sea and gave a name to the Russian

State. They took the trading town of Novgorod and ruled at Kiev. Four times their fleets threatened Byzantium or Micklegarth, as they called the capital of the Greek empire.

Long before this the Danes had struck in force at southern Britain. In 835 "heathen men" landed in the Isle of Sheppey at the mouth of the Thames. Thereafter, every spring, their dragon-prowed boats, glittering with spears and axes, crept up the east-coast rivers. Then, securing themselves on some marsh-encircled island, they seized the horses of the neighbouring countryside and rode out to plunder and slay. If the bewildered farmers combined against them, they formed a ring and, with their massed battle-axes swinging over the "linden wall" of shields, hacked a way back to their ships. Wherever they went they deliberately spread terror. At Crowland, wrote the seventeenth century historian Fuller, "the Danes entering slew Theodore the abbot on the high altar, Asker the prior in the vestiary, Lethwyne the sub-prior in the refectory, Herbert in the choir, Ulric the torch-bearer in the same place, Grimketul and Agamund, each of them an hundred years old, in the cloisters." At Peterborough a single Viking killed eighty-four monks with his own hand; another cut the ribs off an English prince, drew out his lungs and threw salt into his wounds. Breaking open tombs and coffins, and stoning obdurate Christians, "these pagans marched forwards into Cambridgeshire" with waggons full of plunder, and "with a violent inundation, brake into the kingdom of the East Angles." When everyone for whom no ransom was forthcoming had been massacred, they moved on to the next district. Those who paid them enough to go away they left alone till another year, when they returned for more.

"From the fury of the Norsemen," prayed the peasants in their churches, "good Lord, deliver us!"

> "Men's cheeks faded
> On shores invaded
> When shorewards waded
>   The lords of fight;
> When monks affrighted
> To windward sighted
> The birds full-flighted

Of swift sea-kings;
When churl and craven
Saw hard on haven
The wide-winged raven
At main-mast height."[2]

So systematic were these fearful pirates' ravages that, from the
Humber to the Solent, hardly a vestige remained of a Saxon
church within a day's ride of the coast. By the middle of the
century the island seemed their own. In 851 three hundred and
fifty of their ships anchored in the Thames. That autumn,
after the crews had burnt London and Canterbury, they encamped in Thanet. Thenceforward their armies wintered regularly in England. In two decades they systematically destroyed
the kingdoms of Northumbria, East Anglia and Mercia. The
final collapse came after 865, when the sons of Ragnar Lothbrok
—greatest of all Vikings—landed on the east coast. The ancient
realm of Northumbria, with its famous monasteries and beautiful
crosses, crumbled to dust. So did the famous library of York
that had trained Alcuin, and the Fenland abbeys—Crowland,
Peterborough and Ely. In 869 Edmund, last of the East Anglian
kings, after defeat and capture was barbarously slain for refusing to renounce his faith.[3] When three years later the ruler
of Mercia fled to the continent, only one English kingdom remained.

Since the beginning of the century Wessex—once a depend-
ency of Offa's Mercia—had been growing in importance. Absorbing both the small English States of the south-east and the
Ibero-Celts of Devon, its rustic princes, ruling a people half
Saxon, half Celtic, had carried their golden dragon banner to
the Straits of Dover and the Atlantic. A quarter of a century
later, at the battle of Ellendun in the chalk-country near
Swindon, Egbert of Wessex—ancestor of our present Queen—
ended the long Mercian supremacy and established his rule over

[2] Broken pieces of English reliquaries and book-bindings are still preserved
in Scandinavian museums. *The Heritage of Early Britain*, 143.

[3] He was later canonised, and the great abbey of Bury St. Edmunds built
round his shrine. The effigy of the tame wolf which guarded his body during
the night of his death can still be seen carved on the benches of East Anglian
churches—notably at Walpole St. Peter in Norfolk, and Hadleigh and Stonham
Aspal in Suffolk.

the whole island south of the Thames and Cotswolds. Fifteen years later he won the first English victory over the Vikings and their Cornish and Welsh allies at Hingston Down on the hills above Plymouth. In 851 his son, Ethelwulf, again saved his kingdom from invasion after London had fallen.

But by 870, half encircled by sea, and with all England north of the Thames in the Norsemen's grip, Wessex seemed doomed. In that year the Danes entered it in force and, encamping in an impregnable position between Thames and Kennet near the site of modern Reading, started to ravage it as they had done its sister kingdoms of the north and east. Everywhere the Christian cause was failing. In the Mediterranean Moslem pirates, after conquering Sicily, had devastated the whole of southern Italy and plundered the suburbs of Rome.

At that moment the Danes encountered, in a young prince or atheling of the House of Wessex, one of the great men of all time. Alfred, youngest son of King Ethelwulf, was born at Wantage in 849, three hundred years after the Saxons first settled in Wessex. As a child he had been taken by his father on a pilgrimage to Rome. The journey across Europe, the sight of the great city with its noble ruins of the world of learning and order, had stirred his imagination so that all his life he longed to restore learning and order to his fellow men. He had even tried to teach himself to read from one of the beautiful illuminated Latin books which the monks copied by hand and, so the story goes, loved it so much—a strange love in a little Saxon prince—that his mother gave it him. Then, when still a boy, he had had to lay learning aside to be a soldier and fight beside his brothers and their fellow English kings against the Norsemen, who every year were advancing deeper into England.

Unlike many other princes of the time, though he won the love of the rough warriors around him, Alfred refused to take any part in the dynastic quarrels that divided his country. His one thought was not of himself but of serving her. Instead of seeking the crown, he loyally supported each of his three brothers who in turn wore it. At the time that the Danish host invaded Wessex, he was acting as second-in-command to the last of them.

It was due to the presence of mind of this young man of twenty-one that the sole remaining English army was not surprised and destroyed early in 871 on the Berkshire hills at Ashdown. While his brother, the king, was at his prayers, he acted with lightning decision and led his rustic levies, "like a wild boar," against the advancing Danes. "All day the opposing ranks met in conflict, with a great shouting from all men," we are told, "one side bent on evil, the other side fighting for life and their loved ones and native land." By nightfall thousands of corpses lay round the stunted thorn tree in the centre of the battle-field. Among them were a Danish king and five earls or jarls. The remainder of their host fled across the downs to Reading.

Yet Alfred's struggle against the invaders had only begun. Ashdown was one of eight battles fought in that dreadful year. A few weeks later fresh Danish armies poured into Wessex, whose own levies, composed of farmers with homes and fields, began to dissolve. It was this, as much as command of the sea, that gave the Danes their advantage. That spring, when his brother died, Alfred was hastily elected to a falling throne, and left, with a few personal retainers, to defend the last Christian kingdom in England. Hopelessly outnumbered, he managed to hold out till the winter. Then, by paying a ransom or *danegeld*, he was able to secure a brief respite for his unhappy people.

He used it well. During the next few years the Danes were so busy partitioning Northumbria and Mercia and setting up States of their own in what today are Yorkshire, Lincolnshire, Nottinghamshire, Derbyshire, Leicestershire and East Anglia, that they had little time to spare for harrying Wessex. Alfred worked incessantly, reorganising the peasant levies of his half-ruined kingdom and laying the first foundations of an English fleet. When everyone else was in despair and Christians all round the coasts of Europe were meekly submitting to the terrible heathen, this modest, gentle, scholarly man refused to give in. He saw the weakness of the Viking leaders—their greed and savage rivalry—and knew that, if he could win time and sustain the courage of his people, he would beat them in the end.

In the spring of 876 the expected blow fell. The Great Army, as it was called, broke up its camp at Cambridge and marched at high speed across Wessex, ravaging the countryside as it went. Reaching the south coast at Wareham, where it stockaded itself between the Frome and Trent, it seized the approaches to the wide anchorage of Poole harbour. Here Danish fleet-armies from France, Wales and Ireland joined it. For, seeing in Alfred the one man in western Europe who could withstand them, the Norsemen were resolved to crush him once and for all.

He met the challenge boldly. Assembling his levies, he encamped before Wareham and blockaded the invaders. The latter's control of the sea enabled them to receive supplies and reinforcements and to raid the coasts in his rear. But after a time, as he anticipated, they drew weary of their confinement. Uninterrupted summer plundering was essential to the very existence of a Danish army; it could not maintain itself or its morale without. Its leaders therefore asked for a truce, and, on payment of a danegeld, agreed to quit Alfred's realm. Yet scarcely had they sworn to do so, than they treacherously attacked his outposts and broke out on their horses to the west, where, with the help of a fleet, they seized Exeter and proceeded to lay waste Devon. But the stubborn English king followed them, drove them back to their entrenchments and once more resumed his blockade. Then a great storm off the Purbeck cliffs came to his aid and destroyed more than a hundred of their ships and thousands of men who were on their way to relieve Exeter. Before winter fell the besieged offered hostages, made their peace and withdrew to Gloucester across the Mercian border. Nothing like this had happened to a Viking army since Egbert's victory at Hingston forty years before.

But the Danes were not used to defeat. They still believed they could destroy Alfred as they had destroyed his fellow English kings. At midwinter 877–8, a few days after the Christmas feast, their army under King Guthrum suddenly broke into Wessex. Once more they stockaded themselves in an impregnable river position—at Chippenham in Wiltshire—and began to plunder the countryside. Simultaneously a fleet under one of Ragnar Lothbrok's sons swept down on the Devon coast. This time the attack was so unexpected and its ravages so wide-spread that the morale of Wessex gave way, as that of Northumbria and Mercia had done. There was a sudden panic and many of its chief men fled to France. Alfred himself with a handful of followers was forced to take refuge in the lake isle of Athelney, where he lay for a time, we are told, "in great sorrow and unrest amid the woods and marshes of the land of Somerset."[4]

Yet Alfred was no despairer. Quietly and with unconquerable courage he set himself to repair the broken breaches of his kingdom. While he hid among the Parret marshes his messengers, travelling the ancient hill-roads of Wessex, carried his orders to his countrymen to rally. Shortly before Easter the men of Devon, besieged under their ealdorman, Odda, made a sudden sally against the tormentors, routed them and slew their leader. Then, following a plan prepared by the king, contingents from all the western shires, marching through forest and along the grass hill-tracks, began to converge on a secret rendezvous— a lonely landmark and meeting place of ways called Egbert's stone on the downs overlooking the vale of Knoyle east of the forest of Selwood. Here, six weeks after Easter, to their unspeakable joy, Alfred joined them.

Without a day's delay the army set out northwards towards the enemy's camp. On the second day, after halting for the night near Warminster, they encountered the Danish host, hastily assembling in their path on the rolling chalk downs above Bratton and Ethandun, today Eddington.[5] Attacking in a single column of packed shields, after many hours' hard fighting they broke its ranks and drove it in confusion towards Chippenham. In the hour of his victory—perhaps the most important ever won on English soil—Alfred showed one of the rarest attributes of a commander. Exhausted though he and his men were, he pursued his foe relentlessly all the way to their camp fourteen miles off, slaying them in thousands and capturing vast quantities of cattle and stores. He then closely besieged it, preventing every attempt to revictual. After a fortnight, "terrified by hunger and cold and fear," the Danes laid down their arms.

In victory Alfred's full grandeur became apparent. Undiscouraged by their past treachery, he took pity on his enemies. He fed them and offered them peace. Having shown heroism

[4] In after years he loved to tell stories of his adventures there, among them— according to later legend—the tale of the burnt cakes in the cowherd's cottage. Nearly a thousand years afterwards, in 1693, a gold and enamelled jewel bearing his name, *Aelfred Mec Heht Gewyrcan*—"Alfred ordered me to be made" —was found on a farm at Athelney, and is now in possession of the University of Oxford.

[5] Where now the School of Infantry fights its mimic battles. It is believed that the white horse at Bratton was originally cut to commemorate the victory.

in adversity, in triumph he practised the greatest of Christian virtues. He made his cruel foes, who had learnt to respect his valour, realise his nobility. The Danish king at his invitation accepted baptism—the first of his race to do so. "King Alfred," wrote his friend and scribe, Bishop Asser, "stood godfather to him and raised him from the holy font."

Like his victories, Alfred's peace-making at Wedmore marked a turning-point in English history. It made it possible for Danes and Englishmen—the injurers and injured—to live together in a single island, and opened the way to the former's conversion and civilisation. The English king had the wisdom to realise that the sword, though powerful to defend, could settle nothing permanently, and that only a conquest of the heart could endure. And though he and his people had suffered terribly from the invaders, he was too magnanimous to seek revenge and too wise to suppose he could expel them altogether. Christianity and the legacy of Roman order might transform Danes as it had transformed Saxons. No greater act of statesmanship has ever been performed by an English king.

Nor was Alfred, in his far-sighted magnanimity, under any illusion. He knew that, though he might make friends with the invaders who had already homes in the east and north of England, other Danish armies would again attack her from the sea. This patient, courageous man refused to rest on his laurels. While he offered friendship to the defeated, he prepared for new attacks from their kinsmen. He used the peace he had won to give his kingdom a fighting force capable of withstanding the worst that could befall her. Once more, seeing the only certain safety was to defeat the invaders before they could land, he began to build ships. Though he could not hope in his lifetime to defeat a massed Danish fleet—for the pirates' mastery of the northern seas had been unchallenged for generations—the war-galleys he laid down, some twice the size of the largest Viking vessel, made small-scale raiding of the Wessex coast too costly to be profitable. In their first year they destroyed more than twenty pirate ships. On another occasion a Kentish-built fleet, manned partly by seamen whom Alfred had recruited from Frisia, caught sixteen Danish galleys at the mouth of the Suffolk Stour and captured them all.

Even more effective was the English king's reorganisation of his army. To overcome the fatal tendency of a militia of peasants to disperse to their farms after a few weeks' campaigning, he divided the national *fyrd*, as it was called, into two halves, each taking it in turn to serve in wartime until relieved by the other. And to stiffen its amateur ranks, he fostered the growth of a fighting aristocracy by encouraging larger freeholders to assume military rank and responsibility. To every churl with five or more hides of land he offered the right of thaneship and its privileges in return for regular military service with helm, mail-shirt, sword and horse. This semi-professional *corps d'élite*, which in wartime was kept permanently embodied, he also divided into sections, every member in peacetime having to serve for a month in arms for every two at home. This gave him a regular mounted field-force capable of opposing assailants who, living by war, had not, like English fyrdmen, to be for ever thinking about their neglected farms and homes.

The most momentous of Alfred's military reforms was his creation of the fortified burgh or town. The Danish armies had supported themselves by seizing carefully-chosen strategic bases which they provisioned from the surrounding countryside and made impregnable with earthworks and stockades. This had made it impossible for the English either to bring them to action or to maintain themselves in their vicinity. Alfred's answer was to forestall them by turning such sites into permanently garrisoned English strongholds capable of keeping invaders at bay until his field army could destroy them. This device of his original yet practical mind not only gave Wessex a shield which, copied later by other European rulers, enabled western Christendom to survive the Viking attacks, but laid the foundations of urban life in England. Our oldest English towns arose as sentinels to guard the countryside against the Norsemen.

The strength of these burghs lay, not in imposing fortifications, which Alfred's ill-educated and much-plundered subjects had neither the wealth nor skill to make, but in the valour of their defenders. To people them he used the pick of his kingdom's manhood. Every district had to support its burgh, and every local thane to build a house in it and either live there in person or maintain a fighting man to defend it. In this way the veterans of Alfred's wars became the burghers of England's earliest towns. Some of these, like Rochester, Exeter and Chichester, and his capital, Winchester, were built on the sites, and partly from the stones, of Roman cities; others like Oxford and Shaftes-

bury were new creations. The most important of all was London
—formerly inside the Mercian border—which he won and took
over, after it had been destroyed by a Danish raiding party, and
re-populated with English veterans. It proved an acquisition of
immense strategic and political significance. During the last two
decades of his reign, Alfred, overcoming the national prejudice
against urban life, founded some twenty-five towns, or about half
the number the Romans had raised during their three-and-a-half
centuries of occupation.

When towards the end of the reign the Viking Grand Army
again attacked southern England, it was completely frustrated
by this ingenious system. After four years' spasmodic and prof-
itless raiding it was driven ignominiously from the land. Only
one town in Wessex—the little port of Appledore in Kent—was
taken by it, and this had never been an established burgh.
Exeter, Rochester and Chichester all successfully withstood
sieges, and the invaders were repeatedly brought to battle and
defeated by the field-army. The heart of the country was scarcely
touched. The English king had both saved his kingdom and
given new hope to Christendom.

Yet Alfred's true greatness lay not in war but peace. He
wanted to leave behind a kingdom not only secure from foes but
rich in the arts of civilisation. Around him lay, after two generations of warfare, a ruined country—its farms wasted, its monasteries and schools burnt, its people reduced to ignorance and
squalor. Its nobility and even its clergy were almost completely
illiterate. At the start of the reign there was hardly a clerk in
Wessex who could understand the Latin of the services he
repeated. Alone in that ravaged land in his passion for education
—the fruit of his early journey to Rome—Alfred set himself to
teach his people. Nearly half his revenue was devoted to educational ends: to the training of artificers, to the support of the
foreign scholars and craftsmen he brought over as teachers
from every country in Christendom; to the restoration of ruined
monasteries and convents and the foundation of new ones at
Athelney and Shaftesbury; to the great school he established for
teaching the sons of thanes and freemen to read and write and
which in the course of the next generation created something
unique in western Europe: a literate lay nobility. "All the sons
of freemen," he instructed his bishops, "who have the means to

undertake it should be set to learning English letters, and such as are fit for a more advanced education and are intended for high office should be taught Latin also." Even their astonished fathers were made to take lessons. "It was a strange sight," Bishop Asser recorded, "to see the ealdormen, who were almost all illiterate from infancy, and the reeves and other officials learning how to read, preferring this unaccustomed and laborious discipline to losing the exercise of their power." "God Almighty be thanked," Alfred wrote before his death, "we have now teachers in office!"

It was characteristic of this modest, conscientious man that he taught himself before trying to teach others. He worked with his craftsmen, helping to design houses and even inventing a candle clock and a reading-lantern. And he repaired the defects of his neglected childhood and war-riven youth by making himself a master of Latin—the language in which the knowledge of the past was preserved. Even while he was still fighting the Danes he had learned works read aloud to him at every spare moment until he could read them freely for himself. Then, in the intervals of reconstructing and administering a broken realm, he set to work to translate the books which could alone impart to his people the wisdom he wanted them to share. He made no pretence of being a scholar nor thought of himself as a clever man; he sought only to expound the learning of others. But he personally undertook the task—as heroic as any of his feats in battle—of translating into the rough vernacular of his country the most useful works of Christian and classical knowledge. By doing so—for no-one had essayed it before—he became the father of English prose.

Among the books Alfred translated were Bede's "Ecclesiastical History," St. Augustine's "Soliloquies," Boethius's "Consolations of Philosophy," Gregory's "Pastoral Care," and Orosius's "History of the World." Into the latter he inserted chapters of his own, bringing its geographical knowledge up to date and embodying in popular form the information he loved to collect from travellers. Longfellow's poem about "Alfred the lover of truth" taking down from the lips of the old Norse sea-captain, Othere, the account of his voyage round the North Cape into the White Sea is based on one of these insertions. For the warrior who showed Christendom how to defeat the Vikings had an ungrudging admiration for their exploits as seamen and explorers. And his reverence for the past made him recognise their kinship. One of his works was a collection of the ancient heroic songs and poems of the North which were the common legacy of Dane and Englishman—a collection that unhappily perished in the dark and troubled age in which this brave man lit so many candles. The same feeling for the past made him initiate the first history of the English people in their own tongue. For the Anglo-Saxon Chronicle—that record compiled by monks of the chief events in England since its occupation by the English tribes—was probably Alfred's conception. It continued to be kept for more than two centuries after his death and is by far the most valuable of sources for the early history of England. No other nation in western Europe possesses any record of the time to compare with it.

Underlying all Alfred's work was the depth of his Christian faith. "Wisdom," he wrote, "is of such kind that no man of this world can conceive of her as she really is, but each strives according to the measure of his wit to understand her if he may, for wisdom is of God." In the preface to the collection of laws which he published, and in whose administration he took so active and personal a part, he reminded his subjects that, while Christ had come into the world to fulfil the Law, He had bade men be merciful and gentle and do unto others as they would be done by. It was this deeply sincere attempt to model both his life and reign on his Master's that made Alfred's achievement so unforgettable. He not only saved a Christian State by his exertions—and others by his example—but made it worth saving. His legacy to his country and the world was his conception of what a Christian on the throne could be. Long after his death he was remembered by Englishmen as "England's darling."

Because of this, his work—and kingdom—endured. He left no bitterness to be avenged after his death. Having saved Wessex, and with it the English nation, he made no attempt to conquer others. He did not, like Charlemagne, massacre his prisoners or extend his rule by terror, like the Greek emperor who sent 15,000 blinded Bulgars back to their heathen land to prove the might of civilisation. He did as he would be done by. He defeated enemies, not made them. The suzerainty he won outside his own borders was not imposed by the sword, but by character and example. "All the English people," his friend and biographer wrote, "submitted to Alfred except those who were under the power of the Danes." The destruction of the other kingdoms had left the king of Wessex the natural leader and protector of all Englishmen. He married his eldest daughter to the patriot ealdorman who led the resistance in western Mercia after its king had fled and granted him several of his new burghs, including London. Such generosity to less fortunate neighbours made Alfred arbiter of all western England as far as the Dee. Even the Welsh, who had warred incessantly against his race, acknowledged his gentle, unenforced supremacy. So, though their kinsfolk returned for a time to plague his realm, did the Danes he had defeated and who had made their homes in eastern England. Eight years after Ethandun they made a treaty with him by which the frontier between the two races was fixed on the line of the Lea and Upper Ouse and thence along Watling Street. Under it arrangements were made for peaceful commercial intercourse between the two nations.

"I suppose," Alfred wrote in one of his books, comparing seekers after wisdom with royal messengers, "they would come by very many roads. Some would come from afar and have a road very long, very bad and very difficult; some would have a very long, very direct and very good road; some would have a very short and yet hard and strait and foul one; some would have a short and smooth and good one; and yet they all would come to one and the same Lord." He himself had had a very long and hard one, in a hard and barren time. He died soon after his fiftieth year—probably in 899—worn out by his life of struggle and danger and by a painful disease from which he had suffered since youth. But he left to those who came after him a free land recovering from its wounds, and an ideal of kingship that was not of vain-glory but Christian service. He had created two things that were to survive disaster and conquest—a kingdom to which all Englishmen instinctively felt they belonged and a native literature to enshrine their culture and tradition. More than any other man he was the first maker of England.

Chapter Five

THE BONES OF SHIRE
AND STATE

Laws they made in the Witan, the laws of flaying and fine—
Common, loppage and pannage, the theft and the tract of
    kine,
Statutes of tun and of market for the fish and the malt and
    the meal,
The tax on the Bramber packhorse and the tax on the
    Hastings keel . . .

Behind the feet of the Legions and before the Normans' ire,
Rudely but greatly begat they the bones of state and of shire;
Rudely but deeply they laboured, and their labour stands
    till now,
If we trace on our ancient headlands the twist of their
    eight-ox plough.

Kipling

Alfred's kingdom did not perish with his death. Nor did
the wider union of English hearts that he had created. The
Danish conquests had left no ruling native line in the island but
his, and the dream of a Danish empire in Britain had been
destroyed by his victories. There now followed under his heirs
an English one. His son, Edward the Elder, a brilliant soldier,
and his daughter, Ethelfeda, "Lady of the Mercians," regained
East Anglia and the "Danelaw"—the east midland shires which
the farmer-warriors of the Grand Army had settled after their
conquests forty years before. Edward's son, Athelstan, whom
Alfred had girt with his sword as a child, carried the frontiers of
Wessex, or England as it was beginning to be called, beyond
the Humber and established his suzerainty over the former
and now largely Danish realm of Northumbria. At the height of

his power he reigned from the Channel to the Clyde. Even the warlike princes of Wales paid him tribute. And when in 937 Constantine, king of the Scots and Picts, banded with the Britons of Strathclyde and the Vikings of Ireland and the Orkneys in a grand alliance against England, their invasion met with a shattering defeat at Brunanburgh.[1] Five kings and seven earls, we are told, paid that day with their lives.

Not since the fall of Rome had the island known such unity. Alfred's policy had created a framework in which men of different races could forget their hatreds and live together in common allegiance. He and his victorious son and grandson did not drive the Danes out of England. They did something better; they started to turn them into willing and useful subjects. The speech and traditions of the Danes were closely akin to those of the English, and, when they had exchanged their swords for ploughshares and settled down in their new homes, they proved an asset to the nation. They were a vigorous, clear-headed folk: more alert and decisive than their English kinsmen. Like them they were excellent farmers, colonising the North-East, East Anglia, and the eastern Midlands, while Norwegians from the Norse strongholds in Ireland settled in the Lake District, Lancashire, the Wirral, and Isle of Man. Over the whole of this vast area, covering almost the entire country north of Watling Street, the newcomers were left to administer their own laws and customs. Loving liberty, they preferred a multitude of small holdings—tofts or shielings, they called them—to large estates, and covered the map of northern and eastern England with Scandinavian place-names. Like all the men of the North, they managed their own affairs in local public assemblies, gathering in the "thing" to debate questions of law and custom with their neighbours, and leaving high policy and war to their earls or jarls and the professional fighting men who feasted in their bright-painted, dragon-carved, sword-hung halls.

Their love of finery and beautiful objects—jewels, armour, splendid clothes and silver-mounted drinking horns—made the Danes great traders. When prevented from plundering, they

---

[1] The site is uncertain, but Colonel A. H. Burne in his *More Battlefields of England* places it at Brinsworth, near Rotherham, where there is a strong local tradition of a great battle. Another tradition, however, holds that Athelstan laid his sword before the battle on the shrine of St. John of Beverley, which would place the site much further to the east. Perhaps, however, he laid it there after his victory, while pursuing his foes to their ships in the Humber.

took to commerce as the next best thing to piracy, and proved as able with the scales as the battle-axe. They loved to travel for barter and drive a bargain; it was an expression of the sense of adventure in their blood. They loved, too, to build and sail ships. By doing so they brought wealth of a new kind to England. They made its first trading-towns—York, Leicester, Lincoln, Nottingham, Derby, Stamford—and helped to make London again what it had been in Roman times, a great port.

It was largely due to the Danes—for having kinsmen in every maritime country they were an internationally-minded folk— that England took again to exporting surpluses of corn, skins, wool and honey. In exchange for these, foreign merchants imported wine and fish from Rouen, timber and pitch from Scandinavia, and pepper and spices for seasoning the dishes of the great, brought at incredible risk from the East by the traders of many lands—in Arab dhows across the Indian Ocean, on camels over deserts to the ports of the Levant, and thence from Venice across a turbulent Germany to Antwerp and the Thames. Others brought elephant-ivory from Africa and walrus-ivory from Greenland. Such "far-coming men" made London something more than a squalid little wooden town at a river ford in a forest clearing. Its empty spaces among the Roman ruins began to fill again with houses, its *sokes* or "liberties" to trade to be bought up, and its tolls, collected by the royal port-reeve or mayor, to swell the king's treasury at Winchester. With its eight mints under Athelstan, its rules for testing weights and measures, its guildhall and weekly folk-moot in the cathedral precincts, it became by far the largest city in the country, with perhaps fourteen thousand inhabitants by the end of the tenth century. On its wharves from Queenhithe to Billingsgate and in its streets of stalls—the Vintry where the merchants of Rouen traded, Dowgate with its Flanders and Cologne clothiers, Eastcheap with its goldsmiths from Ghent and Ponthieu—the tongues of half Europe could be heard.

These merchants were picturesque folk, with bright, outlandish clothes and a sense of mystery born of their adventures. They travelled in days when most men spent their lives without ever seeing more than the forest clearing around their rustic settlements. "I go overseas," wrote one of them, "and buy purple and silk, precious gems and gold, many-coloured garments and dyes, wine and oil, ivory and brass, copper and tin, sulphur and glass." To protect themselves they travelled in companies, carrying horns which they blew at the entrance to every village to show, like the caravan bells of the East, that they came in peace. At sea, too, where in those days every ship might prove a pirate or raider, they used to sing chants or shanties that other seamen and the watchers at the ports could recognise: signature-tunes like the traditional carol, *leur Kiriele,* which the men of Lorraine sang as they came up the river with Rhenish wine after their voyage from the Moselle.

Trade fraught with so much danger and trouble was naturally slight. Only the smallest quantities of goods could be moved, and only the richest pay the prices that those who risked lives and fortunes had to charge. The vast majority of Englishmen lived, not by selling to strangers, but by raising food for themselves in the place where they were born. Only salt for preserving—carried from village to´village by pedlars—and iron for tools and ploughshares came from a distance. Except in time of war and invasion, the cycle of life in the forest villages never changed: the wheat or rye sown in the autumn and the oats or barley in the spring; the grain dried in the sun and winnowed on the threshing-floor; the scraggy, minute cattle grazing on the common pasture or wintering on the stubble or in the byres; the herds of swine feeding on beech-mast in the woods; the lumbermen felling timber for house and palisade, tool and spear-shaft, and winning year by year more land for the plough. The "leys" and "holts," "dens," "ends" and "bottoms" of so many of our place-names mark the colonies they established, little by little, in the woodland clearings.

The "weorcman," with his bent shoulders striding beside his team of patient oxen, was the foundation on which the Anglo-Saxon kingdom rested. "I go out at daybreak," cried the ploughman in one of the earliest accounts of English rural life, "driving the oxen to the fields, and I yoke them to the plough. However hard the winter, I dare not stay at home for fear of my lord. Having yoked my oxen and fastened the share to the coulter, every day I must plough an acre or more. I have a boy driving the oxen with a goad, and he is hoarse with cold and shouting. I have to fill the oxen's bins with hay and give them water and carry out their litter. Very hard work it is, for I am not free." His fellow labourers, the oxherd, swineherd and shepherd, had the same tale to tell. "I drive my sheep to their pasture at dawn and stand over them with my dogs in all weathers lest wolves devour them. I lead them back to their folds and milk them twice a day; and I make butter and cheese."

Such simple country folk lived, like the peasants of the East today, in rude shacks of wattle and mud with earthen floors, a hole in the roof to let out the wood-smoke, and no lighting save the open door. After working all day—for only by doing so could they exist—they went to bed at dusk, having no means of light but the fire round which they slept or an occasional rushlight dipped in fat. Their shapeless clothes were of goat-hair and unprocessed wool, their food of rough brown bread and vegetable broth, small-ale from barley, bacon, beans, milk, cabbage and onion, and honey for sweetening and mead. In the summer they had boiled or raw veal, and wild fowl and game snared in the forest. In the autumn they slaughtered and salted the cattle for whom there was no more pasture, and during the winter lived hard. When the harvest failed, they starved, and famine was followed—as in India and China today—by pestilence.

In such a life agriculture—its unchanging, unceasing demands, the knowledge and skill handed down from father to son and learnt by a lifetime of experience—occupied men's thoughts almost entirely. Their beasts and crops were their all. Yet under the surface changes were taking place. The Danish invaders of the ninth century had reduced the small farmer to a terrible poverty and insecurity. Against the fierce hosts of raiders, with their serried ranks and splendid weapons, he and his fellow villagers were powerless. They could only die in the flame of their blazing huts or fly into the forests to starve. Protection against the lawless strong became, therefore, as urgent a need as the labour by which they raised their bread. So did the help of some neighbour rich enough to enable them to replace their ruined crops and plundered stock and pay the heavy taxes which Alfred and his successors had to impose to withstand, and then conquer, the Danes.

In this way the small churl or free-holding farmer, with his *yardland* of thirty or so acres—and often his larger neighbour with his *hide* of three or four times as much—sank by degrees into a dependent cultivator. He became a *gebur* or boor: a man whose working capital of beasts, tools and seed had been supplied by a lord to whose descendants he and his heirs paid a tribute of services, fines and produce. Even where he remained a "free" owner, his independence was reduced by the tendency of the Crown to grant some local thane or lord the customary rights the king had always enjoyed over the tribal soil. Lordship had become so essential a bulwark against invasion and anarchy that, in the restoration of his kingdom after the Danish raids, Alfred laid it down that every man should have a lord legally responsible to the Crown for his good behaviour and his service in fyrd or militia. The thane, with his helmet and chain-armour—necessities far beyond the reach of the husbandman—and his burghgate and bell-house round which the community could rally, seemed to his contemporaries the only possible linchpin of public order and security. His function was not to till the ground and gather the harvest, but to guard the peasant's home and fields and, in time of war, turn out at the royal command in their defence. In return his neighbours, in proportion to the size of their holdings, had to contribute to his support.

As always, the price of security against an external danger which had been allowed to grow too great was a loss of freedom. Rights granted by a distant king who seldom visited a locality to an assignee who lived there were far more strictly enforced. The cultivator ceased to be his own master. The very word *churl* in time acquired a servile meaning. He became a bondman working the soil for another as well as himself and bound to it by obligations to him. And the community of free kinsmen, owing allegiance only to the "kindred" and tribal chieftain, became the manorial village of servile holders, compelled as the condition of their tenure to contribute agricultural services to a local lord, who in return protected it against invasion.

These obligations, though based on the size of the peasant's holding, were even more communal than personal. They were enforced not merely by a man's lord, but by his fellows. For the former's rights were over the community's land as a whole, and it mattered little to him who rendered them so long as he received them. The Anglo-Saxon village remained to this extent self-governing; the cultivator's duties to his lord, like those to his neighbour, were controlled by opinion and communal custom. Thus at Leominster in Herefordshire in the eleventh century, 238 *geburs* had between them to plough 140 acres of the lord's land and sow it with their own seed, to do additional "boon" work at special seasons, and contribute between them a fixed amount of capons, eggs, honey and grain. Their stock having originally been provided by the lord's ancestor, each holder's heir had, before succeeding, to redeem it by a *heriot* or fine of some part of it. Lesser holders—the cottars or cottage dwellers cultivating only a few acres each—contributed between them a smaller proportion of services and produce.

As in the past, the working occupier continued, after paying the lord's dues, to enjoy the right to the produce of the land he tilled. His part in the national structure was assured by local law or custom. The lord in turn had to pay similar dues for his lands to his own lord, who might be either the king or, more frequently, some greater lord standing between him and his sovereign. In this way he served not only to protect the local peace, but to administer the national services. He was paid, not like a modern civil-servant or soldier by the Crown out of national funds, but by the king's subjects he guarded. He passed on part of what he received in dues and services to his overlord or king, so helping him in turn to perform his duties. If he failed to do so he forfeited—at least in theory—his tenancy. In a primitive age no better way of ensuring law and order could probably have been devised.

Such was the beginning of what later became known as the feudal system, by which all surplus wealth derived from land came to be enjoyed by those with the means to protect the cultivator from lawless violence. That they did not always do so, and often used their strength to enrich themselves at the expense of the weak, was a defect more of human nature than of the system. And if the local lord took more than the distant king had done, the greater peace and order established and the consequent improvement in the arts of agriculture meant in the long run that there was a little more for all. It was better for the peasant, who had not the time or means to defend himself, to live in the power of an armed protector who was expected to act according to law and could be punished for failing to do so, than to be left at the mercy of every evil-doer stronger than himself. The devastation of the Danish invasions had filled the woods and hills with robbers and outlaws. Some system of organisation for enforcing law and order had become essential if agriculture and the arts of peace were to survive.

And it was a better and kindlier one than the slavery on which both the Roman Empire had been based and the civilisations of the East.

During the ninth and tenth centuries, following the Viking invasions, such changes were taking place in every country in Europe. They were aided by the devices which clerics, with their knowledge of writing, invented to enable kings and other benefactors to convey to the Church rights over land. The word *bookland* was used to describe land over which an assignee, ecclesiastic or lay, held rights granted by written "book" or title-deed as opposed to the older *folkland*—land held by virtue of the oral witness of the "folk." Such assignments could be either, as in the case of folkland, of customary dues and services owed to the Crown by the cultivators, or, in that of royal demesne, of the land itself. And unlike folkland, which being dependent on custom was unassignable, bookland, once granted, could be transferred to strangers. It was a freer and, therefore, superior form of tenure.

Among the royal rights over land granted to local lords by charter was the enjoyment of the fines and profits of local justice, and the franchise—called *"sac and soc"*—of holding private courts of law. These usually covered the enforcement of local order, and the power—*infangthef*—to try and hang a thief caught on land. The grant to a man on the spot, whose interest it was to enforce it, of the ancient tribal right to fine those who failed to attend local courts, helped to check the tendency—one natural as the State grew larger and more remote—of the peasant, absorbed in his own affairs, to leave the enforcement of law to others. To this extent such franchises, though sometimes tyrannically used, enlisted the motive-force of self-interest to preserve the principle that every man should take an active part in the administration of justice.

For the most valuable of all the institutions of the old freedom-loving Nordic tribes was that of communal or folk justice. The law was something that belonged to the whole community: after the soil its most precious possession and one that every man was expected to maintain. The worst fate that could befall him was to be out-lawed or denied its protection. Every "kindred" or locality was traditionally responsible for the behaviour of its members and could punish and be punished for it. And though the new seignorial system lessened the cultivator's right to debate and manage his local concerns, it never in England wholly destroyed it. Early Anglo-Saxon kings had not possessed despotic powers; they had merely been leaders and judges in societies of free men. The lord who took over their functions in the village community did not enjoy such powers either, though sometimes, if a strong or unjust man, he usurped them.

The village or "manorial" court over which the lord or his steward presided remained, therefore, partly dependent—like the tribal court of which it was an offshoot—on the participation of the village community: of all, that is, who held village land. Their right to the soil and enjoyment of its fruits, subject to the lord's dues, was protected and enforced by it. So were the traditional customs of their society, transmitted through its judgments or "dooms" and based on the testimony of the whole body of cultivators.

Communal witness to a neighbour's character lay at the root of English law. A man was publicly judged by his equals or fellow-suitors in the local court or, for graver breaches of the king's peace, like resistance to his officials and the more extreme forms of violence, in the shire and hundred courts. These had grown out of ancient tribal assemblies called folk moots, and, like them, were held on benches in the open-air[2]: usually at some sacred spot marked by a stone and still commemorated in names like Kingston, Stone or Maidstone. The hundred court, which evolved during the tenth century as a division of the shire, probably met monthly; the shire court, presided over by the king's shire-reeve or sheriff, twice a year. The suitors, in theory, were all the freeholders of the shire or hundred, expressing their judgment by the customary cry of "Ja, ja" or "Nay, nay"; in practice, because of the difficulties of travelling, only the more important attended. The shire court in particular was an assembly of large landowners. An appeal lay from these courts to the king himself, who was constantly called on to give judgment. Alfred once dealt with a lawsuit—at Wardour in Wiltshire—"as he was in his chamber, washing his hands."

The deciding factor was the oath. Oaths were weighed rather than counted, and depended on a man's record, status and property. A thane's oath was more valuable than a churl's, and

---

[2] Those presiding over the court—ealdorman, bishop, sheriff—sat on the bench, while the suitors stood.

a churl's than a gebur's. If a sufficiency of "oath-worthy" neighbours or "compurgators" supported an accused man's oath of
denial, he was adjudged innocent. Other things being equal, a
denial outweighed an accusation. But the oath of a man of
suspicious character, or of one who had been convicted of perjury,
could be rejected in favour of that of the plaintiff or accuser
and his compurgators. A man who could not clear himself
by compurgation had to undergo an ordeal by hot iron or water
to determine his guilt.

The most common form of punishment was the fine. This
was a survival from the primitive blood-feud, by which a man's
kindred were both allowed, and in honour bound, to revenge an
injury on the offender's kindred or exact compensation instead.
The Anglo-Saxon kings, seeking to end such vendettas, which
often continued for generations, encouraged composition and,
later, though with immense difficulty, made it compulsory. And
in their occasional laws they laid down tariffs of charges for
expiating particular crimes. Those committed against men of
property were more heavily mulcted than those against humbler
persons. Thus the *wergild* or man-price for the murder of a
"Welshman" or stranger was less than that of an Englishman;
of a Wessex churl only a sixth of that for a nobleman, whose
wergild was twelve hundred shillings—the price of about five
hundred oxen. The scale varied from one part of the country to
another; churls were more highly valued in Kent than in Mercia
or Wessex.

It was a rough and ready system. Under a strong king justice
was regularly enforced; under a weak one it soon degenerated
into anarchy. Its incidence was often brutal; the basis of Anglo-
Saxon law before the Conversion had been an eye for an eye
and a tooth for a tooth. Many of its punishments were those of
barbarous savages. That for arson was burning, for slander
cutting out the tongue, for striking bad money the nailing of the
coiner's hand to the door of his mint. And, for lack of methods
of sifting evidence, the law often inflicted grave injustice.

But for the Church and its creed of mercy, English law might
always have remained savage and cruel. Based on precedent
and custom, it would have ossified like that of so many oriental
States. But because the Church taught that every man possessed

an immortal soul, shared responsibility for his brother's guilt and ought to pity and relieve his distress, it tended, though only very slowly, to make the law more humane. Its beliefs inclined it to take the side of the individual against the impersonal forces of organised society. Though it accepted the existing institution of slavery, it set its face against slave-raiding and slave-dealing, particularly the sale of slaves overseas, and, by doing so, prevented yet another slave society from evolving out of the transition from the tribe to the settled State. And, though it took centuries to eradicate the evil—one from which, like other property-owners, it benefited—it did what it could to mitigate the slave's lot. It recognised his marriage as legitimate, and denied its services to those who beat slaves to death, which the law, by refusing the poor creatures its protection, permitted them to do. And it encouraged the rich, by promises of remission of sin, to redeem and emancipate slaves. "It is made known in this gospel," runs an entry in a contemporary bible, "that Godwig the Buck has bought Leofgifu the dairymaid at North Stoke and her offspring from Abbot Aelfsige for half a pound to eternal freedom, in witness of all the community at Bath."[3] Kings in their codes followed suit. Less than a century after Augustine's landing Ine of Wessex enacted that a slave who was made to work on Sunday should be freed.

From the first, too, the Church used its influence to substitute composition for the blood-feud. It helped to reduce law to writing and was responsible for the first legal codes in England. And it helped to protect the innocent by taking charge of the ancient pagan rites by which those who failed to purge themselves by compurgation were subjected to the judgment of the elements or fate. Before punishment was inflicted by the State the suspect was handed over to the Church for a test called the "ordeal" or judgment of God. After a three days' fast and a Mass at which he was bidden to confess his guilt, he was allowed to let Heaven testify if it would in his favour. This supposed intervention of Providence took one of three forms: judgment by fire, water, or consecrated wafer. Each was carried out under the auspices of the Church and, usually, on holy ground. In the first the accused had to carry a red-hot iron for nine paces or plunge his hand into boiling water; if the scald healed

[3] Dorothy Whitelock, *The Beginnings of English Society,* 113.

within three days he was held guiltless.[4] In the second he was given holy water to drink and was thrown into a pond or stream, which was adjured to reject him if guilty; if the water received him and he sank, he was innocent. In the third he had to swallow a wafer sanctified at Mass; if he choked, it showed that God's body convicted him. Barbarous and haphazard as such methods seem, it should be remembered that they were applied only to those already believed by the courts to be guilty.

The same forbearance towards the man rejected by society was shown in the Church's opposition to the death penalty. It did not question it out of any horror of death; on the contrary, its creed was founded on the conviction that death was only a material and temporary phenomenon. But it wished to give the criminal time in which to repent and save his soul. For the same reason it offered sanctuary at its altars to hunted men flying from vengeance: one that authority came to respect and which, though often abused, gave wrong-doers a second chance and the angry time for reflection.

Little by little the idea that society should protect the helpless, so alien to the fierce warrior creed of the Anglo-Saxons, began to be accepted by Englishmen and their rulers. Ine of Wessex punished a father who denied his child the right of baptism; three centuries later Athelstan exempted children under fifteen from the death penalty. Tenderness, pity, and humility were recognised as virtues to be honoured and fostered; the agelong right of the strong to oppress the weak was more often questioned. Physical strength prevailed as it had done since the world began. But for the first time in Northern Europe those who possessed it were made aware that there was something wrong in abusing it.

The advance of Christianity remained very slow, and for long periods there seemed to be none at all, or even retrogression. As always, it depended on individuals; on the human instruments through whom the Church worked. The first evangelists had all been monks, men bound by vows of obedience to a life of asceticism and piety. They had made vast districts their parishes, and their leaders had become tribal bishops, advising kings in

---

[4] In the St. William window of York Minster there is a picture of a woman showing her hand to a judge.

matters civil as well as ecclesiastical. Archbishop Theodore had given these bishoprics a national unity—one which had preceded by two centuries that of England. Some were still based on monasteries like Durham, Winchester and Canterbury; all, except London, served large and almost wholly rural areas. Many of the sees were in small country-places, like Dunwich and Elmham in East Anglia, Hexham, Abercorn and Whithorn in the north, Selsea in Sussex, Ramsbury, Wells, Sherborne and Crediton in the south-west.

Yet neither the bishop's nor the monastery's influence could reach very far. The early evangelists, like Aidan, Chad and Cuthbert, through their tireless journeyings touched the humblest homes. But bishops soon became more sedentary. Their work was done in the king's and ealdorman's hall rather than on the highway. The monks, too—never more than a few thousand in number—became increasingly static, serving their abbey churches, schools and estates, but leaving the rest of the country to look after itself. To meet the needs of populous districts churches were established called minsters, where services were held and the Christian sacraments—of baptism, confirmation, communion, marriage, penance, and extreme unction—administered by priests living in communities. These were usually "secular" rather than "regular" clergy, unbound by special vows. Many were married.

The vast majority of places in a country of isolated villages could not be reached, however, by either monastery or minster. They had to depend for their religion, as in pagan days, on the village priest or magic-man. Before the Conversion this functionary had been a nominee of the local lord, serving the latter's temple and offering sacrifices and performing magic rites for the local farming-community. He lived, like everyone else, by agriculture, cultivating his allotted strips or glebe—the reward for his services—in the common fields. When the lord became a Christian his people were baptised with him and his priest was ordained by the tribal bishop.

As such the priest was subject to the bishop's supervision and the discipline and teaching of the Church. In practice he continued to be the nominee of a bucolic lord, and his chapel or temple to be the property of the lord whose name it often bore.[5]

[5] Coupled with that of the saint to whom the church was dedicated: e.g. St. Benet Fink or St. Mary Woolnoth.

It was only gradually that he and it were brought under some kind of episcopal supervision and made independent of the lord. The earliest advance was when kings decreed that tithes— the traditional voluntary contributions made to God's service by Christians—should be levied compulsorily on owners of land, and that part of it should be applied to the support of local clergy. Other dues, too, were made payable by law or custom to the village priest—plough-alms for every plough-team in the parish, soul-scot for burials, first-fruits of young stock at Whitsun and of the harvest.

This was the beginning of the parochial system, by which a man dedicated to Christ's service was settled in every village. Appointed to his living by the local lord, who sometimes sold it to the highest bidder, drawn from the same class as his poor, ignorant parishioners, and living without the discipline, training and inspiration of the monastery, the parish priest was often a travesty of the Christian ideal he was supposed to embody. In some ways he was as much a pagan, as steeped in the superstition of fertility-rite and spell, holy water and totem, as the local magic-man he had superseded. Yet the idea of having in every place a man whose business it was to live the good life and set a Christian example had in the course of ages a profound effect on society. And, thanks to the work of the Celtic missionaries, in no land was the knowledge of Christ's personal life and teaching more widespread than in England. Even after the wholesale destruction of monasteries and monastic schools in the Danish raids the tradition survived. It was one of Alfred's many services that, by fostering the translation of Christian literature into the vernacular, he provided a means by which the village clergy —for whom Latin was an unattainable ideal—could transmit the gospel to their parishioners. The greatest of his disciples, Abbot Aelfric, who flourished towards the end of the tenth century, translated part of the Old Testament into English and published two volumes of homilies or sermons, mostly narrative, which, read from the pulpit on Sundays and Saints days, brought the Gospel message and the lessons of Hebrew history to unlettered Englishmen.

After the Viking invasions the old monastic life had been almost destroyed. The great northern houses which had trained the early English evangelists and given the world the work of

Bede and Alcuin, were left blackened shells. So were those of East Anglia and the Fens. Even in Wessex monastic discipline had broken down. The monasteries had become communities of secular canons who lived without vows and treated their endowments as hereditary personal property. Many had wives and children. The old ideals of Benedict and Columba were forgotten.

But in the tenth century a revival of monastic life began in the land of the Franks. From Cluny in Burgundy and Fleury on the Loire a succession of great teachers went out to the little warring kingdoms of western Christendom. It was at this time that King Edmund—Athelstan's brother and successor— appointed a young Wessex monk called Dunstan to be abbot of Glastonbury, by repute the oldest place of Christian worship in England. This sensitive, intuitive scholar made his monastery among the Somerset marshes famous for its teaching, music and beautiful services. In 960, when still only 36, he was made archbishop of Canterbury. Under his guidance—for he was as much statesman as churchman—his royal master, Alfred's great-grandson, Edgar, set himself to restore monasticism to southern England. He was assisted by two great reformers—Ethelwold, who had been dean under Dunstan at Glastonbury and became abbot of Abingdon and bishop of Winchester, and a north-country Dane named Oswald, who, after serving an apprentice-ship at Fleury, was given the see of Worcester and later of York. These two famous men re-established the Benedictine rule at Worcester, Bath, Cerne, Westbury, Winchcombe, Eynsham and Abingdon in the west, and in the isle of Ramsey, Thorney, Crowland, Ely and Peterborough in the Fens. In the latter place, Ethelwold, who helped to rebuild several churches with his own hands, found nothing remaining of its former glories save "old walls and wild woods."

The number of such revived monasteries was never great— perhaps not more then twenty in all England, and none in the ruined north. Many former houses continued in the hands of canons, including York minster and St. Paul's, London. Yet in the next half century these men of the cloister, re-living the old Benedictine life, made England famous again for music and metal-work, bell-casting and organ-building, illumination and embroidery. They re-wrote her books in the Latin that united all men of learning, revived an interest in scholarship, including mathematics, medicine and astrology,[6] and, following Alfred, created a national vernacular prose—the first in western Europe. Through their international organisation they introduced new farming methods, maintaining on their estates higher standards of husbandry than were possible for peasants without capital or rough thanes absorbed in war and hunting. They encouraged the growing of wheat to make the fine bread of the sacrament, and spread a knowledge of manuring and the three-course system of rotation that made more continuous corn growing possible without exhausting the soil. And they re-introduced the arts, forgotten since Roman days, of planting and tending vines, of growing fruit and vegetables, and making gardens.

During the century that followed Alfred's defeat of the Danes the process of rebuilding Christian society went on faster in England than in any other country. Elsewhere the storm the English had stilled, raged unabated; the Vikings, driven from their prey on one side of the Channel, fell with equal fury on the other. A few years after the great king had been laid in his grave at Winchester, one of their leaders, Rollo, secured from Charles the Simple—ruler of all that remained of Western Francia—a permanent settlement in the lower Seine basin which was called after them Normandy. Other heathens attacked a divided Christendom from the east. At the end of the ninth century a nomad race of mounted archers from the Asian steppes overran the Pannonian plain between the Carpathians and Danube. These plundering Magyars, or Hungarians as they were called, swept through East Francia or Germany and at one time reached Aquitaine and the Tuscan plain. Meanwhile Saracen pirates, having driven the Byzantine fleets from the Mediterranean, harried Europe's southern coasts. Two years before Athelstan's victory at Brunanburgh they sacked Genoa. Other bands of Moslem fanatics, camped in the hills of northern Italy, raided the Alpine passes.

England was more fortunate. A great king had taught her people to defend their island home and had endowed it with a realm which was not for ever being partitioned among its princes. His descendants, the fair-haired athelings of the House of Wessex, produced in little more than half a century three

---

[6] The words *circle* and *horoscope* entered our language at this time. L. P. Smith, *The English Language*, 160.

other great rulers—Alfred's son, Edward the Elder, his grandson Athelstan, and his great-grandson Edgar. Had their lives been longer all Britain might have become united under them. Edgar, who was called its Caesar, was rowed up the Dee at Chester in 973 by eight vassal kings, who between them did fealty for almost the entire island. Once a year he sent a great fleet round it; every winter he travelled its highways to hear causes and pronounce judgments. True to Alfred's policy of trust, and following his own father's grant of Strathclyde to a Scottish under-king, he is said to have conveyed to the king of the Scots and Picts the Lothian plain between Tweed and Forth in return for his allegiance. His uncle, Athelstan, was the patron of the Welsh prince, Hywel the Good, who attended meetings of the English Witan and gave Wales her first code of law.[7]

It was at Edgar's coronation that the earliest form of the service still used at the crowning of England's kings was read by its author, the mystic saint and musician, Archbishop Dunstan. Behind the solemn rites—the royal prostration and oath, the archbishop's consecration and anointing, the anthem, "Zadok the Priest," linking the kings of the Angles and Saxons with those of the ancient Hebrews, the investiture with sword, sceptre and rod of justice, the shout of recognition by the assembled lords —lay the idea that an anointed king and his people were a partnership under God. After that sacramental act loyalty to the Crown became a Christian obligation. The ideal of patriotism first began to take vague shape in men's minds, superseding the older conception of tribal kinship.

It was this that helped to give England in the tenth century institutions stronger than those of any western land. Her system of taxation, of currency and coinage, of local government, of the issue of laws and charters were all in advance of those prevailing in the half-anarchical kingdoms and dukedoms of the former Frankish empire. As a result, though a country of little account at the world's edge, her wealth increased rapidly. It was part of her kings' policy to establish in every shire at least

[7] It contained the famous definition of a well-bred cat—"perfect of ear, perfect of tail, perfect of claw, without marks of fire. . . . It should kill mice and not devour its kittens, and should not go caterwauling every full moon." If such a royal beast was killed or stealthily taken from one of the king's barns, "its head shall be held downwards on a clean level floor and its tail held upwards; and after that wheat must be poured over it until the tip of its tail is hidden, and that is its value." *The Heritage of Early Britain*, 111–12.

one town with a market-place and mint where contracts could be witnessed and reliable money coined. By the eleventh century there were more than seventy towns in the country. A dozen— Winchester, the royal capital, York, Norwich and Lincoln, Glouces- ter, Chester, Canterbury, Thetford, Worcester, Oxford, Ips- wich and Hereford—had perhaps three or four thousand in- habitants, and one, the self-governing port of London, four or five times as many. Though most of them were ramparted,[8] and a few walled, their real security and the source of their wealth was the king's peace and the confidence it inspired. So, at least in the south, was that of the countryside. The over- whelming majority of the English were countrymen—a hearty and ruddy-faced race, much given to feasting, drinking and sport. They were lovers of hunting, hawking and horse-racing, cock-fighting and bull-baiting, glee-singing, buffooning and tumbling. Their land was famous for beef, bacon and wheaten cakes, for ale, mead and perry, and for plentiful butter and cheese; a writer recorded that, while Italians cooked with oil, the English cooked with butter. By the eleventh century almost every village possessed a water-mill, and in the rich eastern counties of Norfolk and Lincoln often more than one. The Danish town of Derby had fourteen. The rivers swarmed with fish, and many places had eel-traps; the little Fenland town of Wisbech paid the abbot of Ely an annual rent of fourteen thousand eels. Chester sent its ealdorman a thousand salmon a year, and Petersham in Surrey a thousand lampreys.

The heart of England's culture was no longer Northumbria —now a wasted and depopulated province—but Wessex. Here too, as in the great northern kingdom that had welcomed Aidan and bred Cuthbert, Celtic blood and tradition mingled with Saxon. Even its early kings had borne names which were not Teuton, like Cerdic, Cynric, Ceawlin, and Celtic place- names were intertwined mysteriously in its western shires with English: Axe and Exe, avon for river, coombe for valley. "In Avons of the heart," Rupert Brooke wrote a thousand years later, "her rivers run." The greatest Wessex figure of the age was Archbishop Dunstan, who, like his earlier countryman, St. Aldhelm, had been partly nursed in the tradition of Celtic Christianity. At Glastonbury where his first work was done, legend went back far beyond the English conquest to the tiny

---

[8] As at Wareham in Dorset to this day.

wattle church which St. Joseph of Arimathaea was supposed to have built among the water meadows for the conversion of Roman Britain. Dunstan was a mystic, feeling his way to wisdom through visions and trances; he wrestled with fiends and monsters and heard mysterious, heavenly voices.

Wessex was now a settled land of villages, farms and fields whose names still figure on our maps. Its main outlines—church and parish boundary, mill, ford and footpath—were already what they were to remain for a thousand years. "See you our little mill," wrote a twentieth-century poet,

> that clacks
> So busy by the brook?
> She has ground her corn and paid her tax
> Ever since Domesday Book.[9]

He might have added, earlier. Puttock's End, Cow Common, Crab's Green, Woolard's Ash, Doodle Oak—names of Essex fields and hamlets in the reign of Elizabeth II—were given them when the athelings of Wessex sat on the English throne. So were the boundaries of shire and hundred, and the customs—themselves far older than their new Christian forms—with which men celebrated the changes of the year. Such were Plough Monday, when the village lads, with ribbons and cracking whips, resumed work after the twelve days of Christmas; May Day when they marched to the woods to gather greenery and danced round the May pole; Rogationtide when the parish bounds were perambulated by wand-bearers led by the priest, and small boys were beaten over boundary-stones; Whitsun when the Morris dancers leapt through the villages with bells, hobby-horses and waving scarves; Lammas when the first bread was blessed, and Harvest Home when the Corn Dolly—effigy of a heathen goddess—was borne to the barns with reapers singing and piping behind it. At Christmas the houses were decked with evergreen and the candles of Yule were lit.

With its fine craftsmen and the rule of its strong kings, England was beginning once more to accumulate treasures: to become a rich land worth plundering as she was before the Danes attacked her. Ivories and jewelled crucifixes, golden and silver candelabra, onyx vases and elaborate wood-carvings, su-

---

[9] Rudyard Kipling, *Puck of Pook's Hill*, Puck's song.

perbly embroidered vestments, stoles and altar cloths adorned
the churches and the halls and hunting lodges of the great. As
they sat, in mantles of brightly coloured silks fastened with
golden collars and garnet-inlaid brooches, listening to song,
harp and minstrelsy, the princes and ealdormen of Wessex
were served from polished drinking-horns chased with silver
and wooden goblets with gold. The century of Athelstan and
Edgar saw a new flowering of Anglo-Saxon art. Archbishop
Dunstan himself was a craftsman and loved to fashion jewellery
and cast church-bells. He loved to work, too, in the *scriptoria,*
as he had done as a young monk; in his day the illuminators of
the monastic renaissance, with their gorgeous colouring and
boldly flowing margins, reached new heights of achievement.
So did the sculptors of the Winchester School who carved the
angel at Bradford-on-Avon, the Virgin and Child at Inglesham,
and the wonderful Harrowing of Hell in Bristol cathedral. The
richer parish churches helped to house such treasures: small
barnlike buildings, with primitive rounded arches, high walls
and narrow windows, and bell-towers crowned with weather-
cocks—an English invention. A few survive, like the log church
at Greenstead in Essex, flint and rubble Breamore in the Avon
valley with its Anglo-Saxon text which no living parishioner
can read, stone Barnack and broad-towered Earl's Barton in
Northamptonshire.

In the depopulated north a simpler policy prevailed. Here
Christian missionaries from harried Ireland were busy turning
the Scandinavian settlements along the coasts and dales into
Christian parishes. The wheel-head crosses that marked their
open-air sites of worship show the transitional nature of the
conversion: the carved Odin cross at Kirk Andrea in the Isle
of Man with ravens croaking on a heathen god's shoulder,
while on the other side Christ looks down in majesty; the
Gosforth cross in Cumberland where the resurrected Saviour—
Baldur the Beautiful of northern legend reborn—tramples the
dragons and demons of Hell: Surt the fire-god, Fenris the wolf,
and Loki the serpent. The word cross, derived from the Latin
crux, was introduced by these Irish evangelists, gradually taking the place of the Anglo-Saxon "rood." It first appeared in
northern names like Crosby and Crossthwaite. Other Scandinavian words were being woven into the map of northern Eng-

land; *gate* a street and *thwaite* a clearing; *fell* a hill and *thorpe* a settlement; *foss* a waterfall and *by* a village. Similar Norse names—Swansea, Caldey, Fishguard, Gresholm, Haverford—appeared on the coasts of Anglesey, Pembrokeshire, Gower and Glamorgan.

Like their kinsfolk in the old Danelaw and East Anglia, these northern dalesmen—pirates' brood though they were—had a great respect for law, so long as they themselves made it. The very word entered England through their speech. So did the divisions or *ridings* into which they split the southern part of Northumbria, the juries of twelve leading men employed in the administration of their towns and wapentakes, and their habit of majority decision. For it was a rule among these independent-minded men that, save in a boat or on the battlefield, they were all equal.

Yet all this growing polity and wealth depended in the last resort on the ability of English kings to keep the good order that Alfred had won. Not all the princes of the House of Wessex were great men or able to ride the tides of anarchy in an age still dominated by the Viking invasions. Edmund I, Athelstan's successor, was murdered in a brawl with an outlaw in his own hall; his sickly brother, Eadred, lost York for a time to the murderous Norseman Eric Bloodaxe. And though the lords of the Witan replaced Eadred's feeble and petulant nephew by his able brother, Edgar, the latter died in 975 at the age of thirty-one. Three years later, following a dispute in the Witan over the succession, his eldest son was stabbed near Corfe by a thane of the queen mother's household. The murder of the fifteen-year-old king—"Edward the Martyr"—made a deep impression; "worse deed," wrote the chronicler, "was never done among the English." In the sinister light of what happened afterwards it probably seemed even worse in retrospect than at the time.

For the long reign of the half-brother who succeeded him was one of the most disastrous in English history. Ethelred the *Redeless*—the unready or lacking in counsel—was a spoilt, petulant weakling.[10] Incapable of running straight, his double-dealing set the great ealdormen by the ears even before he

[10] He had an unlucky start, defiling the font at his baptism—a mishap which caused Archbishop Dunstan, who was given to second sight, to predict disaster.

reached manhood. Under his inconstant, passionate impulses, and those of his brutal favourites, England's new-found unity dissolved.

Once more, scenting weakness as vultures carrion, the Norsemen returned. The European mainland was no longer the easy prey it had been; under the challenge of repeated invasion its divided peoples had learnt to defend themselves. The townsmen of Germany, Flanders, Francia, northern Spain and Italy were building walls round their cities, the feudal nobles of the countryside equipping companies of mounted and armoured knights. Even the Hungarians, routed by Athelstan's brother-in-law, the Saxon Otto the Great, had discovered that raiding no longer paid. At the end of the century they gave up their vagrant life and settled down as Christians on the Pannonian plain—henceforward Hungary.

But the Norsemen, whose own land had so little to offer, were not yet prepared to settle down. The northern seas and islands were still full of them. Barred out of Europe, they turned once more to England. Finding from isolated raids on the coast that her people were no longer invincible, they struck in 991 at her south-eastern shires. After a hundred years of victory, the English were confident they could repel them. They received a disquieting awakening.

Before they did so there was one glorious episode. After sacking Ipswich the invaders were opposed on the banks of the Blackwater near Maldon by the ealdorman of Essex—the old, silver-haired, six-foot-nine giant, Britnoth.[11] For an hour three of his retainers barred the only causeway. Then a Danish herald asked that the English should withdraw to allow his countrymen to cross and battle to be joined.

Disdaining any advantage and confident of victory, the chivalrous old earl agreed and the Danes crossed the causeway. But soon afterwards, adventuring far into the Danish ranks, he was cut down and slain. His men, seeing their leader fall, started to fly. But a band of his followers closed round the corpse and, dying to the last man, gave the Danes such "grim way-play" that they were unable to follow up their victory and scarcely, it was said, man their ships to sail home. The sacrifice was in vain—for nothing could save Ethelred's England—but

---

[11] His decapitated skeleton was found and measured at Ely in 1769.

the flame of that day's courage still burns in the Anglo-Saxon epic, *The Battle of Maldon.*

There was little else to redeem the record of the next twenty years. Under their feckless king, who "let all the nation's labour come to nought," nothing went right for the English. "When the enemy is eastwards," wrote the Anglo-Saxon chronicler, "then our forces are kept westward; and when they are southward, then our forces are northward . . . Anything that may be counselled never stands for a month." The English were not only outmanoeuvred; they were betrayed. Some of the ealdormen and the feeble king's favourites threw in their lot with the enemy, shifting from side to side in selfish attempts to increase their dominions. England's only respite was when Ethelred, bleeding her people white with taxes, bribed the Danes to withdraw. But as soon as they had spent the money they returned for more, harrying the countryside until a new ransom or danegeld was raised. They rode at will across Sussex and Hampshire, moored their fleet in Poole harbour, burnt Norwich and Thetford, beat the *fyrd* at Penselwood in the heart of Wessex, and rode past Winchester flaunting the plunder of Berkshire as they returned in triumph to their ships.

Lacking the strong hand they respected, the Danes of northern England turned to their plundering kinsmen. Indeed, Ethelred drove them to it, harrying their homesteads with the same barbarity as the invaders harried his own. "He went into Cumberland," the chronicler wrote, "and ravaged it well nigh all." His crowning act of folly occurred in 1002 when he gave orders for a massacre of the Danes living in York, among them the sister of the king of Denmark. The revenge taken by the bloodthirsty king, Sweyn Forkbeard, was as terrible as deserved.

For a generation the invaders feasted on the carcass of a rich, leaderless land. The monasteries again fell into decay, the farms were plundered, the peasants taxed into starvation and sold as slaves. The worst humiliation came in 1012 when, after a delay in the payment of a danegeld, the invaders pounced on Canterbury and carried off the primate, Alphege, and most of the monks and nuns. And when the brave archbishop refused to appeal for a ransom, he was pelted to death with ox-bones by a pack of drunken pirates.

The next year, after he had reigned for thirty-five years, Ethelred fled to Normandy, leaving his desolate country in the hands of Sweyn. Only London, its walls manned by its warrior gild, remained faithful to the royal cause and Alfred's disgraced line. Then the king's young son, Edmund "Ironside," put up a fight worthy of Alfred himself against Sweyn's son and successor, Canute. For three years the two great soldiers, Englishman and Dane, fought each other among the forests and marshes of southern England. On April 23rd 1016—St. George's Day—Ethelred died and Edmund succeeded. Six months later, after five astonishing victories—at Penselwood on the Somerset-Dorset border, at Sherston in Wiltshire, on the western road to London, at Brentford,[12] and at Otford in Kent—the young king was himself defeated by Canute at Ashingdon in Essex through the treachery of one of his earls, a vile favourite of his father's. A few weeks later, after signing a pact with Canute near Deerhurst on the Severn, by which the country was to be divided, he died suddenly at Oxford.

In that midwinter of disaster the great council or Witan met and made its terms with the conqueror. Preferring strength on the throne to weakness, and unity to division, it elected as king, not one of Edmund's infant sons, but the young Dane, Canute. It proved a wise choice. For though Canute was almost as ruthless as his father, he ended the long Norse scourge. At a meeting of the Witan at Oxford he swore to govern his new realm by the laws of King Edgar. Henceforward he made no distinction between his new countrymen and his old. He followed Alfred.

For if Canute had conquered England, in a wider sense England conquered him. English missionaries, following Boniface's great tradition, had long been at work in Scandinavia; though born a pagan, Canute had been baptised. With his acceptance of a Christian crown the ravaging of Christendom from the north ceased. While in many things still a heathen, revengeful and hard, he became a devout churchman, enforcing tithes, endowing monasteries, and even making a pilgrimage to Rome where he laid English tribute on the altar of St. Peter. A poem of the time describes his visit to a Fenland abbey:

---

[12] Battle-axes, spears, and swords dating from this time have been found in the Thames, some near Brentford and Putney, others close to the site of Old London Bridge. T. C. Lethbridge, *Merlin's Island*, 25–9.

"Merry sungën the monkes in Ely
When Cnut King rowed thereby.
'Row, cnichts, near the land,
And hear we these monkes sing.'"

He rebuilt the shrine at Bury St. Edmunds to the king his countrymen had martyred a century and a half before, and made amends to the murdered Alphege by the honours he paid his tomb at Canterbury.

Had this great, though harsh, man lived, the course of European history might have been different. Being king both of England and Denmark, he tried to make the North Sea an Anglo-Danish lake and England the head of a Nordic confederation stretching from Ireland to the Baltic. After his conquest of Norway he became virtual emperor of the North. But fate was against him. The story of his courtiers telling him he could stay the advancing tide at Lambeth may not have been true, but, like many legends, it enshrined a truth. He was not more powerful than death. He died at forty in 1035, his work incomplete and most of his mighty projects still a dream. He was buried at Winchester among the English kings, while his half-barbaric sons divided his Scandinavian empire between them.

They did not even found a dynasty. Seven years later, when the last of them died "as he stood at his drink at Lambeth," the Witan chose as successor the forty-year-old Edward, son of Ethelred the Unready by his second wife, Emma of Normandy. He was a soft, devout, peace-loving man, with a clerk's long tapering fingers, a rosy face and flaxen hair that turned with age to a beautiful silver. Though exile in his mother's country had made him more French than English, his subjects were much impressed by his piety. He was more like an abbot to them than a king, and they called him the Confessor. His greatest interest was the building of a monastery among the river marshes at Thorney, a mile or two to the west of London. Here, that he might watch his abbey rising—the West Minster, as it was called—he made himself a hall that was one day to become the heart of an empire.

Yet Edward exposed his subjects to almost as many dangers as his father. He was so devout that he refused to give his wife a child and his realm an heir. Absorbed in works of piety, he

left its affairs to the great ealdormen and his Norman favourites.
He made immense grants of land to a Sussex thane named
Godwin, whom Canute had created earl of the West Saxons,
and who, in the dynastic quarrels before Edward's accession,
had been instrumental in blinding and, possibly, murdering his
brother, and later, in securing Edward's election to the throne.
This able but ambitious man induced the king to marry his
daughter and to confer on his spoilt, quarrelling sons the Earldoms of East Anglia, Gloucester, Hereford, Oxford, Northampton, Huntingdon and northern Northumbria. The jealousies
aroused by his greatness and the crimes of his eldest son led to
his eclipse and banishment. But he returned to England at the
head of a fleet, harried its coasts and, with the help of the
Londoners, dictated terms to the throne.

Godwin was not the only subject able to defy the Crown.
Equally masters in their provincial strongholds were his rivals,
Leofric of Mercia—husband of the legendary Lady Godiva,
foundress of Coventry abbey—and the giant Dane, Siward of
York, who met his death like a Norse warrior standing fully
accoutred with breast-plate, helmet and gilded battle-axe. The
power of such magnates was not wholly Edward's fault. It was
a result of the cumulative alienation of royal estates—caused by
the difficulty of raising revenue to pay for public services—
which had been going on for generations and which deprived
the monarchy of its chief and almost only source of income. The
bidding prayer in York Minster might invoke a blessing on king
and ealdorman, but it was the latter, with his castles and retainers, who now had the power to oppress or protect his neighbours. Appointed in the days of Athelstan to lead the *fyrd* and
enforce the royal law in a single shire, the ealdorman by the
eleventh century, with his accumulation of shires and hereditary claim to office, had grown beyond the control of any ordinary ruler. His was the disintegrating force of power without
responsibility. He was neither a chieftain bound by tribal ties
nor a consecrated king with obligations to his people. He was
merely an inflated landowner with proprietary rights in the human beings who lived on his estates. His rivalries and family
feuds cut across the growing sense of nationhood and tore the
realm to pieces.

A similar process had long been taking place on the continent. The problem of the Dark Ages was to make any system of government work except that of force. In tribal times a king had only been able to impose his will when the horde was assembled for battle. Even then his powers were limited; when Clovis, conqueror of Gaul and first king of the Franks, wished to preserve a chalice looted from Soissons cathedral, his sole resource was to split open the head of the warrior who voiced the customary right of veto. Later the tribe had broken on the submerged rock of Roman civilisation; the community of the herd and war-horn could not survive the growing yearning, awoken by Christianity, for individual justice. But the premature attempts of rulers like Charlemagne to recreate an international empire based on law had been shattered, partly by the Norse raids and still more by the difficulty of uniting large areas inhabited by primitive peoples. Without a trained bureaucracy the Roman system of raising revenue could not work; a Frankish king could only levy taxes by farming them out to local magnates. Feudalism—the protection of the locality from predatory strangers by its stronger members—was the only answer until either the old imperialism could be recreated or a national order take its place. Only in island England had patriotism for a time enabled the Crown to hold together a nation.

Alfred's recipe against the Danes and anarchy had been the ramparted town, the royal *corps d'élite* of thanes, and the national State. Against the Norse, Magyar and Saracen invasions Europe's had been the walled city, the castle or château, and the local knight, armed and trained with a degree of specialisation unknown in easy-going England. With his horse, lance, sword and shield, and leather and chain-armour hauberk, he was the answer to the invading horde from which the West had suffered so long. His elaborate smith-made protection, his mobility and striking-power, and his life-long dedication to arms, made him despise mere numbers. Something of the Christian missionary's conviction that faith could conquer all things sustained him; that and a well-placed confidence in his weapons and training.

It was with the knights of East Francia or Germany that Athelstan's brother-in-law, Otto the Saxon, overthrew the Magyar horsemen on the Lechfeld in 955, and re-established the imperial throne of the Germans. It was only a nominal title, for neither in Germany nor Italy, where he was crowned by the pope, did he or his successors ever rule much more than their private feudal lands and castles. Yet it marked a stage in the recovery of Europe's dignity and freedom of action. So in the next century did a later emperor's intervention at the head of his knights to rescue the Papacy from the degrading control of the Roman mob. Another sign of returning health was the resumption, by colonising knights from Germany's frontier Marches and the little Christian kingdoms of northern Spain, of Christendom's long-interrupted expansion towards the east and south.

Yet the feudal knight, while he helped to save and strengthen Europe, added to the problem of its government. If he was invulnerable to his country's foes he was equally so to its rulers, and a scourge to everyone within reach of his strong arm. He lived for war and by it. His neighbours had to seek his protection or be ruined. In Europe it was not the Crown that guarded the peasant and trader, but the local knight and his castle; no village could survive unburnt and unplundered without him. The sole restraint on his power was that of the feudal superior from whom he received his lands. The knight's obligation to his overlord was the counterpart to the loyalty to the Crown Alfred had tried to create in England. He did homage for his fief, swore *fidelitas* or fealty to him, gave him in war the precise measure of military service—neither more nor less—laid down in the terms of his enfeoffment, and attended formal meetings of his court of law.

The squabbling duchies and counties of the shadowy kingdoms of western and eastern Francia, Burgundy, and Italy were based on no other allegiance but this. By the eleventh century the only dominion, save the royal title, left to Charlemagne's last descendant, the king of the West Franks, was the hill town of Laon. The great vassals of the Crown had absorbed everything else. Soon afterwards the chief of them, Hugh Capet, duke of the Isle of France, usurped the vacant and now hollow dignity. He too possessed no more than his personal domain, with its impregnable island capital, Paris. His fellow dukes, and nominal vassals, of Aquitaine, Normandy, Burgundy, Brittany and Gascony, and the Counts of Flanders, Champagne, Toulouse, Maine, and Anjou, could together call on far more knights than he. For ever at loggerheads with one another, they pursued their mutually antagonistic ends by war, for war was their sole resource.

Like *laissez-faire* in a later age, eleventh century feudalism suffered from being too exclusively based on self-interest. And if at first the self-interest was mutual, it soon became contradictory and self-destructive. It reared the State on selfishness alone, and created a society without the cement of love and loyalty: one in which power was sought as a means of self-aggrandisement and men took to themselves lords that they might oppress others. It made for a multiplicity of rival princedoms, duchies and counties whose territories were for ever changing. It produced the very anarchy it was designed to avoid.

The future of European society lay with whoever could discipline and ennoble feudalism. The Church took the lead by trying to limit the ravages of private war. It set aside days and seasons for a "truce of God" when war was forbidden on penalty of expulsion from its communion. By the middle of the century it had succeeded in prohibiting private fighting—at least in theory—from Thursday night till Monday morning. It sought also, by an appeal to conscience, to present knightly power as a trust. It tried to make knight errantry a Christian pursuit: to turn the aggressive, acquisitive Frankish freebooter, armed *cap-à-pie*, into the Christian champion, driving back the heathen, defending Holy Church and punishing iniquity. In chivalry, as it became called, it offered the military class a code of honour. It devised an elaborate ceremony at which the young knight, before being invested with arms, knelt all night in solitary prayer before the altar and, like the king at his crowning, took the Sacrament, swearing to use the power entrusted to him in righteousness and the defence of the helpless. And, for the sake of society, it invested the oath of fealty with mystery and sanctity. It was an offence against God, the Church taught, for a vassal to be false to his liege-lord.

The Church's success was only partial. But in one State at least—the little warlike duchy of Normandy—it early established a working and mutually profitable partnership with the knightly class. Like Canute, Rollo the Viking and his descendants, in acquiring a Christian land, had become fervent champions of the Church. Nowhere was the monastic reforming movement so enthusiastically supported by the laity, so many

monasteries built, and such learned and pious clerks appointed
to well-endowed benefices. It was as though the Norman
knights, the most acquisitive in Europe, were trying to offset
their outrages by the orthodoxy of their ecclesiastical establishments and, while they stormed their way into their neighbours'
lands, to buy an entry to Heaven. They became the greatest
church-builders since the days of Charlemagne and even since
those of imperial Rome, whose giant buildings they tried to
copy. They were not delicate craftsmen like the English; their
chief resource was to build immensely thick walls, and several
of their grander achievements fell down.[13] But they had infinite
ambition and a sense of space and grandeur. It was in the style
of one of their abbeys, Jumièges, that Edward the Confessor,
himself half a Norman, modelled his abbey church at Westminster.

Their buildings expressed their religion. Their patron-saint,
standing above their churches with uplifted sword and out-
stretched wings, was the warrior archangel Michael, guardian
of Heaven; their conception of God a feudal overlord, ready to
reward those like themselves who kept the letter of His law.
With the spirit they troubled themselves little; they were a
practical folk who loved clear definitions. They built, not for
comfort like the timber-loving Saxons, but in stone to endure.
Their serried arches, marching like armies through space, the
vast walls and pillars supporting them, the rude, demon-
haunted figures gazing down from their capitals, symbolised the
crude magnificence and vigour of their half-barbaric minds.
With their grim massiveness and twin-towers rising into the
sky like swords, such churches seemed designed, as Henry
Adams wrote, to force Heaven: "all of them look as though they
had fought at Hastings or stormed Jerusalem."[14]

For war this people had a supreme genius. With their hard
Norse brilliance, they rode their horses through the waves of
battle as their pirate forbears had sailed their ships. They loved
fighting with lance and horse so much that, when they were not
at war, they were for ever challenging one another in mimic

[13] Dean Stanley used to say that when one went round the Norman churches
of England, one was always safe in asking, "When did the tower fall?"
[14] Henry Adams, *Mont St. Michel and Chartres*. "Whenever the Norman
central *cloche* stands, the Church Militant of the eleventh century survives;—not
the Church of Queen Mary but of Michael the Archangel;—not the Church of
Christ but of God the Father—*Who never lied!*"

tourneys where the victors held the vanquished to ransom and plundered their horses and armour.

They were masters too of law and rhetoric and in their own estimation, at least, of courtesy.[15] They knew how to govern, just as they knew how to win battles, because they were absolutely clear what they wanted and how to get it. They never left anyone in any doubt as to what they wished them to do. They meant to get their way and, with harsh, logical insistence, they got it. They were paragons of efficiency. They were what the Romans had been a thousand years before, the natural leaders of their age. Ruthless, almost entirely without sentiment, and though passionate, self-possessed and cool, they had the simplicity of genius. With their round bullet-heads, blue eyes and long aquiline noses, they looked like intelligent birds of prey.

Above all, they had energy. They were as restless as they were greedy and calculating. Like their Norse forbears they would go to the world's end for plunder. In the middle of the eleventh century a few hundred of them succeeded in seizing the south of Italy from the Byzantine Greeks. Then they went on to conquer the rich island of Sicily from the Saracens, the lords of the Mediterranean. An Italian who witnessed that astonishing conquest has left us their picture: dominant, harsh, revengeful, cunning, frugal, yet capable of lavish generosity when fame was to be won by it. "You never know," he wrote, "whether you will find them spendthrifts or robbers. . . . They are headstrong to excess unless they be curbed by the strong hand of justice. They are patient of cold if need be, patient of hunger, patient of hard work; they are passionately fond of hawking, of riding, of warlike armour and of splendid garments."

They had a genius for absorbing other civilisations. So thoroughly did they absorb that of the Frankish-Gaulish folk among whom they settled that within a century of their occupation of Normandy scarcely a word of their old Norse tongue was in use. They had become a Romance or Latin speaking race, with more of the Romans' genius for rule and law than any people since their time. In the chapel-royal of the Norman robber king at Palermo, and in the cathedral his heirs built at Monreale,

[15] "They are the most polite of peoples." William of Malmesbury, *Gesta Regum Anglorum*, cit. *English Historical Documents* II, 291.

they infused the graceful sunshine art of the Saracens and Byzantines with their own northern vigour. Those they enrolled in
their war-bands—and they drew from every race—they turned
into Normans, as proud, ruthless and efficient as themselves.
This too was a Roman trait.

After the collapse of Canute's empire the Normans turned
their gaze on England. Its wealth, so much superior to that of
Normandy, seemed a standing invitation. They viewed its easy-
going, and rather sentimental provincials with a contempt they
hardly tried to conceal: the words *pride* and *proud* first entered the English language to describe the arrogance of the
Normans to whom the Confessor granted estates and bishoprics.
As he had so conveniently refrained from giving his kingdom
an heir, his great-nephew, the young Duke of Normandy,
formed the idea of claiming it for himself. He even succeeded
in persuading his uncle to promise it him—though it was not
by English law his to promise.

The chief obstacle in the Duke's way was Godwin's eldest
surviving son, Harold, earl of Wessex, brother to the queen and
leader of the English and anti-Norman party at Edward's court.
In 1064 Harold was shipwrecked in Normandy, and William—
a great believer, like all Normans, in God's strict sense of le-
galism—used the opportunity to make his unwilling guest swear
to be his liege[16] and help him obtain the English crown. To
make doubly sure of divine intervention he concealed some
sacred relics under the cloth of the table on which the Englishman swore.

The Duke of Normandy was not the only European ruler impatiently awaiting the Confessor's death. The Norse king,
Harald Hardrada the Stern, engaged till now in the civil wars
of Scandinavia, was also ready to claim his kinsman, Canute's,
crown. He possessed the finest fleet in Europe, while that of
England, which Canute had kept to guard her and which Edward in earlier days had taken to sea on rumours of a Danish
invasion, had been disbanded. Harold Godwinson's traitor
brother, Tostig, the exiled earl of Northumbria, was known to
be seeking Hardrada's aid. Their vultures' coalition boded ill for
England.

[16] So William always maintained, though he never suggested any motive
Harold—as rich and great a man as himself—could have had for putting himself
at such a disadvantage.

The other peoples of the British Isles were also restive at the spectacle of English weakness. Since the days of Ethelred, the Britons, Picts and Scots of the far North had increasingly tended to merge, not with their southern neighbours, but with one another and, still more important, with the English and Scandinavian landowners and farmers of the northern half of the old kingdom of Northumbria. It was this corn-growing coastal plain of Lothian between the Tweed and Forth—granted half a century before by King Edgar to his Scottish vassal, Kenneth—that alone offered a real chance of separate nationhood to the rocky and rain-swept lands of Caledonia. In or around 1016, at the close of Ethelred's disastrous reign, a victory won by the kings of Scots and Strathclyde at Carham over the earl of Northumbria helped to ensure the permanence of this northern union of Celt and Englishman. During the first half of the eleventh century the Scots, as the diverse peoples north of the Tweed were beginning to call themselves, made repeated raids into Durham. In 1054 Siward, earl of Northumbria, was forced to lead a punitive expedition as far as the Forth, the old Northumbrian frontier, where he dethroned the Celtic usurper, Macbeth, and installed as king an exiled prince of the old Scottish line—Malcolm, king of the Cumbrians. But Lothian, like Strathclyde, remained part of the new northern kingdom.

The little principalities of Wales, too, for all their constant wars with one another, were drawing closer in the hope of exploiting England's weakness. They also had assumed a Welsh rather than an island patriotism; had become the *Cymry* or fellow-countrymen, uniting in battle, whenever plunder offered, against their wealthier neighbours, even though the English of the western shires were almost as Celtic as themselves. The dream of an earlier, greater Wales, ever victorious against the Saxons, began to haunt their poems and tales: the *Mabinogion* with their legends of Arthur and his chivalry and the great Druid magician, Merlin. Politically this reversal of the unifying trend of the tenth century was to exact a heavy toll in racial war, cattle-raiding and border-baron brigandage. Yet socially it was to enrich, not impoverish, the island, fostering a regional consciousness in which much was preserved of poetry, song and character that would otherwise have perished. "Their God they shall praise," it was said of the Celts, "their language they shall keep, their land they shall lose except wild Wales!" In 1055 the men of this indomitable, hardy race, under a patriot prince, Griffith or Gruffydd ap Llywelyn, ravaged the city of Hereford in alliance with a traitor English earl and burnt the minster which Athelstan had built. Next year they slew its bishop. "It is hard to describe," wrote an English chronicler, "the oppression and all the expeditions and the campaigning and the labours and the loss of men and horses that the army of England suffered."

England had not only lost her chance of uniting Britain. She had lost her freedom of action. Under Alfred she had helped to save Christendom, as she had done two centuries earlier in the days of Bede and Boniface. But when under her last athelings she no longer proved capable of giving leadership, she found herself, as though by some inescapable law of her being, receiving it from others. Canute gave it for a time. And when after Canute's death that failed, the vacuum had still to be filled.

The English were in many ways a more civilised people than any in northern Europe; they seem to have been gentler, kindlier and more peaceably governed. Their national achievement in vernacular scholarship, poetry and literature was unique; their craftsmanship—in sculpture, embroidery, goldsmith's and coiner's work—most skilful and sensitive. They had evolved a union of Church and State for national ends which had no parallel outside the civilised empire of the Greeks; their bishops and ealdormen sat side by side in the Witan and in the provincial and shire courts. To matters of theology and philosophy, like their Irish neighbours, they had given much thought; alone among northern nations they possessed the priceless heritage of the scriptures in their native tongue. Left to themselves, they might even, four centuries before the Reformation, have established on Christendom's western fringe an English Church, based on Celtic scholarship and piety, and free from the cruder superstitions that a stern and revivalist Rome, insisting that the pace of all must be the pace of one, was beginning to impose on the western world. Their great homilist, Aelfric, had repudiated transubstantiation, and the saintly Dunstan tolerated a sober married clergy.

But to the finer minds of the eleventh century England was

a land where the enthusiasm of saints and scholars had become lost in a sluggish stream of petty provincial interests; where married canons lived on hereditary endowments, and boorish, provincial noblemen sunk in swinish and unaspiring drunkenness and gluttony, sold sacred benefices; where the very archbishop of Canterbury was a simoniac and uncanonically appointed; and where bucolic warriors, too conservative to change, still fought on foot and with battle-axe. She had lost touch with the new world growing up beyond the Channel: with the international Church, with its reforming popes and disciplined monasteries, with the new ideals of chivalry, and the mailed knights, battle-trained horses, tall, moated castles which were now becoming the dominant features of the European landscape. Her nerves had grown slack, her sinews had lost their strength. She was living among the memories of the past, static, conservative, unimaginative. She had barred her mind to change; it remained to be seen if she could bar her gates.

On January 5th 1066, a few days after the consecration of his abbey church at Westminster, the gentle Confessor died and was buried in the minster he had built. Next day, without awaiting their northern colleagues, the lords and prelates of the Wessex Witan met in the Godwin stronghold of London. Ignoring the claims of Norman duke, Norwegian king and the young atheling grandson of Edmund Ironside—the last survivor of the ancient line, whom Edward had recently invited to England—they elected Harold Godwinson as king.

Chapter Six

CROWN AND SCEPTRE

The kings of England, lifting up their swords,
Shall gather at the gate of Paradise.
Flecker

When William of Normandy heard the news from England he swore a great oath. He would cross the seas and take the crown from his perjured vassal. He summoned his tenants—his feudal barons and their knights—and called for volunteers from all the Frankish lands to share in his venture. And he asked the pope, who had a quarrel of his own with the uncanonical islanders, to bless the arms that were to punish usurpation, root out simony, and give England a lawful king and primate. It was not as a robber he would come, but as a crusader.

The man who set himself to conquer England was one of the great men of history. His mother was the unmarried daughter of a Falaise tanner; his great great-grandfather had been a pirate. Left fatherless as a child, his boyhood had been spent amid the turmoil caused by the violence of his father's feudal barons. The ruin they unloosed had made an indelible impression on him. Of indomitable will and courage, he soon proved himself their equal in battle. As a statesman he was the master of every sovereign of the age. Far-sighted, patient, prudent, self-controlled, bold but thorough in all he did, and ruthless towards those who stood in his way, he made his little duchy, with its disciplined chivalry of armoured knights and ruddy-faced men-at-arms from the Normandy apple orchards, the most formidable force in Europe. Compelled to wage war in turn against his barons, his jealous neighbours in Maine, Anjou, and Brittany, and his feudal overlord, the titular king of France, he defeated them all. He never lost sight of his aims, never over-reached himself, and steadily increased his domains. When in his fortieth year he began to gather ships for the invasion of England, landless knights from every province of France flocked to his banners. For the warriors of that turbulent land were ready for any risk, however great, that offered a chance of fighting and plunder.

Leopard and wolf, it has been said—Norman and Norseman —were stalking the same prey. Fleets were gathering at the mouths of Norman rivers, in Norwegian fiords and among the Shetlands and Orkneys, in the Danish ports of Ireland, in the forths of Scotland, in Flemish dykes where Tostig was seeking men from his brother-in-law, the count of Flanders, before sailing to harry the English coasts and join Hardrada. Looking down in that summer of 1066, we can see the waiting masts at the mouth of the Dives and the glint of steel on the Norman shore, where William and his few thousand knights have gathered with their horses. And across the Channel Harold's ships cruise off the Isle of Wight and his troops guard little ramparted Sussex and Kentish towns, ready to sell their lives on the beaches.

But as the summer slips by and the wind stays in the north, the English peasant levies, their provisions running short, begin to slip away to their homes and harvests. By September only the thanes remain and the professional house-carls of the royal bodyguard raised by Canute to protect the throne. Even the ships in the Channel return to their ports. For Harold, his kingdom divided under jealous earls behind him, can no longer afford to victual and keep them at sea. Despite her resources England has no organisation for sustained war.

Then the storm breaks. Far among the misty islands to the north of Scotland a great fleet of long-boats moves southward. It carries the army of Harald Hardrada, king of Norway, to conquer England and restore Harold's traitor brother to his earldom. It is joined on its way by the Norse earl of Orkney and by ships from Scotland and Ireland. The wind that keeps William's armada from sailing bears the Norsemen into the Yorkshire and Humber Ouse, where they pour ashore, as their fathers before them, to slay and ravage.

Faced by the news, Harold breaks his camp in the south. We see his house-carls, with their long shields and battle-axes, trotting through wooden London on little shaggy ponies and vanishing into the forests up the straight, grass-grown highroad which the Romans built a thousand years before. For, though the pincers are closing on him, England's king is a master of war. Four years earlier the lightning speed of his marches had broken the power of the great Welshman, Griffith ap Llywelyn. He had driven the king of Gwynedd from mountain to mountain until his desperate followers had deserted and betrayed him. And now the Viking who had come to seize his kingdom should meet the same end. He should have six feet of English earth or, since he was tall, seven!

The king of Norway was a worthy adversary. Six feet six high, he had carried his Viking sword in youth to the walls of Constantinople and won the Norwegian crown in many a pitched battle. He made his landfall on the east bank of the Ouse at Riccall, ten miles south of York. On September 20th, at Fulford, two miles from the northern capital, he fought for its possession all day with the earls of Mercia and Northumbria. By nightfall the English had fled and he was left master of the field. Then, according to Viking wont, he withdrew to his ships to await the city's surrender.

Four days later, by arrangement with the citizens and the two earls, who had promised to join him against Harold, he marched with his men to a rendezvous at Stamford Brig, a small wooden bridge across the Derwent where four roads met, seven miles east of York. That night, unknown to him, the English king and his army, driving furiously up the northern road, reached Tadcaster. Here Harold learnt that, though the earls had been routed, York was still unoccupied. Long before dawn on the 25th he set out with his tired troops to cover the last ten miles to the city. Then, hearing that the Viking host was only seven miles away, he continued his march without a pause. As the Norwegians, many of them without their armour, were awaiting the English hostages in the water meadows beside the Derwent, they suddenly saw a cloud of dust to the west and the chain-mail of Harold's house-carls glistening like ice in the morning sun. So swiftly had they moved that the invaders were caught completely unprepared.

The English king never hesitated. After a brief parley to offer his brother terms, he struck. The Norsemen were divided by the Derwent, with their main strength on the far or eastern side. Bidding those on the west bank fight for time, Hardrada hurriedly formed his polyglot army of Norwegians, Scots, Flemings and Irish into a shield-wall in a meadow still called Battle Flats. But the English, sweeping aside resistance, quickly reached the riverside. For a short while they were delayed by a giant Viking who, straddling the bridge, struck down all comers. Then an Englishman found a swill-tub, paddled it under the bridge, and speared him through a gap in the planks.

Ignoring the risk of fighting with the Derwent in his rear, Harold at once attacked the shield-wall. All afternoon the clangour of axe and sword continued. By dusk Hardrada and Tostig had fallen, and the English king—"a little man sitting proudly in his stirrups"—had made good his boast that the foe should win nothing but a grave. He and his men crowned their achievement by pursuing the survivors twelve miles to their ships at Riccall. At the end of their great march they had covered thirty miles in a day and routed the most famous captain of the age.

Two days later the wind that had stayed so long in the north shifted to the south. At St. Valéry-on-Somme, where William's fleet had been driven by a gale, the trumpets sounded for immediate embarkation. That night the Norman army sailed in more than a thousand ships;[1] it reminded one who was present of the departure of Agamemnon for Troy. There were no English vessels to contest the crossing, for they were laid up in the Thames. On September 28th, with its armoured knights and horses, the armada anchored in the wide waters of Pevensey bay, long since turned to sheep pastures. The local fyrdmen were busy with their farms and harvests and there

[1] William of Jumièges, the chronicler, puts the figure as high as three thousand —an obvious exaggeration. But William of Poitiers' statement, written at William's court a few years after the invasion, that it was a larger fleet than Agamemnon's, sounds authentic. The average carried in each ship was probably not more than twenty men; many vessels also carried horses. Nor were all those who crossed fighting men.

was no resistance. As the Norman duke stepped ashore he stumbled and fell; then rose with his hands full of English earth. It was not a grave he had come to fill.

William was a warrior of a different stamp from Harold. Bold though his venture was and vast the stake, he did nothing by impulse. He took no needless risks. He moved into the peninsula formed by the Brede estuary and Bulverhythe, built a castle of earth and timber at the little fishing port of Hastings, and secured his bridgehead. Then he sent out cavalry patrols to explore and harass the countryside. He meant to make Harold or Hardrada—whichever had triumphed in the north—meet him on ground of his own choosing, where his war-horses could be kept fed and fresh. For the nearer he stayed to his ships, and the farther his foe marched, the greater the latter's problems and the less his own. William knew Harold's impetuous temperament; he had campaigned with him in Brittany. If he could make him fight where the Norman was strongest and the English weakest, he might win England at a blow. For once Harold and his army were destroyed, everything else would follow. The Duke, therefore, stayed where he was. He left the English—or Norsemen—to do the marching.

The news of the landing, galloped through the forests or flashed by hill-beacons, took two days to reach York, where Harold was celebrating his victory. Without a moment's hesitation the English king and his battered house-carls set out again for the south. In six days they covered the 190 miles to London —an average day's march of 32 miles. They waited there a few days until the fyrd of the southern shires could join them. Then, at dawn on October 12th,[2] they marched again for Hastings. For uncertain of his kingdom's loyalty, and fearful lest the northern earls should play him false, Harold dared not leave William at large. He had to burn out the southern wasp's nest like the northern.

Late on the evening of the 13th, sadly reduced in numbers by their victory, the house-carls reached the rendezvous in front of William's bridgehead—a "hoar apple tree" on a spur of the downs where the Hastings trackway emerged from the Sus-

[2] There is a conflict of evidence as to whether Harold left London on the 11th or 12th, but I follow Colonel Burne in believing it to have been the 12th. *Battlefields of England,* 20.

sex oak-forest. They had covered the 58 miles from London in
two days. A large part of the fyrd was still straggling through
the woods behind them, half of it a day's march or more away.
This was the hour for which William had waited. That night,
as soon as the news of Harold's arrival reached him, he ordered
his troops to stand to and march at dawn.

At daybreak on October 14th, the Norman army set out
from Hastings in a long column—"a countless host", a chronicler wrote, "of horsemen, slingers, archers and foot-soldiers."
It probably consisted of between 7000 and 10,000 men. Before
it was borne the papal banner which the pope had sent to William, the champion of orthodoxy and reform. In front marched
archers with bows and cross-bows, then the men-at-arms in long
padded shirts or hauberks covered with thin chain mail, and
then the squadrons of armoured knights on which William relied for victory, riding their great horses and bearing lances
with fluttering pennants and brightly painted shields.

An hour after they set out, they sighted the English host
on the summit of a low ridge just beyond the little Sandlake
or Senlac[3] brook. Only about half Harold's army had arrived,
and perhaps not more than a third was ready for battle. According to one account, he himself had been riding all night.
Though he had come to attack, there was nothing now but to
stand on the defensive. He had as many troops as his adversary
but few archers and armoured knights, for the English, stubbornly set on ancient ways, despised foreign and new-fangled
weapons. They liked to fight on foot, as their fathers had done,
with axe and spear. The house-carls, with their chain-covered
tunics and double-handed battle-axes, were perhaps the finest
infantry in Europe, and they were fresh from victory. But the
rest of Harold's force, apart from the thanes, was an antiquated
rabble of peasants, equipped with spears, javelins, clubs, and
even pitchforks and sickles. Many were local farmers, out to
revenge their plundered beasts and crops.

The king, therefore, drew up his force with the house-carls
in front, forming the traditional shield-wall of the North—a thin
line of armour, spears and axes, extending from about half a
mile along the low, scrubby ridge. Behind them congregated
the densely packed shire-levies, ready to assail the Normans

[3] The way the French-speaking Normans pronounced it.

when the house-carls had broken the first force of the attack. Harold himself, with the great flapping royal banner of Wessex, took his stand in the centre beside the hoar apple tree, just on the site of the abbey which William afterwards built to commemorate the battle.

The fight began at about nine o'clock. "The terrible sound of trumpets on both sides," wrote the Duke's chaplain, "signalled the start of battle." As soon as the Normans had deployed, their bowmen moved forward and, halting about a hundred yards from the English line, opened fire. Their technique, derived from the Vikings or possibly learnt from the Hungarian invasions of a century before, was not very advanced, their bows short, and their arrows flimsy. But the English, having scarcely any archers, could not reply and had to endure the flickering hail in patience. It did not, however, last long, for their assailants' ammunition was limited to what each man carried.

When, therefore, William's infantry moved forward to the attack, the shield-wall was still unbroken. "The English," we are told, "resisted valiantly, each man according to his strength, hurling back spears and javelins and weapons of all sorts, together with axes and stones fastened to pieces of wood." It was how they had always fought. The house-carls waited on the summit with their battle-axes poised over their heads and cracked open the skulls of every Norman who reached them. The Breton auxiliaries on the attackers' left—kinsmen of the Britons whom the English had defeated so often in the past— liked their reception so little that they fled down the hill. Many of the defenders, forgetting their king's orders, followed after them, shouting in triumph.

At that moment there was nearly a panic in the Norman ranks. The rumour went round that the Duke had fallen, and there was a movement towards the rear. Then William, removing his helmet to show himself, galloped among the knights and rallied them. "He dominated the battle," wrote his chaplain, "bidding his men come with him more often than he ordered them to go in front of him." Wheeling his shaken squadrons, he launched a counter-attack against the pursuing and now breathless English. It was completely successful. In a static fight the Anglo-Saxons were still a match for anyone, but in mobility the trained Norman horsemen were far their superiors. The fyrdmen were cut down in hundreds, and few who had left the summit regained it.

William now launched his cavalry at the ridge itself. They came up the slope, in their hauberks and pointed helmets, like the long line of fighting horsemen painted above the north arch in Claverley church in Shropshire. But the main force of house-carls who had obeyed Harold's orders were still unbroken on the ridge. Like the infantry before them, the knights and their horses were met with a shower of spears, clubs and javelins. Those who were able to spur their terrified steeds to the summit, encountered the swinging English battle-axes and harsh cries of "Out! Out!" Once more there was almost a panic, and many fled down the hill. And once more the less disciplined defenders followed them. But this time William was ready for them; it was said that he had given orders for a feigned retreat to draw them to their doom. As soon as they reached the open ground below the hill, they were ridden down and pounded to pieces by waiting knights.

William now launched his third attack. This time he used all arms simultaneously. His archers, who had replenished their ammunition, were ordered to fire high in the air, while the infantry and cavalry, walking or riding together in a dense mass, moved forward under cover of their high-angle barrage. The dropping arrows distracted the defenders; one pierced Harold through the eye and, though, with an effort, he wrenched it out, the report of his wound spread quickly through the English ranks. Many of the shire-levies, few of whom can have fought before, began to retreat into the darkening forest. By this time there were many gaps in the shield-wall, and little groups of Normans were everywhere penetrating it, moving forward in wedges around some famous knight like immense battering-rams. Among them, according to one account, was the Duke's minstrel, Tallifer, who had begged his master to let him lead the charge.

> "Tallifer who was famed for song,
> Mounted on a charger strong
> Rode on before the Duke and sang
> Of Roland and of Charlemagne,
> Oliver and his vassals all
> Who fell in fight at Roncesvals."

He found the death he sought on the hedge of English swords, helping, unconsciously, to make the England of the future.

The ring of house-carls round the stricken king was now shrinking fast. Yet the tradition of five hundred years held; the flower of the English infantry went on fighting, after all hope of victory had faded, for something more than victory. "The valour of the English," wrote a Norman, "and all their glory raged." While the victors' cavalry pursued the fugitives into the forest, the house-carls fought on. They were so closely packed that the dead had scarcely room to fall. One tall thane struck a Norman's horse in two with a single blow before being struck down himself by Roger de Montgomery's lance. Then—it was "about twilight"—a band of knights closed in on the king, as he bent, bleeding over his shield, and hacked him in pieces with their swords. "In the English ranks," wrote the Norman chronicler, "the only movement was the dropping of the dead; the living stood motionless. . . . They were ever ready with their steel, those sons of the old Saxon race, the most dauntless of men." But, as darkness fell, the ring of living dwindled until all the Wessex thanes and house-carls lay round their king and the banner of the Fighting Man.

William followed up his victory ruthlessly. He had waited for the key to the kingdom; he now turned it and flung open the door. Yet even in victory he acted with his usual deliberation. He made no attempt to advance directly on London, but marched first to Dover to secure its castle. Then, harrying the countryside, he followed the line of the Kentish downs towards the capital. But, as its citizens were not yet prepared to open the gates, he left its formidable river and wall defences alone and, burning Southwark, proceeded westwards through Surrey and Berkshire in search of a ford. He deliberately left behind him a trail of blazing villages. He had only a small force in a populous kingdom, and he wanted no trouble in his rear.

He met little resistance. After Harold's death the Londoners, the two archbishops and the northern earls proclaimed Ironside's grandson, the young atheling, Edgar. But they were neither prepared nor able to meet William in the field. The only disciplined force in the south of the country had been destroyed, and the peasants and farmers of the fyrd had returned to their homes. So had the earls of Mercia and Northumbria, who were far more concerned with their provinces than with the fate of England. When, having crossed the Thames at Wallingford, the invader struck east, like Caesar, to cut off the capital from the north, the dispirited Londoners hastily sent envoys to Berkhamstead to treat. On Christmas Day he was crowned in the Confessor's abbey at Westminster with all the familiar ceremonies of English kingship.[4] As Canute had done before him, he swore to defend holy Church, rule justly and keep good law. As he did so his followers, mistaking the traditional shout of acclamation for a riot, set fire to the houses outside.

A few thousand Norman knights and men-at-arms had conquered a nation of between a million and a half and two million people. Six centuries had passed since the Angles and Saxons had established their kingdoms in the Roman province of Britain, and four since England's conversion to Christianity —distances of time as great as those which divide us from the days of Edward III and Elizabeth. England had led western Europe in monastic learning when the Normans' ancestors had been savages. Her craftsmen were famous throughout Christendom,[5] and her patient, industrious husbandmen, with their love of the soil and genius for managing their local affairs, had given her the framework of village and shire. She was still what Alfred's successor had made her—the best administered and richest of all the western kingdoms.

William had no wish to destroy such an inheritance. Adventurer though he was, he had his race's genius for creative order. At first, like Canute, he tried to govern his new realm with the help of the English lords and prelates who accepted his conquest. Many of his earliest officials were English, and some of his first writs and charters issued in English. But he was faced by two inescapable difficulties. One was the necessity of rewarding the followers with whom he had won and without whom he could not maintain his throne. The other was the obstinacy of the English and their hatred of foreigners, par-

---

[4] In words almost the same as those still used after 900 years he was enjoined to "stand firm, and hold fast from henceforth the seat and state of royal and imperial dignity, which is this day delivered unto you, in the name and by the authority of Almighty God; and by the hands of us the bishops and servants of God, though unworthy."

[5] So were her craftswomen. The beautiful Bayeux tapestry, which was made to record the story of the Conquest, is now believed to have been English work.

ticularly the French. William began by confiscating only the lands of those who had fought against him at Hastings and whom, in keeping with his claim to be the Confessor's heir, he treated as traitors. But the discontent aroused by the arrogance of his acquisitive barons and their rough knights forced him to carry the process of confiscation further. A widespread rising three years after the Conquest he suppressed with terrifying ruthlessness. During the next generation, seizing on every act of disobedience or rebellion, he transferred the ownership of almost every large estate from English hands to Norman. At the end of his twenty years' reign there were only two major English landowners left—Thurkill of Arden and Colswein of Lincoln—one English bishop, the saintly Wulfstan of Worcester, and three English abbots. Almost every Englishman held his land at the will of some Norman.

In this way William substituted for the old aristocratic direction of the State a new and far more efficient one. He resumed the royal rights over the nation's land that his Anglo-Saxon predecessors had improvidently "booked" away. He kept a fifth for himself and his family, and a quarter for the Church. Of the remainder he redistributed all but an insignificant fraction—the property of small English and Danish freeholders—among his hundred and seventy chief Norman and French followers on strictly defined conditions of military service. Nearly half of this went to ten men. Having learnt from his harsh life that no State or throne was safe unless organised for instant war, the king attached to every grant of land an inescapable martial obligation. In return for their great fiefs or "honours," as they were called, his tenants-in-chief, including bishops and abbots, had to swear to support the Crown with a fixed number of mounted and armoured knights, to pay specified dues at stated times, and to attend the royal courts and councils. To meet these commitments they in turn had to farm out their lands on similar terms to professional knights or fighting-men, whom they "enfeoffed" as their vassals.

Thus every substantial holding of land, whoever its immediate occupier, was made to furnish and maintain an armoured, mounted and battle-trained knight ready to take the field at any moment. As well as serving the needs of its peasant cultivators, who had to perform the same manual services, or more, for its new owner as its old, it became a knight's fief or fee, itself part of some greater fief or "honour." If its feudal holder failed to perform his military services, it reverted to the overlord to whom he had sworn allegiance for it. It could neither be broken up nor sold without the latter's consent, and on its holder's death his heir, after paying a fine and doing homage, had to render the same services.

To a large extent this system had already been established in France and other parts of western Europe. Yet it was unique —a mark of William's creative genius—in its identification of the protection of the fief with that of the realm. It was the absence of this that had so troubled his own early life in Normandy and broken up the old English kingdom. In the Conqueror's new England the holder of every substantial military fief had to do homage for it, not only to his overlord, but to the Crown.

For after William had crushed two rebellions in which disloyal Norman tenants-in-chief had called out their vassals against him, and at a time when a new rising and a Danish invasion were threatened, he held, at the Christmas feast and council at Gloucester in 1085, "very deep speech with his wise men." Next year he summoned a meeting at Salisbury, not only of his tenants-in-chief, but of all principal landholders in the country. And by making them swear to obey him even against their own overlords, he made them directly responsible to the Crown as in no other state in Europe. By this simple device he turned feudalism, without weakening its military efficiency, into an instrument of royal power. He became not only, like the king of France, the nominal lord paramount of the realm, but the actual one. He was able to do so because, having conquered England and its land, he started with a clean slate.

Nor did William make his nobles rulers of provinces like their English predecessors or their counterparts in France. Whether by accident or design, he scattered their estates about the country. This not only made it harder for them to rebel, but forced them to think in national as well as regional terms. Abroad the feudal count, like the old Anglo-Saxon earl, thought only of his country or province; in England, like the king himself, he had to think of the country as a whole. Henry de Ferrers, rewarded with 114 manors in Derbyshire, was given 96 in thirteen other counties. A still greater tenant-in-chief, Robert de Mortain, held his 793 manors in twenty different shires. The only exceptions were on the Welsh and Scottish borders, where the local magnates needed vast powers to keep the tribesmen of the Celtic west and north at bay. The prince bishop of Durham, and the earls of Chester, Shrewsbury, and Hereford, ruled what were later called counties palatine. Yet even these were small compared with the independent provinces of France, and the king appointed to them only men he could trust. He watched them very closely. Within half a century of the Conquest only two of these compact, semi-independent jurisdictions remained.

William thus restored to England what it had lacked since the days of Edgar and Canute—an effective central power. She had collapsed because, in the absence of a king strong enough to control them, her nobles had refused to work together. Having spent the greater part of his life trying to teach those of his own land to do so, William shaped the kingdom's feudal law so as to compel her new lords to render common service to the Crown. Like the master statesman he was, he made this their interest as well as their duty. If, through passion or impulse, they ignored it, they soon discovered their mistake. So did their fellows who witnessed their fate.

Within these limits—a framework of discipline in which every baron enjoyed his just feudal rights but no more—William scrupulously respected the "liberties" of his nobles. They were the instrument by which he ruled. Less than two hundred French-speaking barons—closely inter-related and accustomed to working together—and five or six thousand knights became the principal land-holders of England. Having both a duty and incentive to protect the Conquest, they guaranteed its permanence. They formed a new ruling caste; a warrior aristocracy that possessed not only privilege but creative energy. The names they brought from their Norman homes are writ on our maps and across our history—Montgomery and de Mandeville, de Warenne and Giffard, Baldwin and Mortimer, Mowbray and Beaumont, Neville and Lacy, Bohun and Courcy, Beauchamp and Percy.

Beneath this military superstructure the Conqueror had the sense to leave England much as it was. Instead of uprooting its complex polity, he adapted it, with his flexible Norman genius, to his own ends. He kept the Witenagemot, which became the Great Council of his tenants-in-chief, lay and ecclesiastical. He kept the elaborate secretarial and financial machinery which the English kings had devised for raising gelds and land-taxes, and for sending out enquiries and orders to their officers in the shires. He kept the old divisions of shire and hundred; the shire-courts where, under the royal sheriff's eye, the freemen interpreted the customary law of the locality, and the hundred-courts where representatives of the villages—priest, reeve and leading peasants—settled their disputes and answered for breaches of the peace. He left unchanged the free communities of the Danelaw, and the ancient tenures by which the Kentish cultivators were protected in their holdings. He left, too, with the Norman manor superimposed on it for military and taxing purposes, the Midland English village, with its strip-divided fields, its hereditary rights of cattle-pasture and pig-pannage, its communal system of cultivation and wide variety of tenures. He left the Londoners the rights they had always enjoyed under their elected portreeve and burgesses. "I will," he wrote, "that ye be worthy of all the laws that ye were worthy of in King Edward's day and . . . that every child be his father's heir . . . and I will not endure that any man offer wrong to you." And he kept the old Anglo-Saxon shire fyrd or militia—an invaluable counterpoise to the Norman feudal array. It was this even more than the Oath of Salisbury that gave the monarchy in England a power enjoyed in no other European State.

Above all, William kept the English conception of service to the Crown as the basis of landed tenure, and the English tradition that an oath of fealty to the king was more binding than an oath of homage to a liege-lord. It made him something more than a leader of Norman freebooters in a conquered land. In his charters and proclamations to English and Normans alike, he repeatedly stressed that he was the successor of the English kings. Their institutions, however decayed under the last feeble athelings, became in his strong, capable hands, the instruments of a growing monarchical power. By building on the foundations of Alfred and his heirs, he made England what it had been a century before—the most united and therefore strongest State in Christendom.

Wherever an English institution could serve his end, William improved on it. Having got rid of the independent provincial earls who under Ethelred and the Confessor had acquired the un-English right to own and rule land without relation to the service to the Crown for which it had been granted, he used in their place the sheriffs or royal officials with whom his predecessors had vainly tried to check the earls' powers. The Norman sheriff administered the royal estates in the shire, presided at its court, collected the taxes, and led the shire militia in time of war or rebellion. This linked the Crown with the forces, so strong in medieval society, of local patriotism and self-interest and made for national unity. So did the system—possibly brought from France, but adapted also from Anglo-Saxon and Danish practice—by which sworn juries or panels of neighbours were made judges of local questions of fact. William used these repeatedly to discover the rights of the Crown against his powerful Norman followers and the taxable value of their estates.

For most Englishmen all this was a terribly painful process. It was like some drastic operation carried out on the body of a prostrate nation without an anaesthetic. "Cold heart and bloody hand," wrote a Norse poet, "now rule the English land." William was guilty, in his own dying words, of "the barbarous murder of many thousands, both young and old, of that fine race of people."[6] To many the Conquest brought bitter tragedy; the families of those who died in battle, the peasants on the line of march, the thanes whose lands were seized to provide fiefs for William's foreign barons and knights. All who made the least resistance were ruthlessly stripped of their estates in pursuit of the royal policy. Most of the old English nobles and thanes who survived Hastings and the later rebellions in the west, north and midlands, became mere farmers; at Marsh Gibbon in Buckinghamshire—the Conqueror's great tax-survey records— Aethelric, the former owner, "now holds it of William, the son of Ansculf, in heaviness and misery."[7] Some fled to Scotland, where they strengthened the Saxon elements of that wild land, or took service in the Varangian bodyguard of the Greek emperor at Constantinople. A few brave men, preferring liberty to life, took to the marshes and forests as outlaws, like Hereward the

[6] "I have persecuted its native inhabitants beyond all reason. Whether gentle or simple, I have cruelly oppressed them; many I unjustly disinherited; innumerable multitudes, especially in the county of York, perished through me by famine or the sword." Ordericus Vitalis, *The Ecclesiastical History* cit. *English Historical Documents*, I, 286.

[7] "*Graviter et miserabiliter*"—one of the few human touches in that grim, invaluable record.

Wake, a small Lincolnshire landowner who held out in the Fens till 1071. "Most," as William Fuller wrote six centuries later, "betook themselves to patience, which taught many a noble hand to work, foot to travel, tongue to entreat."

Humbler folk were left in possession of their holdings; Norman and English alike would have starved otherwise. Yet many of them were subjected to the tyranny of the special courts which the Conqueror set up in the forests, still covering more than a quarter of the land, to preserve the red and fallow deer for his hunting. "He loved the tall stags like a father," we are told. To guard them his forest officers put out the eyes of any man found killing hart or hind, and mutilated poor peasants caught in the woods with dogs or arrows. In these sacred precincts even the lopping of a bough was punished. Rich and poor alike murmured at the king's forest laws, but "he was so sturdy that he recked nought of them."

William was hard and ruthless: "so stark a man," an English monk called him. When some rebellious townsmen in his native Normandy mocked him for his tanner's blood, he had them flayed alive and their skins hung from the walls. After the second rising of the northern counties in 1070, when five hundred Norman knights were massacred at Durham, he so harried the countryside that along the road from York to Durham not a house remained standing. Even the northern capital and its famous minster were burnt. It took the north generations to recover. Seventeen years later the royal commissioners, surveying the tax capacity of Yorkshire, entered against place after place the grim word, "Waste."

Above all, William was a merciless taxer. His first act after his coronation was to "lay on a geld exceeding stiff." Close-fisted and grasping—a monk complained that, while the Saxon kings gave their courtiers four meals a day, he gave his only one—he had compiled after 1085, mainly that he might tax his realm more closely, a record of all feudal holdings directly or indirectly liable to the Crown. "So narrowly did he cause the survey to be made," wrote an English chronicler, "that there was not one single hide nor rood of land, nor—it is shameful to tell, but he thought it no shame to do—was there an ox, cow or swine that was not set down in the writ." Using commissioners to hold local enquiries or inquests in every shire and hundred, he had recorded, with meticulous efficiency,[8] the ownership and taxable value of every manor or village under lordship, both at the Conquest and at the time of the survey. This included the number of its hides or ploughlands,[9] of the freemen, villeins, cottars and slaves living on it, of its mills, fish-ponds and plough-teams, the extent of its woodland, meadow and pasture—every-thing, in short, that was capable of being taxed. Originally drawn up on long parchment rolls stored in the Treasury at Winchester, the survey was copied into two volumes christened by the English "Domesday" because there was no appeal against it.[10] It was the most remarkable administrative document of the age; there is nothing like it in the contemporary annals of any other country. It enabled the king to know the landed wealth of his entire realm; "how it was peopled and with what sort of men," what their rights were, and how much they were worth.

The taxation William imposed fell directly on the rich, but, as the rich could pass it on, even more severely on the poor. The peasants' burdens, the labour and boon-services demanded of them by their lords, became heavier. The English thane, who had taken part of the village produce as his due and oc-casionally summoned its reluctant young men from the plough to serve in the ealdorman's levies, was supplanted by a Norman or Frenchman. There was a new face—and a new tongue spoken —at the manor house. It is never pleasant to have to pay taxes and rent. It is far worse to have to pay them to a foreigner. And these foreigners were great sticklers for their rights. They left no-one in any doubt that they were the masters of the country and regarded the natives as a conquered race. In those harsh years when Norman knight and English churl were learn-ing uneasily to live together, many an English back must have smarted from the lash of a French man-at-arms. So must many a sullen English heart.

Behind the Norman knight's bailiff, with his bullying ways and grasping demands, was the castle which his master built to house his retainers and overawe the neighbourhood. Every-

---

[8] He employed a second body of commissioners to check the findings of the first. F. M. Stenton, *Anglo-Saxon England*, 609.

[9] Usually reckoned at about 120 acres, though its size varied in different parts of the country.

[10] *Dialogue of the Exchequer.* One volume was for the rich counties of Essex, Norfolk and Suffolk, and the other—in less detail—for the rest of England south of the Tees. F. M. Stenton, *Anglo-Saxon England*, 648.

where, on strategic hill and vantage point, the castles rose-little islands of foreign power in a subjected countryside: the high, circular, moated mound, raised by English labour and crowned by a wooden, and often later stone, keep or tower; the outer bailey with its earthwork enclosure and barracks, whence knights and men-at-arms rode forth to police and terrorise the countryside; the moat with its drawbridge. Even proud London was overawed by its Tower, begun in wood immediately after the Conquest and in stone a generation later.[11] The heavily armoured Norman warriors—retainers or *cnihtas,* as the English called them—who garrisoned these strong-points had the whip-hand of the countryside. A poor man, if he was to live and till the soil in peace, had to make what terms he could with them. Otherwise he might find his house burnt over his head, his wife and children driven into the woods, and himself thrown into a stinking dungeon.

Yet the Norman Conquest brought compensations to the underdog. William the Conqueror conquered something more than England. He used the heritage of Alfred to curb his own turbulent nobility. He brought feudalism under royal control. He prevented men like Hugh of Avranches and Roger Montgomery and his own half-brother, Odo of Bayeux, from exercising in island England either the independent provincial sovereignty they and their like enjoyed on the continent or the usurped native powers of a Godwin or a Leofric. The stark king fastened his English version of the feudal system, with all his Norman thoroughness, on the free-booter barons and knights who had so long kept western Europe in an uproar with their selfish civil wars. In such strong hands as his, in an age when violence, falsehood and treachery were the normal background to political relationships, feudalism helped to create the social virtues—fidelity and loyalty—from which love of country can alone arise. "I become your man for the tenement that I hold of you," the feudal tenant swore as he knelt before his lord with his hands clasped between his, "and faith to you will bear of life and limb and earthly worship, and faith to you shall bear against all folk."

[11] The White Tower, with its 15-feet thick walls, is the only surviving part built by the Conqueror. The words *castle* and *tower* both entered the English language at this time.

For an Anglo-Norman knight after 1086 that lord was not only his local overlord, but the king.

It was this that completed the work that Alfred had begun. It made England again—and as she had never been before—a disciplined land, disciplined not only at the base but at the summit. A man could cross her, it was said, with his bosom full of gold. By stamping out private war between the rich and strong, William re-created a kingdom in which State loyalty counted for more than feudal loyalty, and where the unarmed peasant could till the soil in security. He refused to allow anyone, however powerful, to challenge his peace. "So very stern was he and hot," wrote the Anglo-Saxon chronicler, "that no man durst do anything against his will." He did many harsh things; conquest is a cruel, bloody business, and any nation that allows itself to be conquered must suffer. But, in enforcing public order without respect to persons, he fostered in his subjects that sense of obligation to the State which is the beginning of patriotism.

By making England one, William saved her too from future conquests. He closed the door on the northern barbarians who had ravaged her for three centuries and who now withdrew into the Scandinavian mists. Twice during his reign the Danes were invited by rebellious subjects to land on the east coast, and twice were driven out with no profit to themselves and disastrous consequences to their sympathisers. Though Scotland, with Norsemen settled round her northern and western coasts, still looked for another generation to the barbarian North, England ceased to be a frontier land between the Viking world and the reviving civilisation of western Europe. Henceforth her lot lay wholly with the lands that had inherited the memories and traditions of Rome. Having under Canute been part of a Scandinavian empire spanning the North Sea, she became part of a Norman-French empire spanning the Channel.

Her military forces were now far more formidable than they had been even in the days of Athelstan. In open country the Norman knights on their war-horses were the masters of every field. Six years after his conquest of England William invaded the lowlands of Scotland, whose king, Malcolm Canmore, had married the atheling's sister, Margaret. His mounted armour quickly reached the Tay, where he forced Malcolm to do homage and surrender his eldest son as a hostage. A later punitive force, following a Scottish raid into England, advanced as far as Falkirk and built a fortress on the Tyne called Newcastle to guard northern England.

The Welsh cattle-raiders learnt the same lesson. From the great "Marcher" earldoms of Hereford, Chester, and Shrewsbury the Norman barons went out to seize strategic positions in every lowland valley, driving the natives into the hills. The kingdom of Gwent became Norman; so did Chepstow and Monmouth, Gower and Cardigan, Radnor and Brecknock, Montgomeryshire and the Vale of Clwyd. In all of them stone castles rose to dominate the countryside. Even in the far west beyond the mountains, the Marcher lords planted their power in the Pembrokeshire plain. Early in the twelfth century they settled it with English and Flemish farmers, so that it became known as "little England."

In a society so warlike and predatory kingship called for rare qualities. An eleventh century king had to appoint and dismiss his own officers, preside over councils and law courts, raise and lead armies, and, if his realm was not to relapse into anarchy after his death, choose his successor and secure for him the loyalty of his lords. He had to hear and determine lawsuits, give judgment in person, and constantly travel the country both to preserve order and feed his Court. An Anglo-Norman king had not only to do so in England but in Normandy, Brittany and Maine. Wherever he went, he was followed by throngs of suitors, seeking favours and redress of grievances. Even the poor villeins used to surround William on his progresses, holding up their wooden ploughs to draw attention to their woes.[12]

Above all, the king had to overawe the rough, half-barbaric warriors who surrounded him and on whom his power depended. When he wore his crown in public at the great annual Easter, Ascension and Christmas Feasts at Winchester, Westminster and Gloucester—ceremonies attended by the entire baronage—the peace of the realm turned on the majesty with which he spoke and moved. In days before even the greatest could read and write, formal pageantry—coloured, gilded robe, heraldic de-

---

[12] "For they were oppressed by innumerable burdens because they had to transport provisions great distances from their own homes." The *Dialogue of the Exchequer. English Historical Documents* II, 516.

vice on banner, shield and tent, splendid trappings for horse and throne, glittering arms and armour—were the medium through which the might of the State was expressed. So was the king's presence.

It was England's fortune that during the first centuries after the Conquest so many of her rulers possessed kingly qualities. William himself had tremendous presence. "He was of moderate height," wrote the historian, William of Malmesbury, "immense corpulence, going rather bald in front; of such strength of arm . . . that no-one could bend the bow which he drew when his horse was at full gallop. His dignity was of the highest, whether sitting or standing, despite the deformity of a protruding stomach." It was because his able, tough, short-set, second son, William, had character too that the Conqueror on his death bed in 1087 sent his English crown, sword and sceptre to him instead of to his weak, good-natured, eldest son, Robert of Normandy. "Rufus" or the Red King as he was called from his flaming hair, was a bad man—reckless, vicious, illiterate, cruel and blasphemous. But his English subjects, shocked though they were by his life, remembered with gratitude "the good peace he kept in the land." "He was very strong and fierce to his country," wrote one of them, "and to all his neighbours and very terrible." He feared, it was said, God little, and man not at all. When the Norman barons, who turned his eldest brother's duchy into an inferno, raised trouble in England, they got short shrift. He had his cousin, who was one of them, whipped in every church in Salisbury and hanged. And when he needed help against his stronger subjects, he did not hesitate to arm his weaker: his "brave and honourable English," as he called them. Seeing in him the defender of the order which enabled them to cultivate their fields in peace, they turned out for him with a will.

After William II's death in 1100 from a mysterious arrow in the New Forest, it was the English who enabled his successor, the Conqueror's youngest son, Henry, to wrest Normandy from his brother, Duke Robert. At the battle of Tinchebrai, forty years after Hastings, English infantry, fighting side by side with Anglo-Norman knights, overthrew the baronage of the duchy and annexed it to the English crown. They were trained by the king himself, who showed them how to repel cavalry. Though he was as grasping as his father, the English, whose despised tongue he learnt to speak, made a hero of Henry,[13] who, unlike his brothers, had been born in their land. His title to the throne being doubtful, he proclaimed his adherence to English law, swore in his coronation oath to maintain justice and mercy, and promised to "abolish all the evil practices with which the realm was unjustly oppressed." He claimed that he had been called to the throne in the old electoral way, "by the common counsel of the barons of the realm." Soon after his accession he married a daughter of the Scots king, who through her English mother was descended from Edmund Ironside and Alfred. In later years he loved a Welsh princess, Nest, wife of one of his Marcher barons, who helped him—ruler of a realm speaking three different languages—to understand not only his English subjects but his British.

Henry I, "the Lion of Justice" as he was called, deserved his people's confidence. "There was great awe of him," testified the Anglo-Saxon chronicler; "no man durst misdo against another in his time; he made peace for man and beast." For thirty-six years this squat, avaricious, smooth-spoken man[14] gave the English that political stability which those who have known anarchy value most. He was a tremendous worker, a man of business who could read Latin, understood the importance of administration, and introduced into government regular habits and routine. His father had given England a taxing system more accurate and honest than any in Europe; building on his foundations, Henry gave it a permanent officialdom. He made it out of the domestic officers of his household—the treasurer; the chamberlain who looked after the bedchamber; the constable of the knights and the marshal of the stables; the steward, who presided in the hall where scores of ushers kept order with rods; the reverend chancellor with his seal and writing-office—an innovation of the Confessor's—where writs were prepared for the sheriffs.

Henry, a particularly parsimonious man, kept these functionaries in the strictest economy. Their wages and "liveries"

13 It was said that during the siege of Bridgnorth, the stronghold of the rebellious Robert de Bellême, the Norman barons, who sympathised with the defender, were prevented from abandoning the siege by the English soldiers.

14 According to William of Malmesbury he was plain in his diet, hated drunkenness and snored very loud.

of bread, wine and candles were meticulously laid down in the royal accounts. The chancellor, the most highly paid of all— for he had to maintain a large staff of clerks—received five shillings daily, three loaves, one of the best quality and two less good, two measures of wine, a wax candle and forty candle-ends. He was also allowed two meals a day at the king's table. A humble official, like the man who looked after the cloths in the pantry, only got three halfpence a day and his food; the ewerer had an extra penny a day when the king went on a journey—for drying his clothes—and threepence whenever he had a bath. The state baths before the three great feasts of the year, however, had to be provided free.

His officers stood in great awe of Henry. One of them has left us a story of his gentler side. It was part of the Court custom for the chamberlain and his servants to pour out every evening a measure of wine in case the king should need it in the night. As, however, the latter never asked for it more than once or twice a year, they fell into the habit of drinking it themselves. But one night the king called for the wine after it had been drunk. When the trembling chamberlain confessed what had happened and threw himself on his master's mercy, Henry replied, "Do you get no more than one measure a night? That is very little for the two of us; in future get two measures from the butlers every night, one for you and one for me!" The name of Painscastle in Radnorshire still preserves the memory of the king's affection for this worthy official, Pain FitzJohn, and the lands he gave him.

The greatest of all the royal servants, the justiciar, who kept order when the king sat in judgment and deputised in his absence, became, in the person of Roger of Salisbury, a poor Norman priest whom Henry made a bishop,[15] head of the national administration. He and his fellow officers formed a kind of inner standing court of the Great Council known as the Curia Regis, to which both judicial appeals and affairs of State were referred. With their staffs of trained clerks and chambers where suitors could wait on them, they were the first fathers of our civil service. In the great stone hall of Westminster —today the oldest public building in England—which Rufus

[15] Chosen, it is said, by Henry because of the time-saving speed with which he read the offices in chapel.

raised over the marble bench where the English kings had done justice in the open air, public business continued even when the Court was travelling. Here twice a year, under the chairmanship of king or justiciar, officials called barons of the Exchequer sat at a table with counters and a chequered cloth, carefully checking with the sheriffs the taxes, rents, fines and debts due to the Crown. Every penny had to be accounted for. There was nothing else like it at the time in western Europe.

This capacity for organisation, for creating institutions which continued irrespective of great persons, made a deep impression on Henry's subjects. They admired the unhurried regularity and dignity with which he did business: his daily reception before the midday meal of all who came for justice, the sober recreation after it, the carefully planned arrangements for State progresses through his dominions. His influence was felt in every county, where the sheriffs were kept perpetually busy, receiving writs, making records and collecting the revenue under the eyes of the royal officers at Westminster.

After Henry's death in 1135 from a surfeit of hunting and lampreys Englishmen again had an experience of life under a weak king. His only legitimate son having been drowned crossing the Channel, he had nominated as successor his daughter, the empress Matilda, widow of the German emperor and wife of the count of Anjou, Geoffrey Plantagenet—so called from the sprig of broom he wore in his helmet. But the Council, deeming a woman unfit to rule and exercising the old English right of election from the royal house, offered the crown instead to his nephew, Stephen of Blois, son of the Conqueror's daughter. This good-natured monarch lacked the qualities for kingship. "A mild man, soft and good, and did not justice," an English chronicler wrote of him. He "began many things, but never finished them." Though he reigned for nineteen years—"nineteen long winters," the chronicler called them—he left little behind save a chapel at Westminster bearing his name and an abiding memory of the anarchy unloosed by his weakness. Taking advantage of his indecision, the Welsh descended from their mountains to sack farms on the Dee and Wye, and a savage horde from Scotland marched into England, massacring the inhabitants and driving off the women and girls as slaves, roped naked together.[16] It was only halted by the resolution of the aged archbishop of York—Thurstan, friend of St. Bernard and founder of Fountains—who called out the fyrd of Yorkshire. Fighting under the banners of the north-country saints and led by a handful of Norman nobles—one of them named Bruce and another Balliol—the Yorkshiremen routed the invaders at the Battle of the Standard near Northallerton.

In 1139 Matilda, too, invaded the country from Anjou. For eight years England was racked by civil war, while local barons, playing their own selfish game, threw in their lot, first with one side, then the other. It was hard indeed for them to avoid doing so with two sovereigns claiming their allegiance. Freed from the control of the officials of the Curia Regis, the worst of them built castles from which they plundered their neighbours and indulged in all the licence—so familiar in Europe, but now almost forgotten in southern England—of private war. Some, like King Stephen himself, brought murderous foreign mercenaries into the country, and turned royal fortresses of which they were custodians into private strongholds. In the Isle of Ely—the district that suffered most—the terrible Geoffrey de Mandeville, earl of Essex, made life a hell with his savage foreign soldiers. "They put men in prison for their gold and silver, they hung them up by the feet and smoked them with foul smoke. . . . They put knotted strings round their heads and writhed them till they went into the brain. They put them into dungeons crawling with adders and snakes. . . . Men said that Christ and his saints slept." The fields were untilled, the crops destroyed, the cattle driven away. On the continent such doings were normal. In England, after seventy years of strong rule and royal justice, they were not. The result was to create a universal longing among Englishmen and even among Norman knights and barons for the strong monarchical rule their fathers had enjoyed.

In the end the disorder was resolved by a compromise. It was agreed that Stephen should reign till his death and be succeeded by Matilda's twenty-year-old son, Henry Plantagenet, count of Anjou. His father—the most powerful of all the in-

[16] "That execrable army, more atrocious than the whole race of pagans . . . spread desolation over the whole province. . . . The sick on their couches, women pregnant and in childbed, infants in the womb, innocents at the breast and on the mother's knee, with the mothers themselves, decrepit old men and worn-out old women . . . they put to the edge of the sword or transfixed them with their spears." Richard of Hexham, cit. *English Historical Documents* I, 314.

dependent vassals of the French king—had left Henry ruler, not only of Anjou, Maine and Touraine, but of Normandy which he had conquered in Matilda's name. Six months after his accession the young count doubled his dominions by marrying the gay, divorced runaway queen of Louis of France, Eleanor of Aquitaine. Twelve years his senior and the greatest heiress in Europe, she brought him the fiefs of Gascony, Guienne, Poitou, Saintonge, Limousin, La Marche and Auvergne, and control of more than half of France.

In the spring of 1153, Henry came to England to rally his mother's supporters. In a whirlwind campaign he transformed the military situation. That November at Winchester, amid tumultuous rejoicing, he was accepted by Stephen as his "son" and heir. When a year later, on the king's death, he was crowned and invested at Westminster with the regalia of England—golden crown and sceptre, silver-gilt rod and spurs, embroidered sandals and mantle of white silk—every bell in London rang for joy.

Chapter Seven

THE LAWYER KING

All our struggles for freedom smack of law.
Disraeli

At twenty-one fortune had made Henry II the richest ruler in Europe. He was well-read, eloquent, courteous, a lover of learned conversation, and a good linguist. Yet he was as at home in the field as the court; indifferent to hardships and never happier than when jesting with rude soldiers round a camp fire. His short, homely cloak and frugal meals were a by-word; when he cut his finger he sewed it up with his own needle. He bore the press of suitors that surrounded a medieval king with cheerful good-humour; even when vexed by importunity, he let the crowd bear him from place to place while he listened patiently to every man's case. With his round head and eager, freckled face, his sandy, close-cropped hair contrasting with the effeminate locks of the nobles and troubadours of his wife's glittering court, his squat, sturdy frame and long boxer's arms, he looked rather like a good-natured lion; affable, modest and open to all.

Beneath these winning attributes lay a steely will, determination to achieve his ends at all costs, and tireless industry. "In night-watches and labours," wrote one of his secretaries, "he was unremitting." He never forgot a face or a lesson. He was as businesslike and methodical as his grandfather. And like him he was adamant in reducing his affairs to order. Those who opposed him were met with unrelenting, unscrupulous resolution. Beneath his urbane manner ran the diabolical temper of the Angevins; there were times when he tore off his clothes in rage and gnawed the straw from his mattresses. "From the devil we come," boasted one of his sons, "and to the devil we shall go!" Yet in Henry, as in them all, ferocity and subtlety were deceptively mingled. And in him both were subjected to a strong commonsense and prudence.

For this formidable, restless, broad-chested young man, with his harsh, cracked voice, ruddy face and grey eyes that could glow in anger, regarded war as a costly gamble. Swift to strike, unrelenting in pursuit, he was in victory unusually merciful and magnanimous. The greatest master of diplomacy of the age, he liked to settle accounts without bloodshed. He preferred mutilation as a punishment to death and a fine to either. For an avaricious man he was even moderate in fining. And, though he gave his heart to none save his undeserving sons, he was seldom cruel or vindictive. He made enemies, as all who reform with passion must; his vitality drove both his wife and children to rebellion. Once an exasperated courtier threw a stone at him—an indiscretion that cost him the manor of Didcot.

Yet those who worked with Henry loved him. The praises of his judges and Exchequer officials were founded on more than flattery. For his devotion to their common task—the creation of order in his kingdom's affairs—was the consuming passion of his life.

At the core of his being lay a daemonic energy. He was always moving, always active, and so rentless that even in chapel he chattered and scribbled incessantly. He rose before cock-crow, and only sat down to ride or eat. Slaving like his grandfather far into the night over public business, he shared the passion of all the Conqueror's line for the chase; on his journeys he hunted and hawked along every stream. He never brooked or wasted a minute's delay.

Like Napoleon he wore out everyone round him. "You will see men running as though they were distracted," wrote a courtier of the early morning start of his progresses, "horses rushing against horses, carriages overturning carriages, players, gamesters, cooks, confectioners, morris-dancers, barbers, courtesans and parasites making so much noise, and in a word such an intolerable, tumultuous jumble of horse and foot, that you would imagine that the abyss had opened and Hell poured out its inhabitants." The pace of Henry's travels was one of the wonders of the age; he seemed to fly.

He had need to, for his realm stretched from the Northumbrian moors to the Pyrenees, an enormous distance in the primitive transport conditions of the time. The mere fact of governing such an empire was a wonderful personal performance. Only a Henry of Anjou or a Charlemagne could have achieved it. The thirty-five Christmases of his reign were spent in places as far apart as Bermondsey, Bordeaux, Lincoln, Cherbourg, Winchester—where the English regalia and treasure were kept—Falaise, Westminster, his native Le Mans, Berkhamsted, Argentan, Bayeux, Woodstock—his favourite English hunting lodge and the home of his menagerie of leopards and lions—Poitiers, Nantes, Windsor, Bures, Dublin, Chinon, Marlborough, Caen, Nottingham, Angers, Domfront, Guildford and Saumur. From 1158 to 1163, and again from 1166 to 1170—periods when he was consolidating his own and his wife's continental dominions —he was continuously abroad. At no time was he away from France for more than two years. He made up for it by the thoroughness of his perambulations when in England. Few sovereigns can have seen so much of the country. In a single year he held his court at Winchester, Windsor, Feckenham, Cirencester, Westminster, Nottingham, Marlborough, Winchester palace in the city of London, Reading, Canterbury, Dover, Wye, Bury St. Edmunds, Ely, Geddington, Beaumont hall in Oxford where his son Richard was born, Amesbury, Bishops Waltham, Woodstock, Stokes, Stanstede and Portsmouth.[1]

As soon as he ascended the throne this restless genius began, with furious energy, to restore his kingdom. He sent away the foreign mercenaries, dismantled the unlicensed castles, and demanded back the filched Crown lands. When the earls his mother and Stephen had created ignored his writs, he marched against them, scaring the Midland magnate, Peverel of the Peak, into a monastery, and making the great Marcher lord, Hugh de Mortimer, yield up his castles of Bridgnorth, Cleobury and Wigmore. Having restored order in England, he turned against the Welsh princes and Scottish king. He chased the former back to

[1] *The Chronicle of Benedict of Peterborough*, ed. W. Stubbs II cxxix–cxlviii.

their mountains, and made the latter restore the shires of Northumberland, Westmorland and Cumberland taken during the troubles of Stephen's reign, and do homage at Chester. After which, in the autumn of 1158, this tireless man set out for France to apply, from the Vexin to Toulouse, the same treatment to his own and his wife's continental vassals.

Yet Henry was too shrewd to suppose that much could be won by war. Dominion had come to him so early that conquest made little appeal. What he wanted was to consolidate his possessions and make them a reality instead of, as with other medieval empires, a shadow. He was a realist. The campaigns he fought were either to repress rebellion or secure his frontiers. His reduction of Brittany was to safeguard the long, narrow corridor of his French provinces; his chastening of the Welsh and Scots to save the English Marches from raiding and rapine. Wherever possible, he protected his dominions by diplomacy or family alliances.

Most of all, he sought to make his rule endure. It is this that constitutes his claim to greatness. The supreme object of his crowded, stormy life was to create institutions that could preserve his inheritance after his death from the disintegrating forces threatening it. The chief of these was the power that had made it: military feudalism. In the hands of a ruler like the Conqueror or Henry I, feudalism gave strength and security to a nation. Under a weak one, as Stephen's reign had shown, its dynamic of self-interest could tear the State to pieces. It was not enough, Henry saw, to discipline it during his lifetime. He had to leave the means of doing so to his successors.

Yet feudalism was an inherent part of society. It could only be destroyed by destroying society itself. In England it was the mainstay of the foreign monarchy. Every earl, baron and knight, as well as being a leader and organiser of the local community, was a trained fighting man, dedicated to arms from boyhood and ready for instant war. He had to be able to leap fully armed into the saddle without touching the stirrups, to wield lance, sword and shield, to wear all day without tiring the heavy armour of his caste. This grew ever more elaborate, and the knight's advantage in battle correspondingly greater. By now even his face was completely covered by a ponderous visor, which let down like a castle portcullis, and which after being dented in action, had to be hammered off his head at the nearest smithy.[2]

The members of this warlike caste, who viewed everyone else with contempt, had two interests: fighting and landed property. They thought of them as synonymous, for each sustained the other. They fought for land, not only under their liege-lords on the battlefield, but in the feudal courts of law, where the sole process for determining ownership was trial-by-battle. If a man was not fit to fight for land, the knightly class felt, he was not fit to own it. His only resource was to hire or enfeoff a young knight or champion to fight for him.

The knight's goal—the end of all his prowess—was the fief. The Church and the ladies, and the gay troubadours of southern France, were beginning to evolve a romantic code of chivalry: of courtesy and devotion to the weaker sex, of defence of the Faith, of battle against pagan and heretic. But this was more for the young and idealistic than for workaday knights. The price of a fief was feudal loyalty. And the sole point of honour with most of the hard-bitten men who lived by knighthood was fidelity to the overlord who had enfeoffed them. Every great lord kept his court of armed vassals—"all his barons and men French and English," as one charter put it: his courtiers and officials, marshal and constable, treasurer, seneschal and chamberlain, dapifer, dispenser and butler. The principal seat of his honour, like Castle Acre in Norfolk with its hundred knights' fees or Pleschey in Essex, was a capital in miniature. At Bridgnorth Robert de Bellême housed a thousand knights and retainers in the castle; the palatine earls of Chester dispensed open hospitality all the year round, with feasting, sport and minstrelsy. The great feudal lord sat enthroned in his court like a king, with his tenants-in-chief below him, his "barons"[3] on one side and abbots on the other, ready, like the peers of the realm, to give him aid and counsel, witness his charters and adjudicate disputes.

[2] "They discovered William kneeling with his head on the anvil while the smith laboured with hammer and tongs to draw off his helmet which had been beaten out of shape and driven on his head by the force of the blows received in the tournament." S. Painter, *William Marshal*, 40.

[3] As late as the eighteenth century the head of the untitled family of Venables was still addressed by his Cheshire neighbours as the "baron of Kinderton," his medieval forbears having been barons of the palatine court of the earls of Chester. *Shakerley MSS.*

In France, where his feudatories could evoke against him his own overlord, the French king, Henry was never really able to discipline such magnates. He was one himself. But in England his grandfather and the Conqueror had already curbed their power. Even the relapse into anarchy under Stephen had not turned them into independent war-lords and rivals to the monarchy like their continental cousins. They were still what the Norman kings had made them, part of the realm. For all their retainers, imposing armour and battle-horses, they shrank from war against their acknowledged sovereign. Perhaps it was because they knew that the English people, who ploughed their fields and served as infantry in the fyrd, were on his side; perhaps there was something unsympathetic to lawlessness and blood-letting in the very air of the island. Even the tournament —that substitute for private war, in which fully-armed knights jousted, often to the death, for horses, armour and ransoms— was regarded with disfavour in this peaceful realm.[4] Compared with the glittering, bloody pastime it had become in chivalric France, it was so tame an affair that many young Anglo-Norman knights took service under some continental duke or count who could show them proper sport. Only in a few places did the English civil war degenerate into the ferocious, town-sacking, village-burning slaughter habitual abroad. When Stephen was barred out of his castle of Newbury by his own marshal, instead of hanging the latter's little son, who had been left with him as a hostage, or catapulting him as he was urged to do into the defiant fortress, he merely paraded him under a tree in view of the battlements and then carried him back to his camp. He refused even to gouge his eyes out. A few days later he was seen outside his tent playing conkers with the boy.

It was this gentler strain in English feudalism that enabled Henry to disarm his barons so quickly. So long as he respected their just rights and avoided violence, he knew they were unlikely to combine against him. Having got rid of their mercenaries and unlicensed castles, he subjected them, like his grandfather, to fiscal discipline. He recalled to their old work of punishing

---

[4] Even when licensed by the Crown under Richard I, it was restricted to a few specified areas, like the open rolling country near Salisbury, and between Brackley and Mixbury in Northamptonshire. D. M. Stenton, *English Society in the Early Middle Ages*, 80.

infringements of royal rights the Exchequer officials whom the latter had trained. At their head he placed his treasurer, Nigel of Ely—nephew of the great Roger of Salisbury, gratefully remembered now as "that man of prudence, far-sighted in counsel, eloquent in discourse and, by the grace of God, remarkably qualified to deal with great affairs."

The methods of these watchdogs were described in the *Dialogue of the Exchequer,* written by Nigel's son, Richard Fitzneal. Its guiding principle—still enshrined in Treasury practice —was "devotion to the king's interests with a single mind, due regard being paid to equity." In its pages we can watch the presiding justiciar, with the treasurer, chancellor and barons of the Exchequer, sitting on the covered benches round the black-and-white squared table, as each sheriff presented his accounts, and the official calculator, as in some gigantic chess-match, moved the piles of coins or counters that represented money. We see the humbler officials of the Lower Exchequer—silverer, melter, ushers, chamberlains and tellers—receiving and weighing the cash, and sometimes assaying or "blanching" it in the furnace, while the tally-cutter notches and splits the wooden talleys which serve for receipts. And we can still read the Latin entries on the sheepskin pipe-rolls on which were recorded the state of the sheriff's annual account with the Exchequer, the debts due to the Crown, the farms and rents of the royal estates and woods, the legal fines, the escheats of those whose fiefs had become vacant, and the year's feudal reliefs and tallages. Among the latter was a war-tax on knights' fees called scutage or shield-money, initiated earlier to meet the case of ecclesiastical tenants unable to serve in the field and which Henry adapted to give lay tenants, too, an alternative to accompanying him on his foreign campaigns. It suited both them and him, for, by using the proceeds to hire Flemish, Welsh and Basque *solidarii* or mercenaries, he partly freed himself from independence on the baronage in war. For the same reason he substituted for the personal service of castle-guard[5]—one that had been much abused by Stephen's disloyal vassals—a tax called ward-money,

---

[5] Land was sometimes held by a tenure called sergeanty involving the performance of special personal duties. Such were carrying the king's standard in the field or providing him with falcons for hunting or napkins while he dined. One manor was held by sergeanty of holding the royal head during Channel crossings; another tenant had to bring his sovereign a dinner of roast pork whenever he hunted in Wychwood forest.

which, while relieving the tenant of a vexatious duty, enabled the Crown to hire professional soldiers to garrison its fortresses.

But the field in which Henry mainly mastered his barons was not that of arms but law. At the time of his accession there were at least five different systems of jurisdiction in England. There were the great franchises of the baronial honours, and the village manorial courts, both private property. There were the old public courts of shire and hundred, presided over by the sheriff—nominally a royal officer, but in practice a local magnate who farmed their profits and the taxes of the county and who, during Stephen's lax rule, had often encroached on the Crown's rights and, in some cases, even tried to make his office hereditary. And there was the king himself, who not only sat in his *curia regis* as supreme feudal overlord, but, as successor of the athelings, was the traditional fountain of national justice.

Henry first sought control of the shire and hundred courts. He revived his grandfather's practice of sending out Exchequer barons *in itinere* or *eyre* to sit beside the sheriffs and enforce his fiscal rights. Before long he had made these progresses annual events. And since there was little distinction between the profits of jurisdiction and jurisdiction itself, he empowered his officers, not only to look into revenue matters, but to hear and try local pleas of the Crown. To these he added offences which had hitherto been dealt with by the sheriffs. By two assizes or royal councils—one held at the Wiltshire hunting palace of Clarendon in 1166, and the other ten years later at Northampton—trials of murder, robbery, larceny, rape, forgery, arson and harbouring criminals were reserved to the justices *in eyre*. The criminal jurisdiction of the Crown—formerly confined to *lèse majesté* and breaches of the king's peace on the royal domains and highways—was made nation-wide, and the sheriff's chief judicial powers transferred to officers under the sovereign's eye.

These Henry chose carefully for their loyalty and impartiality, and, as he and they gained experience, for knowledge of the law. At first he had to rely on bishops, Exchequer officials and minor barons temporarily executing judicial commissions. But by experiment he gradually created a body of trained judges whose business it was "to do justice habitually." Some were clerics, others laymen, but all were drawn from the lesser Anglo-Norman families whom he used as a counter-poise to the feudal magnates. Among their names were those of Basset,

Thorold, Belet, Peck, and Comyn. They were assigned to six, and later four, regular circuits of counties, round which, escorted by sheriffs and javelin men, they rode on annual progresses. Others, sitting on a marble bench in Westminster Hall, formed a permanent judicial tribunal of the *curia regis*, which later grew into the courts of King's Bench and Common Pleas. One of its members, Ranulf de Glanvill—or, possibly, his still more famous clerk, Hubert Walter, who succeeded him as chief justiciar—wrote the nation's first legal classic, a Latin treatise on the laws and customs of England and the procedure of the royal courts.

It was through such procedure that Henry traversed the power of the feudal jurisdictions. One of the commonest sources of disorder during the civil war had been the baronial habit of forcibly seizing land on some trumped-up excuse. The victim had two alternatives: to counter-attack with similar force if he could command it, or to appeal in his overlord's court to the only process recognised there, trial-by-battle. In this, whether fought by the principals or by professional champions, victory almost invariably went to the strongest or richest, the largest purse securing the longest lance.

By adapting the old English principle—enshrined in the coronation oath—that it was the king's duty to see that justice was done and that every freeman had a right of appeal to him, Henry and his judges devised writs or royal commands restoring possession to any freeman forcibly dispossessed of his land. They offered these for sale to all, Norman and English alike, whose tenures were free from servile services: to all, that is "free to go with their land where they would." A writ of summons called *praecipe* directed the sheriff to order the overlord of any seized land to restore it immediately or answer for his failure in the royal court. Another called *novel disseisin* commanded him to reinstate any dispossessed freeholder pending trial and summon "twelve free and lawful men of the neighbourhood" to "recognise" and declare, under oath before the king's judges, to whom its possession had belonged. A later writ called *mort d'ancestor* similarly protected the peaceful possession of a freeholder's heir against all claimants not able to prove a superior right in the royal courts.

These possessory writs, as they were called, had three effects. They protected a man's right to possession as distinct from his legal ownership—a matter which might otherwise be disputed for ever. They made everyone with a claim to a freehold plead it, not in the court of the feudal overlord, who was powerless against a royal writ, but in the king's. And, through the procedure laid down for investigating such claims, they substituted for the barbarous custom of proof-by-battle a sworn inquest or "recognition" by "twelve free and lawful men of the neighbourhood," summoned by the sheriff to "recognise" with whom the disputed possession lay.[6]

These "recognitors" or jurymen were not the doomsmen of the old, formalistic English law, swearing in support of a neighbour's oath. Nor were they necessarily witnesses to acts that had happened under their eyes. They were men of substance assembled to answer questions of common knowledge put to them under oath by the king's judges. The Conqueror had used such inquisitions for fiscal purposes. His great-grandson used them for judicial. It is immaterial whether they derived, as some think, from a long-disused device of Charlemagne's or from that of the twelve thanes of the Anglo-Danish wapentake swearing to accuse no innocent man and conceal no guilty one. What matters is that, imposed by the royal prerogative, they were at once accepted in a country where presentment and judgment by a man's neighbours had been part of popular law from time immemorial. Through the ingenuity and good sense of this strong, subtle-minded and original ruler, the corporate conscience of a group of neighbours, acquainted with the persons and facts involved and sworn to speak the truth, was substituted for the unpredictable arbitrament of battle. It seemed a more sensible way of ascertaining God's will, in other words the truth. And it was certainly a better way—and this may have appealed even more strongly to Henry—of keeping the peace.

The same procedure was extended to actions to determine legal ownership. By a process called the Grand Assize a freeholder whose title was challenged could decline trial-by-battle in his overlord's court and, opting for a trial in the king's, put himself "upon the testimony of the country." In this twelve knights of the shire declared in the presence of the royal judges

[6] "Summon by good summoners," ran the writ of *mort d'ancestor* to the sheriff, "twelve free and lawful men of the neighbourhood of X to attend before me or my justices on such-and-such a day, prepared to declare on oath if O. the father of the aforesaid G., was possessed of his demesne as of fee of one virgate in that village on the day of his death." Glanvill, cit. *English Historical Documents* II, 473.

which of the litigating parties had the better right. Once determined, such recognition by Grand Assize was final. "So effectively
does this procedure," wrote Glanvill, "preserve the lives and the
civil condition of men that every man may now legally retain
possession of his freehold and at the same time avoid the doubtful event of the duel."

Through these writs—"infinitely diversified for different causes"
—Henry achieved a major and peaceful revolution. He did so
under the guise of restoring "the good old laws." Appealing to
native English tradition, he used the prerogative to bring the
whole system of freehold tenure under national law. By making
the smaller landowner's right to his property dependent on
the royal instead of the feudal courts, he struck at the root of
the great lord's power over his military tenants. And he dealt
a death-blow to trial-by-battle and private war. He did not
abolish the feudal courts and their processes; like the lesser,
and very active, private manorial courts, they survived for
centuries. He merely drove them out of such business as im-
perilled the unity and safety of the State by offering their clients
cheaper, surer and quicker justice in the royal courts. His writs
attracted to the latter an ever-growing volume of litigation and
revenue. "The convincing proof of our king's strength and justice," wrote a grateful subject, "is that whoever has a just cause
wants to have it tried before him."

Henry's enemies—the great and strong—complained that he
wore out their patience with his perpetual assizes and cunning
legal formulas: his "mousetraps," as one of them called them.
His justification, in Richard Fitzneal's words, was that "he spared
the poor both labour and expense." Selfish, crafty, unscrupulous,
the great lawyer-king wielded the sword of justice "for the
punishment of evil-doers and the maintenance of peace and
quiet for honest men." His judges made his remedies available
in every corner of the realm. With the precedents they enshrined
in their judgments, they little by little created a common law for
all England. Even that of the shire and hundred courts had
varied from district to district; Kent, Wessex, Mercia, the Danelaw, London and the Celtic West had all had their separate
customs and practices. Henry's judges established the same system for north, south, east and west, for town and country, for
Norman, Englishman and Welshman. They nationalised, as it
were, the Law.

In doing so they drew from the principles which Italian jurists had recently rediscovered in the great legal codes left behind six centuries before by the Emperor Justinian. But, while the continental lawyers who studied Roman jurisprudence in the new universities of Bologna and Paris had little chance of applying it except in the church courts, law in England, thanks to Henry's triumph over the feudal jurisdictions, was no academic study confined to learned doctors and pursued only in palace courts, but a practical, day-by-day business affecting the whole nation. However much they might admire the logical maxims of imperial Rome, Henry's judges had to administer the kind of law to which ordinary Englishmen were accustomed. In their judgments, based on the decisions of their predecessors, they embodied from popular and local custom whatever seemed compatible with a common national system.

The growth of such case-law, as it was called, was a two-way process. It was not merely imposed from above but grew from below. It was, above all, a collaboration between professional judges stating the law and laymen drawn from different classes of society, deciding questions of fact. The classic example, pregnant with far-reaching consequences for the future of England and the trans-oceanic nations that sprang from her, was the use in criminal jurisdiction of the old Anglo-Saxon principle of enlisting local worthies to sift local accusations. The assize of Clarendon in 1166 directed the itinerant judges to enquire of twelve "lawful" men from every hundred and four from every township whether any of their neighbours were reputed to have committed felony. Only those so presented were to be put upon their trial. So resolved was Henry to stamp out the violence unloosed by civil war[7] and such the weight he attached to the verdicts of these local worthies that even when those they accused were proved innocent by the customary "judgment of God" or trial by water, they were banished the realm.

This principle of allowing representatives of the neighbourhood to decide questions of fact in criminal law was applied to the trials not only of Englishmen but of Normans. So was the rule—unknown to ancient Rome—that every case should be tried

[7] At a single assize at Lincoln the justices had to try 114 cases of homicide, 89 of robbery, 65 of wounding, and 49 of rape. A. L. Poole, *Domesday Book to Magna Carta*, 392.

in public, as in the presence of the Anglo-Saxon tribe. The secret tribunal, that instrument of imperial tyranny, was never allowed a lodgment in English Common Law. When, long afterwards, the kings of other lands brought the feudal jurisdictions under their control, the authoritarian maxims of Roman civil and canon law, deeply rooted in the minds of continental royal lawyers, often became instruments of despotism. In England, where law was founded on popular custom and the open participation of the ordinary man in its processes, it proved a bulwark of public and private liberties.

Henry's achievement was far in advance of his age. No other ruler could offer his people such a system of national justice. So unique was it that when the kings of Castile and Navarre became involved in a quarrel about one another's lands, they brought an action in his court like a pair of English knights seeking a remedy by Grand Assize or inquest of *novel disseisin*. By the end of Henry's reign there was no major offence against the public peace which could not bring the offender within range of a royal writ. Even the killing and maiming of villeins and cottars were punished by his courts. Within five years of his death an ordinance of his greatest disciple, Hubert Walter the justiciar, created in every county officials called coroners to hold inquests on all sudden and suspicious deaths.

All this prepared the way for the rule of law that was to become the dominant trait in England's life. Henceforward, whoever gave law to her, was to have a machinery by which it could be enforced—against the strong as well as the weak. The professional judges Henry trained, the regular courts in which they sat, the writs they devised to meet popular needs, and the judgments they left behind to guide their successors, helped to ensure that justice should be done even in the royal absence or in the reign of a weak or unjust sovereign. By making his Common Law the permanent embodiment of a righteous king sitting in judgment, the great Angevin established the English habit of obedience to law which has been the strongest of all the forces making for the nation's peaceful continuity and progress.

Because of Henry's firm hand on the lawless strong, England grew richer during his thirty-five years' reign than ever before. Save under Stephen, she had known the blessings of stable government for more than a century. Feeling they could count on the future, the more enterprising took the long-term risks without which wealth cannot be made. The country, still more than half forest, fen and moorland, began to fill up, as landlord and peasant made fresh clearings and colonies in the woods and wastes. By one of those paradoxes which posterity, looking back, can see, but which men fail to observe at the time, the peace Henry and his predecessors gave their subjects constituted a long-term threat to the forests that Richard Fitzneal called "the secret places of kings and their great delights."[8] The "rich feedings" for royal game in their green recesses which this faithful Treasury official wished to preserve for his master's heirs for ever, were a standing temptation to an acquisitive rustic folk with an eye for pasture, rich loam and cheap firewood. The more secure their lives became, the more inevitably they encroached on the royal forests. Even the ferocious punishments of the forest courts failed to deter them. Henry II and his grandfather, with their flair for turning everything to money, established a regular tariff for licensed "assarts," as the making of agricultural clearances were called. Every few years forest-eyres or "regards" were made to harvest the fines. And the royal wardens and verderers waged a ceaseless, sanguinary war against humbler poachers and timber-cutters, who were "wont to do evil in the forest" and staked life, limb and freedom to do it.

Yet nothing could stay the advance of the plough. The wastes as well as the woods were shrinking, and, on the edges of the huge fens, dykes and embankments were being dug to turn mudflat and marsh into pasture. Even the desolate north was slowly being won back by its sturdy knights and freeholders. And on the hills and downs, among the thorns and thickets, the flocks were growing, as men found that sheep could graze secure from thief and raider. It was the Common Law as much as England's climate and herbage that for the next two centuries made her wool export the most valuable in Europe and her fleeces the mainstay of the Flemish looms.

The Norman and Angevin connection stimulated the flow of goods across the Channel. Small but growing quantities of corn

---

8 "Thither they repair to hunt, their cares laid aside; . . . there, renouncing the arduous but natural turmoil of the court, they breathe the pure air of freedom for a little space." *Dialogue of the Exchequer,* cit. *English Historical Documents* II, 528.

from East Anglia and Kent for the cloth-towns of Flanders,
fat cattle, hides and Yarmouth herrings, butter and cheese from
the great vaccaries beside sluggish Lincolnshire and Yorkshire
rivers, Cornish tin for Flemish metal-workers, and Derbyshire
and Mendip lead to roof Norman cathedrals, were exported in
exchange for fine cloth from Flanders, furs from Iceland and
Scandinavia, German silver and Baltic timber, pepper, ginger,
gold and jewels from the Orient, wines from Spain, the Rhine-
land and Gascony. The Bordeaux trade with Southampton
and the south coast ports was immensely stimulated by Henry's
marriage with Eleanor of Aquitaine. His reign was a time of
dawning maritime activity, of fishing fleets launched from sandy
East Anglian estuaries to harvest herring and cod; of the growth
of the Cinque Ports—Hastings,[9] Romney, Hythe, Dover, Sandwich, Winchelsea, Rye—paying for trading privileges by keeping
the Channel between the king's dominions free of pirates. And
because his forbears had banished the fear of the Norsemen, old
inland ports like York, Norwich and Lincoln began to be superseded by new ones on the sea like Hull, Boston and Lynn. The
coast no longer belonged to pirates.

All this was part of a process common to much of western
Europe in the twelfth century: the age which saw the rise of
the merchant and craft cities of Flanders and Lombardy and
the semi-independent urban communes of France. The demand
of the rich for beautiful objects set others to work making and
distributing them and so growing rich themselves. Fine and
intricate chain-mail closely fitted to the body took the place of
the clumsy leather hauberks and metal scales of earlier days.
Wonderful swords and crested helmets, gilded shields and pavilions, silken surcoats worn over armour and emblazoned with
heraldic devices to distinguish their wearers in battle and tourney, all stimulated craftsmanship and trade. So did the gorgeous
robes and furs which the rich were forced to wear to keep themselves warm in the large, draughty halls and churches they
built themselves. One of Henry's sons spent £33—an immense

---

[9] "I grant to my barons of Hastings . . . their liberties and quittances of
toll and lestage. . . . and freedom from all customs throughout the whole of
my land. . . . And I give them treasure trove in sea and land . . . And in return
for these liberties they shall provide for me each year twenty ships for fifteen
days at their own cost; and, if further service is needed, they shall have full
payment." Charter of Henry II to Hastings, cit. *English Historical Documents* II,
968.

sum at that time—on "three robes of scarlet and three of green, two baldekins, one mattress and other necessities" for the knighting of a favourite.

Unlike the Anglo-Saxon nobles, who according to William of Malmesbury were "more inclined to dissipation than the accumulation of wealth" and were content with "mean and despicable houses,"[10] the Normans were frugal in their personal lives but splendid in their architecture. They raised larger buildings than any in Britain since the Roman occupation. During Henry's reign the great square keeps of Dover, Bamborough and Newcastle-on-Tyne were built, and lead was brought from Cumberland to roof his castle at Windsor. Like his predecessors he was an enthusiastic builder; he had the walls of his chamber at Winchester decorated with paintings, and adorned his hunting palace at Clarendon with marble columns.

At first the Conquest had checked the growth of town-life in England. In York and Lincoln, the two chief cities of the north, as well as in lesser boroughs like Cambridge, houses were demolished to make room for castles; others were burnt by plundering soldiery or deliberately destroyed as a punishment for rebellion. But during the reigns of the two Henrys there was a steady growth in the size and number of towns. The Crown and the great secular and ecclesiastical lords found the sale of free burgess-tenures and the tolls of markets and fairs a valuable supplement to agricultural revenues. Both kings encouraged commerce by selling to the citizens and gild-merchants of favoured towns—among them Bristol, Winchester, Gloucester and Hastings—charters of freedom from the countless tolls and custom-dues which impeded the flow of goods at every city gate, port, and river crossing. In no other European land was there so large a comparative measure of internal free trade. "Let all the men of London and their property," ran Henry I's charter to its citizens, "be quiet and free from toll and passage and lestage and from all other customs throughout all England and at the seaports." And though the second Henry, alarmed by the growth of independent communes in the walled cities of France, was chary of granting self-government to towns, his grandfather had already given the Lon-

10 "They were wont to eat until they became surfeited and to drink until they were sick." William of Malmesbury, *Gesta Regum Anglorum*, cit. *English Historical Documents* II, 291. He was, however, being a Norman, a prejudiced witness.

doners the right to appoint their own sheriff and "farm" and assess their taxes.[11] By the end of his reign the city—by far the largest in England—had over 20,000 and perhaps as many as 30,000 inhabitants, and was spreading into the fields beyond its ancient walls. Most of the houses were still flimsy single or two-storied wooden structures; one winter gale flattened more than six hundred, and fires often swept away whole wards. But the richer merchants' and knights' houses were already being built of stone, and red-brick tiles were gradually replacing thatch. Two years before Henry's death the Londoners began their first stone bridge; a monument of faith in the country's stability, that took thirty years to complete and lasted for six centuries.

One of the king's subjects, William Fitz Stephen, wrote a glowing account of contemporary London: the clear river bordering it on the south, the royal palatine castle in the east whose keep was set with a mortar tempered with the blood of animals, the high and massive walls with their seven doublegates and towers, the thirteen conventual and hundred and twenty-six parish churches. He described the merchandise that flowed up its river from the ends of the earth—gold and spices from the East, arms from Scythia and purple silk from China; the wine and cook-shops where travellers could buy hot dishes at any hour of the day or night; the market outside the walls in the meadow called Smithfield, where highstepping palfreys with gleaming coats were put through their paces, and where country folk brought their goods and livestock for sale—"swine with long flanks, cows with full udders, oxen of immense size and woolly sheep." And he drew the picture, the first in our history, of the Londoners at play; their summer evening walks among the suburban wells—St. Clement's, Holywell, Clerkenwell—and the sparkling streams whose mill-wheels made so cheerful a sound; the hunts in the great Middlesex and Essex forests after stag, fallow deer and wild boar; the apprentices and schoolboys playing football in the fields while "the fathers and wealthy magnates came on horseback to watch the contests and recover their lost youth"; the archery, running, jumping, wrestling, dancing and stone slinging, rowing and skating, with which the youths and maidens regaled themselves on holy days.

Henry himself was a careful husband of his kingdom's re-

---

[11] Henry II deliberately abstained from confirming this part of his predecessor's charter.

sources, and left behind a vast treasure. Twice he reformed the coinage, suppressing unlicensed mints and punishing forgers with a, for him, unusual ferocity. He set his face too against wrecking—a popular practice along the western coasts—and "ordered that humane treatment be accorded to mariners saved from the perils of the deep." To the scandal of the pious he was a great patron of Jews, and for the very reason which, after the crucifixion, was the chief source of their unpopularity. By giving them his protection he turned their practice of usury—forbidden to Christians—into a kind of sponge to absorb the revenues of rich barons and abbeys. For when these borrowed money for their costly enterprises at interest-rates[12] based on the belief that defenceless Jews would never be able to enforce them, he gave the latter the assistance of his Exchequer courts. For this he made his Hebrew *protégés* pay dear. If they hesitated to pay he threatened to pull out their teeth, as his son John did and—but for him—his barons would have done. When they died, since the Law no more safeguarded their inheritance than that of slaves, he acquired their estates. Like the royal forests they were his private property, and all they had was his.[13] In this way the king enjoyed the profits of usury without its odium. The hatred and pogroms it aroused fell exclusively on the Jews and only increased the fines and profits of the Crown. So remunerative did this royal patronage prove that on the death of the great money-lender, Aaron of Lincoln, who had financed the building of some of the finest abbeys and castles of the age, a special department of the Exchequer was set up to deal with his estate.[14]

The feudal barons despised traders. Henry did not. He used them to swell his revenues. It was characteristic of his freedom from the prejudices of his age that the man he chose as his first favourite and counsellor was the son of an Anglo-Norman merchant who had migrated from Rouen to London and rose to be the city's port-reeve or chief officer. Young Thomas Becket was a student of the new canon or church law, and at the time of Henry's accession had become, through his great

---

12 Sometimes as high as 60 per cent. 43½ per cent was considered normal.

13 "The Jew can have nothing that is his own, for whatever he acquires he acquires not for himself but for the king." Bracton.

14 His clients included the archbishop of Canterbury, the king of Scotland, the cathedral of Lincoln, and the abbeys of Peterborough and St. Albans. A. L. Poole, *From Domesday Book to Magna Carta*, 422.

talents, archdeacon of Canterbury and the primate's legal adviser. Dark, handsome, and immensely tall, with a great hooked beak and wonderful vitality, the brilliant ecclesiastical lawyer became the young king's inseparable companion. He was made chancellor and loaded with gifts and favours; the woodchopper, the contemptuous nobles called him after his homely origin. His wealth, splendour and vast train of retainers became the talk of England and France. The very bits of his horses' harness were made of silver. When in 1158 he went on an embassy to Paris to negotiate a marriage between his master's seven-year-old son and the French king's three-year-old daughter, he rode, like the great actor he was, on a magnificent charger, preceded by hundreds of knights and liveried choristers with richly-caparisoned packhorses ridden by monkeys in silks and velvets. A year later he led the royal army in Aquitaine and captured the city of Cahors, unseating a French champion in open tournament.

In 1162 the king, wishing to have a loyal and subservient ecclesiastical collaborator, raised this low-born clerk to the supreme office of archbishop of Canterbury. With his aid, he felt, he would be able to bring the practice of every court in the land into line with the principles of law and order he was trying to enforce.

Chapter Eight

BELL, BOOK AND CANDLE

There is no power but of God; the powers that be are ordained
of God.
St. Paul

The papacy is no other than the ghost of the deceased Roman
Empire sitting crowned upon the grave thereof.
Thomas Hobbes

In trying to subject every part of the nation's life to the
Law the great Plantagenet fell foul of the one Power which in
that age no prince could safely challenge. By doing so he suffered a defeat that impressed his contemporaries more than all
his triumphs. For even the proudest of kings—born to the purple and gold of the throne, riding in glittering armour to the
sound of trumpets, feasting and hunting and giving law—were
members of Christ's Church. Every day they knelt before the
altar or by their gilded, painted beds and confessed themselves
sinners and penitents. In their pride and the lust of their pleas-
ures they might pay small heed to the words of their prayers,
yet, in the eyes of themselves and their subjects, they were
children of God.

"Non nobis, Domine!" they heard their priests chant, "Not
unto us, O Lord, but unto Thee the power and the glory!"
Behind their crowns and sceptres lay the memory of the "mocking reed and crown of thorns."[1] They acknowledged a Faith
that proclaimed that whoever exalted himself should be hum-
bled, bade the rich give to the poor and all men be merciful
and brothers to one another. When sickness came and death
threatened—and death was never far from the filthy, disease-

[1] Lord Radcliffe, *The Problem of Power*, 22.

haunted towns and villages of the Middle Ages—even the strongest trembled. It was at such times that princes, barons and merchants made gifts to the Church—to endow abbeys, schools and hospitals, to teach the young and nurse the sick, to pay monks and priests to offer prayers for their souls and intercede for them. So when the Conqueror lay dying, remembering the rivers of blood he had shed, he "hastened to make provision for the future welfare of himself and others, ordering all his treasures to be distributed among the churches, the poor and the ministers of God."[2] Even his vicious, braggart son, Rufus, who "kept down God's Church" and blasphemed against every hallowed belief, became a craven when death threatened, crying for the saintly Anselm whom he had so long refused to instal as archbishop in order that he might filch the revenues of Canterbury. For without the Church's intercession, it was believed, there was no salvation from the powers of evil and the eternal torments over which they presided. The greatest ruler and poorest peasant thought the air was full of fiends, that the Devil lay in wait to cast men into hell-fire, that the sole hope of salvation lay in the prayers and services of those ordained of God. Into the hands of their supreme head, the pope, had been given, it was supposed, the keys of Heaven and Hell.

For despite six centuries of barbarism Christ's religion had lost none of its hold on human hearts. As was natural in an ignorant time it had become overlaid with the superstitions of the pagan creeds it had supplanted. Its philosophy of love and forgiveness was not easily grasped by men whose forbears had offered sacrifices to demons. In converting successive waves of heathen, the Church had allowed them to cling to many foolish fancies so long as they accepted the truth that Christ, the Son of God, loved mankind and had died for the remission of its sins. The fertility-rites of primitive tribes, the magic cults of

[2] Ordericus Vitalis, *The Ecclesiastical History*, cit. *English Historical Documents* II, 281. "At length, on Tuesday, 9 September, the king woke just when the sun was beginning to shed his rays on the earth, and heard the sound of the great bell of the cathedral of Rouen. On his inquiring what it meant, his attendants replied: 'My lord, the bell is ringing for Prime in the church of St. Mary.' Then the king raised his eyes to heaven with deep devotion and lifting up his hands said: 'I commend myself to Mary, the holy mother of God, my heavenly Lady, that by her blessed intercession I may be reconciled to her well-beloved Son, our Lord Jesus Christ.' Having said this he instantly expired." *Idem* 289.

the Orient, the hell and fiends of northern mythology were so intermingled with the tale of Christ's life and teaching that it had grown hard to distinguish truth from error.

The God in whom medieval man believed was an intensely personal God, for ever appearing in acts of nature, visions and apparitions, plagues and cures, storms, fires and miracles. And not only God, but the whole hierarchy of Heaven, angels and saints, apostles and martyrs, lay on the frontiers of the visible, tangible world, ready at any moment to reveal themselves. So did the Devil and the fiends, witches and ministers of evil. A flight of crows seemed a swarm of demons come to fetch the soul of a usurer, the howling of the wind the cries of some wicked lord borne through the middle air to Hell. When Henry I granted the abbey of Peterborough to a simoniac—a notorious purchaser of Church preferments—the country folk throughout the fens heard horns blowing in the night and saw hunters, "black and big and loathsome," riding in the woods with satanic hounds.[3] At a time when men knew little of the laws of nature or the world outside their village homes, they accepted such tales with no more question than their twentieth century descendants the latest scientific marvels.

Behind all this superstition lay a conception shared by rich and poor alike, educated and ignorant. It was that the universe, from its greatest to its minutest part, was governed by divine law. Everything that happened in the world—that had happened, was happening, or was going to happen—was part of the same majestic rule, only partly intelligible to man's puny intellect. It was within his power, either at the instigation of the Devil to oppose that law or, with Christ's grace and the guidance and intercession of his Church, to further it. The Church existed to explain it, to help man obey it and, through Christ's love and sacrifice, to obtain forgiveness for him when he broke it.

And that Church existed for everyone. Alone in a world of inequalities it opened its doors to all. It was not merely for certain families or tribes, for kings and landowners, for the successful or learned. It was for fools and failures, for the weak and sick, for women and children, for prisoners and paupers,

---

[3] Anglo-Saxon Chronicle (Peterborough), cit. *English Historical Documents* II, 194.

for saints and sinners. Two things bound the whole of Christendom: believe in Christ and membership of his Church.

It was this universal quality that made its appeal so overwhelming. It gave purpose and significance to every life. The priest praying for souls, the king doing justice, the knight fighting the infidel and invader, the peasant working in the fields, the woman rearing children, the artist and craftsman glorifying creation, all were members of one body and in God's eyes equally important. And it was the Church that united the members of this great family, dead, living and unborn, interceded for their sins and helped them to everlasting bliss. Within the wide limits of human frailty—for which the Church made full allowance—medieval man relied on its guidance at every point. There was a place in its creed and ritual for everyone and everything.

Wherever in western Europe man turned his eyes, he was confronted by the majesty of the Church. He could not read a book that churchmen had not written and copied by hand; unless he was a churchman trained by churchmen, he almost certainly could not read at all. In an age when most people lived in huts little bigger or cleaner than pigsties, the Church's buildings towered above the landscape, and blazed within with colours, jewels and vestments. They were filled with the carvings and paintings of great artists who had employed their genius to make the Christian story familiar to everyone. For the Church did not teach as today only by books and sermons. At a time when not one man in a thousand could read, it drove its lessons home in sculptured stone and vaulted space, in painting, glass and embroidery. Through stone and wooden panel, altar-piece and reredos, it depicted the Nativity or the Adoration of the Shepherds, St. Michael leading the heavenly host or St. George slaying the Dragon, the Lamb of God or the flowering Tree of Jesse. In a thousand forms it illuminated the lives of saints and apostles, martyrs and prophets; the clash between Virtue and Evil, Truth drawing the tongue of Falsehood or Sobriety dosing Drunkenness over the door of the Chapter House at Salisbury, the devils carting the souls of the damned to Hell in rustic wheelbarrows whose colours still blaze down from the great fifteenth-century window of Fairford church in Gloucestershire. So too the lovely and dramatic ritual of its services helped to shape the imagination of every man, rich and poor, in Christendom. On Good Friday the Crucifix was taken from the altar and hidden in a curtained wall called the Easter sepulchre, from which on Easter morning it was borne in triumphant procession before the rejoicing congregation.[4] The poorest peasant took part, as actor and audience, in the never-ceasing pageantry, drama and music with which, in even the remotest village, the Church invested the changing year. His holidays or "holy days," were its feasts; his daily work was performed against the familiar background of religious intercession and rejoicing, prayer and ceremony.

Everything medieval man did was blessed or cursed, approved or disapproved, explained and solemnised by the Church. He was baptised by it, married by it, buried by it. He went into battle calling on its saints to aid his arms; he sought a cure for all his ills at its martyrs' shrines or in its holy waters and wells; he made his oaths on its sacred relics. Its superstitions, often touchingly beautiful, were part of his daily life. He prayed before the painted images of its saints and angels for help, comfort and forgiveness. The bells rang, and the familiar gargoyles grinned from the village church tower, to guard him from demon or storm; he brought his corn to be blessed at its altars, and, repeating its hallowed Latin incantations, danced round his apple trees to make them fruitful. The very oxen of the fields, he believed, knelt in the byres on Christmas night in remembrance of the manger birth.

The Church not only controlled men's minds and imaginations. It enjoyed immense wealth. It commanded in every country a host, not of warriors, but of men and women vowed to its service. They ranged from scarlet-robed cardinals and mitred archbishops to humble parish-clerks, bellringers and church-sweepers—members of the Minor Orders, as they were called; from judges, lawyers and physicians to the poor ragged students who begged and sang their way along the roads of Europe to hear the Church's famous doctors lecture on theology and canon law in its cathedral schools and universities. In its heyday in the twelfth and thirteenth centuries, it has been reck-

---

[4] See Helen Waddell's description of "the Office of the Sepulchre and the Office of the Star, the amazing moment when for the first time the three white-clad figures come slowly up the cathedral aisle, as those who seek something and the challenge, 'Quem queritis in sepulchro, O Christicolae' first rang from the tomb itself." *The Wandering Scholars*, 65.

oned, one out of every thirty adult males in western Europe was a cleric of some kind.[5]

The flower of this vast army were the "regulars," the monks and nuns who had forsworn the world and embraced that of God, living in disciplined communities under rules or orders stricter than those of any other existing society, military or civil. In hundreds of monasteries and convents in every land these dedicated men and women followed a life of routine whose end was Christ's worship and the service of his Church. They rose from their pallets in the dormitories an hour or two after midnight[6] to troop down cold corridors to celebrate Matins and Lauds in chapel; assembled in the chapter house for admonition or punishment and to discuss the business of the day; dined in silence in the refectory, where the officers and their guests sat in state on the dais and the monks at long tables below, as in an Oxford college today, while one of the brethren read aloud a Latin homily; laboured in the monastic fields, gardens and workshops, or copied and illuminated books in the scriptorium, whose desks looked through unglazed arches on to the grass garth of the cloisters; taught the novices and prescribed to the sick until the hour of Vespers recalled them once more to their devotions. From the first moment of the day to the last, when Compline was sung before they withdrew at dusk to their dormitories, their lives were ordered by the chapel bell—a sound familiar in every corner of Christendom.

It would be hard to exaggerate the part played by the monastic houses in forming the character of English and European institutions. They were the centres and creators of civilisation, and the principal meeting places of learned men. Our schools, universities and charitable foundations have all grown out of their rules and ordered life. The names of their officers still survive in our societies and collegiate bodies: the precentor in charge of the music, services and books, the chamberlain of the clothing and bedding, the sacristan of the church fabric and sacred vessels, the cellarer of the provisioning and the bursar of the finances, the infirmarer of the hospital, the almoner of the charities. In that simple rustic world there was

[5] As compared with roughly one in a thousand in modern Britain. But it included virtually the entire professional class.

[6] "And when they rise for the service of God, they shall exhort each other mutually with moderation on account of the excuses that those who are sleepy are inclined to make." *Rule of St. Benedict.*

nothing to compare with these establishments, with their chapter-houses, dormitories and guest-houses; their libraries whose books were lovingly copied by hand in the cloisters even in winter frosts; their workshops, kitchens, butteries, bakehouses, breweries, laundries and dairies; their granges, barns, fish-ponds, orchards, vineyards and gardens—the first in Britain since Roman times—water-pipes, drains and filter-tanks. Far in advance of the richest layman they possessed even lavatories, with long stone or marble washing-troughs, brass water-cocks and towels. And in their infirmaries, where the monks were periodically bled,[7] bath-houses were provided for bathing the sick and aged and, before the great Christian feasts, the entire chapter.

Such institutions were teachers and examplars, not only of learning and piety, but of the arts and graces of life. In the Customary of St. Augustine's, Canterbury, which William the Conqueror's Italian archbishop, Lanfranc, restored to its ancient monastic constitution, the monks were enjoined not to crack nuts with their teeth, not to make signs across the refectory or lean on the table. "The dishes are not to be broken or dirty or smeared on the underneath," ran the Rule of Barnwell priory near Cambridge; "the brethren ought all to be careful not to wipe their noses or rub their teeth on the napkins or table-cloths."[8] Every three weeks the monastic linen was washed, and in summer every fortnight. In the guest-house, where travellers were entertained, the hosteller kept a store of clean towels and sheets, well-scrubbed saltcellars and porringers, silver spoons and basins, fresh rushes for the floor and straw for the beds, candles, candlesticks, and writing materials.

During the twelfth century the wealth of the monasteries grew with every generation. At the magnificent services which were held at their shrines—the greatest events of the medieval year—offerings were showered on them by multitudes of deeply moved Christians. Most visitors left donations with the houses that sheltered them; every rich man wished to win prestige on earth and a friend in Heaven by some gift or legacy to the saint or martyr commemorated by the local shrine; blessed Alban or

---

[7] "A season of blood-letting, when the cloistered monks were wont to reveal the secrets of their hearts in turn, and to discuss matters one with another." *Chronicle of Jocelin of Brakelond* (1907 ed), 21.

[8] D. H. S. Cranage, *The Home of the Monk,* 23–4.

Edmund, Peter or Paul, or the tender, merciful Virgin. In men's minds the monasteries were personally identified with these divine personages. Their jewelled shrines and crosses, golden and silver vessels and candlesticks, silken and embroidered altar-cloths, chasubles and dalmatics, their rare books bound in gold, and the hallowed relics brought from afar by visiting kings and princes were the glory of neighbourhood and kingdom. Their wealth was immense. An abbey like St. Albans or Bury St. Edmunds might have estates in a dozen counties. Its officers were constantly travelling to collect its rents and dues. Every fortnight Ramsey drew from the village whose turn had come to supply its kitchens twelve quarters of flour for the monks' and guests' bread, 2000 loaves for its servants, ten fat pigs, fourteen lambs, 120 hens, 2000 eggs, and vast quantities of malt, honey, lard, cheese, butter, beans and horse-fodder.

The abbot of a major monastic house was a prince of the Church, ruler of a famous society, and lord and administrator of a vast property. It was not enough for him to be, like old Abbot Hugh of Bury, "a good and kindly man, a godfearing and pious monk but in temporal matters unskilful and improvident." If he was, the abbey soon fell into debt to the Jews —ever offering tempting loans on its treasures—or was cheated of its rents and services by grasping knights and cunning peasants. When in the last years of Henry II's reign Samson, the sub-sacristan of Bury, was elected in Hugh's stead, the holy Edmund himself appeared to one of the brethren in a vision, predicting that the new abbot—unlike his senile predecessor— would be "constant in labour, alike when disputing with the archbishop of Canterbury about the pleas of the Crown, when striving with the knights of St. Edmund for the payment of scutage, with the burghers about encroachments on the market, or with the sokemen for the suits of hundreds." Samson proved all that the saint had foretold, holding inquests into the abbey's rights on every manor and into the obligations of all its villeins and freeholders. He cleared wastes and brought them into cultivation, made and stocked parks and fishponds, rebuilt halls, granges and chapels, replaced reed and straw roofs with stone and lead, and paid off the abbey's soaring debts to the Jews— Benedict of Norwich and Rabbi Joce—entering all in a book which he kept daily, "as if he saw in it the image of his probity in a glass."

Many abbots left such minor details to their subordinates; Samson was as exceptional and untiring as the great Angevin king who approved his election. And an abbot normally had enough to do without being an accountant. He was the father confessor of a community whose influence was nation-wide and had to bear in mind that "the rule of souls is the art of arts, the highest form of knowledge." He sat in the council of the realm, and presided over the feudal court of the abbey's barons, knights and freeholders. He played a leading part in the affairs, not only of the monastery but of the neighbourhood, and acted as a judge in a wide range of secular affairs. When, for instance, a poor girl begging her bread from door to door, was assaulted by one of the sons of Richard FitzDrogo, it was Abbot Samson who imposed a heavy fine to compound the wrong and settled it on the girl and a passing pedlar who agreed to marry her. And, like the monastery itself, he had to provide hospitality for a constant succession of great travellers, including the king himself. Samson, we are told, "whenever any important guest arrived, used to sit with his monks in some retired grove and watch the coursing for a while." For an abbey played as large a part in the social life of the nation as in the religious, political and economic. Its prestige, and that of its saint's shrine, was a matter of widespread concern. A broil between the burghers of Bury and the abbey servants during the Christmas feast led to the abbot discontinuing his customary hospitality and threatening the offenders with excommunication, whereupon "they all went out from the church and, having taken counsel, stripped themselves and, naked except for their underclothes, prostrated themselves before the door."[9] Even the smaller houses were the leading institutions of the countryside in which they stood; when, after a riot, the Mayor of Oxford surrendered the keys of the town to the prior of St. Frideswide's, he did so on bended knees.

In days when there were no hotels, newspapers or posts, the monasteries, with their international organisation, were the means of communicating news, learning, crafts and discoveries. They

[9] "All were heavily scourged and absolved, and all swore that they would abide by the judgment of the Church for the sacrilege which had been done. . . . When everything had been restored to peace, the burghers ate with the lord abbot on the days following with great joy." *Jocelin of Brakelond* (1907 ed., 146–7).

provided the schools, hospitals and libraries[10] of the age. They trained its artists, scientists, physicians and writers. A monk of Malmesbury invented a flying machine that flew a furlong,[11] the same house had a medical school started by an Italian to which patients came from every part of the country. Most of the larger abbeys maintained a succession of historiographers who compiled elaborate, if somewhat inaccurate, chronicles of their times; William of Malmesbury, Florence of Worcester, Eadmer and Gervase of Canterbury, and the two thirteenth century chroniclers of St. Albans, Roger of Wendover and Matthew Paris, are among the fathers of English history. And from the cloisters the Christian kings, who were slowly creating England and the other infant States of Europe, drew officers trained in regular habits of routine, business and accountancy, and, still more important, in ideals of public service. The monastic officers were called "obedientiaries"; they commanded because they obeyed. Nowhere else could those who had to keep order over large areas find men so fit for their business. For the Church offered a far wider choice of trained servants than the feudal families whose sons were usually taught only to hunt and fight. Through its hierarchy unaccounted men could rise to the proudest posts in Christendom; could become bishops and abbots, justiciars, chancellors and royal ministers. So the great statesman, Suger, who, as minister to two kings, laid the foundations of French monarchical power in the second quarter of the twelfth century, began his career as an acolyte, serving the altar of the monastery for which his father had worked as a serf. His contemporary Adrian IV—the only Englishman ever to become pope—had begged his boyhood's bread at the gates of St. Albans abbey.

The Norman conquest had coincided with a monastic revival throughout western Europe. In 1066 there had been only thirty-five monasteries in England, and only in two or three had the monk's habit been worn. One alone—Burton—lay north of the Trent. During the next half century, not only were the older Benedictine houses revitalised by the French and Italian abbots whom the Conqueror imported from the Cluniac foundations

---

[10] These in the 11th and 12th centuries were seldom large. Christ Church, Canterbury—probably the largest in England—had rather over 600 books in Lanfranc's time. At the beginning of Lent they were all laid out on a carpet in the chapter-room so that each monk could choose one for his Lenten reading.

[11] It fell and broke his leg because he forgot to give it a tail.

on the continent and from the monastic schools of Normandy, but, for the first time since the Danish invasions, monasteries re-appeared after a lapse of two hundred years in the ravaged lands beyond the Humber. In the second decade of William's reign a Norman prior and two English monks from the abbeys of Winchcombe and Evesham set out on foot for the north with a donkey laden with sacred books and investments to restore the tradition of Aidan and Bede to Northumbria. Two great abbeys, St. Mary's at York and St. Cuthbert's at Durham, sprang indirectly from this act of faith.

But the real revival of monastic life in the north occurred in the reign of Henry I with the coming of the Cistercians. The splendour, wealth and magnificent ritual of the Benedictine houses, even after the Cluniac reforms, left the more austere spirits of the age unsatisfied, and a movement began in France to restore the simplicity and poverty of early monastic rule. In 1084 the first Carthusian settlement of the Grande-Chartreuse was made among the lonely Grenoble mountains. Fourteen years later six Benedictine monks founded the abbey of Cîteaux near Dijon. In this little community among the Burgundy marshes the stern, earnest life of the primitive ascetics was revived. It was its third abbot, Stephen Harding, an Englishman from Sherborne, who in 1119 drew up the famous Charter of Love which became the rule of the Order of Cistercians. Under the inspiration of the great Burgundian preacher, St. Bernard, abbot of the daughter house of Clairvaux—the "bright valley"—and the most compelling apostle of Christianity since St. Boniface, its colonies spread across Europe, reaching Poland, Hungary and the Scandinavian mountains.

In 1128 the first Cistercian house in England was founded at Waverley in Surrey. But it was among the desolate Yorkshire hills and the remote valleys of the Welsh Marshes that the Order made its chief settlements. It was part of its Rule that its monks should live far from the haunts of men, in silence and austerity, and support themselves by their own labour. Even their rough, homespun woollen tunics and cowls were undyed, giving them their name of white monks in contrast to the black monks of the older Rule. Their simplicity of life and love of solitude and country pursuits made a deep appeal to the English. By the end of Stephen's reign there were twenty Cistercian monasteries in Yorkshire alone, and forty in the kingdom.

Fountains, founded in 1132 on waste ground in Skeldale by a dozen pioneers from St. Mary's, York, grew from a few huts under an elm tree into the great abbey of St. Mary's. Rievaulx, Jervaulx, Byland and Kirkstall, Tintern, Valle Crucis, Neath, Abbey Dore and Margam, raised in the twelfth and rebuilt in the thirteenth and fourteenth centuries, were among the grandest achievements of the Middle Ages. Bare of ornament, sculpture and painting, their grave, simple outlines have still the power, even in ruin, to stir the heart, after five centuries. Equally impressive were the woods the monks planted round their homes and the sheep-runs the lay brethren or *conversi* —drawn from the peasant class—made on the bleak northern and western hills. They were the most enlightened landlords and finest farmers of the age, sowing alternate corn and grass leys and transforming scrubby wilderness with flocks that grazed by day on the uplands and folded at night on the barley plough-lands. Theirs was an instinctive genius for blending the works of God and man; in the Great Coxwell barn in Berkshire we can still see the reverence and skill with which they turned nature to human ends while enriching and beautifying it. "Labo-rare est orare," was their founder's motto: to work is to pray. They built roads and bridges, drained marshes and planted trees, quarried stone, wrought in wood and metal, laid out gardens and vineyards, and bred fine horses, cattle and sheep. To them England owed the noble Lion breed whose golden hoof raised the Cotswold towns and villages. They made her wool as famous as their brother monks of Cîteaux made the vineyards of the stony Côte d'Or. And if the great names of Chambertin and Clos de Vougeot still recall for lovers of wine the skill of the French Cistercians, their brethren in England are commemorated by the homely cheese which the monks of Jervaulx made from ewe's milk in lonely Wensleydale.

Nothing gives a clearer idea of the might of the medieval Church than to stand in one of the cathedrals, still towering above the roofs of our modern towns, that were first raised as monastic churches. They express the universal sense of the im-portance of religion and the soaring imagination and practical genius of men who had mastered the lost Roman art of vault-ing great spaces in stone. Most of them were originally built on the site of smaller Saxon churches by English masons in the massive Norman style under the prelates whom the Conqueror imported from Normandy, and rebuilt in a still more ambitious style under their successors in the latter twelfth and early thirteenth centuries. Canterbury, whose choir Lanfranc started to build with Caen stone in 1072, Rochester begun seven years later, Gloucester in 1080, Ely, with its magnificent nave, in 1083, Worcester in 1084, and the incomparable Durham in 1093, with its ribbed vaulting—the earliest of its kind in Europe—and its still surviving Norman nave and choir; Norwich, Winchester, Coventry, Carlisle and Chester—were all originally made for monks. So were the abbey churches of St. Albans—built partly from Roman tiles and stones—Gloucester, Westminster, Peterborough, Chester, Malmesbury, Tewkesbury, Pershore, Sherborne, Romsey and Bury St. Edmunds, whose nave, over 300 feet long, surpassed that of our largest cathedral today.

These vast edifices were miracles of construction. So were the non-monastic cathedrals served by secular canons, which the Normans raised in London, York, Old Sarum, Lichfield, Lincoln and Winchester; for the last a whole royal wood was felled. They were built without any but the most elementary mechanism for moving and lifting large weights, by men whose wealth consisted almost entirely of crops, flocks and herds and whose sole means of transport were wheeled carts drawn by oxen.[12] To realise the magnitude of their achievement one has only to reckon what it would cost, even with modern machinery and power, to rebuild in stone every cathedral and parish church in England. Yet this is what the men of the twelfth and thirteenth centuries did at a time when the population was only a small fraction of its present size. "It was as though," a chronicler wrote, "the very world had shaken herself and cast off her old age, and was clothing herself everywhere with a white robe of new churches." Faith alone could have caused men to sacrifice and accomplish so much.

The architecture of these cathedrals expressed the unity of existence in which their builders believed: the ordered vaulting; the pillars rising out of the earth like trees; the stone walls and arches carved with flowers and leaves, animals and men; the light of heaven flooding in through windows, at first plain

---

[12] The beams for the church of Abingdon abbey—now destroyed—were brought from Wales in carts drawn by twelve oxen apiece, which took six or seven weeks on the double journey from Shrewsbury to Abingdon. M. Bateson, *Medieval England*, 84.

but later painted, like the ceilings, in brilliant colours; the arches
soaring into the sky, and the whole made one by the idea,
implicit in every image and symbol, of God over all and judging
all, and Christ and his Mother, the Virgin, pitying and loving all.
In the enthusiasm of the time tremendous sacrifices were made
by clerics and laymen alike to raise these monuments to their
faith; one abbot gave the entire wool-crop of his manors for a
year to provide a tapestry hanging, while the monks of Abingdon
sold the gold and silver from their shrines to build their new
church. Relics of saints and martyrs—the monasteries' most precious possessions—were taken on tours round the country to raise
money from the laity, who gave, not only gifts in money and
kind, but in the cities of France even their labour to help the
travelling bands of professional masons and craftsmen to whom
the work of construction was entrusted. "Who.has ever seen,
who has ever heard tell," an eye-witness wrote of the building
of Chartres, "that nobles, men and women, have bent their
proud and haughty necks to the harness of carts, and, like
beasts of burden, dragged to the abode of Christ waggons
laden with all that is needed. . . . One sees old people, young
people, little children, calling on the Lord with a suppliant
voice and uttering to him, from the depths of the heart, sobs
and sighs with words of glory and praise."[13] Such enthusiasm did
not last; it was succeeded, as always, by selfishness, torpor and
corruption. But it was sufficient, not only in England but in
every country in Christendom, to change the face of Europe.

It was no wonder that an institution that evoked such love
and loyalty possessed power. Alone in a world of warring feudal
States, it was united and permanent. Alone it recognised the
rights and human dignity of the poor. It enjoyed, through its
monopoly of teaching and writing, the control of education
in every western land. Above all, in an age ridden by terrors
and disasters, it confronted simple, credulous men with the
threat of Hell and promise of Heaven.

The recovery of the Roman Church after the long anarchy of
the Norse, Hungarian and Saracen invasions, was an event far
more momentous even than the conquest of England. Eighteen
years before the Normans landed in Sussex a German emperor,

[13] Henry Adams, *Mont St. Michel and Chartres*, 102–3.

marching into Italy, had ended the scandal of three popes—
one a man of notorious life and all puppets of the feudal nobility
of Rome—competing with one another for St. Peter's throne.
By rescuing the Holy See from its dependence on local factions,
he restored to the Western Church its unity and initiative.
Within a generation the papacy had become a self-renewing
oligarchy, with its head chosen by a papally appointed college
of European cardinals. The bishops of Rome ceased to be petty
Italian princelings, with a vague aura of universal sanctity derived from remote antiquity, and became, as in the days of
Gregory I, the active leaders of western Christendom. They
even tried to establish a suzerainty over the Eastern or Greek
Church—an attempt, however, which ended in the final schism
between the two halves of Christendom.

During the next century the papacy was the chief instrument
for reforming the abuses which had long disgraced the Church.
A succession of great popes sought to carry the austere standards
of the Cluniac monasteries into the world of the diocese and
parish. Their objectives were twofold. One was to make the parish
clergy live stricter lives and remain celibate. The other was to
end the commerce in sacred benefices, which were sold by
lay patrons to purchasers who treated them as hereditary fiefs.
In the anarchy that followed the Norse invasions simony, as it
was called, had become the normal link between lay proprietor
and ·cleric. Just as feudal tenants paid reliefs on entering their
fiefs, bishops paid kings at their consecration and recouped themselves from those they ordained, and patrons of livings exacted
tribute from parish priests, who in turn charged their parishioners
for the Church's offices. At one time even the papal throne was
bought for a boy of twelve, who later sold it back to his godfather.

Many of the rulers of northern Europe had already been won
to the reformers' ideals by the Cluniac monks. Among them
was William the Conqueror, who entrusted the reorganisation of
the English Church to the great Italian lawyer and teacher
Lanfranc, abbot of Caen in Normandy. Lanfranc proved a most
able administrator and, with the possible exception of Dunstan,
the greatest holder of the English primacy since Theodore of
Tarsus. He revived regular and diocesan synods, removed rustic
sees to more populous centres like Salisbury and Chichester, reasserted the precedence of Canterbury over York—lost during

the Scandinavian conquest of Northumbria—and strengthened the episcopal supervision of parishes. Like a wise statesman, he introduced changes gradually, separating spiritual courts from temporal, so that bishops ceased to sit beside laymen in the hundred courts, and appointing archdeacons in every diocese to administer ecclesiastical law and look after Church property. And, without carrying matters to extremes or forcing those already married to put away their wives, he forbade ordination to married clerks. In this however he was less successful, for the rustic English were a stubborn folk, who, being used to their parish priests having wives, could not see why they should be deprived of them or believe that they would lead better lives without them.[14]

William and Lanfranc held that the best way to reform the religious life of a State was through its ruler. In this they followed the view of Edgar and Dunstan, Alfred and Charlemagne, and nearly all the early Christian kings and missionaries. But it was not that of the great man who in 1073 was elected to the papal throne. Hildebrand—or Gregory VII as he called himself—was a squat Tuscan peasant who, as his predecessor's chief minister, had been the moving spirit in the attack on simony and clerical incontinence. His aim was to make the Church independent of all secular control. An idealist of strong will and high administrative ability, he reached back to the conceptions of Gregory I and St. Augustine, claiming for his office a universal supremacy over all Christians.

Against the dream of the vanished Roman Empire that Charlemagne had failed to recreate and in which a Frankish emperor had been the secular head of western Christendom—one that

---

[14] Half a century later the position was unchanged. "By the advice and permission of the king, Archbishop William of Canterbury sent over all England and ordered bishops and abbots and archdeacons and all the priors, monks and canons that there were in all the cells in England, and for all those that had to care for and look after Christianity all to come to London at Michaelmas and there to discuss all God's dues. When they arrived there, the meeting began on Monday and continued right on to the Friday. When it all came out, it turned out to be all about archdeacons' wives and priests' wives, that they were to give them up by St. Andrew's Day, and anyone who would not do so should forgo his church and his house and his home, and never more have a claim to it: this was ordered by William of Canterbury, the archbishop, and all the diocesan bishops that were in England, and the king gave them all permission to go home, and so they went home, and all the orders availed nothing—they all kept their wives by permission of the king as they had done before." Anglo-Saxon Chronicle (Peterborough), cit. *English Historical Documents*, 195–6.

still lingered on in the shadowy *imperium* of the German or "Holy Roman" emperors—Gregory VII opposed the ideal of an ecclesiastical empire transcending all frontiers. He claimed that in this world as in the next all men were subject to spiritual authority, and that the pope, as Christ's representative, had been entrusted with its exercise. In the event of a clash between the spiritual and temporal ruler—between Church and State, pope and king, prelate and lord—the latter must give way to the former. "The Christian religion has so disposed," he wrote to William the Conqueror, "that after God the royal power shall be governed by the care and authority of the Apostolic See.

Some such claim for the Church had been made by the first Gregory more than four centuries before. But, in the barbarism and chaos of the age in which he lived, it had never been realised and had only been applied locally and occasionally. The tendency of churchmen during the dark ages had been to withdraw from the world rather than to rule and reform it. They left that to Christian kings like Charlemagne and Alfred. But now that the heathens had been rolled back from Christendom's beleaguered frontiers and the might of armoured barons and knights protected church and monastery from barbarian rapine, Hildebrand saw, in a politically divided continent, a chance to make his vision good. A City of God, ruled by the men of God, might be founded on earth.

His first object was to establish discipline and unity in the Church. He set himself to organise its resources as his contemporary, William of Normandy, set himself to organise those of the English kingdom. He brought to the task the same dominating sense of purpose, logic and energy. Over the great international army of the tonsured he and his successors claimed an authority as direct as that which William claimed over his barons and knights, and one far more absolute. He sought to create a rival and international feudal system for clerics. Every parish priest, regardless of the rights of the lay patron, was to be the liege of the bishop of his diocese, every bishop of the metropolitan of his province, every metropolitan of his overlord, the pope. International frontiers and feudal rights must be disregarded in establishing this holy hierarchy, for the Church was above earthly laws or divisions. And to the pope, as Christ's vicar on earth, lay an appeal from every man and woman in orders in Christendom. A ladder of graded courts, administered by ecclesiastical lawyers, should carry the appeal of the humblest clerk to the papal *curia* in the Holy City itself. A system of ecclesiastical or canon law, derived from early Christian and Roman practice, and constantly added to by popes and councils and the Church's doctors of law, was to provide the machinery —meticulous, bureaucratic, authoritative—for enforcing papal control over all clerics.

The difficulty was to apply such a system to the turbulent feudal world of the eleventh and twelfth centuries. At first it seemed not incompatible with the control that enlightened secular rulers like the Norman and Angevin kings were trying to impose on their nobles. For both the spiritual and temporal authorities were seeking the same end: the substitution of order for anarchy. Yet the greater their success, the more inevitable became a clash between them. For, as their powers widened, they found themselves trying to control the same thing.

One of these was the investiture of bishops and abbots with the symbols of their authority. In the early days of Christianity the Churches had been democratic, and bishops had been elected by the clergy and congregations of their dioceses. But when the barbarian tribes overran the West this ceased to be practicable. Their kings and chieftains having always appointed their priests, they continued to do so after they became Christian. And having liberally endowed them and their sees and abbeys with land, they tended to treat them, not as the heirs of Christ's apostles, which the Church claimed they were, but as feudal tenants-in-chief. In return for conferring on them the insignia of their office—the episcopal staff and ring—and the broad domains bequeathed for their support, they demanded homage and fealty.

To the Gregorian reformers, in their zeal for the Church's independence, this seemed a shocking infringement of spiritual rights. To them the staff and ring symbolised no earthly lordship but the charge Christ had laid on his apostles. That they should be conferred by a layman—even a consecrated one—was sacrilege. No layman, they contended, ought to have the right to choose those who were to exercise such sacred functions. It might be tolerable in a godfearing king like William the Conqueror, who filled sees and abbeys with reformers and loyal churchmen. It was unendurable when the crown was worn by a blasphemous wretch like his son, Rufus, who appointed evil-living favourites to bishoprics and kept the primacy vacant for years while he enjoyed its revenues, though the saintly Anselm, abbot of Bec, was at hand to fill it.[15]

Yet this new conception of the priesthood's exclusive sanctity ran counter to the belief—still held by conservative churchmen, especially in England—that anointed sovereigns were like Melchizedek, both priest and king. And by the end of the eleventh century the Church probably owned about a quarter of the land of every realm in Christendom. To deprive a sovereign of the right to control the possessors of such wealth and power was to strike at the very roots of government. In a still tribally divided and decentralised country like Germany, where the prelates were the traditional support of the Crown against the feudal lords, it was a denial of political unity to the nation. In 1075, by a decree forbidding lay investiture and insisting on the canonical election of bishops, Hildebrand paralysed the machinery of the vast but half-formed State whose rulers had rescued the papacy from its dependence on the Roman nobility. For though the emperor, reigning over a realm that stretched in theory from the Frisian coast to Tuscany, at first ignored his former ally's *diktat*, the latter was able to use against him a weapon whose effect in such an ill-knit land proved cataclysmic. By the dread curse with bell, book and candle that excommunicated a man from the Christian communion, the pope made Henry IV an outcast to his own subjects. Deriving authority as emperor, not from tribal or national ties like other rulers, but from his title as bearer of the temporal sword of Christendom—one conferred by papal coronation and consecration—his excommunication and deposition by the Holy See destroyed the grounds of their allegiance. The great feudal vassals who were for ever disputing his right to govern Germany declared that unless he obtained absolution within a year they would elect a successor. That winter of 1077 the first prince in Europe stood barefooted in the snow outside the castle of Canossa to implore the pope's forgiveness for claiming his ancestral rights over his own clergy. It was the only way he could keep his throne.

[15] "By the holy face of Lucca," he swore before a bout of fever reduced him to his senses, "neither he nor anyone else shall be archbishop but myself!" At the time of his death Rufus was enjoying the revenues of two other sees and eleven abbeys.

In England attempts to make the Church independent of the State were less effective. It was not that the Church was less respected, but that the Crown was much more so. It had a nation behind it. And, though the English had a tradition of loyalty to the papacy, Rome was a long way off. William the Conqueror, while continuing to pay the customary Peter's pence to the *curia*, disregarded a request from Hildebrand for homage as a return for the papal blessing on his invasion of England. "I have not consented to pay fealty," he wrote, "nor will I now, because I never promised it, nor do I find that my predecessors ever paid it to your predecessors."[16] Nor would he allow a papal legate to be received without leave or permit Lanfranc to obey the pope's summonses to Rome. For in his view the archbishop was what Dunstan had been before him, the religious counsellor of the king of England and not the servant of the Holy See.

For William, like his successors, was a realist. He and they saw that Hildebrand's claims were not compatible with the law and order which was their subjects' overriding need. A bishop might be responsible to God for men's souls but he was responsible to the Crown for their bodies. He was the holder of a great feudal landed estate and jurisdiction, with as many knights' fees and castles as a lay baron. He was the custodian, not only of spiritual, but military power. "You may talk as much as you please," declared Rufus to the bishop of Durham at the latter's trial for conspiracy, "but you will not go out of my hands until you have yielded me your castle." Churchmen were not always peaceable subjects. They were sometimes as turbulent as their kinsmen, the lay lords with whom they plotted treason. When Hildebrand protested at the Conqueror's imprisonment of his bishop half-brother, Odo of Bayeux, William sent him the mail-shirt in which that warlike prelate had been taken, with the scriptural quotation, "Is this thy son's shirt?" And the ordinary Englishman, to whom a proud Norman bishop was as much a foreigner, and sometimes as much an oppressor, as a Norman baron, agreed with the royal attitude.

---

[16] "Pray for us and for the state of our realms," he added politely, "for we always loved your predecessors, and it is our earnest desire above all things to love you most sincerely and to hear you most obediently." *English Historical Documents* II, 647. "No statement," Sir Frank Stenton comments elsewhere, "has ever settled a major issue in fewer words or more conclusively."

For this reason the lay investiture contest in England did not end in a Canossa. It ended in a working compromise. During the violent Rufus's reign there was an *impasse* between him and the saintly Italian scholar and philosopher whom under fear of death he had made his archbishop. At one time Anselm left the country rather than compromise the Church's rights, and, because of his gentle goodness, the whole nation, ecclesiastical and lay, sympathised with him. But after Henry I's accession a settlement was negotiated. In 1106 that shrewd monarch, recognising that the public was behind the Church's demand for independence in purely ecclesiastical affairs, granted it the monopoly of investing bishops with the episcopal staff and rod. He also agreed that cathedral chapters should elect them. But their right to do so was made dependent on his leave and his own right to nominate a candidate and veto those of others. And before consecration prelates had to do homage to the Crown as in the past for their stewardship of lands and castles, which were conferred by royal writ. In this way the King retained control of the nation's wealth and political power, while acknowledging the Church's right to confer spiritual authority. This sensible compromise was adopted in other lands, and, after the concordat of Worms in 1122, in Germany itself.

For Hildebrand's claim was too wide to be compatible with the governance of society. Like other unnatural victories won by force or fear, it could not be maintained. It was an imposing ideal to liken the relation of Church and State to that of heaven and earth, sun and moon, soul and body. But the moment the attempt was made to apply it in the physical world and to enforce the doctrine that the pope, as Christ's vicar, could never be lawfully resisted, the papacy was confronted with the dilemma which Christ had met with the counsel to render unto God the things that were God's and to Caesar the things that were Caesar's. The Church could only deny authority to the temporal government—the feudal instrument which had rescued Europe from anarchy and the invading horde—at the price of itself assuming responsibility for ruling society. And to do this it had to employ agents who could fight its battles with the weapons, not of Heaven, but of the brutal physical world around it. It sought them in the Norman robber barons of Sicily, who responded to Hildebrand's alliance by sacking Rome, in the separatist feudal princes of Germany, in the mobs and merchants of the Lombard cities, whose republican communes, harking back to an earlier classical tradition than the Empire, also wished to shake off the restraints of a Teuton emperor. It did not bring about the rule of divine justice and peace. It merely unloosed angry passions and deeds which in turn provoked others. It encountered the eternal nemesis of violence.

Chapter Nine

THE HOLY BLISSFUL MARTYR

From every shire's end
Of Engleland to Canterbury they wend
The holy blissful martyr for to seek.
Chaucer

Yet at Canossa the papacy had tasted blood. Throughout
the twelfth century the initiative lay with the canon lawyers who,
seeking to organise the Church as a completely self-governing
institution, tried to free it from all secular control. Even in England, where during Stephen's reign it was able to bargain with
rival claimants to the throne, it established the right of clerical
appeal to Rome and the freedom of papal legates to exercise
independent powers within the realm. And its courts, with their
superior procedure and unique advantage of a written code,
extended their jurisdiction, not only over churchmen and
church property, but over a wide range of matters affecting
laymen, including marriage, divorce, adultery, defamation of
character, testamentary disposition and, in certain cases,
breaches of contract. For these, it was contended, involved the
moral, and therefore ecclesiastical, offence of perjury.

The Church also won for its members almost complete exemption from the processes of criminal law. If a cleric—even a
church-sweeper or poor ragamuffin student—committed a murder, burglary or other breach of the peace, it claimed the exclusive right to try and punish him. And as the canon law
forbade the use of mutilation and the death sentence, and as
the keeping of prisons was costly, it relied for punishment

mainly on penance and spiritual penalties. Any malefactor who could read or mumble over a Latin text from the Bible—the common test of clerical status—and so claim "benefit of clergy," could escape the king's judges. The worst that could befall him was a fine or brotherly scourging or, in the last resort, defrocking, in which case he still remained free to repeat his offence.

Thus Henry II, seeking to restore order after the civil war and establish a common law for all Englishmen, was confronted by ecclesiastical privileges incompatible with his object. The Church's punishments were far too light to maintain order in a violent and unpoliced age. During the first years of the reign more than a hundred murderers are said to have escaped death by pleading clerical immunity. To the king's orderly and and autocratic mind it was intolerable that episcopal tenants-in-chief should have the right to appeal over his head to foreign courts and leave the realm to advance their suits against him. It seemed equally so that papal legates, over whose appointment he had no control, should exercise judicial powers inside his dominions and constrain, by threats of excommunication and suspension, those who were his vassals and ministers.

Yet Henry could only end such immunities by putting back the clock and reversing the trend of half a century. It was far harder to attack ecclesiastical privilege than baronial. For only barons regarded the latter as sacrosanct, while all Christians honoured the Church's rights. They thought of them as the personal property of Christ and his saints. For a layman to punish a monk or even a menial servant of St. Peter's or St. Mary's abbey was to usurp the household rights of these holy personages; to scourge a consecrated priest whose hands could perform the miracle of the eucharist, the vilest sacrilege. An affront to the Church was an affront to all the powers of Heaven. Its effects might be incalculable.

For the medieval mind, even when educated, found it hard to distinguish between theory and practice. Schooled in Latin law and abstractions on a foundation of barbaric legend and superstition, it tended to be logical rather than realistic. In a universe of inexplicable wonders it accepted almost any premises, however fantastic, and then reasoned, closely and rigidly, from them. If, it argued, the Church's ministers were the representatives of God, the wider their powers the wider God's sway.

And it proceeded to ignore the fact that churchmen in their worldly capacity displayed most of the weaknesses of laymen and were quite as capable of error.

Had a majority of clerics been what they were supposed to be and what the best of them were, the Church's claim to immunity from national Law would have been reasonable. But most of them were merely ordinary men in clerical dress leading clerical lives. Their leaders—though a few were saints and many men of ability and learning—were as given to pomp and luxury as the lay lords by whose side they presided over realm and neighbourhood. They entertained in halls off plate of gold and silver, wore jewels, rings and costly garments, kept fine horses, hounds, hawks and armies of retainers, and travelled with magnificent cortèges. Monks, who in theory had withdrawn from the world to mortify the flesh and exalt the spirit, lived in startling variance, not only with their own professions, but with the poverty-stricken life of the countryside around them. Gerald of Wales, the Pembrokeshire archdeacon who wrote the best travel book of the age, described a Trinity Sunday dinner at Christ Church, Canterbury, where sixteen exquisitely cooked dishes were served with wines to match. Many Benedictine houses were as comfortable and exclusive as the common-rooms of modern Oxford and Cambridge colleges. Tonsured head and monk's habit might be the garb of a St. Bernard or Hugh of Avalon; more often their wearers were worldlings with the same pride and class-consciousness as their kinsmen in court and castle. Other churchmen not in regular orders did not even trouble to wear the outward garb of piety, but went about, like the fashionable chaplains of the feudal magnates, with curled hair, pointed beards and effeminate clothes or, like secular canons in non-monastic cathedrals, in fine linen instead of sheepskin. And some, though mostly in minor orders, were knaves and malefactors, as dangerous to the public peace as any other criminals. In Worcestershire, in the early part of Henry II's reign, one of them raped a girl and then murdered her father; another, a canon of Bedford, slew a knight at Dunstable and, after being acquitted in the teeth of the evidence by the bishop's court, insulted a royal judge who had been sent to investigate the matter. It was such men that Henry II wished to bring under the Common Law.

For the Church sheltered so many beneath its ample cloak

that it formed a complete cross-section of humanity. Its members mirrored all the vices and passions, as well as virtues, of their age. Vulgar vituperation, litigiousness, misrepresentation of opponents, even downright brawling were common clerical failings. At a time when society was only half-tamed, it was as hard for churchmen as laymen to restrain the primitive impulses to violence. A gang of scuffling prelates at a coronation broke a buckle of the king's crown, and an archbishop of Canterbury and bishop of London had to be sent away from the royal table for squabbling over rival claims to say grace. When, at the Council of Westminister in 1176, an altercation arose between the English metropolitans as to who should sit on the papal legate's right hand, the monks of Canterbury knocked down the archbishop of York and sat on his stomach.

Even grave statesmen and scholars, who lived austere lives and would have died for their faith, suffered from spiritual pride, vanity and the jealous passion for being in the right. Abbot Samson of Bury, who by his noble devotion restored St. Edmund's abbey to its former glory, contended with the archbishop of Canterbury for the precedence of his house like an ambitious *grande dame*. And the munificent Henry of Winchester, who distributed a fortune among the poor and built the beautiful church and hospital of St. Cross, with its thirteen aged bedesmen and daily stint of ale and bread for the bona fide traveller, helped by exaggerated claims for his Order to create conflict between Church and State in a land where before the Conquest it had been almost unknown.

It was this personal element that magnified ecclesiastical pretences beyond reason. In their self-righteous anger priests sometimes lost all sense of proportion and blunted the instruments which were the sources of their power. A bishop of Norwich anathematised with every dreadful curse the poachers in his park, and an abbot of St. Albans excommunicated a neighbour for cutting his timber. Even the saintly archbishop, Edmund Rich, in the next century denied the consolations of religion to the royal butler, the earl of Arundel, because he had impounded some episcopal hounds in his Sussex woods. The arrest by the secular authorities of a shoemaker for homicide in the grounds of Waverley abbey provoked the monkish cry, "Our places are as free as our altars!" and a claim that not merely consecrated land but even monastic farms were outside the royal jurisdiction. The case ended in the release of the murderer and a public whipping by the entire chapter of the bailiff who had made the arrest.

Yet in standing up for the Church's rights and the ideals they helped to safeguard clerics often showed splendid courage. They were without arms in a society of hot-tempered warriors. During the struggle between Pope Alexander III and the Emperor Frederick Barbarossa clerks bearing letters to Rome were seized by imperial partisans and either hanged or sent on their way without their noses or lips. It was still an age of fearful brutality, in which the punishments of secular courts matched the atrocities they sought to suppress. Felons were blinded and mutilated, traitors tied to posts in the Thames and left to drown. Men were burnt alive for arson, their hands cut off for forgery and their tongues for slander. When such cruelty was habitual, national law non-existent over the greater part of Europe, and force, corruption and bad faith still decided most disputes between men, any extension of the scope of the canon law and of the power of ecclesiastical courts seemed an advance in justice. It helped to create enclaves of gentle and civilised dealing in a brutal world.

Even in England, where the State kept better order than anywhere in Christendom, this still appeared to be so. Henry II was a king whose work for justice endured for centuries after his death. His attitude towards the Church, where its claims did not conflict with his own rights, was devout and generous; towards a true saint, like the Carthusian Hugh of Avalon, whom he made bishop of Lincoln, he showed a touching humility, suffering his rebukes even in anger. Yet, like most princes of the time, he was a man of violent passions, unscrupulous and licentious, and, during his rages, almost a madman. His ends served the good of society, but his means were harsh and tyrannical. The steps he took to bring his subjects under the law did not appear to contemporaries in the same light as to posterity. Nor could what he was trying to achieve be appreciated before he had achieved it.

Henry, therefore, proceeded with great caution. As in his attacks on the powers of feudal magnates, he merely claimed that he was restoring ancient customs that had been infringed during the civil war. This was largely true, and calculated to appeal to a people who, since the Conquest, liked to look back to an imaginary time when all laws had been good and justice invariably done. And, as with the baronial franchises, the king relied on subtly disguised and harmless looking legal devices to bring the ecclesiastical courts under his control before anyone could realise what was happening.

In this he was assisted by the brilliant ecclesiastical lawyer whom he had made his chancellor and who, while serving in that capacity, showed almost as small respect as he for clerical claims which conflicted with the needs of royal revenue and justice. Seven years after his accession the death of the archbishop of Canterbury presented Henry with what seemed a wonderful opportunity. In the summer of 1162, brushing aside all opposition, he induced the monastery-chapter to elect to the vacant see his gorgeous counsellor and boon-companion, Becket—one who, though a cleric, was not even ordained a priest until the day before his consecration as head of the English Church.

In doing so, however, the king made a grave miscalculation. For Thomas Becket, who received his sacred office with reluctance, had no sooner accepted it than, at the age of 45, he completely changed his way of life. The most resplendently arrayed and attended man in England, who had taken the field at the head of seven hundred of his own knights, worn the long-embroidered sleeves of a baron and once told his sovereign that his royal cloak was unfit to give a beggar,[1] he now donned the black robes of a Canterbury monk, attended midnight masses, and daily—and with his habitual ostentation—entertained and washed the feet of the filthiest beggars in Canterbury. A shameless pluralist who had collected benefices and prebendal stalls to support his magnificent entertainments, he insisted on resigning the chancellorship regardless of the entreaties of his sovereign, who had seen in the union of the primacy and the royal chancery the solution of all his problems. He gave up the coursing and hunting and the hawks and hounds in which he delighted.[2] Most surprising and, for the king, disconcerting, he embraced the extreme theories of the clerical reformers. He became an ardent, unbending champion of the papacy. When the

[1] The king retaliated by making Becket give the poor man his own.
[2] Once in after years, a fugitive in disguise from the king's anger, he was all but detected by the look of recognition he cast at a fine hawk on a knight's wrist. M. D. Knowles, *Archbishop Thomas Becket. A Character Study,* 14.

pallium—the symbol of spiritual authority—arrived from Rome, he walked barefoot through the Canterbury streets to receive it.

For, with the thoroughness with which he did everything, Becket refused to serve two masters. Having been the most loyal of royal lieutenants, he now transferred his allegiance to a more powerful master and, as it seemed to the king most ungratefully, sacrificed his interests. Instead of applying his vast legal and business experience to subject ecclesiastical encroachments to Exchequer scrutiny, he used them to extend the rights and revenues of his see. He revived long-dormant claims, demanded the restoration of estates alienated by his predecessors, and insisted on receiving homage in place of the Crown from knights holding church-lands. When a fellow tenant-in-chief usurped an advowson, he summarily excommunicated him, thus depriving the Crown of his services,[3] for no-one could have dealings with an excommunicated man. Nor would he yield an inch to the king's demands about criminous clerks. A tax reform, to which as chancellor he would have given whole-hearted support, was fiercely resisted by him in the Council. "By the eyes of God," declared the furious king, "it is not seemly for you to gainsay me." "By the reverence of those eyes by which you have sworn, my lord king," Becket replied, "not a penny shall be given from all my land or from the jurisdiction of the Church."[4] Even when Henry sought a papal dispensation for his bastard brother to marry an heiress within the prohibited degrees, instead of facilitating matters as a normal archbishop would have done, the primate refused to consider it. He seemed to go out of his way deliberately to enrage his former friend and benefactor.

Thus the king's attempt to bring the Church under the law was frustrated by the very man who had been his chief assistant and who, as the repository of his secret plans, was ideally situated to defeat them. His love for his brilliant lieutenant turned to bitter hatred. With all his resolution and cunning he set himself to remedy his mistake. He had to get Becket at all costs out of the key position in which he had so injudiciously placed him.

[3] Later, under intense pressure, he withdrew the excommunication, but so ungraciously as to make the king contemptuous as well as angry.
[4] *Materials for the History of Thomas Becket*, II, 373, cit. *English Historical Documents* II, 714.

The two men—the one with the strongest throne in Europe, the other representing the international Church—seemed well matched. They had been the complement of one another and now became the antithesis. Each had the same imperious, overbearing will, each was thorough, persistent, and electric with restless energy, each had behind him a career of unbroken triumph. And each knew, or thought he knew, his opponent by heart, for they had worked together in close companionship for seven years, and, so far as either was capable of love, had been fascinated by one another.

Yet within a year the king had completely outmanoeuvred the tall, gaunt, dark archbishop. For, with all his boldness and courage, Becket lacked the virtues in which Henry, the Achillesheel of his temper apart, was so strong. He had none of his capacity for patient statesmanship and *finesse* in handling political opinion. He was a perfectionist rather than a man of the world. During his seven years as chancellor he had shown himself a tireless organiser and worker, with a wonderful quickness and versatility. He possessed dazzling address and charm; could be all things to all men and, so long as he was not personally concerned, show considerable tact, and, though revealing his heart to none, win from subordinates affection and even devotion. But while he appealed to the multitude by his dramatic genius and emotional power, his equals could not depend on him. He was far too much of an egotist to be a good colleague. He lacked constancy and stability: was a man of extremes who lived on his nerves. He seemed capable of every attitude except moderation. He constantly laid himself open to criticism and suspicion by sudden changes of mood which appeared to responsible men insincere and in bad taste. They saw him as an exhibitionist who could never stop playing a part. To Gilbert Foliot, the austere and learned bishop of London who had been the leader of the Church party before Becket's elevation to the primacy, he seemed as much an upstart ecclesiastically as to the feudal magnates socially: a careerist who had never been a monk or even a priest and whose pretences to devotion were utterly insincere.

The king, who had been so well served and delighted by his chancellor's genius, understood his weaknesses perfectly: his vanity and hypersensitiveness, his inability not to overstate and dramatise his case, his pathological desire—the result of a lonely childhood—to win applause and justify himself. And in their triangular relations with the English bishops and the pope, both of whose support was essential to Becket's position, he played the brilliant, excitable archbishop like a fish. First he joined issue with him over what was by far the weakest point in the Church's position—the trial of criminous clerks, to which a notorious murder and an equally notorious acquittal had just drawn everyone's attention. It was an issue on which the Church was divided and about which doubts were felt even by the pope. In October 1163 at a Council at Westminster Henry outlined his proposals for dealing with this pressing scandal. He did not challenge the Church's right to try its members, but demanded only that clerics found guilty by ecclesiastical courts of major crimes should be degraded and handed over to his officers for punishment. Those who could not be restrained from such outrages by the thought of their sacred orders, he pointed out, could scarcely be much wronged by the loss of them.

To this Becket, incapable of moderation and taking up, as always, the extreme position in any cause with which he was identified, replied that it would be a monstrous injustice to punish a man twice for the same offence. In a long, passionate speech he urged the king not to introduce into the kingdom a new discipline contrary to the decrees of the ancient fathers— "a new law of Christ," he called it, "by a new and strange kind of lord." At this Henry asked angrily whether he and his fellow bishops were prepared to swear to abide by the ancient customs of the realm. This put them in a quandary, for in the time of Henry's grandfather the Church had been subjected to many restraints which it had since shaken off. Yet in England an appeal to ancient custom was always hard to refuse. After a consultation, therefore, the archbishop replied that they would swear as their liege-lord requested, but with the customary proviso, "saving the rights of their order." At this Henry became extremely angry and stamped out in a rage, leaving the bishops to digest the fact that they were in for an uncomfortable and dangerous struggle. Next day he demanded from the primate the return of the castles and honours of Berkhamsted and Eye which he had granted him during his chancellorship.

Having set the issue before the world—one in which he appeared to be asking nothing of his bishops but what was fair and reasonable—the king proceeded to drive a wedge between them and their leader. His instrument was the pope, Alexander III, a sensible man and no extremist, who, being engaged in a life-or-death struggle with the emperor Frederick Barbarossa during which he had been forced to take refuge in France, was exceedingly anxious to stand well with the English king. He therefore responded willingly to Henry's suggestions that he should hint to his quarrelsome metropolitan that it was no service to the Church to insult the Crown by refusing to swear to the ancient customs of the realm, and that some reasonable compromise over the trial of criminous clerks would be in the Holy See's interest. Confronted by surrender in such a quarter Becket —still a parvenu in the Church—felt that he had no choice but to give way. He therefore privately, and it seems rather impulsively, informed the king that the next time he was asked to swear to the ancient customs of the realm in public, he would do as he wished. It was characteristic of him that in taking this step he consulted nobody, and refrained from informing his fellow bishops who had stood behind him so firmly at Westminster.

Immediately, in the January of 1164, the king called a council at his hunting-lodge at Clarendon. In that simple, childlike age, when men's minds were swayed by outward forms and ceremonies, it seemed essential to obtain from the archbishop and his colleagues a solemn and public declaration of what had been promised. Once more the primate was asked, in the presence of the barons and bishops, whether he would agree to clerics, found guilty of felony by ecclesiastical courts, being degraded and handed over to the king's judges for punishment. And once more the archbishop, who seemed almost incapable of meeting his old master in public without falling into a furious altercation, contended that it was contrary to divine law to punish a man twice for the same offence, and that a priest was a sacred being who could no more be sentenced by a layman than a father by his own child. Thereupon the king reminded him of his promise to swear to the ancient customs and constitutions without insulting qualifications. Then he sprang a bombshell on everyone by producing these in written form and asking the prelates to acknowledge them.

These sixteen carefully-prepared clauses, known to history as the Constitutions of Clarendon, set out, not unfairly, the relationship that had existed between Church and State in the time of Henry I. Some of them, like the proviso that no peasant's son should be ordained without his lord's assent, were undisputed. Others traversed what in the past thirty years had become the accepted practice of the Church. They included provisions for trying in the king's courts disputes about advowsons as a species of landed property, and for regulating reckless and blackmailing accusations brought by archdeacons against laymen for moral offences. And they laid down a procedure for dealing with criminous clerks: preliminary investigation before a lay judge, trial in the ecclesiastical courts in the presence of a royal observer, and, where guilt was proved, degradation and delivery to the king's officers for sentence and punishment.

The most contentious provisions were that no tenant-in-chief should be excommunicated, no cleric leave the realm and no appeal be made to Rome without the king's leave. And appeals in ecclesiastical disputes were to go from the archdeacon's court to the bishop's, from the bishop's to the archbishop's, and, unless permission were given for an appeal to Rome, from the archbishop to the king, who was to direct the archbishop's court how to decide the issue. This was tantamount to making the king supreme ecclesiastical judge in the realm—a principle which, however much it might conform with ancient English practice, ran diametrically counter to existing canon law. It struck at the international sovereignty of the Church and made the crown, as in Saxon and early Norman times, the constitutional link between the pope and the English clergy.

It was one thing for Henry to try to restore the ancient unwritten and peculiarly English relations between Church and State in a tacit agreement with his own bishops, some of whom at least were sympathetic to views which had been held only a century before by such a primate as Lanfranc. But it was another to reduce these to writing and demand from churchmen a public avowal of principles which violated the disciplinary canons of their Order. The episcopal bench was appalled. For three days, in a series of violent arguments, the bishops stood solidly behind the primate in defence of what they deemed the liberties of the Church.[5] Even when "the princes and nobles

---

[5] "We stood by you then because we thought you were standing courageously in the Spirit of the Lord. We stood immovable and undismayed. We stood firm, to the ruin of our fortunes, ready to suffer bodily torment or exile, or, if God so willed, even the sword." Gilbert Foliot, Bishop of London, to Archbishop Thomas Becket, 1166. *Materials for the History of Thomas Becket* V, 521, cit. *English Historical Documents* II, 748.

of the realm, waxing hot in their wrath, burst into the chamber, muttering and clamouring," and, shaking fists in their faces, declared that those who resisted the king were in deadly peril, they remained firm.

At this point Becket—vehemently reproached by the king for promising his agreement in private and humiliating him by breaking it in public—suddenly gave way. Without consulting his colleagues he announced that, as his lord and sovereign would have him perjure himself, he must do so. By refusing to add his seal to this grudging agreement, he made his surrender seem as great an insult to Henry as it seemed a betrayal to his colleagues. Subsequently he made his position still more invidious by suspending himself from the service of the altar as a penance for perjury. He also sent an emissary to the pope to ask forgiveness for betraying the Church.

The archbishop could hardly have played his cards worse. His colleagues, hopelessly confused and divided, had lost all confidence in him. Even those who most strongly upheld the principles for which he had contended felt that, as he had abandoned them, it was a needless and dishonest continuance of a regrettable controversy to qualify and repudiate his undertaking. The view of responsible laymen was that he had made himself ridiculous and, by his vanity and ungrateful provocation of his royal master, compromised the Church's position.

Henry had put his adversary in a cleft stick; his resignation now seemed inevitable. Yet, in his determination to crush him, he had blundered himself. By setting down his claims in black and white, he had put the Church's defenders on their guard. This became apparent when he sent the Constitutions to the pope for ratification. For though the Holy Father, confronted by an imperialist anti-pope in Rome, was in greater need than ever of the English king's support, he could not publicly repudiate the doctrines for which his predecessors had fought. The denial of the right of ecclesiastical appeal struck at the Church's independence and unity and at one of the papacy's principal sources of income. While agreeing to six of the clauses, Alexander, as tactfully as possible, withheld his assent from the remainder. And he released Becket from any oath he might have made to observe them. He did not approve of the archbishop's attitude, but he could not do otherwise.

The pope's refusal to underwrite his Constitutions only made

Henry the more determined to get rid of the man to whom he attributed the refusal. Meanwhile the latter further prejudiced his position by trying to escape from the country in a fishing-smack. That October the king called a meeting of the Council at Northampton and summoned the archbishop to appear before it for a technical breach of feudal law—the lonely, passionate man's failure, in his alternating moods of defiance and despair, to respond to a sheriff's writ, which should never in any case have been addressed to him. There, working himself into one of his famous rages, Henry browbeat the Council, whose members needed little encouragement to avenge themselves on the primate, into sentencing him for his contempt of the royal court to the loss of all his own and his see's moveable goods. Then, without notice, he called on him to account for the vast sums which had passed through his hands as chancellor. When Becket, seeing that the king was resolved on his ruin, offered a compensation of 2000 marks, it was contemptuously refused.

At that moment Henry seemed to hold all the cards. He was the most powerful ruler in Europe, and the head of a State in which respect for the Crown was more deeply rooted than in any other. He had behind him a baronage which he had taught to join with him in governing the realm, and a knighthood deeply attached to the throne. Becket, in the eyes of every king's man and of many of his fellow prelates, was a low-born clerk, a parvenu whom his royal master had raised from a merchant's counter. In opposing his benefactor he had laid himself open to charges of the basest ingratitude.

Yet, by making him desperate, Henry drove his adversary back on something greater than either himself or the Church. He forced him on to the rock of the inner spirit. Though ill and afraid, the archbishop resolved to compromise no more and to take his stand, not merely on the Church's tenets, but on the cross of suffering and sacrifice it enshrined. By doing so he became the champion of thousands to whom the rights and wrongs of the constitutional principles under dispute meant nothing. Becket was not by nature a religious man; he was self-centred, egotistical, an artist and an autocrat. Though pure in life, and generous to his servants and retainers, he did not in-stinctively love men or turn the other cheek. He was neither meek nor humble. Indeed he was more arrogant than the king, who, for all his blind rages and high-handed ways, had a vein of everyday simplicity which the primate lacked.

Yet for the lonely, spectacular role he now chose Becket was superbly equipped. His towering height, his pale, sensitive face, the aquiline nose and restless penetrating eyes, the white feminine hands and quick eager movements made him look what he aspired to be, a saint and martyr. And the very theatricality and emotionalism that so annoyed high-born men of the world appealed to the hearts of common folk who only saw him from afar and knew nothing of his weaknesses. Here was a man who even in that age of pageantry and outward symbols made his meaning ten times clearer than anyone else, speaking to them across the immense barriers of rank and wealth. Almost alone among the rulers of the time he laid himself out to please the masses—the peasants and craftsmen of England who were without the rights and privileges, laws and liberties of the feudal lords. When he rode on visitation and the children of the poor were brought to him to confirm, he did not, like other prelates, bless them from the saddle. He dismounted and went through the formalities of the sacrament like a humble priest.

Through the king's vindictiveness Becket had reached solid ground. From that moment, despite all the odds against him, he never quitted it. "If you desire success in this world," one of the monks at his side counselled him, "make peace with the king. But if you wish to serve God, act fearlessly." It was what the archbishop had resolved to do. His enemies on the episcopal bench and many of his friends, faced by Henry's unrelenting fury, urged him to resign rather than to bring ruin on the Church. He refused either to do so or to plead in an issue which, if lost, would place every churchman at a despot's mercy. Declaring that all temporal power derived from God and that a son could not judge his spiritual father or a sheep his shepherd, he traversed his adversary's whole position and announced, in defiance of the Constitutions, that he would appeal to Rome against any sentence passed on him.

On the 13th October 1164 Becket was summoned before the Council to receive judgment. Before setting out from the monastery where he lodged he deliberately said a votive mass of St. Stephen, the first Christian martyr. Then, ordering the assembled bishops to excommunicate any who dared to lay hands on him, he entered the royal castle, wearing his archbishop's cope and pallium and bearing his own cross. When the bishop of London protested, saying, "If you brandish your cross, the king will brandish his sword," Thomas replied, "The cross is the emblem of peace; I carry it for the protection of the whole English Church." All day, while the king and his barons sat in one room and Becket in another, and pleading bishops and threatening envoys constantly passed between them, the archbishop sat alone, hugging his cross and gazing on the crucifix. To his adversaries he seemed merely an angry, unreasonable man clinging to an untenable position—one who, as the bishop of London said, had always been a fool and always would be.[6] To himself he seemed to be wrestling with wild beasts at Ephesus. "This is a fearful day," murmured one of his followers as angry baron after baron came in with summons and threat. "Ay," replied the archbishop, "but the Day of Judgment will be more fearful!"

As the bishops—even those most opposed to Becket—dared not, in face of his prohibition, join in judgment against him, the king demanded it from his earls and barons alone. But when the magnates made their way to the archbishop's chamber to inform him of the sentence, he rose and refused to hear them. "You are come to judge me," he cried, "it is not your right. . . . It is no sentence; I have not been heard. You cannot judge me. I am your spiritual father; you are lords of the household, lay powers, secular personages. I will not hear your judgment! Under protection of the Apostolic See I depart hence." Then, rising to his full height and bearing his cross, he swept into the darkening hall and towards the door, while knights and royal servants, rising from the straw-strewn floor and benches where they had dined, shouted, "Traitor!" "Perjurer!" Outside in the wet streets the people thronged round him to beg his blessing so that he could hardly control his horse.

That night, while the triumphant king issued a proclamation that no-one was to do him physical hurt, Becket rode out of Northampton in driving wind and rain and made his way in disguise to the coast. Three weeks later he landed in France.

[6] If Zacchaeus like Becket had refused to come down from his tree, Foliot remarked, he would never have entertained Christ in his house.

For six years the archbishop remained an exile. The revenues of his see were confiscated, his kinsfolk banished, and his office declared forfeit.[7] From the position he had taken up—that ultimate appeals affecting the Church must lie to the pope and not the king, and that no lay court had the right to lay hands on an anointed priest—nothing would move him. Attempts were made to negotiate a compromise by the pious king of France, who gave him shelter out of dislike for his English rival, by the pope who, despite his disapproval of the constitutions of Clarendon, was still deeply anxious to retain Henry's goodwill, by the bishops who found themselves between the devil and the deep sea and could not obey their temporal master without disobeying their spiritual. All were in vain and broke down on the enmity of two resolute and legalistically-minded men of genius, who brought out all that was most stubborn and violent in one another. From time to time, whenever the temporising pope permitted, Becket emerged from the French monasteries into which he had retired to a life of the sternest austerity, to hurl anathemas and excommunications at his fellow prelates for compromising with the king. Only the papal prohibition stopped him from treating the latter likewise.

Henry was equally unappeasable. But in the end the logic of events was too much for him. He could not govern Christian England without the Church. And, in an international age, himself an international ruler, he could not cut the English Church off from the universal Church and make himself, instead of the pope, its ruler. To ensure the peaceful succession of the crown and secure his inheritance from the uncertainties of civil war—the fate that had befallen his own on his grandfather's death—he wished to have his eldest son crowned during his lifetime—a constitutional practice familiar in France though one hitherto unknown in England. But the consecration, which in a Christian realm was the binding part of a coronation, could only be performed—according to the custom both of Church and realm—by the archbishop of Canterbury. After waiting five years and trying vainly to get a papal dispensation to allow the ceremony

[7] "Of a truth," declared Louis of France when he heard the news from England, "like the king of the English, I also am a king, but I have no power to depose even the least of the clerks of my realm." Becket retaliated by surrendering his see to the pope, who restored it to him, thus immeasurably strengthening his position.

to be performed by deputy, Henry took the law into his own hands and in June 1170 had the young prince crowned by Becket's enemies, the archbishop of York and the assisting bishops of London, Durham, Rochester and Salisbury.

Yet the king was well aware of his danger. He knew that the pope, who was by now on firmer ground in his duel with the emperor and anti-pope, was unlikely to condone such an invasion of the Church's control of its own hierarchy, and that opinion, both in England and on the continent, was hardening against him; unless he could soon negotiate some kind of public settlement with the archbishop, his dominions would almost certainly be laid under interdict and himself under excommunication. He knew too that Becket's host and champion, the king of France, was arming against him, and that many of his own barons, galled by his firm rule and strong measures, were awaiting an opportunity to rise.

He therefore intimated to the papal legates and French king, who were still trying to negotiate a settlement, that he was ready to make his peace with the archbishop, restore his forfeited estates, and receive him back into his realm. Nothing was said about the Constitutions, but the presumption was that, as neither archbishop nor pope had accepted them, their enforcement was to be tacitly dropped. The great thing was to achieve a public reconciliation and the restoration of peace and normal religious life in England. A meeting between the two disputants took place in the French king's presence and they were apparently reconciled. But, though the restoration of the archbishop's lands and dignities was agreed, the customary kiss of peace, which he had demanded at a previous abortive meeting and which had been refused by the king, was neither given nor requested. The quarrel—and at heart both men knew it—had been patched up but not appeased.

In agreeing to return to England the primate knew the risk he was running from a passionate and injured autocrat of unpredictable moods. But his own safety was by now the last thing with which he was concerned. His only thought was of spiritual victory. Nor did he return unarmed. Before setting out he secured from the pope letters of suspension and excommunication against his fellow metropolitan of York and two of his own suffragan bishops for their part in crowning the young king. Just as he was about to embark, he learnt that they were on their way to join the king in Normandy to consecrate royal nominees to five vacant English bishoprics. Faced with the prospect of a packed and hostile episcopal bench, Becket at once used the discretionary powers with which Alexander had armed him and launched the sentences of excommunication and suspension, hastily despatching them to England before him.

Then on December 1st, 1170, having shown that he was prepared to abate not one tittle of the Church's authority, and avoiding the royal officials who, infuriated by his latest act of war, were waiting at Dover to seize him, he landed at his own cathedral's port of Sandwich. All the way to Canterbury the roads were lined with praying and rejoicing multitudes; it was like a triumphal procession.[8] In the city he was welcomed with trumpets, psalms and organs. As he took his throne in the cathedral his face was transfigured with happiness. "My lord," one of his monks whispered to him, "it matters not now when you depart from the world. Christ has conquered! Christ is now king!"

When Henry in Normandy learnt what had happened and that Becket had announced that, though ready to absolve his suffragans on their doing penance, he had no power to withdraw the papal sentence on his fellow metropolitan, he flew into an ungovernable rage. "What idle and coward knaves have I nourished as vassals," he shouted, "that faithless to their oaths, they suffer their lord to be mocked by a low-born priest!" Four knights—Reginald FitzUrse of Williton in Somerset, William de Tracey, Richard le Breton, and Hugh de Morville of Knaresborough—took the king at his word, and, without informing anyone of their intention, set out for England. There they made their way to Saltwood castle in Kent, the home of Becket's bitterest enemy, Sir Ranulf de Broc, the man who during his

---

[8] "The poor of the land . . . received him with the victor's laurels and as the Lord's annointed. So wherever the archbishop passed, a swarm of poor folk, small and great, young and old, flocked to meet him, some prostrating themselves in the way before him, others tearing off their garments and strewing them in the way, crying aloud, again and again, 'Blessed is he that cometh in the name of the Lord'." Herbert of Bosham, cit. *English Historical Documents* I, 757.

absence had farmed his see's revenues and who, with his retainers, was already waging open war against him.[9]

On December 29th the four knights, with a rabble of de Broc's followers, arrived at Canterbury where the archbishop was sitting after dinner in his chamber. Ostentatiously refusing his servants' offer of food, they strode up to his chamber, and sat down on the rushes before him, watching him in grim silence. When after a time he addressed them they broke into curses, telling him that they had something to say to him by the king's command and asking if he would have it said in public. Then they told him that, unless he absolved the excommunicated bishops, he must immediately leave the realm. To which the archbishop replied that they should cease from brawling and that, as his trust was in Heaven, no sea should ever again come between him and his church. "I have not come back to flee again," he said; "here shall he who wants find me."

At that the knights sprang to their feet and began shouting. But the archbishop answered them in kind: "I am not moved by threats, nor are your swords more ready to strike than my soul is for martyrdom. Go, seek him who would fly from you. Me you will find foot to foot in the battle of the Lord." And as, amid tumult and insults, they withdrew to their waiting men, there was a flash of the same fiery spirit that had caused the archbishop six years before in the castle hall at Northampton to round on the king's mocking brother and call him bastard. He followed the intruders to the door and cried out after them defiantly, "Here, here, will you find me!"

Becket was now expecting immediate death. Indeed, it had become clear during the past few days that he was deliberately seeking it. In his Nativity sermon on Christmas Day he had told his hearers in the packed cathedral that they had already one Canterbury martyr—St. Alphege who had been pelted to death by drunken Danes—and that they might soon have another. And on the day before the knights arrived he had secretly sent two of his monks to the pope and, in bidding them farewell, shown that he never expected to see them again. That night at supper he remarked to those about him that he who must lose much blood must drink much wine.[10]

---

[9] They had pillaged a storm-bound ship laden with Becket's baggage and ambushed the packhorses carrying what remained to Canterbury.

[10] A remark which made him the patron saint of the London Company of Brewers. M. D. Anderson, *Looking for History in British Churches*, 193.

By now it was nearly dark, and the monks had repaired to the cathedral for vespers. A few minutes later the four knights, having donned their armour in the courtyard, returned to the hall. But they found the door barred. While they were seeking another and battering in a shutter with an axe seized from a carpenter, Becket's clerks repeatedly urged him to take refuge in the cathedral. Fearing that they wo. .d all be massacred together, they dragged and pushed hin. ʹ far as the church door. But when the monks, leaving their vespers, ran to meet him and tried to bolt the door behind him, he sternly refused, saying, "It is not meet to make a fortress of the house of prayer." Then, "driving all before him as a good shepherd doth his sheep," he made his way into the dark, silent cathedral. Almost immediately its peace was broken by the knights and their retainers pouring through the open cloister door, led by FitzUrse, in hauberk and with drawn sword, shouting, "Hither to me, king's men!" Then they all began shouting together, "Where is Thomas Becket, traitor to the king and realm?" The knights were completely covered in armour save for their eyes, and their swords were naked. At the sight the monks fled into the shadows and the dark crypt below.

Only three of his household now remained with the archbishop—William Fitz Stephen, his future biographer, Robert of Merton, his confessor, and an English monk named Grim who was holding the cross. As the clamour behind increased Becket suddenly stopped and, descending the steps from the choir, called out in a clear voice, "Lo! here am I, no traitor to the king but a priest. What do you seek from me? I am ready to suffer in His Name who redeemed me by His blood." Whereupon the armed men came shouting and clattering through the darkness to where he stood beside a pillar in the transept. As they closed in to seize him, apparently intending to carry him off, they again called on him to absolve the excommunicated bishops. Rising above them in his great height, he answered: "There has been no satisfaction made, and I will *not* absolve them!" "Then you shall die this instant," cried one of the knights, "and receive your deserts." "I am ready to die for my Lord; may the Church through my blood obtain peace and liberty!" As he resisted their efforts to drag him away, the knights, fearing a rescue, began to strike furiously at him with their swords. A blow cut off his scalp, while another severed his cross-bearer's arm. Two more blows brought him to his knees, and a fourth scattered his brains on the pavement. Then the murderers burst out of the cathedral to plunder his lodgings and make their escape before the city could be roused.

When that night in the desecrated cathedral the monks bent over the body of the proud, fastidious archbishop and stripped off his bloodstained Cistercian's habit to replace it by his pontifical vestments, they found to their amazement a covering of filthy sackcloth and a horsehair shirt, long-worn and alive with lice.[11] Beneath it they saw the festering weals of repeated selfscourging. Then, through their grief and fears, they rejoiced exceedingly. For they knew that he had been a true monk and a saint of God.

By death the archbishop had triumphed. As the news became known a thrill of horror ran through Christendom. The king against whom Becket had contended, collapsed in an agony of lamentation. Exchanging his robes for sackcloth he shut himself in his chamber, where for three days he refused all food and consolation, groaning and crying exceedingly and from time to time falling into a stupor. When he at last calmed down, he threw himself and his realm on the pope's mercy. If it was not to disintegrate, it was the only thing he could do.[12]

But it was not the great alone who were shaken. The common people left their rulers in no doubt as to their attitude. Within a few hours of the murder rumours of miracles began to spread outwards from Canterbury. Four times, it was said, the candles round the bloodstained pall had been lit by invisible hands. A monk in the abbey had seen the archbishop in a vision going towards the high altar in episcopal robes; his deep, beautiful voice had joined in the singing of the introit. A blind woman who touched her eyes with a handkerchief dipped in his blood had regained her sight; others similarly afflicted who had prayed to him had been restored. "The blind see, the deaf hear, the dumb

[11] As the faithful Grim put it, "anyone would have thought that the martyrdom of the day was less grievous than that which these small enemies had continually afflicted."

[12] The pope himself was so shocked at the news that for a week he refused even to speak of it and issued a general order that no Englishman should have access to him. When an envoy from the excommunicated bishops, who were still trying to get their sentences suspended, at last succeeded in doing so, it cost them five hundred marks.

speak" wrote John of Salisbury, "the lame walk, the devils are cast out!" Meanwhile the de Brocs, who had threatened to move the body, were besieged in their castle by a furious crowd. The murderers, who began by boasting of their deed, are said to have fled to Scotland, where the people tried to hang them.

It was easy for twelfth century kings and lords to ignore the rights of the individual poor. But they could not ignore popular beliefs. In matters of faith neither monarch nor prelate had the last word. The Church represented and embodied the beliefs of the people. Because they were convinced that Becket was a saint, the pope, who had so often tried to restrain him during his life, was forced within two years of his death to canonise him. His shrine at Canterbury, blazing with jewels and surrounded by the discarded crutches of those he had cured, became the most famous place of pilgrimage in England. For a time the cult of St. Thomas almost rivalled that of the Virgin Mary. Churches were dedicated to him and memorials erected in lands as remote as Scandinavia and Iceland.

In his own land, whose fame he had blazoned through Christendom, Becket's name became better known and more honoured than any other of his age. Before the Reformation there can have been few English churches that did not have a retable, wall-painting, window or other treasure depicting some scene in his troubled life. Even today, despite the wholesale destruction by sixteenth and seventeenth century iconoclasts, many survive, like the boss in the roof of the Norwich cloisters with its demons standing over the Canterbury murderers or the panel at Elham in Kent in which the saint defies the royal anger at Northampton. By a strange paradox—for it had been to strengthen the realm that Henry had fought against him—Becket lived on, not merely as a martyr, but as a national hero to a submerged and conquered people. A Norman born in England who had stood up to her foreign rulers and died at their hands, he became, in a modern writer's words, "one of the people of England as well as one of the saints of God."[13]

In a constitutional historian's sense the martyrdom achieved comparatively little. It saved for English clerics the right of appeal to Rome in purely clerical matters. It established the immunity of criminous clerks from lay justice. And it brought

[13] Douglas Jerrold, *An Introduction to the History of England,* 506.

the English Church, beyond doubt or cavil, into line with the universal practice of the Roman Catholic Church and the canon law, even though that practice conferred on churchmen a greater independence than had been customary in the Anglo-Saxon and early Anglo-Norman state. As a result power in England, as elsewhere in western Europe, continued to be regarded, not as force to be operated by a single untrammelled will, but as a balance in which rulers were subjected to the check of the organised Christian conscience expressed through the Church. When four centuries later the rulers of England repudiated the authority of Rome, the habit of thought remained—a potent check to tyranny.

In everyday administrative practice, after the first shock of the murder had passed, it was the commonsense views of Henry that prevailed rather than the extreme and unrealist claims of the archbishop. Of the sixteen Constitutions of Clarendon only those governing the freedom of appeals to Rome and the trial of criminous clerks were abandoned. The royal courts extended their control over advowsons and kept their jurisdiction over pleas for debt, except when the latter arose from wills and marriages—matters which had always been dealt with by ecclesiastical courts. The Crown continued to control, subject to certain formalities, the election of bishops and abbots, and to deny to English prelates the right to excommunicate their fellow tenants-in-chief without permission.

Yet Becket's martyrdom created an emotional content which for centuries remained of immense significance in English life and helped to form the enduring values of England. The Canterbury martyr created "The Canterbury Tales" and all the generations of pilgrims riding or tramping through the Kentish countryside "the holy blissful martyr for to seek." It was not the worldly ends for which Becket had fought that mattered after his death. It was the spiritual means with which he had fought for them. The immunity of clerics from lay jurisdiction meant as often as not the protection from justice of rogues and scoundrels; the right of appeal to Rome meant the submission of disputes, which might have been more expeditiously and justly settled at home, to the costly processes of bureaucratic procrastination and corruption in a foreign land. But that a man in high place who had notoriously loved, and to excess, the wealth and fine things of the world and enjoyed them in dazzling splendour, should voluntarily renounce them and live in exile and poverty, should mortify his body and at the end return to his native land to brave and suffer a violent death for the sake of an ideal, was to reveal the power of Christ and enhance the spiritual dignity of man. It is not easy for one who has lived fine to subdue the flesh, to face unarmed the naked swords of brutal warriors, to place himself in the power of insulting foes. Whoever voluntarily chooses these things is, whatever his failings, a great man. In this sense Becket was great—"great," as one of his followers put it, "in truth always and in all places, great in the palace, great at the altar; great both at court and in the church; great, when going forth on his pilgrimage, great when returning, and singularly great at his journey's end."[14] Historians, who condemn him for contending against administrative measures which were in themselves reasonable, sometimes forget this. But his contemporaries who witnessed his martyrdom or those who heard of it from their fathers and went on pilgrimage to kneel on the steps where he died or touch with trembling fingers the bloodstained hem of his garments, saw it very clearly. For all the world's coarse obsessions and stupidity and blindness, the saints and martyrs have the last word. It is their triumph over the frailty of the body that causes man to believe in God.

It was a measure of Henry Plantagenet's greatness as a statesman and of the resilience of his character, that he and his work for England were able to survive the flood of horror and indignation by which, when the news of the murder became known, they were threatened. His continental dominions were placed under interdict, and, for a time it was uncertain whether, with the outraged feeling at Christendom against him, he would not be excommunicated and his throne declared forfeit. The pope refrained only because of the importance of retaining his aid in his struggle with the emperor and because of the frankness with which the contrite king admitted his responsibility for the unintended consequences unloosed by his passionate outburst.

Now that his anger of the past seven years was spent and

[14] Herbert of Bosham, *Materials for the History of Thomas Becket III*, 471, cit. M. D. Knowles, *Archbishop Thomas Becket*. Proceedings of British Academy XXXV (1949), 23.

turned to repentance, Henry's patience, wisdom and statesmanship reasserted themselves. He let time do the work that time
alone can do. Leaving the cauldron to simmer, he vanished
from his troubled dominions and went on a crusade. It was
characteristic that it was a crusade that served his own ends
as well as the Church in whose name it was undertaken.

Sixteen years before, when Henry had succeeded to the English throne, he had persuaded an English pope—Adrian IV—to
entrust him with a mission. It was to conquer for the Roman
Church the heretical, slave-raiding island of Ireland which
Patrick had converted to Christianity seven centuries before
but which, since the Viking invasions, while remaining nominally Christian, had relapsed into its primitive Celtic savagery.
Among the Church's claims—enshrined in the forged "Donation
of Constantine," a document long accepted by the faithful—was
one of the sovereignty of all islands. In its name an earlier
pope had blessed the Conqueror's invasion of England and
claimed homage from that unresponsive monarch. And it was
in its pursuit, and the more reasonable one of introducing some
kind of order into the chaotic ecclesiastical life of Ireland, that
Henry had been presented by Adrian with an emerald ring and
a papal bull authorising him to subdue and rule the island
"for the enlargement of the Church's borders, the restraint of
vice, the correction of morals and planting of virtue, the increase of the Christian religion and whatsoever may tend to
God's glory and the well-being of that land."

An opportunity for pursuing this holy task now presented
itself. A few years earlier one of the rulers of Ireland's ever-
warring kingdoms—Dermot of Leinster—had sought aid against
his subjects and fellow kings at the English court. Unable at
the time to help him, Henry, in return for his homage, had
furnished him with letters authorising any of his subjects to do
so. Such aid Dermot had found among the warlike Norman
adventurers whose ancestors had conquered and settled south
Wales a century before. In May 1169 Robert Fitz Stephen, son
of a Marcher lord and a Welsh princess, landed at Bannow in
Leinster with thirty Norman knights and four hundred Welsh
men-at-arms and archers. With this minute force, and five hundred Irishmen under Dermot, he captured the Viking port of
Wexford and re-established the exiled king on his throne.

In the following year the other Irish kings and the Danish

traders or *ostmen* of Dublin, alarmed by the exploits of these armoured, mounted strangers, combined to expel them. But their hopes were defeated by the arrival of two more contingents —one under a half-brother of Fitz Stephen named Fitz Gerald, and the other under a far more important Marcher lord—the ruined earl of Striguil and Pembroke, Richard de Clare, who, in an attempt to repair his fortunes, had promised Dermot help in return for his daughter's hand. In the late summer of 1170 this great soldier and adventurer, commonly known as Strongbow, with a force of 1200 men stormed, first the Danish port of Waterford, and then Dublin. Six months later, on the death of his father-in-law, he claimed the kingdom of Leinster.

The news caused Henry to act. He could not afford to let his vassals set up an independent feudal power in an island so near England. During the summer after Becket's murder, while Europe waited for the curse of Heaven to fall on him, and a handful of Norman knights performed prodigies of valour defending Dublin against a Viking fleet and an Irish host, he assembled four hundred ships in Milford Haven. In October 1171, swiftly crossing southern England and Wales, he sailed for Ireland with five hundred knights and several thousand archers and men-at-arms. He took with him an ample store of supplies, including portable towers for siege warfare. Like the Romans in their invasion of Britain, he was resolved to impress the natives. His object, he assured them, was to protect them from lawless oppression.

Against this disciplined force the unarmoured foot-horde of Ireland, armed with stones and javelins, was as impotent as the ancient Britons against the Romans. The kingdoms of Leinster and Meath fell without a blow. That winter Henry spent in a palace of wattle outside Dublin built by his new subjects. Here he accepted homage from the Norman-Welsh adventurers who had preceded him and from the native kings and princes. And here he received the submission of the Irish bishops, who swore to conform to the canon law and practices of the Catholic Church and to acknowledge him and his heirs as kings of Ireland.

Thus, in the winter following Becket's murder and as an indirect consequence of it, the foundations of the English government of Ireland were laid. It was an alien one but seemingly better than none at all. For all the poverty of its people,

Ireland was potentially a rich land, "excelling," as a chronicler put it, "in serenity and salubrity of climate, abounding in pasture and fisheries, and its soil only lacking for fertility the industry of a skilful cultivator."[15] Politically it was much what it had been a thousand years before—a disunity of warring Celtic tribes. Ecclesiastically, it had scarcely progressed beyond the primitive organisation set up by the first evangelists, with colonies of missionary priests living in bee-hive wattle huts round monastery churches whose abbots wielded episcopal powers. The austerity, scholarship and enthusiasm of three centuries earlier had vanished: most of the monks were married, and until the elevation of the saintly Malachy as bishop of Armagh in 1132, the metropolitan see had been held as an hereditary fief by a family of local chieftains.

By setting up an orderly government at Dublin Henry did what neither the Roman emperors nor the native princes of Ireland had done. Around the east-coast ports that the Vikings had founded, his English "Pale" became a civilised province, with royal castles and castellans, regularly enforced laws, a justiciar and justices, and a settled agriculture. To stimulate trade with England and the continent the monopoly of the Scandinavian pirates and slavers was ended, and a colony of Bristol merchants established in Dublin with the same liberties as in their native town. And to provide hereditary warriors, administrators and prelates to maintain order, organise manorial estates and build castles and cathedrals, Irish land was confiscated and granted on the usual feudal terms to members of the ruling Anglo-Norman caste.

It was a realm, however, with little depth and with fluctuating frontiers, beyond which, among the bogs and mountains of the west, the kings and clans of Connaught and Munster, admitting only a nominal allegiance, maintained their ancient and savage independence. The work that Henry had begun, and which only such a man could perform, was never completed. In the spring of 1172, growing daily more anxious for news from England and the continent—from which no word had come throughout that stormy winter—he hastened back to the world of affairs. At midnight on Easter Day he sailed from

---

[15] William of Newburgh, *Historia Rerum Anglicarum*, cit. *English Historical Documents* II, 339–40. "But its people are uncivilized and barbarous in their habits, almost wholly ignorant of law and order."

Wexford never to return. A few days of his usual rapid travelling carried him from St. David's to Portsmouth and thence to Normandy, where the pope's legates were impatiently awaiting him.

There, at Avranches, he made his formal submission to the mighty Church, swearing on the gospels to accept whatever penance the legates might impose. He agreed to allow appeals to Rome, to restore the possessions of Canterbury as they were before his breach with the archbishop, and to compensate all who had suffered in the latter's cause. And he promised to expiate the evil done in his name by taking the cross and serving, with two hundred knights, in a crusade against the Moslems, either in Palestine or Spain. Those present, we are told, "observing his humility and devotion, could scarcely restrain their tears." Then he was solemnly forgiven and allowed to resume his place as one of the pope's champions against the foes of Christendom, without and within.

But Henry's troubles were not at an end. During the past year a formidable coalition, emboldened by his loss of prestige, had been forming against him. It included most of the great feudal lords of Aquitaine, Normandy, Poitou and Brittany, and his fellow feudatory, the count of Flanders. At its head was the French king, whose wife Henry had stolen twenty years before and who had been Becket's patron. What made this conspiracy against his French dominions so galling to Henry was that it was joined, not only by his queen, Eleanor of Aquitaine, but by the young sons, greedy for power and freedom from paternal control, upon whom he had lavished affection and on whom, in an attempt to keep together his vast international empire, he had bestowed the titular sovereignty of its provinces. The eldest—his namesake, the "young king" of England and duke of Normandy—fled to Louis of France's court in March 1173, and, though the queen was captured on her way, the fiery fifteen-year-old Richard, duke of Aquitaine, and the crafty fourteen-year-old Geoffrey of Brittany joined him there. The wolf-pack had rounded on the old wolf.

Forced to fight, Henry met his enemies with his usual resolution and energy. With the speed that made him so formidable a soldier, he outmanoeuvred the slow feudal chivalry of France with an army of Brabantine mercenaries. Once that summer he rode 140 miles in two days. "Oblivious of food and sleep," wrote William of Newburgh, "he arrived so quickly that he seemed to have flown."

Yet while he was chasing Louis back to his own domains and reducing Norman and Breton castles, rebellion broke out in England. Its nobility, long uneasy at encroachments on their jurisdiction, had been particularly alarmed by a purge of sheriffs in the year of Becket's death and their replacement by Exchequer officials. Encouraged by the example of the young king, to whom at Henry's request they had sworn allegiance, the bolder of them took up arms. The earl of Leicester, head of the great Anglo-Norman family of Beaumont, landed in Suffolk with an army of Flemish mercenaries, while Hugh Bigod, the old earl of Norfolk—a veteran of the civil war who had already raised his standard once against the king—tried from his castle of Framlingham to rouse the eastern counties. Simultaneously William the Lion, king of the Scots, laid siege to Carlisle and with an army of Lothian knights and naked savages from Galloway swept across Northumberland, which the young king had treacherously offered him as a bribe.

Yet though Henry was forced to remain in France, the island realm that his forbears had made withstood the shock. Led by the justiciar, the official nobility of service that he and his grandfather had created out of the lesser baronage proved as strong as the forces of the provincial feudatories. The "new men"—the de Lacys, Bohuns, Glanvills, de Veres, Trussebuts, Vernons, Balliols and Bruces—counterbalanced the mighty Beaumonts, Mowbrays, Bigods, de Masseys and Tancarvilles. The Church, too, having made its peace, remained true; only one prelate, the bishop of Durham, had dealings with the traitors. Even the Welsh princes stood by their allegiance. And the English people, who had no love for French-speaking earls and still less for plundering foreign mercenaries, supported the Government vigorously. When an army of Flemish weavers landed at Walton, singing their arrogant marching song,

> "Hop along, hop along, Wilekin, Wilekin,
> England is mine and thine!"[16]

---

[16] "Hoppe, hoppe, Wilekin, hoppe, Wilekin, Engelond is min ant tin." Matthew Paris, *Historia Minor* (ed. Madden I, 381), cit. A. L. Poole, *Domesday to Magna Carta*, 336. They are said to be the oldest Flemish verses extant.

they were met near Bury St. Edmunds by "the host of England"—the fyrd of the eastern countries under the constable, Humphrey de Bohun—and cut to pieces by Suffolk peasants with forks and flails.

Yet with his vassals in the field against him from the Pennines to the Pyrenean passes, Henry had to fight for his life for more than a year against the disintegration that threatened every large medieval dominion. Not till the spring of 1174 was the position in Aquitaine and Normandy sufficiently stable to allow him to return to England. When he landed at Southampton on July 7th a new invading force—the vanguard of a great host awaiting a wind at Gravelines under the "young king" and count of Flanders—had just sacked Norwich, William the Lion had again overrun Northumberland, and the royal justiciars were cut off from one another by a cordon across northern England of rebel castles—Chester, Dunham-Massey, Stockport, Tutbury, Duffield, Leicester, Groby, Mount Sorrel, Kirkby Malzeard, Malessart, Thirsk and Northallerton. Meanwhile London, freed from the surveillance of the king's justices, had relapsed into a state bordering on anarchy; bands of young men roamed the streets at night breaking into houses and shops and slaying all who resisted.

Henry had made his peace with the Church. But he had still to purge his crime in the eyes of the common people. Before marching against the rebel and invader he made a hurried pilgrimage to the tomb of his former archbishop. At Harbledown, a mile out of Canterbury—the village of "Bob-up-and-doun" of Chaucer's poem—he dismounted and made his way on bare feet through the cobbled streets to the cathedral. Here, surrounded by prelates and watched by a vast crowd, he prostrated himself before the archbishop's tomb while the monks, at his entreaty, scourged him. At dawn, after kneeling all night before the shrine and showering endowments on it, he rode in haste to London.

Here wonderful news reached him. At midnight on the 17th a travel-stained messenger from the sheriff of Lancashire arrived at the palace gate with a demand for immediate admission. Asked what brought him, he replied that his master, Ranulf de Glanvill, held the king of the Scots in chains in his castle of Richmond. Four days before, on the morning after

Henry had knelt all night at Becket's shrine, a handful of English knights under Glanvill and the sheriff of Yorkshire, Robert de Stuteville, had made a raid from Newcastle into the heart of the Scottish army then ravaging Northumberland.[17] Riding through thick mist, they had surprised the king of the Scots outside Alnwick castle. Despite the odds against them they had resolved then and there to carry him off. "Turn back who will," cried Bernard de Balliol, "I will go forward sooner than be branded a coward!" Such courage met its reward. A day later, his feet tied beneath his horse's belly, William the Lion was carried into Richmond castle and the drawbridge raised behind him. As the news spread, the bells of all the English churches began to peal.

After that miraculous delivery everything came Henry's way. The Scottish host, deprived of the leader who was the focus both of its own and the nation's unity, dissolved into its component parts and, fighting furiously among itself, vanished into the northern mists. The English rebels, despairing of help, surrendered their castles to the king and his officials. Within three weeks of the prostration at Becket's tomb, the revolt was at an end. By the beginning of August Henry was able to return to Normandy with his Brabantine and Welsh mercenaries. Seeing that the attempt to bring him down was hopeless, Louis sued for peace.

In victory Henry behaved with great magnanimity. To his sons he offered half his wealth and honours, keeping only control of the government and justice on which the peace of his realm depended. From the captured barons he asked nothing but the demolition of their unlicensed castles. He took no revenge and shed no blood.

Thus ended what William of Newburgh called "the foul and detestable strife" between the king and his sons, the one supported by the English people and the naturalised Norman barons and knights whom the Crown had invested with the old

[17] "Everything was consumed by the Scots, to whom no food was too filthy to eat . . . and while they sought out their prey it was the delight of that inhuman nation, more savage than wild beasts, to cut the throats of old men, to slaughter little children, to disembowel women and to commit other atrocities of a kind too horrible to mention." William of Newburgh, *Historia Rerum Anglicarum*, cit. *English Historical Documents* II, 348. The culprits were apparently the wild kerns of Galloway; the English chronicler admitted that the Scots king was attended by "a more honourable and civilised body of soldiery," the Norman-Scottish lords and knights of Lothian.

national authority of the Anglo-Saxon State, the other by the greater feudal earls who, having lands on both sides of the Channel, had not yet accepted the native conception that power in England could be exercised only within the framework of royal supremacy. It was the last time that older nobility dared to challenge the joint forces of Crown and Law.

For the remaining fifteen years of the reign, whatever his difficulties elsewhere, Henry had little trouble in England. His peace, and the writs, judicial eyres and juries by which it was enforced, were steadily strengthened and extended. So was the native *levée-en-masse* or shire militia that had proved so powerful a counterbalance in his hands to the forces of provincial feudalism. In 1181 he issued an ordinance named the Assize of Arms, defining the ancient obligation of every free man to serve in it and the scale of equipment required from him. Almost as much as his new judiciary and the Common Law, it was a guarantee of the realm's endurance.

Outside England Henry was less successful. He remained on good terms with his vassals, the Welsh princes, and received the reluctant homage of the king of Scots and the custody of the castles of Edinburgh, Stirling, Berwick, Roxburgh and Jedburgh. And he retained, though with difficulty, his precarious hold on the coastal Pale of Ireland. In the midwinter of 1176–7 one of the Norman knights he had settled there, John de Courcy, fell with three hundred followers on the kingdom of Ulster and, in the course of an amazing campaign, conquered it.

But south of the Channel Henry's prestige never recovered from his humiliation by the dead saint. Though, as vassal of the French king, he still ruled nearly two thirds of France and its entire coastline from Somme to Bidassoa, and though his daughters were married to the rulers of Sicily, Castile and Saxony, he was no longer master in his own house as in the northern island whose people neither shared his blood nor spoke his tongue. His French fiefs were constantly threatened with rebellion and disruption, provoked and sometimes fomented by his own unruly sons. Only in his native Anjou, where the ruined fragments still stand of the great castles he built at Tours, Angers and Chinon, did he know anything approaching peace.

In the end, after his fascinating and unreliable eldest son had died in arms against him, Henry was betrayed and defeated by a sudden coalition between his second son, Richard of Aquitaine, and Louis's successor, the cunning Philip Augustus of France. Caught in an hour of weakness and without an army, he saw the home of his youth, his beloved Le Mans, burnt under his eyes and was forced to fly for his life with a handful of retainers. Compelled to accept a humiliating peace from his son and his French overlord, he died on July 6th 1189 at the age of 56, betrayed by those he loved and surrounded by enemies. At the last—for no heart can survive in isolation—even that imperious will broke, and, learning of the treachery of his youngest son,[18] the beloved prince John, he turned his face to the wall with the bitter farewell, "Shame, shame on a conquered king!"

Save for his expedition to Ireland, Henry never went on his promised crusade. His claim in history is that he was the first European king to make a nation out of a feudal State. But in his day the ideal that appealed to men's imaginations was not the nation—scarcely conceived as yet outside England—but Christendom: an ideal derived from the memory of the *pax Romana* and the longing of Christians for the brotherhood prescribed by a common Faith. It was that conception, constantly thwarted by the brutal passions of the age, that had defeated Henry in his struggle with Becket. In 1188, however, in the face of a terrible disaster to Christendom, it again seemed about to become a reality, transcending the narrow ambitions of princes.

For in the last year of his life Henry, like all the rulers of Christian Europe, was called upon to go crusading. Ever since the armoured, mounted knight had saved the West from its heathen invaders, the frontier chivalry of Christendom had been trying to win back the lost lands on its circumference. For two centuries the process had helped to absorb the energies of the restless knights of Europe's southern and eastern States.

---

[18] "He sat up on the bed on which he was lying and gazing round fiercely said, 'Is it true that John, my very heart, whom I have loved before all my sons, and for whose advancement I have endured all these ills, has deserted me?' When he discovered that this was indeed the case, he sank back upon his bed and, turning his face to the wall, and groaning aloud, cried, 'Now let all things go as they will, I care no longer for myself or anything else in the world.'" *Giraldus Cambrensis, De Principis Instructione,* cit. *English Historical Documents* II, 384.

The little Christian kingdoms of Spain—Leon, Castile, Aragon, and Navarre—had begun the counter-attack even before the Viking invasions had spent themselves, taking the offensive against the Moors who had overrun their country. During the years when the Conqueror and his sons ruled England a Castilian king captured the great hill fortress of Toledo, and the Spanish national hero and *guerrillero,* the Cid Campeador, founded the principality of Valencia. Other Christian warriors in eastern Europe carried their banners into the lands of the Slavs, Balts and Wends. The twelfth century saw a great quickening of this advance under Henry II's contemporaries, Albert the Bear of Brandenburg and Henry the Lion of Saxony, and under a new crusading Order called Teutonic Knights. Behind them followed the industrious German peasants, and the stone castles, abbeys and church-spired cities which were everywhere the outward symbols of Christendom.

It was between the Cross and Crescent in the south that the struggle was fiercest. Here there was small place for the missionary and proselyte. In eastern Europe, where the tradition of Boniface lived on, whole peoples, like the Poles and Magyars, had accepted Christianity. But in the long drawn-out war waged between Faiths from one end of the Mediterranean to the other there was neither charity nor understanding. England, in the forefront of Christendom's defence against the Norsemen, had far less part in this conflict than the continental States. But in 1147 a fleet drawn largely from her ports had helped the count of Oporto to liberate Lisbon and found the kingdom of Portugal. The first bishop of Lisbon was a Winchelsea monk.[19]

The most spectacular scenes in this merciless strife were played in the land from which Christianity had come and to which, though long lost to Islam, all Christians instinctively turned. To them, as England's earliest maps show, Palestine was the centre of the earth. To its holy places went, even in Europe's darkest age, a long procession of Christians, with palmer's staff and scrip, ready to brave every hardship and hazard in order to kneel on the soil made holy by Christ's blood. In the generation before the Norman Conquest an English archbishop, suffering violence on the way, had made the

[19] He introduced the Sarum missal into the new State. Poole, 149.

long journey to Jerusalem to lay at the Saviour's tomb "a golden chalice of very wonderful workmanship."

Soon afterwards the dangers of the Jerusalem pilgrimage had been intensified by the conquest of the Arab caliphates of Bagdad, Syria and Egypt by fanatic tribesmen from the Asian steppes. In 1071 the Seljuk Turks, with their curved scimitars and mounted bowmen—a people as masterful as the Normans— had overthrown the army of the Byzantine empire at Manzikert in Armenia and captured the emperor. This disaster to eastern Christianity and the increased persecution of western pilgrims aroused a wave of intense feeling through Europe. Two popes, the great Italian, Hildebrand, and his French successor, Urban II—preached an international crusade to save the Greek empire and recover Jerusalem. Thousands of knights took the crusader's vow and cross. And, in the first flush of enthusiasm, multitudes of humbler men followed them. Led by the fierce Norman warriors who had conquered the Saracens of Sicily and southern Italy, they crossed the Mediterranean in the ships of the Italian trading cities or trekked through the wild Balkan mountains to Constantinople and Asia Minor. The West, so often in the past six centuries invaded from the East, struck back with its mailed feudal chivalry and new technique of war.

In the last years of the eleventh century by a wonderful exploit the crusaders captured Jerusalem and founded the Latin kingdoms of Outremer or beyond the sea—Edessa, Antioch, Tripolis and Jerusalem. These little States were organised on the feudal pattern of western Europe, with fiefs, nobles and knights, bishoprics and seignorial courts, castles and cathedrals. Around them lay the deserts of the East and the great Moslem caliphates with their teeming cities. But, though there was a steady influx of crusaders from the West, their base was too narrow and their numbers too small to withstand the unceasing inroads of climate, disease and war. Their barons and knights fought, too, among themselves, indulging to the full the perilous luxury of feudal strife. In the face of the watchful and revengeful East it was one they could ill afford.

Because of this the attempt to widen the bounds of Christianity by force failed, as Christ had taught it always must fail. Those against whom the Crusades were undertaken resisted, and those who made them plundered the conquered and quarrelled over the spoils. The Frankish warriors were as ruthless and grasping in the land of Christ's gentle and selfless life as at home. The kingdom of Jerusalem, founded in the name of a religion that preached that the meek should be exalted, proved, like the Moslem dominion it supplanted, a place where the strong oppressed the weak. For all the nobility that inspired its foundation it was Christian only in name. When after eighty years it was assailed by the Saracens under a great leader, Salah-ad-Din or Saladin, sultan of Egypt, it was without friends in the Levant. Even the Greek Christians of the Byzantine empire had learnt to distrust and hate it.

In the year before Henry II died the news reached Europe that the crusaders had been routed and that Jerusalem had fallen. The shock was tremendous; when Abbot Samson of Bury was told, he donned a horsehair shirt and gave up flesh and wine.[20] Once more the leaders of the Church preached the crusade. It was acclaimed with enthusiasm by the warriors of every western land. All Christendom's rulers answered the call, and the kings of England and France, temporarily burying their quarrel, met in the presence of a vast concourse to dedicate themselves. Subsequently Henry, who two years earlier had refused the crown of Jerusalem, summoned a Great Council at Geddington to approve a national levy, called the Saladin tithe, of a tenth of every man's personal possessions or movables. It was the beginning of a new kind of taxation in England.

Yet it was not the shrewd, calculating Henry who led a crusade to recover Jerusalem, but his son, the golden-haired, blue-eyed warrior giant, Richard—the first of Europe's princes to take the cross on hearing the news from the Holy Land. This romantic, chivalrous young knight of 32—poet, musician and true son of the lovely and passionate Eleanor of Aquitaine—could think of nothing else. He was so eager to raise an army that, on his accession to the throne, he declared that he would sell anything, even London, if he could find a bidder. He released the Scottish king, William the Lion, from his vassalage to the English crown in return for cash for men and arms. That he left his country's frontier exposed to attack from northern barbarians did not trouble him.

Yet, though he turned his back on his kingdom and sailed

---

[20] *Chronicle of Jocelin of Brakelond* (King's Classics), 63. He also secretly made for himself a cross of linen cloth and sought, though in vain, the king's leave to sew it on his monk's robe and go crusading, *idem* 85.

away into the Orient, he proved a magnificent soldier and
leader. Despite the fiery temper that made enemies of all his
fellow sovereigns, he was the hero of the Crusade. Within a
few weeks of his arrival he had put new heart into the dispirited, plague-ridden army besieging Acre. The zeal with which,
though stricken with fever, he pressed home the attack, led to
the city's early fall. Two months later, by his great victory at
Arsuf, he opened the road to Jaffa and Jerusalem. And though
the final prize eluded him and he was forced in the end to
return with his work incomplete, he concluded a treaty with
the Saracens that secured the beleaguered Christian kingdoms
of the Levant and the pilgrims' road to the holy places for
another half century. He made the name of the northern land
over which he ruled more honoured than it had ever been before; "his kingliness," it was said "could not be hid." Even
Saladin praised him. And though hated by crafty and intrigu-
ing princes, he was loved by simple fighting men for his lion-
heart, his constancy to his word and his frank, open nature and
generosity. His shield of golden lions and scarlet crusader's
cross became part of the heritage of England.

Until Richard's accession that country had taken little part
in the crusades. She was too remote from the scene of the conflict—many months' weary and dangerous travelling from her
shores—and from the Mediterranean ports from which the crusading armies sailed. But the work of her Norman and Angevin
kings had made her rich and strong, and her warrior lords,
stopped from fighting one another at home, were eager for adventure. Like their kinsmen beyond the Channel, they shared
in the chivalrous frenzy roused by the great French and Italian
clerics who preached the third Crusade. They gladly followed
their lion-hearted king, and their English men-at-arms and bowmen followed them, to die of wounds and torture, pestilence
and thirst, battle and drowning under the blazing eastern sun.
The crusaders' tombs in our country churches, lying in sculptured stone or alabaster beside the wives from whom their zeal
parted them, still preserve the memory of that far-off time and
antique devotion. So do the names and traditions of some of our
oldest institutions and buildings: the Temple where our barris-
ters have lived for six centuries but which was first built as
the home of the Knights Templars who guarded the road to
Palestine and whose round church, shattered by enemy bombs

in 1940, was inspired by the church of the Holy Sepulchre in Jerusalem; the fourteenth century gateway in Clerkenwell of the Hospitallers of St. John of Jerusalem who defended and cared for poor and sick pilgrims; the ancient Mercers' Company, which began as an association to support the crusaders of the Hospital of St. Thomas of Acon, founded by the sister of Thomas Becket in memory of his martyrdom.

Yet the chief immediate effect of the Crusades on England was the amount Englishmen had to pay to support them. The drain on their purses did not even end with the cost of equipping Richard's fleets and armies. For when after three years' absence he was shipwrecked on his way home and captured, disguised as a scullion, by one of the many continental princes with whom he had quarrelled, they were called upon to pay the greatest tax in their history as his ransom. It was a testimony of the hold the monarchy had taken on their hearts that they paid it willingly. It was a sign of their growing wealth that they were able to pay it at all.

The Crusades had another consequence for England. Except for a few months of his brief ten years' reign Richard was continuously abroad. Even when he returned from captivity he recrossed the Channel as soon as he could raise another army to defend his dominions against his fellow-crusader, Philip Augustus of France. What was remarkable was that the anarchy that had divided an impoverished England under Stephen and before the Conquest did not recur. The permanent officials and judges Henry II had trained and the institutions he had created continued to ensure justice and order. As soon, it is true, as his strong hand was withdrawn there was a dreadful outbreak of anti-Jewish rioting and massacre in York, Lincoln and the rich East Anglian towns—part of a wave of hysteria against that hapless race that swept across Europe with the preaching of the Crusade. And there were rebellions, caused mainly by Richard's scheming younger brother, John, and by the intrigues of the French king. But they were sternly suppressed by the justiciar, William Longchamp—a swarthy, stunted cripple of little tact, humble birth, but much fidelity[21] —and, after his fall, by his successor, Hubert Walter, arch-

---

[21] His grandfather is said to have been a runaway French serf.

bishop of Canterbury and one of Henry's former judges. Indeed—and this was the test of the dead king's statesmanship—the nation continued to grow now even under a sovereign who neglected his business. For Englishmen, set on the true course of national development by the great Angevin, were learning to govern themselves. The absence, not only of the king but of so many great lords in the Holy Land, actually helped them to do so.

Chapter Ten

THE CHARTER

The King is under no man,
but he is under God and the Law.
Bracton

"And still when mob or monarch lays
Too rude a hand on English ways,
The whisper wakes, the shudder plays,
Across the reeds at Runnymede.
And Thames, that knows the moods of kings,
And crowds and priests and suchlike things,
Rolls deep and dreadful as he brings
Their warning down from Runnymede!"
Kipling

By the beginning of the 13th century a remarkable thing
was happening. The people of England, conquered a hundred
and fifty years earlier by a foreign aristocracy who had seized
their land and despised their language, were becoming more
conscious than ever before of their unity and nationhood. And
though their kings and lords still spoke French and boasted
French descent, even they had begun to think of themselves as
English and of their country as England. Within a generation
of the Conquest an Italian archbishop of Canterbury was writing of "we English" and "our island."

For there seemed to be something in the land that naturalised foreigners and, adapting their ways, absorbed them. It
was due largely to its being cut off from Europe by sea, so that
its diverse folk gradually came to think of themselves, not
merely as barons or knights, churchmen, merchants or peasants,
but as members of a distinct community that was both part of
western Christendom and yet apart from it. Before Frenchmen

had come to regard themselves as Frenchmen, Germans as Germans or Italians as Italians, Englishmen, including the Normans settled in England, thought of themselves as Englishmen. This sense of separateness was aided by their kings' insistence on the unity of the realm and on a common system of law. And it was stimulated by the difficulty the conquerors—a few thousand warriors speaking a foreign tongue—experienced in ruling so stubborn a race. A hundred years after Hastings there were still Englishmen who persisted in going unshaved as a protest against the Conquest. The Norman knights, living in this misty land of rain and deep clay forests among an alien population, could only exploit their conquest by meeting the natives half, and more than half way. They needed English men and women to plough their fields, tend their homes, nurse their children and help them in battle. And the English did so—on terms: that their conquerors left them English and became in the end English themselves. For, though they took what their new lords brought them—the centralised monarchy, the French and Latin ideas, the feudal discipline, the capacity to make laws and build in stone—they were most successful in retaining their own institutions and customs. They kept the shire, the shire-court, the village jury, the tithing, and watch and ward; the habit of open justice: the Anglo-Saxon and Scandinavian love of debate and talking things over; the sense of public and neighbourly responsibility. They were quick to absorb, but even more tenacious to preserve.

To strengthen itself against an over-powerful nobility with interests on both sides of the Channel, the monarchy had deliberately encouraged this process. When Henry II had to reduce a rebellious baron's castle he was able to assemble several hundred English village wrights from the surrounding eastern shires to construct his siege-engines. His principal military engineer and architect was an Englishman called Ailnoth. He was not the only man of his race whom the Crown employed and rewarded. And many Normans of knightly rank, and even some of the higher aristocracy, intermarried with the despised natives. "When Normans and Englishmen live close together and wed each other," wrote an observer, "it can scarcely be determined who is of English and who of Norman birth."

Since their numbers were very small, the conquerors soon

became bilingual. They continued to think and converse among themselves in French, but spoke English with their subordinates. They learnt it from their nurses and servants, reeves and ploughmen, and, after the conquest was complete, from their men-at-arms. Abbot Samson of Bury—head of the richest monastery in the land—preached to the common people in the dialect of Norfolk where he had been born and bred. And by the end of the twelfth century even Normans were coming to take a pride in the history and traditions of the country they had won, and to treasure the legends of its saints and heroes. The monkish historians, Henry of Huntingdon and William of Malmesbury, collected the ballads and tales of old England, and Gerald de Barry, the Marcher's son, loved to boast of his Welsh ancestry and the beauties and antiquities of his Pembrokeshire home. It was a Norman—Geoffrey of Monmouth, bishop of St. Asaph—who wrote the romantic tale of King Arthur and his British court and made it almost as favourite a theme with the French-speaking ruling-class as the exploits of Charlemagne and the Song of Roland. It helped to make Britain's inhabitants—Normans, Britons and English alike—believe that they had a common history.

From all this sprang a new force with which kings and barons and even the Church had to reckon: that of national opinion. It was hard to define, but easy to feel. It was based both on Christianity and on the love of liberty and open-speaking which the English had inherited from their remote ancestors. It was fostered by a common subordination to the Law and of thankfulness for its blessings. At its core lay a strong belief in justice: of fair dealing between lord and vassal, prince and subject, neighbour and neighbour, of a rough working balance in keeping with divine law and human conscience. "Take away justice," St. Augustine had written, "and what are kingdoms but dens of thieves?" The English felt this in their bones. And with it went a practical sense—derived both from the new royal judiciary and from that customary law of neighbours which Englishmen had so long administered among themselves—of how justice could be best ensured.

The chief repositories of this feeling were the men who were growing up between the greater feudal barons and the inarticulate peasant mass of the nation. It was an upper middle-class composed mainly of descendants of the Norman knights who had been enfeoffed as owners, or rather feudal holders, of the soil and whose fiefs, though originally granted for life, had become, like other property, hereditary. As their military functions fell into abeyance with the substitution of scutage for service in the field, they became, instead of professional soldiers, landed gentlemen with administrative responsibilities. They served on the new juries of the Grand Assize and in the "oversight" of the royal forests, performed the customary duties of suit of court in the shire and hundred moots, and gave testimony on oath in the periodical inquests of kings and sheriffs. They were still mainly of Norman descent, name and speech, but intermingled increasingly with the wealthier English free-men and landholders and with the Anglo-Norman traders of London and the new towns. Many of our oldest families—Berkeleys and Nevilles, Lumleys and Cromwells, Leghs and Clavells—sprang from this twelfth century knighthood rising into gentility. It found its natural leaders in the officials and judges whom the kings had set up as a counterpoise to the higher feudal aristocracy and ennobled with grants of land. It was employed by the Crown for an evergrowing host of local administrative and legal tasks. It provided a supply of laymen of trust and character with the time for public service, and of ecclesiastics with sufficient personal status to make the Church in England rather more independent of foreign control than anywhere else.

The Norman and Angevin system of common law and central administration helped to train this new upper or upper-middle class. So did the ancient Anglo-Saxon institutions of local government. The shire and hundred courts, the juries impanelled to pronounce on questions of fact, the larger towns just beginning to win rights of self-government from their overlords, all gave men opportunities of learning to act in co-operation, of administering corporate affairs and finance, and of reaching practical decisions after ordered discussion. As the nation grew in wealth and civilisation, more and more public business was left to local men of worth rich enough to take communal responsibility under the Crown yet not strong enough, like the greater feudal lords, to act without it. It was the policy of Richard's justiciar, Hubert Walter, to trust the rising merchant class far more than it had been of his old master, Henry II, who had always feared that the towns might acquire the dangerous independence of the city communes of Flanders and northern Italy. During Walter's administration townsmen were encouraged to buy charters giving them the right to elect mayors and councils, make regulations for trade and markets, and assess their individual contributions to the national taxes.

Both Henry's immediate successors approved this process—Richard because he wanted cash for crusading, and his brother, John, because, with his restless, insatiable, improvident nature, he always needed money for something. Traders were eager to pay for freedom from regal or feudal restrictions, for the freer they became, the richer they grew. During John's reign London acquired the right to elect its sheriffs, mayor and councillors, and more than seventy other towns received charters. This tough, sallow, moody, highly intelligent little man—he was only five feet five inches high—who succeeded Richard in 1199 after the latter had been fatally wounded besieging a Limousin castle, had much of his father's energy and genius for administration. He had been taught in boyhood by the great justiciar, Ranulf Glanvill, and all his life took a keen interest and pleasure in public business. He frequently sat on the judicial bench, and once swore, when a London mob had threatened the Jews, that, if he granted his peace to a dog, it should be inviolably observed. But, having been spoilt in childhood by both parents—who, though they quarrelled bitterly, doted on this precocious and entertaining child of their middle age—he could never discipline himself, and, though a ruthless tyrant when his passions were roused, was never able to discipline others. A sustained course of action was usually beyond him. His ever-changing, unpredictable moods made him his own enemy and, sooner or later, almost everyone else's. He lacked balance. At bottom, for all his ferocity and very real ability, he was something of a *farceur*. He could not resist a joke, even a dangerous one.

Having been born after his father had divided the succession to his empire among his other sons,[1] John could never rid him-

---

[1] Henry called him *Jehan sans terre*—John Lackland. The classical picture of John's character was drawn by Stubbs, and Miss Norgate. Since Professor Galbraith's demonstration of the unreliability of his chief accusers—the St. Albans chroniclers—Dr. A. L. Poole, Lady Stenton and Dr. S. Painter, in his *Reign of King John*, have modified the picture, but, though they have justly stressed the king's exceptional difficulties, great ability and intermittent administrative virtues,

self of a suspicion that everyone was trying to defraud him or of the habit of grabbing whatever he could. Suspicion and greed were the leading traits of his character. He rarely trusted any man or missed a chance of cheating one. Unfortunately for himself he had great charm, and neither his parents nor his generous, impulsive elder brother, whom he repeatedly betrayed, could bring themselves to treat his lapses as anything but the peccadilloes of a wayward boy. With his sly, vulpine face, slanting eyes and deceptive geniality, he grew up without morals or a sense of responsibility. At 17, when his father made him lord of his new dominions in Ireland, he caused an uproar by his childish mockery of his vassals, and during his coronation in Westminster abbey, at the age of 31, he is said—though this may have been a monkish libel—to have joined in the laughter of his ribald favourites at the sacred rites. His whole nature was paradoxical and unpredictable. Sensual and grossly self-indulgent with a passion for jewels and rich garments, he could be both munificent and absurdly mean. He compounded for his gluttonous excesses by providing meals for vast numbers of beggars—sometimes as many as a thousand at a sitting—yet when he visited St. Edmunds abbey, instead of leaving the princely oblation expected, borrowed a silken-cloth from the sacrist and never paid for it. He owned a library of theological books and was exceptionally clean in his person, once taking as many as eight baths in half a year,[2] yet loved nothing better than to watch prisoners being tortured in filthy dungeons.

To these traits England's new ruler added the wild temper of his race. He suffered from maniacal rages when his body became so contorted as to be unrecognisable, when his eyes flashed fire and his dark, sallow face turned livid, and he rolled on the floor, gnawing the rushes. He was as restless as his father and seldom spent more than two or three nights in one place. Intensely jealous and suspicious, he frequently engaged in sly intrigues against his ministers, partly because he distrusted them and resented their power and partly for the amusement of it. He seemed to take a pride in lying and breaking

the fundamental case-history remains of a man who, with all his erratic genius, was a criminal enthroned. Nothing else can fully explain the attitude towards him of his contemporaries.

[2] He always gave William, his bathman, a few pence on these occasions in addition to his official stipend of a halfpenny a day. Poole, *From Domesday Book to Magna Carta*, 427.

faith. Though, therefore, often successful in the short run—for he was capable of great, though unsustained, resolution—his ventures seldom ended well.

He began by losing the Angevin empire. Ever since he had succeeded his father in 1180, Philip Augustus of France had been trying to break up the vast aggregation of English-held fiefs that made it so hard for him to unify his realm. Despite his unexpected victory over the dying Henry—won for him chiefly by the latter's rebellious sons—and some success during Richard's captivity, he had been thwarted by the latter's return and brilliant defence of Normandy. Philip Augustus was no more a warrior than his father, the pious Louis VII, and was completely outmatched by the fury of Richard's marches—"more swift than the twisted thong of a Balearic sling." But he was a master politician—patient, calculating, far-sighted—and as unscrupulous in pursuit of his unchanging purpose, the unity of France, as John in that of his selfish, wayward impulses. He took advantage of his new opponent's every mistake, and John made many. The first occurred in the second year of his reign when, having discarded an uncanonical and childless wife, the English king married the 14-year-old heiress of Angoulême and bride-elect of one of his Poitevin vassals. By doing so in flagrant defiance of his feudal obligations and then refusing to answer a complaint in the court of his overlord, the king of France, he forfeited his French fiefs for contumacy. This would have mattered little had he been able to defend them like his father and brother. But, though a far better soldier than Philip when he exerted himself, he did so only spasmodically, and, according to the monkish chroniclers, spent months in lethargic idleness with his young bride while his foe reduced one after another of his Norman and Angevin fortresses. A far more important factor in his defeat was the difficulty he had in inspiring his feudal tenants, both French and English, to fight for him. His moral instability made even victory useless. For by a dreadful crime he threw away his one great military triumph, when in 1202, after marching eighty miles from Le Mans to Mirabeau in forty-eight hours to relieve his octogenarian mother, he captured the chiefs of the besieging army. Among them was his nephew, Arthur of Brittany, to whom Philip had offered his French fiefs. After vainly trying to extract an oath of allegiance from the 16-year-old lad, who had his full share of Plantagenet arrogance, he secretly did away with him—according to general belief with his own hands in a debauch.[3] It was a slip of which the king of France made every use.

In three years John lost two-thirds of the Angevin empire. Everything went north of the Loire, including Normandy. He failed to hold even the almost impregnable fortress of Château-Gaillard—the key to Rouen and the crowning triumph of twelfth century fortification which Coeur de Lion had built on the Seine at Les Andelys on the model of the Byzantine castles of the Levant. John listened to the growing tale of disaster with apparent indifference. "The king of France," he was told, "is in your land; he is taking your castles; he is binding your seneschals to their horses' tails and dragging them shamefully to prison!" "Let him alone," was his reply, "some day I shall win all back." By 1205 he was left with nothing but the Channel Islands, part of Poitou, and his mother's distant and unruly inheritance of Aquitaine.

Thus, after being joined to Europe for a century, England reverted to her former island state. The Channel again became her frontier. Her people viewed the loss of Normandy with mixed feelings. The feudal magnates resented it, for some had lands in the Duchy which they could now hold only by doing a homage to the French king incompatible with the service they owed for their English land. Though they tried to avoid the necessity, they were forced to choose between them and become either English or Norman. The rank and file, though they felt the shame of their king's discomfiture—"Softsword" they called him—regarded with indifference the end of a connection which had always been remote to them and from which they had derived little advantage. When, however, Philip Augustus, intoxicated by his success, threatened to invade their own land, they responded to their king's summons with an enthusiasm which showed that patriotism, still scarcely existent elsewhere, was already a force in England. With general approval the Council imposed a tax on all merchandise—the first

---

[3] "After dinner, being drunk and possessed by the devil." *Ann. Margam,* cit. Norgate, *John Lackland* 91. John is said by one chronicler to have previously ordered Arthur to be blinded and mutilated and to have been thwarted by the refusal of Hubert de Burgh, castellan of Falaise.

in English history—and ordered a national *levée-en-masse*, under which, in the event of a French landing, every male over the age of twelve was to turn out under the shire, hundred and parish constables on pain of forfeiting land or freedom. About a quarter of the royal revenue went that year on armaments. Ships from the Cinque Ports, to whose burgesses John gave the rank of barons, patrolled the Channel, and foreign vessels were made to lower their sails to his flag: a precedent on which later kings based their claim to "dominion" of the narrow seas.[4] Ceasing with the loss of Normandy to hold both shores of the Channel, England fell back instinctively on her true line of defence, the Channel itself. A few years later she won her first naval victory, when several hundred little ships under the king's bastard brother, the earl of Salisbury, caught a French invasion fleet at anchor off the inland port of Damme, near Bruges, and largely destroyed it. John may not have grasped the full importance of sea-power, but with the help of William de Wrotham, archdeacon of Taunton and keeper of the royal galleys he created a permanent naval establishment. He once stated that it was easier to drown invaders than to kill them on land. Like his father and brother before him, he was a patron of seamen, though, as in everything else, an erratic and arbitrary one.[5] Richard, who employed a fleet of English merchant ships to take his army to the Levant, built and enfranchised the town of Portsmouth. John, who added its dockyard, walls and arsenal, also helped to choose the site of a new port called Liverpool and gave it its first charter.

Having suffered defeat in a continental war, John now involved himself in a struggle with a still more powerful foe. Pope Innocent III was perhaps the ablest statesman that had ever sat on St. Peter's throne. A quarter of a century earlier his predecessor, Alexander III, had ended his long struggle with the emperor and anti-pope by establishing the Roman *curia*, not only as the supreme court of Christendom, but as ruler of central Italy and patron of the republican cities of the Lombard League. To save his tottering empire after its defeat by

[4] It was a point to which Samuel Pepys, that indefatigable official of the Navy Office, devoted much research four and a half centuries later as he pored over his cherished volume of Selden's *Mare Clausum* in search of precedents.

[5] In 1208 he threatened to hang some Welsh sailors if they did not enter his service. A. L. Poole, *From Domesday Book to Magna Carta*, 436.

the Milanese pikemen at Legnano, the great emperor, Frederick Barbarossa, had done obeisance at his feet. Now Barbarossa's grandson, Frederick II—claimant to the imperial crown
and heir to the Norman kingdom of Sicily—was a papal ward,
and Germany itself had dissolved into anarchy and civil war.

The papacy was thus at the height not only of its spiritual
but worldly power. In 1200, in a secret address to the cardinals,
Innocent III claimed the right to dispose of the empire. Two
years later he launched the Fourth Crusade, which, carried in
a Venetian fleet, turned aside from its objective and stormed
the capital of the Christian East, Constantinople. There, in the
greatest city on earth, Frankish and Venetian crusaders set up
by force a Latin instead of a Byzantine empire and attempted,
though in the teeth of bitter resistance, to subject the Greek to
the Roman Church.

Such was the background against which the English king
embarked on his duel with the papacy. It arose from the election of a successor to Hubert Walter, archbishop of Canterbury.
Ever since Henry I's settlement of the investiture dispute of a
century earlier, the English kings, while conceding the Church's
right to elect and consecrate, had continued to control the appointment of bishops by writs directing cathedral chapters
whom to elect.[6] On this occasion a group of the younger monks
of Christ Church, Canterbury, jealous of the influence on the
Crown of the diocesan bishops, anticipated the royal *congé
d'élire* by provisionally electing in secret one of their own number and sending him to Rome to seek papal approval. Later,
terrified by the royal displeasure, the chapter unanimously
chose the king's nominee, John de Grey, bishop of Norwich.

When however the pope received the formal request for confirmation of the appointment, he refused to give it and set aside
the election as uncanonical. He also refused to confirm the
earlier election and directed the Canterbury monks to send
delegates to Rome with powers to make a new one. His aim was
both to widen the papal power and ensure the appointment of
one who was neither a cloistered monk without experience of
the world nor of a mere Crown official and man of affairs like

---

[6] "Henry, King of the English, to his faithful monks of the church of Winchester, greeting. I order you to hold a free election, but nevertheless I forbid
you to elect anyone except Richard my clerk, the archdeacon of Poitiers." Writ
of Henry II, cit. A. L. Poole, *From Domesday Book to Magna Carta*, 220.

the late archbishop, whose work as justiciar and chancellor had
left him notoriously little time for ecclesiastical business. He
did not deny the king's right to be consulted; the Canon Law
required the acquiescence and advice of the lay ruler in order
to ensure the harmony of Christian society. But it was his duty
as supreme pontiff to refuse the pallium to any but the best.

And the best was available. Living in Rome was a great
theological teacher, a canon of York and Nôtre Dame who had
been a master in the cathedral schools or university of Paris
and had been lately raised to the rank of cardinal. Stephen
Langton was a Lincolnshire man, cadet of a family of small
Anglo-Danish landowners who farmed the manor of Langton-
by-Wragby.[7] He was a scholar and a gentlemen; a thinker and
man of the world, trained in the supreme function of statesmanship—the decision of practical questions in the light of first
principles. But he was also a poet and, in his quiet, unpretending way, something of a saint. His work as a scriptural com-
mentator rearranging the text of the Bible[8] had won him a
European reputation, and he was the author of the great Latin
hymn, *"Veni, Sancte Spiritus"*—"Come, Holy Ghost!" It was of
him that the pope was thinking when he bade the Canterbury
monks elect "whomsoever they would, so he were but an earnest and capable man, and, above all, an Englishman."

When John heard of the election he flew into one of his
famous rages. He billeted his mercenaries on Christ Church,
Canterbury, and drove the monks from the kingdom. He would
not, he said, accept as primate one of whom he "knew nothing
save that he had dwelt much among his enemies." His most
sacred prerogative had been violated. The pope might refuse
to confirm his appointment but had no right to persuade the
monks to elect a nominee of his own. And the king appealed—
indignantly and with justice—to English history and custom.
Yet, like his father in his struggle with Becket, he forgot that
times had changed and that what had been the custom of
England might not be eternally acceptable to the rest of the
world. The Church was not merely an ecclesiastical conven-
ience of the English Crown—a part of the machinery of State;

[7] "Langton, sir," said Dr. Johnson of his young friend, Bennet Langton,
"has a free warren from Henry the Second, and Cardinal Stephen Langton in
King John's reign was of their family."

[8] His arrangement of the books of the New Testament is still largely followed,
both in the Catholic and Protestant Churches. M. Powicke, *Stephen Langton*, 38.

Becket himself had died to prove it something more. And at that moment its supra-national authority was more widely acknowledged than ever before.

The pope tried to overcome John's opposition. But after Langton had been denied admission to his see for a year, Innocent placed England under an Interdict. Throughout what had become, through its king's defiance, a schismatical realm, almost all religious services ceased, the churches were closed, and the church-bells were silent. It was a blow that would have dissolved most continental kingdoms. But, though many leading churchmen fled the country, with their strong national cohesion the English endured the ban for five years. They had a rooted respect for their Crown, and the more politically-minded believed with John that the pope had infringed its rights. They were much afraid of the spiritual consequences of the Church's displeasure. But they were even more afraid of the king's. His officers continued to be obeyed, his law observed and his taxes collected.

John himself did not appear to mind the Interdict. It enabled him to increase his income. Like his great-great-uncle, the wicked Rufus, he had never shared in the general veneration for priests and sacraments; at his coronation, according to his enemies, he had even broken with hallowed precedent by declining communion. As the clergy refused to carry out their duties, he confiscated their revenues. From the proceeds he gave them—so long as they remained passive—a small subsistence allowance, supervised in the case of village priests by four "lawful men" of the parish. With his harsh, cackling laughter he ordered his officers to raid their parsonages and take their uncanonical wives into custody for ransom. Meanwhile he cut down the woods of Canterbury and threatened to have Langton hanged if he entered the country.

Even when the pope excommunicated him the king remained defiant. He refused to let the papal messengers land, and for a time made it impossible to publish the sentence in England. When an Exchequer clerk quitted his employment on the grounds that it was an offence to serve an excommunicated person, he is reported—on doubtful authority—to have had him incarcerated in a dungeon, where he could neither stand nor lie, and then crushed to death under a leaden cope. For five years he gave a demonstration of what could happen to a Christian land ruled by a despot without restraint of Church. Despite the enormous wealth seized from the ecclesiastical estates—and several monasteries, including the great Cistercian house of Waverley, were completely ruined—he imposed taxes on the realm that doubled his revenue. He was able to do so, not merely because he stopped at nothing to achieve his ends, but because he had inherited the most efficient mechanism of State seen in the West since the days of imperial Rome.

It is not easy to follow the exact course of the events during which, in his struggle with the papacy, John made an enemy of his own baronage: still, in that policeless age, the principal agency through which the government of the countryside was conducted. The contemporary records are incomplete, while the monkish chroniclers of the next reign, bitterly prejudiced against the king, are inaccurate and unreliable. Many of their stories about him are unsupported by other evidence and some are clearly untrue. What is certain is that John lost the trust of almost the entire nobility and incurred the active hatred of a part of it. It was a hatred—and fear—aroused by specific injuries. Some of these were inflicted by John's wanton and petulant passions, others by his deliberate methods of government.

For behind the king's erratic conduct lay a purpose. It was to increase the already vast power of the Crown which his father and father's officers had bequeathed him and to use it to create a war-chest with which to recover his lost dominions. At the back of his mind lay a deep resentment. His defeat in France, he felt, had been due not to his own fault but to his English barons' reluctance to fight his battles. He therefore addressed himself to the congenial task of screwing out of them everything he could. With the taxes, fines and aids he took he filled his castles with barrels of silver marks and with jewels and precious fabrics against the day when he should once more be able to take the field against the French king. By 1208 he had accumulated 40,000 marks in the treasury at Winchester; four years later he had another 50,000 marks stored in Nottingham castle.[9] At Devizes after his death were found a hundred-and-

[9] S. K. Mitchell, *Studies in Taxation under John and Henry III*, 344.

seven rings set with emeralds, a hundred-and-eleven with sapphires, fifteen with diamonds, twenty-eight with rubies and nine with garnets; at Corfe, with other jewellery, a hundred-and-nineteen rich garments of silk, twenty-nine of samite and four splendid baldekins from Bagdad.

In accumulating such treasure John used every known tax and a good many original variants of his own. The most important was scutage—the composition which tenants-in-chief and their military vassals had to pay their lord, the king, in lieu of service in the field. As it was the tenure by which they held their lands, the king had the right to demand it whenever he went to war. But the extent of the service and, therefore, the amount of the composition accepted instead of it, had always been limited by feudal custom. John varied it at his pleasure. He also levied scutage before instead of after a campaign, and so got his money whether he was involved in the expenses of a war or not. While his father in thirty-five years levied only eight scutages, and his crusading brother only two, John in sixteen years imposed eleven, several of them for service on campaigns that never took place. The rate at which the highest was assessed was almost double that of his brother's day.

As well as scutage and the customary feudal aids from his tenants-in-chief, the king during his brief reign imposed two national levies on the capital value of all personal and movable goods—a special impost originally instituted for Richard's crusade to recover Jerusalem—and at least seven general tallages on the manors and boroughs of the royal demesne. These were in addition to the annual farm of the demesne leased by the Crown to the sheriffs. The tallage of 1210—to pay for a short summer campaign in Ireland—was by far the largest ever raised in England. Some royal boroughs, like Worcester, Northampton and Oxford, paid three or four more times as much as they had paid before.

In addition to these regular taxes the king employed many other means of filling his coffers. When his tenants' estates, through death, wardship or other cause, fell into his custody he stripped them by special tallages of almost their entire realisable capital. He sold heiresses to low-born foreigners, so in the term of the day "disparaging them," while widows in ward—who were allowed by feudal custom a right of veto—were compelled to marry against their will or subjected to heavy fines.

One lady, whom John had disposed of three times, had to pay the enormous sum of 5000 marks for the right to enjoy her inheritance after the death of her third husband. Mercenary captains were made sheriffs and simultaneously allowed to hold judicial office, thus enabling them, with royal connivance, to blackmail property-owners with vexatious writs and false accusations. Summonses were issued to extract fines for non-attendance, writs were withheld or sold at exorbitant rates, crushing penalties imposed without regard to the nature of the offence or means of the accused, justice delayed or even denied altogether. The elaborate fiscal and legal system of the two Henrys and the great justiciars was turned into a merciless machine for extortion.

The most remunerative of all the king's devices for raising money was to get, by just such means, his richer subjects into debt either to himself or the Jewish usurers whom he employed as sponges. Once they were unable to pay, however temporarily, he had the legal right to imprison them and seize their lands. They were then at his mercy. He could impose on them any fine he liked as the price for their liberation and the restoration of their estates. The only limit was their capacity to pay.

In all this, which was done with an aggravating regard for legal niceties, John kept within the letter—though seldom the spirit—of the Law. Like his father he stretched his rights as far as they could be made to go legally, but, unlike his father, much further than was politically wise. In doing so he showed an ingenuity and an application worthy of a better cause. He acted, when it did not clash with his own interests, as a careful and conscientious judge, and spent laborious hours devising with his Exchequer officials new ways of increasing the revenue. He made frequent inquests into the debts of the Crown and even instituted plans for a new Domesday survey. To free himself from the restraint of the great officers-of-state, who were mostly old-fashioned men of honour, he evolved an office called the Wardrobe where he kept, with his clothes and jewels, a private or privy seal with which to issue orders over the heads of the chancery clerks. Meanwhile—for he was no ascetic—he amused himself with full-blooded Angevin zest, over-eating and drinking, making free with the wives and daughters of his nobles, and "hunting woods and streams, delighting in the pleasure of them."[10] "He was a very bad man," wrote a horrified chronicler, "cruel towards all men and too covetous of pretty ladies." There is no evidence that he felt any compunction for the latter, though it made him bitter enemies, but when, instead of attending mass, he caught seven cranes on Holy Innocents' Day, he compounded for the offence by feeding fifty paupers a crane! Throughout the demoralising years of the Interdict his edicts grew ever more arbitrary and erratic. He removed the Exchequer to Northampton to annoy the London merchants, ordered the fences of the forest assarts in Essex to be levelled for his game, and, reserving every river bank for his hawking, forbade, according to one account, the killing of birds in England.

By the fifth year of the Interdict John had built for himself an apparent position of immense strength. He employed part of the money raised from taxation to hire bands of Poitevin, Welsh and Flemish mercenaries—a savage race of men who lived by war and struck terror into every place they visited. With their help and the law's he imprisoned his enemies, torturing some and letting others, for whom no ransom was obtainable, die of starvation in his dungeons. From all of whom he was suspicious —and at one time or another this included nearly everyone of importance—he took hostages for good behaviour. That this was no formality he proved in the summer of 1212 at Nottingham castle when, on news of a rising in Wales, he hanged twenty-eight boys—the sons of Welsh chieftains—who had been left in his custody. When the wife of a former favourite—the great Marcher baron, William de Braose[11]—tactlessly recalled the fate of Arthur, she and the son she tried to withhold from the king's officers were thrown into a dungeon at Windsor and left to starve with a sheaf of oats and a flitch of raw bacon. Eleven days later their corpses were found, propped together against the wall, the boy's cheeks gnawn through by his mother in her anguish.

By such methods John intimidated everyone. The Welsh, the Irish and the Scots were equally afraid of him. In 1209, with the help of his fleet and mercenary army and a vast feudal array, he made the princes of all Wales do homage and the aged

[10] The map of woodland England is still marked by his hunting-boxes, a few, like the old house in Tollard Royal at the edge of Cranborne Chase, still standing.

[11] At the height of his power de Braose had held sixteen castles and 352 knights' fees. S. Painter, *The Reign of King John*, 46.

William the Lion of Scotland pay an enormous fine and give his daughters as hostages. Yet though there was no one who "did not obey the rod of the king" and fear him, the effects of the Interdict were cumulative. The strain of it affected the mind, not only of the king's subjects, but in the end of the king himself. He became afraid of what his people were thinking, and went about perpetually armed and surrounded by a foreign bodyguard. In the summer of 1211 the breakdown of negotiations to end the deadlock with Rome enabled a visiting papal emissary to pronounce the sentence of excommunication in the presence of the Council. When in the next year John assembled the feudal host at Nottingham for an expedition against the Welsh princes, his nerve suddenly gave way. Warned that the barons were plotting either to seize and slay him or deliver him to the Welsh, he dissolved the host. About the same time a wandering hermit known as Peter of Wakefield predicted that by Ascension day John would have ceased to reign. The seer was seized and carried off to Corfe Castle, but his prophecy received wide credence.

It was against this background that the pope in the spring of 1213 threatened to declare the English throne forfeit, and the king of France, like a second Conqueror, gathered a fleet and army at Boulogne to seize England as the Church's champion. Once more the English responded to the threat of invasion, assembling at the royal summons in such numbers that most of them had to be sent home for lack of provisions. "If they had all been of one heart and mind for king and country," wrote a chronicler, "there was no prince under heaven against whom they could not have defended the realm." But whatever the native patriotism of those too humble to have had direct experience of John's methods of government, he knew now that their leaders loathed and feared him. He could not hope to contend simultaneously against his own nobility, the Church and a foreign invader. He therefore executed a sudden and brilliant *volte-face*. He made his peace with the papacy on its own terms and, by declaring himself a penitent, won the goodwill of the strongest Power in Europe. He went further and did what the Conqueror had refused to do at the bidding of Hildebrand. On May 15th, 1213, at the Knights Templars' house at Ewell near Dover, he knelt at the feet of Pandulf, the papal legate, and solemnly surrendered the kingdom to the pope, receiving it back as his feudatory. From being the champion of English freedom from foreign interference he became in the course almost of a night the most submissive of the sons of Holy Church. "The lord king," declared the delighted legate, "is another man by God's grace!"

With his usual resource and lack of sincerity, John had turned the tables on his enemies. His realm being under papal protection, the French impending crusade had lost its meaning. A few weeks later the earl of Salisbury carried out his victorious raid on the invasion fleet at Damme and returned with a rich haul of captured ships. And on Ascension day, his prophecy having failed, Peter of Wakefield was dragged behind a horse's tail from Corfe to Wareham and hanged. The triumphant king celebrated the occasion with a magnificent feast in a painted pavilion. "And a right joyous day it was," wrote the historian, Roger of Wendover, "the king taking his pleasure and making merry with the bishops and nobles who had come together at his call."

But with one of his foes John had not done. The injured barons may or may not have meant to betray him, but they had resolved to put an end to the reckless and irresponsible rule of the past few years. They and other property owners had endured an almost intolerable persecution. Tax after tax and aid after aid had been wrung from them, their children had been taken and held as hostages, the wardships of minors and the marriages of heiresses trafficked to the basest agents. Some of them had suffered, too, personal insults of the gravest kind. They alone, with their armour, horses, castles and men-at-arms, had the means to withstand such a tyrant. Even for them it involved intense danger. But they had been driven to desperation. They were of many kinds. Some were selfish bullies who wished to free themselves from royal control in order to oppress their weaker neighbours. Some, especially in Essex and East Anglia—where the Bigods and Bohuns, Mandevilles and Clares still hankered after their lost independence—were reactionaries who wished to restore provincial feudalism. But most of the malcontents were the descendants of royal officials: Stutevilles and de Vescys, Fitz Walters and Fitz Peters, de Vauxs and de Lacys, Mowbrays and Percys—members of the new aristocracy of office which the Henrys had used to discipline the older nobility and which had helped to fashion the administrative machine that had now been turned into an instrument of irresponsible tyranny. They were strongest in the north, where authority had always been left to the man on the spot and where local magnates were used to defending themselves against Scottish raiders. In the summer of 1213, when John, heartened by his naval victory at Damme and his alliance with the Church, was raising immense sums to finance a grand coalition of German, Provençal and Flemish princes to crush the rising power of France and recover his French dominions, a number of these northern barons, summoned to join him at Portsmouth, refused on the ground that their tenure did not compel them to serve abroad. In the following summer while the king was campaigning against Philip Augustus on the Loire, goaded beyond endurance by the demands to support his costly alliance and expeditionary force, they refused his demand for scutage. In this they were acting beyond their rights. For it was part of the feudal law that an overlord could tax his tenants-in-chief to support his wars. But these stubborn northerners maintained that such a right could be denied if it was not used justly and within the limits set by custom.

For, in the light of his son's use of it, Henry II's achievement had presented England with a terrible dilemma. The great Angevin had convinced the nation and even its feudal magnates that, after the disorder of Stephen's reign, happiness and prosperity for all depended on the supremacy of the Crown. He had created a legal and financial machinery for making that supremacy effective and a self-renewing school of trained administrators to operate it under his successors. That the first of them was almost continuously out of the realm had mattered comparatively little; the mechanism of State had continued to function in his absence and the officials Henry had trained to strengthen and improve it. But when the next heir proved a diabolical maniac, who used the royal power to make life intolerable for his subjects and alienated everyone in turn, those whom Henry had made the agents of that power were, little by little, driven into making a choice. They had either to destroy it, and with it the order and unity on which the prosperity of the realm depended, or subject the wearer of the crown himself to it. The first course might have been easy; the second was superlatively hard. It is the supreme measure of Henry II's achievement in educating his greater subjects that the best of them chose the second, and carried their reluctant fellows with them.

Yet the very cunning and ability of his son also impelled men to that wiser choice. Had John been a weakling as well as an impossible king, the monarchical power which had become the expression of England's unity could scarcely have survived the storms raised by his misdeeds. Yet for all his periodic lethargy, when driven into a corner he fought back with a fury that made even the most reckless or arrogant opponent chary of going to extremes. It was no child's play to dash from his hands the sceptre and rod he misused. The alternative of restraining and controlling him—and with him the royal power—was thus kept open.

It was an alternative, too, to which Englishmen now instinctively turned. It was of the Crown that they thought when they used the word England, for without it there would have been no England. Ever since the days of Alfred the monarchy had been implanting in them the habit of acting together. The great alien princes who had grasped in their strong hands the athelings' sceptre—Canute the Dane, William and Henry the Normans, Henry the Angevin—had each strengthened it. It had become natural even to Anglo-Norman barons to act with and through the Crown. They still tried to do so when its wearer of the hour became their oppressor and enemy.

For the functioning of their local institutions, their personal dignity and honours, the tenure of their lands, the administration of justice and order were now inextricably bound up with the Crown's existence. As everywhere in the Middle Ages society in England was intensely local; men lived and thought in terms of neighbourhood. Yet, as a result of three and a half centuries of evolution, her political and legal organisation had become, not provincial like that of France and Spain, Germany and Italy, but monarchical. The Crown was the motive-spark of public activity and the fount of honour. An English landowner thought of himself not merely as the vassal of a provincial earl, but as a liege of the king; an English justice not only as a functionary of a provincial court but as a guardian of his peace. Social organisation was not federal as on the continent; it was

national. From top to bottom ran this chain of unity. The great
men who ruled the provinces were also the officers of the royal
household, judicial bench and feudal array. They governed the
neighbourhood and they served the king. In a descending
scale the same principle applied to every division of the nation:
to those who operated the institutions of shire, hundred and
village, the baronial honour and the manor. All stood, in one
capacity or another, on the rungs of a ladder, feudal or administrative, that stretched upwards to the throne.

The trustees of this unifying system were, after the wearer
of the crown, the officials and judges of the royal court. Those
whom Henry II had trained were so imbued with his spirit
and so resolved to make his rules prevail that even the heir
to the throne was powerless against them. When, before his
accession, John, in his brother's absence, had raised the standard
of rebellion against the unpopular justiciar, William Longchamp,
Roger de Lacy—constable of Chester—without a thought of his
own future hanged the castellans of Tickhill and Nottingham
for surrendering their castles, and, when the squire of one of
them tried to drive away the birds from his corpse, strung
him up beside his lord for his affront to the royal dignity.

Most of John's chief advisers had formerly opposed him in
the king's name. And despite his ungovernable temper, they
continued to do so after his accession whenever his erratic
projects endangered the royal power of which they were the
loyal executants and guardians. The king's majesty had become
to them more important than the king himself. For all his threats
and intrigues against them, John for a time sulkily acquiesced
in this state of affairs. When in 1205 Hubert Walter died—the
great archbishop and former justiciar to whom posterity owes
the Chancery rolls—John is reported to have exclaimed, "Now,
by the feet of God, for the first time am I king and lord of
England!" His successor as justiciar, Geoffrey Fitz Peter, maintained the same honourable tradition.[12]

Such men continued to stand by the king even when the
country erupted under his feet. They were his traditional advisers, and, out of loyalty to the royal state of which they were
the honoured upholders, refused to leave him to the counsel of

[12] And earned from his royal master, according to the not very reliable St.
Albans chronicler, Matthew Paris, a similar epitaph: "When he gets to hell,
he may greet Archbishop Hubert, whom he is sure to meet there!"

those who never questioned his acts and with whom he increasingly surrounded himself: creatures like his harsh Poitevin justiciar, Peter des Roches, who in 1213 succeeded Geoffrey Fitz Peter, and the reckless foreign soldiers of fortune—Falkes de Bréauté, Engelard de Cigogné, Hugh de Boves and Waleran the German—who commanded the mercenaries. The greatest of the loyal magnates was William the marshal, now close on his seventieth year and once the little boy whom King Stephen had refused to catapult into his father's castle at Newbury. He had grown up, a landless younger son, to become the ideal of every English knight: fearless, upright, truthful, chivalrous, the greatest champion in the tournament-lists of his age, and unfailingly faithful to his pledge and feudal oath. He had stood by his dying liege-lord, the "young king," when all the world had forsaken him. Later he had served Henry II with equal fidelity and had been one of the faithful few at his tragic death. Towards Richard, whom he had opposed in his father's cause,[13] he had shown the same frank and flawless loyalty. He had been rewarded for his loyalty to the Crown with the hand of the greatest heiress of the realm, Isabel de Clare, Strongbow's daughter, and had become Earl of Pembroke and Leinster and lord of vast estates in Wales, Ireland and nine English counties. And when his brother died he had inherited the office of marshal. But whether as a penniless knight or a great feudal lord, he had remained the same: outspoken, fearless and invincibly staunch. John strained that faith to the utmost and took delight in doing so, but came in the end to know that the marshal's loyalty to the Crown was unbreakable. "By the legs of God," he said, "I deem him the most loyal knight who ever was born in my lands."

Yet the dilemma which faced loyalists after thirteen years of this disastrous reign was beyond the solution of even this shrewd old paragon of knightly virtue. The nation was drifting into war, not only between its best elements and its worst, but between the best themselves. Men were appealing from the king to the king's law, and taking their stand, in the name of the just laws of the king's father and grandfather, against the

---

[13] "Sirs, I do not repent me of what I did," he replied to friends who volunteered to try to save him from the new king's wrath for his uncompromising defence of his father. "I thank you for your proffers; but, so help me God, I will not accept that I cannot return. Thanks be to Him, He has helped me ever since I was made a knight; I doubt not He will help me to the end."

king's government. The perils inherent in the situation were intense.

To resolve it called not only for loyalty and selflessness, but for the most subtle, comprehending statesmanship. And in its archbishop the nation found what it needed. Langton was a scholar trained in the close logic of the medieval Church, with a vision that embraced all Christendom. Unlike his famous predecessor, St. Thomas, though a man of the strictest principle, he was an idealist who understood human nature and the need for saving the self-respect of stubborn disputants. His temper was essentially moderate, conciliatory and unassuming. He had the kind of good sense and quiet, rather whimsical humour that takes the hysteria out of strained situations. He was always seeking to achieve what men of goodwill, after calmly hearing and debating all the arguments, considered both just and expedient. His aim was reasonableness even more than reason. In this he was most English. So was he in his respect for established custom and dislike of extremes.

It was not Langton's wish to see the Crown overthrown, the law ignored, the realm divided, the barons petty sovereigns as in the days of Stephen and Godwin. What he wanted was that the king should preserve the law his predecessors had created. And it was to law that the archbishop appealed, not only of man, but of God. For it was the essence of medieval Christian philosophy that God ruled the earth, and that men, and kings above all men, must further His ends by doing justice. The earthly order, like everything else, existed to help them do so. Government must be founded in justice or it was not in Christian eyes government at all. Law was the expression of justice, and kings were its upholders and dispensers. It was their duty to enforce what Christian men, through long custom, had learned to regard as just. And whenever it became necessary to re-state or extend the law, sovereigns, as bearers of the sword of justice, were under an obligation to consult with the leaders and wise men of the realm.

The first of these were the princes of the Church, for the Church was the medium through which God's law was communicated to men. Its political function was to remind kings of what justice was, to impress on them its importance, and recall them to it when they strayed from it. "Will you to your power cause law and justice, in mercy, to be executed in all your judgments?" the archbishop of Canterbury asked the king at his crowning. It was natural, therefore, that he should take the lead in reminding him of his obligation to rule justly. Ever since the days of Augustine this had been the function of the head of the English Church. He was to the king, in the traditional phrase, his "father in God."

Having long flouted his coronation oath, John, in his submission to the Church, had offered England on the altar, and the offer had been accepted at its face value by a magnanimous but distant pope who knew neither John nor England. It had been accepted too, and in the spirit in which it had been made, by the worldly Italian financiers and lawyers who surrounded the papacy and who saw in it a licence to sell the benefices of the English Church for the profit of the Roman *curia* in return for leaving the king free to do as he pleased with his lay subjects. Langton, while he deplored what seemed to him an unnecessary surrender of his country's freedom from foreign control, was resolved to make John's hypocritical oblation a real one. From the start he used his traditional position as his chief adviser to induce him to do what he had promised at his coronation: to use power as a trust from God and govern justly.

As soon, therefore, as he returned to England the archbishop reminded the king of his coronation oath. On St. Margaret's day 1213 he received him at the door of Winchester cathedral where, before absolving him from excommunication, he made him swear to defend and maintain the Church, to recall the good laws of his ancestors and, judging all with the just judgments of his court, render to every man his right. Then he allowed him to enter the cathedral and resume that part of his royal functions which, in ecclesiastical eyes, alone distinguished him from a vulgar tribal tyrant. Afterwards king, prelates and nobles dined together "in joy and merriment."

For the next two years—among the most crucial in English history—Langton struggled against immense difficulties to keep the king true to this conception and to the oath he had sworn. He had to contend, not only with a treacherous and tyrannical nature, but with the factious interests, self-seeking and violent passions of those who were trying to use the resentment John had aroused to destroy the peace and the unity of the realm. When in the autumn of 1213 the king returned in a towering rage from an abortive campaign in Poitou and marched with his mercenaries to the north to punish the barons whose truancy he regarded as the cause of his discomfiture, Langton pursued him, first to Northampton and then to Nottingham, threatening to excommunicate his army if he made war on any man without prior trial and sentence. And when the northern and East Anglian lords spoke of renouncing their homage and resorting to arms, Langton urged them not to carry matters to extremes in defiance of the law. Both with king and barons he repeatedly appealed to precedents, to the wise laws of the Confessor and the solemn compacts to govern justly which the Norman kings had made before their reigns in the presence of Christ's ministers and their chief subjects. All that was needed to restore justice and peace to England, he claimed, was to renew such compacts. "A charter of Henry I has been found," he told the barons, "by means of which, if you desire, you may regain your lost liberty." And he tried unceasingly to induce them to base their demands on its terms.

In this struggle to avert civil war and preserve both the royal authority and the liberties of the subject, Langton was aided by the little group of loyalists of whom William the marshal was chief. But he was aided still more by the temper of the people of whom he was so characteristic a representative and whose nature he understood so well. He was, as Pope Innocent had said, above all an Englishman. And he pursued the road which Englishmen had already begun to take and which the monkish biographer of Abbot Samson of Bury defined in the phrase, "Blessed are those who steer a middle course!"[14] By patiently following that road in a time of fierce passions and overwrought tempers, Langton saved the monarchy as the unifying force of the realm. And—though this was no part of his purpose—he unconsciously set the future course of English constitutional development.

The crisis which resolved that future occurred in the autumn of 1214. During the summer of that year John's long-planned alliance to crush the French king took shape. While his nephew, Otto of Brunswick, claimant to the imperial throne, threatened Philip Augustus from the north with two of the latter's own

[14] Or, as the good abbot himself loved to say, "Let a middle course be taken!" Jocelin de Brakelond, 23.

vassals—the counts of Flanders and Boulogne—John struck at the Loire from his territories in Gascony and Poitou. But the Poitevins proved a broken reed, and the English king was forced to beat a precipitate retreat on La Rochelle and on his ships. Meanwhile Philip, freed from pressure in the south, used his advantage of interior lines to throw his entire strength against John's northern allies. Their defeat at Bouvines near Tournai in July decided the campaign, and with it the future of France and England. When John landed three months later at Dartmouth, an angry and disappointed man—his treasure wasted and his mercenaries dispersed—the English malcontents' opportunity had come.

That November the northern and eastern barons met at Bury St. Edmunds under pretence of a pilgrimage and swore an oath before the high altar that they would withdraw their allegiance if their "ancient and accustomed liberties" were not restored. Throughout the winter Langton and the marshal struggled to obtain from the king a guarantee sufficient to satisfy them and save a recourse to arms. John did everything he could to postpone and evade the issue, appealing to the pope and taking the crusader's cross in order to drive a wedge between the Church and barons, while his seneschals in Gascony and Poitou sought feverishly for new mercenaries.

Yet the growing pressure and number of the malcontents forced him to accept the advice of his counsellors and, however insincerely and reluctantly, meet their demands. In the early spring of 1215 the northern and East Anglian lords, who were by now in the ascendancy, joined forces on the Wansford Heath tournament-field beside the great north road near Stamford. Thence they advanced to Brackley, another tilting-ground nearer John's Windsor headquarters. When the king rejected their conditions—communicated to him by the archbishop and marshal[15] —they resorted to open force and, after an unsuccessful attempt to capture the royal castle of Northampton, marched on London where the mayor and leading citizens were waiting to open the gates. By taking the capital, which they entered on May 17th, they gained a base from which to threaten Windsor.

John was now *in extremis*. Apart from the mercenary garrisons of his castles he had only a handful of personal retainers

---

[15] "Why do these barons not ask for my kingdom at once?" he asked indignantly.

upon whom he could depend. Faced by reports of a new baronial rising in the south-west, he could do nothing. Until the barons had occupied London and its large circumference of wall and river, he might have crushed them, for they lacked both major castles and professional troops. He had been prevented by the moderating counsels of the loyal lords, who still stood by him but wished, with Langton, to see their fellow barons, and all men, enjoy their just rights. The whole weight of that sober influence was now thrown into the scales to achieve peace and a fair settlement. The earls of Pembroke, Chester, de Ferrers, Surrey and Arundel commanded between them several hundred knights, the Welsh Marches and the western Midlands, as well as part of the home counties. There was nothing to do but to take their loyally proffered advice and make terms.

That John did so with his tongue in his cheek is certain. He was in secret correspondence with Rome, attempting, and not unsuccessfully, to present, not only the rebel barons as traitors to Church and king, but Langton as their dupe and abettor. He was trying too to gather mercenaries in Europe. Yet during the second week in June he sent William the marshal to London to tell the eastern and northern lords that, "for the sake of the welfare and honour of the realm, he would freely concede to them the laws and liberties for which they asked." It was what the archbishop had been labouring for ever since his return to England two years before.

On June 15th, the barons, among them the mayor of London, met the king in a meadow beside the Thames called Runnymede. For five days their pavilions remained pitched by the river. With John were the archbishops of Canterbury and Dublin and the papal legate, seven other bishops, the loyal magnates of the Council, his brother, William of Salisbury, and his chamberlain, Hubert de Burgh. The Charter to which at their advice he set his seal was ostensibly a restatement of ancient law and custom. It began by guaranteeing the liberties of the Church: a reply, not only to John's confiscation of its revenues, but to his father's Constitutions of Clarendon of half a century before. It promised that the king should not without "general counsel," that is without the consent of the great council, demand scutage or aid from his tenants-in-chief other than the three regular aids long recognised by feudal custom; that the heirs of earls and barons should be admitted to their inheritances on payment of the customary reliefs; that the estates of heirs-in-ward should not be wasted during their infancy nor widows robbed of their dowries or forced against their will to marry royal nominees. It laid down that no free man should be imprisoned or dispossessed save by process of law and the just judgments of his equals[16]; that he should not be taxed or fined unreasonably or to his ruin; that his means of livelihood, including the merchant's stock, the craftsman's tools and the peasant's wainage, should be free from amercement; that London and the chartered boroughs should enjoy their ancient liberties; that merchants should come and go safely in time of war; and that the foreign mercenaries should be dismissed. It provided for the regular administration of the judicial system; ordered that the common pleas should be held at Westminster and not follow a perambulating court; that none should be made justices, bailiffs or constables who did not know the law of the land; that sheriffs should not sit in judgment in their own shires; that two justices with four knights-of-the-shire should hold assizes in every county every quarter; that royal writs should not be sold at exorbitant prices or withheld from those entitled to them. "To none," the king was made to swear, "will we sell, to none will we deny or delay right or justice."

In all this the Charter, which consisted of more than sixty clauses, was a recital of the wrongs suffered by Englishmen under a tyrannical king. And, as men of property—and, above all, landed property—were the only subjects with legally enforceable rights, it confined itself in the main to setting out particulars of the redress granted them. It was a charter of "liberties," and to the medieval mind a liberty was a right to the enjoyment of a specific property. It was a freedom to do something with one's own without interference by the king or any other man.

Called Magna Carta because of its length, the Charter was not, therefore, a declaration of general principles, let alone of human rights. Medieval men thought of these only in connection with religion. The Charter enunciated no theories; it was nothing if not specific and practical. Yet, though its chief beneficiaries were tenants-in-chief of the Crown, it was a national as well

---

[16] "No free man shall be taken or imprisoned or disseised or exiled or in any way destroyed, nor will we go upon him . . . except by the lawful judgments of his peers or the law of the land."

as feudal document. It made no distinction between Norman and English, and guaranteed the liberties of small property-owners as well as large. Thirty-two of its sixty-one clauses dealt with the relations of the king and his subjects and not merely his tenants-in-chief. "We grant," it declared, "to all the freemen of our realm, from us and our heirs forever, all the under-mentioned liberties to have and to hold for them as our heirs from us and our heirs." And it established two precedents of immense significance for the future. One was that when an English king broke the feudal compact and gave his vassals the right—universally recognised by feudal law—to renounce their allegiance, it was not necessary to dissolve the bonds of political society and disintegrate the realm. Magna Carta was a substitute for deposition: a legal expedient to enforce customary law that left the king on the throne and the sword of civil war undrawn. Government in England, though exercised by the king, was to be rooted in justice and based on law, or it was not to be accepted as government at all. This was Langton's supreme achievement, and England's. Magna Carta was the first great political act in the history of the nation-state—itself an institution of which the English had been the pioneers.

The unity of the barons in the face of John's injustice, and their decision to act within the law, had created a new phenomenon: a corporate estate of the realm to prevent the unjust exercise of power by the realm's ruler. The taxpayers had combined to control the tax-imposer. Magna Carta was the product not of a rebellion, as it seemed at the time to the king and his more bitter opponents, but of a revolution carried out by process of law. By the provisions for summoning the great council before any new aid or scutage could be granted, it made a representative assembly of feudal tenants a preliminary to taxing those tenants. This was something wholly new. And in establishing the principle that the king must conform to the law which he administered, it created a constitutional device for compelling him to do so. In addition to provisions for regulating the summons of lords to the council—archbishops, earls, bishops and greater barons by individual writ, and lesser barons by collective summons through the sheriffs—the Charter contained a clause by which twenty-five representative barons, chosen by their Order, were to become its guardians. They were to "observe, keep and cause to be observed, with all their might" the liberties it guaranteed. Should any of them be infringed, and just redress be refused, these twenty-five lords—almost all of whom had served, or were the sons of men who had served as royal officials—were empowered to take up arms against the king to enforce the Charter. The indignant John was made to admit his subjects' right to restrain the wearer of the Crown whenever he infringed their liberties. "These barons," he had to announce on behalf of himself and his heirs, "with all the commons of the land shall distrain and annoy us by every means in their power; that is, by seizing our castles, lands and possessions, and every other mode, till the wrong shall be repaired to their satisfaction, saving our person, our queen and our children. And when it shall be repaired, they shall obey us as before."

By this device, though a clumsy and primitive one, the men who had wrung Magna Carta from the king sought to ensure its permanence. It was dictated by fear and the just belief of the barons that the moment their force was dispersed John would try to destroy both them and their settlement. Even in the hands of men less distrustful of the sovereign they were seeking to bind, it would probably have been unworkable. Its dangers were clearly foreseen by Langton who tried, though in vain, to introduce a mediating body between the king and the barons' council. "They have given me," declared the furious monarch, "twenty-five over kings!" Yet the pattern of constitutional thought thus set was to be reproduced in a thousand forms in the history of the English nation. It is still enshrined, after seven centuries, in the words of our national anthem:

> "May he defend our laws
> And ever give us cause
> To sing with heart and voice
> God save the king!"

It was a prayer that the best of those who stood by the king's shoulder at Runnymede had tried to realise.

They did not succeed. The spirit of wisdom and accommodation which for a few weeks had seemed abroad that summer did not last; the revengeful passions and fears of the king and those he had wronged were too strong. The peace which the archbishop and a handful of wise men had made between them was, in the words of the chronicler, Ralph of Coggeshall, only "a sort of peace." Though copies of the Charter were despatched to every county in England, within a few weeks it was a dead letter. For a short time John gave an appearance of trying to implement it—dismissing mercenaries and foreign sheriffs, issuing writs for the release of hostages and for inquests into evil customs, and appointing the faithful and honourable Hubert de Burgh to succeed the unpopular Peter des Roches as justiciar. Yet it was an appearance that deceived no-one who knew John personally, though, with the help of his emissaries in Rome, it fulfilled its main purpose of deceiving his overlord, the pope.[17]

Nor were the malcontent barons in London any wiser. By their arrogance, tactlessness and incompetence they proceeded to provoke the very reaction they were trying to avoid. They treated the royal surrender which more loyal men had helped them to win as a personal triumph. They sent the king arrogant and insolent messages and, though he lay sick, refused to stand in his presence. Nor would they execute the charters of loyalty by which their renewal of homage was to have been sealed. Bent on revenge and self-aggrandisement, they remained in London, kept the castles they had seized, and prepared for civil war. Feeling that all he struggled for had been in vain, Langton bitterly reproached them. But when the pope, advised by Italian clerics who did not know England, ordered him to excommunicate them as contumacious vassals, he refused on the ground that the pope had not been informed of the true facts. The great archbishop had already incurred the *curia's* displeasure by opposing the wholesale grant of English benefices to Italians and by his championship of the claims of English churchmen for compensation for their losses under the Interdict—wrongs which the papacy seemed to have forgotten now that John was its vassal. He maintained his belief in natural justice against the pope himself. But true to his unfailing rule, though he protested at what he believed to be wrong, he accepted his punishment in silence. Suspended from office by the papal legate and the Poitevin bishop of Winchester, Peter des Roches, he left England

---

[17] The latter's attitude is summarised by Sir Maurice Powicke in his exquisite miniature, *Medieval England*, 239-40. "In the eyes of the great Pope Innocent, looking from afar, England was a sort of madhouse. Here was a penitent king, who had surrendered his realm to the Holy See, had taken the Cross, and was anxious to go to the rescue of the Holy Land; and over against him was a band of reckless, irresponsible and wicked men."

to lay his case, and that of the Englishmen who had opposed his tyranny, before his master in Rome. When he found that it was not to be heard, he withdrew, broken-hearted, intending to end his days in a Carthusian cell.

His departure and the gathering of the harvest were the signal for war. At the end of August letters arrived from Rome, annulling Magna Carta as a diabolical and unauthorised agreement and releasing the king from his oaths. John was now ready to strike. The mercenaries he had been recruiting on the continent were beginning to reach England, and most of the principal fortresses were in his hands. And the great Marcher earls of Pembroke and Chester, disgusted by the excesses of the baronial leaders in London, were still true to him.

In the campaign that followed, the king was brilliantly successful. His professional army was pitted against an assembly of amateurs without plan or leader. The feudal nobility of the peaceful English shires had ceased to be men of war. Except for a valiant, though unavailing defence of Rochester castle by William d'Aubigny—lord of Belvoir—the barons did little to oppose their fate. Instead they remained, indecisive, behind the walls of London. Meanwhile the king's foreign captains, from their castle strongholds, raided their manors and burnt their farms, while John wasted the north in a terrible winter campaign.

Then the tide turned. The barons appealed to England's enemies. The young Scottish king, Alexander II—"the little sandy fox," as John called him—laid siege to the great border fortress of Norham and burnt Newcastle. Declaring John to be deposed, the rebel lords offered the throne to Louis of France—the son and heir of Philip Augustus and husband of Henry II's granddaughter, Blanche of Castile. During the winter three French contingents landed in the Thames estuary. In May Louis followed with a large force of knights. The fleet which John had confidently expected to destroy them was dispersed by a storm. Then four of his chief supporters—the earls of Salisbury, Arundel and Warren and the count of Aumale, holding between them four hundred knights' fees and thirteen castles—went over to the enemy. Faced by a union between his own vassals and the chivalry of France, commanded by the overlord of his own unpaid mercenaries, the English king dared not face a pitched battle. He withdrew to his stronghold of Corfe in the south-west, leaving eastern England in the hands of his foes.

The war that followed was conducted with a fearful ferocity. During a nightmare summer England was ravaged by two foreign armies. In his fury against his subjects John swore that he would make the halfpenny loaf cost a shilling before the year was out, and is said to have set fire each morning to the house in which he had spent the night. His marches were marked by blazing ricks and smoking, corpse-strewn villages. But though, sometimes marching forty miles in a day with his tough merce-naries, he showed at the end a genius for war worthy of his brother, Coeur de Lion, he could not contend against fate. In reality he was fighting against his own past. And the people of England, whose king he was, raised no hand to help him.

On September 2nd, he set out from Cirencester for Oxford and Reading in an attempt to relieve Windsor Castle, then besieged by the French. A fortnight later he drove at lightning speed into East Anglia. On the 16th he was at Cambridge in the heart of the enemy's country; a day later, as his foes vainly laboured after him, at Clare in Suffolk. Then, doubling on his tracks, he marched north to harry Lincolnshire and the Fens. He burnt the great abbey of Crowland and the manors of the Soke of Peterborough and the Lincolnshire harvest fields. Hav-ing reached Grimsby, he turned back, and on October 9th entered Lynn—one of the few towns in eastern England still loyal to his cause. Two days later he again set out for the north. But in attempting, with his usual impatience, to cross the Wel-land without waiting for the ebb tide, he plunged his army into disaster. Most of it, with the whole of his baggage train, in-cluding his treasure and crown—"everything in the world that he held most dear"—were swallowed up in the quicksands. Reaching Sleaford with the survivors on the 14th, he was stricken down by dysentery—brought on, according to a monkish chronicler, by a debauch of peaches, wine and fresh cider. Then he was carried, "panting and groaning," in a litter made of willows, to Newark where, on the night of October 18th/19th, 1216, he died at the age of forty-eight.

Chapter Eleven

THE STRUGGLE FOR
LIBERTIES

The friend of pity and alms-deed,
Henry the Third whilome of England king,
Who this church brake, and after, at his meed,
Again renewed into this fair building,
Now resteth here, which did so great a thing.
John Stow

"Let us not be divided from the common counsel, for . . .
if we are divided, we shall all perish."
Robert Grosseteste

Before John died he "sent word to William the marshal,
earl of Pembroke, that he placed his eldest son, Henry, in God's
keeping and his." "Beg the marshal," he whispered, "to forgive
me the wrongs I have done him. He has always served me
loyally, and he has never acted against me no matter what I
did or said to him." Then he bade his mercenary captains bear
his body across a war-riven land and lay it, not in conquered
Anjou with his father and brother, but in Worcester cathedral
beside the shrine of St. Wulfstan, last of the Anglo-Saxon saints.

At that moment the rebel lords and the French controlled
nearly all south-eastern and most of eastern England. Their ally,
the Scottish king, had been free to march during the summer
from Berwick to Kent to do homage to Louis. But though
many, including the earls of Salisbury and Warenne, had now
abandoned what seemed a lost cause, the west still stood by the
hereditary throne. The French advance remained barred by
the great midland fortresses of Lincoln, Newark, Nottingham
and Northampton, of Oxford, Wallingford and Windsor in the

Thames valley, of Devizes on the Wiltshire plain, and Corfe guarding the waters of Poole harbour. And Dover castle—"the key to England"—continued under Hubert de Burgh, the justiciar, to defy every assault.

On October 28th, after burying John at Worcester, the papal legate and William the marshal had the nine-year-old Henry crowned in the abbey church of Gloucester. "Standing before the high altar," wrote the St. Albans chronicler, "with Jocelin bishop of Bath dictating the oath, he swore in the presence of clergy and people . . . that he would give honour, peace and reverence to God and His Holy Church and its ministers all the days of his life. He swore that he would show strict justice to the people committed to him, that he would destroy evil laws and unjust customs, and would observe the good and make everyone else observe them. Then he did homage to the most holy Roman Church and to Pope Innocent for the kingdoms of England and Ireland; and he swore that so long as he held his kingdom, he would faithfully pay the thousand marks which his father had bestowed upon the Roman Church."[1] Then the two bishops crowned him with a golden bracelet of his mother's. As they stood before "the little pretty knight," the stern, warlike barons were moved to tears. The marshal, who in half a century's service had "proved himself in time of need as gold is proved in the furnace," declared he would carry him "on his shoulders, one leg here and one there, from land to land" and never give in. The oaths of fealty were repeated, the Charter reaffirmed, the crusader's cross taken, and a Holy War declared. But it was a Holy War with a difference: of Englishmen fighting, not for the Church alone but for their homes, threatened by a lawless foreign soldiery, and for their own just polity.

For the dreadful struggle of the past year had wrought a miracle. Had the dead king won, Magna Carta—the expression of that polity—would have perished, and England's future would have been shaped, like that of other western lands, by a royal bureaucracy. Had the barons, who called in a foreign army, triumphed, the Charter would have been discredited by feudal licence and anarchy. Instead, with its more extreme clauses modified, it was reissued by the young king's advisers to rally

[1] Matthew Paris, *Chronica Majora* (Rolls Series) III, 1–2, transl. M. Hennings, *England under Henry III*, 1–2.

his subjects. Blessed by the representative of the pope who had denounced it, it became an instrument for re-uniting Crown and people under the sovereignty of law.

The greatness of Langton's achievement was now apparent. Though half England had disowned her allegiance to a sovereign who ruled without law, she had repudiated neither the monarchy nor the law. She had resisted John but rallied to his son. The disturber of her peace was no more, and in his place was a little golden-haired Plantagenet boy who embodied the just laws and the good order and peace that his forbears had given her. In his veins ran the blood of the two Henrys, the Conqueror, Athelstan and Alfred. And by his side as regent, raised to his office by the unanimous acclaim of warriors as loyal as himself, was the paladin of English chivalry. "No, marshal," Earl Ranulf of Chester declared when the old man tried to decline the trust, "that cannot be. You are so good a knight, so fine a man, so feared, so loved and so wise that you are considered one of the first knights in the world. I will serve you and carry out to the best of my power all the tasks you may assign me."

It was through this inspiration and example that the nation returned to the throne. At first only a handful of churchmen and Marcher earls appeared to be defying Louis. Yet every week, as the new Government's character became clearer and the old marshal showered letters of pardon and safe-conduct on his enemies, more and more lords rallied to the royal cause. Though they bore French names and were of French descent, they did not wish to be ruled from outside the island. England's century-and-a-half of union with France, dissolved by John's loss of Normandy, was not to be renewed under the Capet princes. Its dissolution was permanent. The marshal's policy was to unite the "native born" and drive out the French. Each end served the other. When in the spring of 1217 he took the offensive and regained Marlborough, Southampton and Winchester, the king's uncle, the earl of Salisbury, and more than a hundred knights and barons returned to the fold.

The royal advance that April to Farnham and Chichester revived the threat—relinquished by John a year earlier—to the rebel communications with France. With Hubert de Burgh holding out in Dover and the marshal driving in from the west, the seamen of the Cinque Ports began to attack French shipping in the Channel. Meanwhile, on the forest borders of Sussex and Kent, a Flemish knight named William de Casingham—nick-named by his English followers Willikin of the Weald—"gathered together a thousand bowmen, lodged in the wilderness and woods with which that country abounded, and gave the French great trouble, slaying many thousands of them."

With his communications threatened and his way to the interior still barred by the royal fortresses along the limestone belt from Lincolnshire to Wiltshire, Louis made the fatal mis-take of dividing his forces. In May he sent a strong column of French knights to reduce Lincoln castle whose castellan, Dame Nicolaa de Hay, had been holding out for more than a year. It was the marshal's opportunity. Summoning the garrisons of the midland castles to join him at Newark, he surprised the besiegers in their lines on May 20th. It was the happiest day in the old man's life: he was so excited that he forgot his helmet and had to go back to fetch it before the fight. A day-long tourney up and down the narrow streets of Lincoln ended in the capture of almost every man of standing in the French and rebel army. Only one English knight was killed. The plunder was enormous. There was so much that the day was called the Fair of Lincoln.

When Louis heard the news he broke up his lines round Dover and retired to London. Three months later—on St. Barthol-omew's day—Hubert de Burgh put out from Sandwich with the Cinque Ports fleet to intercept the French reinforcements upon which Louis' last hopes of conquering England depended. The English had the weather-gage and bore down, under cover of a hail of arrows, to board the invaders. Only fifteen French ships escaped. Among the dead was their commander, a rene-gade monk and pirate, who was reputed to be a wizard![2]

Peace followed at once. The marshal showed no bitterness or wish for revenge. His one object was to get the French out of the country. Before the end of September, speeded by an indemnity for their expenses, they were gone. In October the young king re-entered London, and in December the king of the Scots came in to pay his homage. And in the following spring,

[2] The plunder was divided between the victorious seamen and the hospital of St. Bartholomew in Sandwich—a home for maimed mariners and aged men and women of the town which still exists.

Langton, exonerated by a new pope, returned to England in triumph.

That winter the Charter of Liberties was affirmed for the third time in three years. An accompanying forest-charter deforested all royal woodlands enclosed since Henry II's day, pardoned those outlawed for breaches of forest law, and gave the right to kill a beast or two to every baron and prelate passing through the forests who gave warning by horn to the verderers. Every freeman was to be at liberty to drive his swine through them, and no-one was to lose life or limb for venison.

A year later, in the spring of 1219, the marshal, who felt his end approaching, laid down his office. In words that epitomised, not only his ideal, but his country's, he addressed his young sovereign. "Sire, I pray God that if ever I have done anything displeasing to Him, He will give you the grace to be a gentleman. If it should happen that you follow the example of some evil ancestor, I pray Him not to grant you a long life." A few weeks later his body was borne from his castle at Caversham down the Thames to London to be laid in the church of the Knights Templar. "Lords," declared Cardinal Langton at the graveside, "you see what the life of the world is worth. Behold, all that remains of the best knight who ever lived. . . . We have here our mirror, you and I. Let each man say his paternoster that God may receive this Christian into His Glory and place him among His faithful vassals, as he so well deserves."

The reign of Henry III that followed was one of the longest in English history.[3] It covered the greater part of the thirteenth century. It was a period of political consolidation and of great artistic achievement. Yet from the start it was checkered by the problems and embarrassments which John's reign had created or left unresolved. Anarchy and civil war had bequeathed a heavy burden of debt. In its first autumn the young king's Government had been forced to beg the papal Curia for time in which to pay the comparatively small annual tribute due. Prices were rising, the yield of almost every tax had been reduced by the ruin wrought by war, and new sources of supply were denied by the Charter. When in 1222 the justiciar, Hubert

[3] It lasted for 56 years. Only the reigns of Victoria and George III were longer.

de Burgh, tried to enlarge the revenue, he was sternly rebuked by Archbishop Langton for restoring "evil customs." In its embarrassment the Government had to resort to every shift. It ransacked royal castles for John's silks and jewels, paid its creditors in sacks of wool and leather, and appealed to the Council for consent to a poll tax. This device, which assessed earls at three marks, barons at one, knights at a shilling and freeholders and burgesses at a penny, aroused a storm of opposition. Many taxpayers refused to pay, maintaining that the Council had no power to bind them individually.

The Government had another problem. It had inherited a legacy of anarchy. Its first problem was to bring men back to peaceful habits. The records of the courts reveal how great was the need. Humble malefactors like the Essex priest's son who robbed and murdered victims all over the county, or the multitude of poachers armed with bows and arrows who assaulted Hugh Hop-over-Humber while he was guarding Earl de Warenne's park at Cuckfield and slew his fellow park-keeper, were only imitating their betters. In 1221 William, earl of Albemarle, rebelled and seized several castles in the north and midlands, including the great fortress of Fotheringay. Even the bishop of Winchester, Peter des Roches—the king's guardian and the first man in the kingdom after the justiciar—behaved as though he was above the law and refused to pay his taxes. The foreign captains to whom John had entrusted the royal castles proved particularly hard to discipline. They and their men had been the kernel of the force which had driven the French from the country and they felt they could do as they pleased. Philip Marc's retainer who burned a neighbour's house, abducted his sister, and stole his horse, nine cows, four pigs and fifty-two chickens,[4] was the type of their lawless kind.

The worst offender of all was Falkes de Bréauté, the fiery little Norman whom John had made sheriff of Oxfordshire and five other counties and entrusted with the castles of Windsor, Oxford, Northampton, Bedford and Cambridge. His services in the war had been brilliant, but in the end the Government was forced to act against him. In 1224 he was found guilty by the justices-in-eyre of more than thirty acts of unlawful disseisin against his neighbours' lands. He retaliated by seizing one

[4] *Rot. Claus.* I. 336, cit. S. Painter, *William Marshall*, 244.

of the royal judges. This was too much, and, after the host had been called out to besiege Bedford castle, he was deprived of his offices and banished the country, while eighty of his men were hanged.

In their work of enforcing the law the king's ministers were hampered by a decision, in the year of Magna Carta, of an international Church Council held at the Lateran palace at Rome. This had decreed that the clergy should no longer take part in the practice of ascertaining legal guilt by the time-honoured ordeal of fire or water. This sign of growing reliance on human reason, which the Church, through its educational institutions, was slowly if unconsciously creating, robbed the primitive "judgment by God" of its religious sanction. It presented courts of law throughout Christendom with the problem of finding some alternative method of reaching verdicts when there was a clash of evidence. In southern lands, where there were plenty of clerks trained by the law-schools of Ravenna and Bologna in the re-discovered principles of classical jurisprudence, resort was had to the Roman rules of evidence. In England, impoverished by civil war and far removed from the fount of classical learning, a simpler and more native substitute was found. A few months before the marshal died the Council issued to itinerant justices a direction that, sooner than keep persons charged with felonies indefinitely in jail, they should use their discretion.[5] They were to experiment and make use of their experience in ascertaining and estimating local opinion. Just as Henry II's judges had accepted, as proof of a man's right to his lands, a sworn oath from an assize or jury of his neighbours, so his grandson's judges met the Lateran Council's repudiation of trial-by-God by summoning similar, though humbler, juries to resolve the guilt of those accused of felony. Juries of presentment, drawn partly from the knightly class and partly from representatives of the villages, were already presenting suspected criminals to the king's justices. The latter now adopted the idea of using the small freeholders or sokemen assembled by the sheriffs for this purpose to resolve, with a simple yes or no, whether those presented were actually guilty

[5] T. F. T. Plucknett, *Concise History of the Common Law*, 112.

of the crimes of which they had been accused. They took counsel, as the saying was, of the neighbourhood.[6]

Thus for the supposed verdict of God through the elements was gradually substituted the conception—a curiously English one—of a verdict through the inspiration of a dozen decent, honest freemen, equipped with local knowledge and sworn under a solemn religious oath to speak the truth in open court. *Vox populi*—not of an anonymous mob, but of a group of "worthy and lawful" men who knew their neighbourhood—was to be accepted as the voice of God. The accused could take his choice of submitting to such a verdict, of putting himself, as it was called, upon the country, or of remaining in gaol. It was a rough and ready way of getting at the truth, but one whose roots lay deep in English history. And in the course of their everyday practice—though it was a process that took centuries to complete—the trained judges of the Crown contrived methods of making evidence available to such petty juries that eventually proved more realistic than all the elaborate rules of Roman Law. The judges expounded and interpreted the Law, and the jurymen, who began their long career as corporate witnesses to the opinion of the locality, became in the end judges of fact and assessors of evidence.

[6] Two early examples of how this worked, translated from the Chancery Inquisitions, are given by Margaret Hennings in her invaluable little book, *England under Henry III*. "I have diligently made an inquisition," the sheriff of Derby reported, "into the death of Robert son of Henry de Bretteby . . . by the oath of good and legal men . . . . who say on their oath that Henry son of William de Bretteby killed his son Robert by misfortune and not by felony, and the misfortune was as follows. Henry was ploughing in the field of Bretteby on Friday the morrow of St. Mary Magdalene, and his son Robert was driving the plough. Henry whirled the staff of the plough violently round to frighten the oxen and horses. The iron of the staff being slightly fastened came off and struck Robert on the back of the head, so that he died of that wound, as the jury believes, on the Tuesday following. They say also that they know for a truth that Henry would rather have killed himself than his son because he had no other." A similar inquisition of twenty years later by a Northumberland jury into the death of a servant of Hugh Galun of Worpath found that "Margery, who was in the service of Hugh at Thyrwhyt, had been baking oat-cake on a griddle; and there came a calf of Hugh's which had a habit of stealing and eating oat-cake, and tried to get some. Hugh, who was in the house, took up some tongs and threw them at the calf, which was between him and Margery. The tongs hit the calf on the back, and then went over its back and struck and wounded Margery on the head. She survived ten days, received the sacraments and then died. There was no quarrel between Hugh and Margery, nor did he intend to hit anyone but the calf. Hugh killed Margery by the greatest misadventure, and not feloniously nor of malice aforethought." Hennings, 265–6.

Co-operation between central officials, paid and trained for their specialist functions, and unpaid amateurs, representing the interests, property and good sense of the local community, was the method by which England after the civil war repaired the broken thread of her social life and resumed her organic growth. The English ideal was a working partnership between Crown and people: between, that is, the hall of justice at Westminster and the local courts, officers and jurymen of the shire, hundred and vill and the delegated jurisdictions and franchises of the feudal landowners. These last remained as numerous as ever, but now derived their strength, not, as in many other parts of Europe, from their separateness but from their participation in the royal machinery of government. On that participation the State depended. The sword and rod of equity with which the king did justice were the earls and barons of the realm, the sheriffs and knights of the shire, the constables of the hundred and vill. And they in their turn depended on the royal authority for the peace, order and growing prosperity of their society.

The connecting link between throne and neighbourhood was the law—the king's or Common Law, as it was called; the law, that is, of the whole community. During the two long reigns which succeeded the troubled era of John the legal institutions Henry II had given England grew steadily. It was an age of fertile judicial invention, when a little group of royal justices— sitting on the Bench of Common Pleas at Westminster, travelling the country on eyre, or attending the sovereign's person in the King's Court—were devising and offering the subject an ever-growing number of writs, and building up by their judgments a body of law that made England the justest land in Europe. Among them were some very great men—Martin Pattishall, the justice who had condemned the terrible Faulkes de Bréauté and whose tireless industry on assize wore out all his fellow judges, William Raleigh of Devonshire who became bishop of Norwich and Winchester, and his still more famous pupil, Henry de Bracton—another west-country man who held the rectorships of Coombe-in-Teignhead and Bideford, and who lies buried in Exeter cathedral of which he was chancellor. His text-book on litigation, *The Laws and Customs of England*, citing more than five hundred decisions collected from the plea rolls of the

King's Court, was the most germinating legal work of the century.

Though case-law was not yet binding on the courts, it was fast becoming so, for the professional judges were the sole interpreters of the "custom of the king's court" which became through them the common law of England. Its strength lay in its popularity with all classes of free Englishmen. It was in the thirteenth century that the words judgment and plea, inquest, assize and heir, acquit and fine, first became part of English speech. Even the poorest freeman felt that he could get justice from the royal courts and at a cheaper rate than that offered under any other system of law.[7] For it was a point of honour with the king's judges that, while the sale of writs formed an important source of revenue, a poor litigant should always obtain an essential writ for nothing.

Behind the courts was the "community of the realm." It consisted, not only of barons and prelates, but of the lesser landowners of the shire, of the petty freeholders of the villages and the burgesses of the free towns. The first, increasingly styled knights of the shire, performed a multitude of duties. They served as sheriffs, escheators and coroners, and as justices on special commissions of gaol-delivery to relieve the overworked royal judges; they sat in judgment in the shire court at its monthly meetings in the county-town, and attended the two great annual assemblies when the lords, knights and freeholders of the shire gathered to meet the justices on eyre. They took the leading part in the fortnightly meetings of the hundred or wapentake courts—held, "within the four benches," in some time-hallowed spot in the open air, like Scutchamore Knob on the Berkshire downs or the hollow still visible on the west side of the Fosse Way near its crossing with the Grantham-Nottingham highway.[8] They served on the committees which scrutinized the presentments of the hundreds and villages, and carried

---

[7] "Of his own free will," our greatest legal historian has written, "the small freeholder passed by his lord's court and the county court on his way to the great hall. He could there obtain a stronger and better commodity than any that was to be had elsewhere, a justice which, as men reckoned in those days, was swift and masterful." Pollock and Maitland, *History of English Law* I, 203.

[8] "A certain pit on the top of the hill on the contrary side of the Fosse Way, near the most westerly corner of Bingham lordship, called Moot House Pit, where the Hundred Court is or ought to be still kept." R. Thoroton, *History of Nottinghamshire*, cit. Lady Stenton, *English Society in the Early Middle Ages*, 133.

the record of the shire court to Westminster when summoned there by the king's judges. They acted as jurymen on the grand assize, assessed, as elected representatives of their fellow knights-of-the-shire, the taxes due from each hundred, and investigated and reported on local abuses and grievances. They were constantly being called on for their views in questions put to them on oath by the king's judges and council.[9] So were the humbler freeholders and sokemen who also, as elected representatives of their neighbours, assessed the village taxes. Even outside the privileged ranks of "free men," the community of the unfree was represented by the six *villani* or villein-farmers who presented, with the parish priest and reeve, the local malefactors and answered for the village's offences and omissions before the terrible, all-enquiring eyre.

From all this sprang a growing sense of unity and nationhood. French and English place-names were becoming blended on the map; English place and Norman owner grown English: Norton Fitzwarren, Pillerton Hersey, Sturminster Marshal, Berry Pomeroy. And the marriage of Church and State, spiritual and secular, was consummated, too, in this land where everything ultimately merged and became part of something else; Abbots Bromley and Temple Guiting, Toller Monachorum and Salford Priors, White Ladies Aston and Whitchurch Canonicorum. The great bishop, Richard le Poore, who built Salisbury cathedral, left his heart to be buried in the little Dorset village of Tarrant Crawford. The pride of Englishry—of being native-born, though one's name and blood were wholly French—had become a dominant force. When William Longespée or Longsword, earl of Salisbury—bastard son of the great Angevin, Henry II—wanted to blacken Faulkes de Bréauté, he said that he had called "all the native-born men of England traitors, saying also that all we native-born men of England longed for and desired was war." No more prejudiced Englishman or greater contemner

[9] To a remarkable degree the machinery of State depended on the oaths of ordinary Englishmen: of those "good and lawful" men to whom judges and sheriffs constantly turned for the execution of royal commands. "Every man," ran the writ commanding the tax of one-fifteenth on moveables in 1225, "shall take an oath as to the number, quantity and value of his own moveables and likewise of his two nearest neighbours. And if by chance there shall have arisen dissension on this head . . . the knights themselves by the oaths of twelve good and lawful neighbouring men . . . shall inquire the truth and shall take the fifteenth according to that truth." Stubbs, *Select Charters*, 352, cit. M. Hennings, 175.

of foreigners ever existed than the monkish chronicler who bore
the name of the French capital and wrote the chronicle of St.
Albans abbey in the middle of Henry III's reign. His violently
partisan portrait of his sovereign is only surpassed in ridicule
by Macaulay's of James II—an English ruler who also loved
foreigners and foreign priests. Matthew Paris' attitude towards
Henry's alien favourites and—devout monk though he was—
towards papal emissaries who tampered with his country's institutions, set the tone of English thought and history for generations; it is hardly an exaggeration to say that it was still being
echoed by the great Whig historians six centuries later.[10]

It was this that made things so difficult for Henry when he
grew up. The young king took pride in being an Englishman.
He had been born in Winchester, the old English capital, and,
unlike his predecessors, spent almost his entire life in England
—a thing that no English monarch had done for more than two
centuries. His patron saint and examplar was the last of the
Anglo-Saxon kings, Edward the Confessor—a man whom in
many respects he resembled. It was in the Confessor's name
that he christened his eldest son and heir, and it was to him
that he dedicated his greatest building. But he had an affec-
tionate and clinging nature—what his critic, Matthew Paris,
called "a waxen pliability"—and was easily swayed by those he
loved, particularly the relations of his Poitevin mother among
whom he grew up, and, later, by his beautiful Provençal wife.
For the first few years after he came of age in 1227—for Stephen Langton died soon after—the kingdom was governed by
the bluff justiciar, Hubert de Burgh. But when in 1232 de
Burgh's many enemies—for he was a high-handed, tactless man
—combined against him, Henry turned to his father's old favourite, Peter des Roches, the Poitevin bishop of Winchester, who
had been his early guardian. The great barons, who grumbled
at the low-born de Burgh, found that they had exchanged a
King Log for a King Stork. Within a few months Henry's foreign favourites had absorbed most of the great offices of England. One of them, Peter des Rivaux—a nephew of the bishop
of Winchester and a most able man—became treasurer, keeper
of the wardrobe and privy seal, keeper of the royal forests and
ports, and at one time sheriff of twenty-one counties. "Little by

[10] See Professor V. H. Galbraith's brilliant paper on "Roger Wendover and
Matthew Paris."

little," wrote the disgusted Matthew Paris, "the king invited such legions of Poitevins that they almost filled the whole of England, and wherever he went he was surrounded by hosts of them. Nor could anything be done in the realm except what the bishops and the crowd of Poitevins chose."

Yet it was not merely that Henry liked to be surrounded by his French kinsfolk. As was natural in a young man whose father had been forcibly constrained by his own barons, he wanted to be master in his own house. Though he had pledged himself to abide by the Charter and meant within limits to do so, he conceived kingship as something to be exercised, not in consultation with the "lawful men" of the realm, but by himself alone. Holding his throne as a fief from the papal *curia,* which had authorised him, when he came of age, to assume the royal power, he had a particularly exalted view of a king's sacred function. For his more politically-minded subjects' notion of a community of the realm he had nothing but an impatient contempt. And if he was prevented by his assent to Magna Carta from levying the older kinds of feudal taxation except with the consent of his chief vassals, he could pursue his father's device of employing the instruments of his private household—the Wardrobe and Privy Seal—to enlarge his revenue and power in other ways. It was to do so, and not merely to exalt a deserving favourite, that he and the bishop of Winchester concentrated in 1232 so many key offices in the hands of that able and experienced household official, Peter des Rivaux. There was more method in their design than the foreigner-hating Matthew Paris supposed.

For under the industrious des Rivaux the Wardrobe—the office that administered the king's personal expenditure—had become a major department of state with an elaborate and highly efficient machinery. Henry's object was to subordinate to it the entire financial system of the kingdom, including the treasury, the exchequer and the fiscal management of the shires. By doing so he hoped to by-pass, as his father had done, the older executive offices and the great baronial families who had acquired a prescriptive right to them. After Hubert de Burgh's fall the post of chief justiciar was not even filled.[11]

[11] It was revived under pressure, a generation later, but as a judicial rather than a political office: that of Lord Chief Justiciar or Justice.

Yet the very efficiency with which des Rivaux and his clerks sought to enlarge the revenue by a strict inquisition into royal rights provoked a violent reaction against the authority of the Wardrobe and the clever, industrious foreigners who controlled it. Many of their enquiries, especially into the corrupt and extortionate practices of sheriffs, were badly needed and helped to check, in the common interest of Crown and nation, the private peculation and encroachment which were the bane of all medieval government. Like the ceaseless inquisitions of the judges of the *curia regis* and exchequer into the usurpations and evasions of franchise and property owners, they effected a permanent improvement in the country's administration. And by taking a far closer account of the income of the shires—hitherto farmed by profit-seeking sheriffs for a fixed annual sum—they turned the sheriffs from speculating contractors into salaried revenue-collectors.

But what struck men at the time was that these reforms were carried out without the consent of "the natural men of the realm," the hereditary or official representatives of the nation's chief taxpaying classes or "estates." And, being effected by agents who were regarded as foreigners and upstarts, they led, not only to an improvement in public administration, but to a passionate demand that such administration should be controlled by those who had a right to represent the community. The chief spokesman of that demand, and of the movement against "the foreign people about the court," was the son of the old marshal—Richard Marshal, earl of Pembroke and Leinster, and hereditary marshal of England. When the Poitevin ministers, who were bringing back foreign mercenaries into the royal castles, seized the manors of two of his chief adherents, he upheld their claim that, by breaking the feudal compact and the law, the king had forfeited his right to their allegiance. In the summer of 1233 he and his fellow barons refused a royal summons to Oxford and pledged themselves to act together until Henry should dismiss his foreign ministers and rule by the counsel and aid of "the national and noble-born men of England." When the king and his foreign advisers retaliated by outlawing him and laying siege to his castles, he insisted on his right to be tried by his peers and took up arms in self-defence. The principle for which the Charter had been fought was again at stake; government in England had to be government by law or it was not to be regarded as government at all.

As the marshal was the better soldier, and was supported by the most experienced fighters in the country, including his fellow Marchers and the great north Welsh prince, Llywelyn ap Iorworth—a veteran of Magna Carta days—the young king's appeal to the sword was ineffective. True to his father's principles, Richard scrupulously avoided any personal conflict with his sovereign, but made short work of his half-hearted supporters. By the beginning of 1234 he had driven the royal forces ignominiously from Wales and captured Shrewsbury.

The king was furious. The ingenious plans of his bureaucrats for enlarging his revenues and power had been frustrated by the brute force of conservative English barons who insisted that he could not even choose his own advisers. And the barons were almost equally embarrassed, for, though they had taken up arms to prevent the royal authority from being delegated to outsiders, they had no wish to endanger either it or the throne. They were not seeking power for themselves, but merely fighting to prevent it from being monopolised by strangers and to preserve their rights. The dilemma was only resolved by the intervention of the leaders of the English Church who passionately urged on the king his sacred duty to govern in accordance with the Charter and the counsel of his natural advisers. At their head was the archbishop-elect of Canterbury, Edmund Rich of Abingdon, the most saintly Englishman of the day. His eloquence, his fame as a theologian—he had been one of the first to lecture on Aristotle in the new schools at Oxford—and his life of fierce austerity towards himself and selfless tenderness towards everyone else,[12] had given him immense authority. His plea, in the tradition of Stephen Langton, for justice between sovereign and subject and for an investigation into the acts of irresponsible ministers, coming at the moment of the royal defeat, induced in the young king a fit of highly emotional penitence. Returning in the spring of 1234 from a pilgrimage to his favourite shrines of Walsingham, Ramsey and Peterborough, he suddenly dismissed his foreign advisers, including Peter des Rivaux, and ordered the bishop of Winchester "to turn his at-

---

[12] He was canonised within eight years of his death. Among the legends about him was the story of his boyhood's meeting with Christ, in the likeness of a child, among the Oxford water meadows. He is said to have worn a sack pressed to his skin by an iron plate, and to have refused the fees of his needy Oxford scholars. His name is commemorated in St. Edmund's Hall in his old university.

tention to the care of souls and meddle no more with royal affairs." In the midst of this *volte-face* news arrived from Ireland that the marshal, who had been visiting his lands there, had been lured into a trap by his enemies and, on the strength of orders sent by the Poitevin ministers under royal seal, treacherously done to death. Though Henry denied all knowledge of the order, which was laid at the door of his discredited counsellors, his claim to govern England without the counsel of its native nobility had been dramatically and successfully challenged. And Magna Carta had been sealed by a martyr's blood.

Henry's susceptibility to foreign influences arose largely from the very piety that made him yield so suddenly to the archbishop's prayers. He was the most devout of men. Every day he heard three masses, and, when the officiating priest raised the sacred bread of the sacrament, he used to seize his hand and kiss it.[13] The early thirteenth century was an age of intense religious faith, and Henry—in many ways an ordinary man— was a child of his time, and a very simple one at that. He had grown up when men's minds were obsessed with the great crusades against the infidels without and the Waldensian and Albigensian heretics within, and loyalty to the Church, and its head, was second nature to him. It was from the papal legate that he had received his throne.

Among those who had tried to bring about a reconciliation between the king and his baronage was an Italian cleric named Agnellus, leader in England of a new international Order called Minorites or Franciscans. They had come into existence to combat the heresies which had swept like a plague across southern Europe at the close of the twelfth century. These had proved most dangerous wherever increase in wealth caused by the Crusades and maritime commerce with the East had filled court, castle and monastery with luxurious and ostentatious ways of living and new and disturbing ideas. It was the contrast between such wealth and pomp and the selflessness ordained by Christ that caused simple men, who were beginning to think for themselves, to condemn the excessive endowments of monks

---

[13] Even his saintly cousin, King Louis of France, thought this too much, saying, "that he himself was not always free to hear mass but rather to hear sermons. The king answered him graciously, but said that at any time he would rather see his friend than hear one speak of him, however well he spoke." Rishanger, *Chronica* 74, cit. Hennings, 146.

and prelates. The Waldensians or "poor men of Lyons," founded at the time of Becket's death by an enthusiastic merchant of that city, had started by demanding that Christian ministers should renounce all worldly goods, and had gone on to the heretical thesis that an honest layman was as competent to expound Holy Writ as a priest. The "Cathari" or Albigensians, taking their name from the Provençal city of Albi, had maintained in their puritan zeal that all matter was evil, including man's body. In doing so they denied one of the fundamental tenets of the Church: that God had really become man in the person of Jesus and that Christ's body had risen from the dead.

Angered by these attacks on its wealth and dogma, the Church, under the great pope Innocent III, had preached a merciless crusade against heresy and ordered the temporal arm, in the person of Philip Augustus of France, to extirpate it from Provence with fire and sword—an invitation to which that sovereign and his warlike nobles had eagerly responded, seizing the chance to bring the rich lands of the south under their dominion. But though the Provençals were disciplined by a long and ferocious war—waged while Magna Carta was being fought for in England—massacre, torture and the dungeon could never be the final answer to criticism of the Church and its ministers. Such an answer could only come from within the Church itself: from those who realised that the heresies that threatened Christendom's unity sprang from the disillusion caused by clerical pride, sloth and luxury and could only be combated by Christian ministers free from these failings.

Of such was the Castilian ascetic, Dominic—an Augustinian canon who, travelling from Spain to Rome at the beginning of the century, was so struck by the universal heresy of the Provençal people that he settled in their midst to preach God's word and win them back to orthodoxy by simple and austere living. A few years later a still more remarkable man, a rich Italian clothier's son named Francis of Assisi, abandoned a life of wealth and gaiety to minister to the lepers and paupers of the growing trading-towns of northern Italy. Both these great reformers founded international Orders which were recognised by the Church and whose members, called brothers or friars,[14] renounced all worldly wealth and devoted themselves to a life

---

[14] After the French *frères* and the Latin *fratres*.

of service. The preaching friars or Dominicans were concerned mainly with the teaching of orthodox dogma and of the dialectical processes by which it was propagated; the Franciscans or Minorites—so named because they were the *minores* or "lesser brethren" and ministered to the lesser or lower classes. The one concentrated on winning men's minds, the other their hearts. Both, insisting on vows of poverty and chastity, were open to laymen as well as clerics, and both abjured the static, conventual life of the older monastic Orders. They made the world their parish, and the street and market-place their cloister. And both in their earlier years shunned the possession of all property and land. To the Franciscans in particular poverty seemed a supreme good: "our lady Poverty," their founder called it.

The two Orders, meeting a universal need, spread rapidly, founding missions in every European land. The black-robed Dominicans first came to England in 1221 under the patronage of Peter des Roches. They were welcomed at Canterbury by Stephen Langton himself, and at once established branches in London and Oxford. But it was the Franciscans who aroused the enthusiasm of the English. In 1224 a band of nine, including three Englishmen, landed at Dover under brother Agnellus of Pisa. Penniless, barefoot and bare-headed, in coarse grey gowns with girdles of rope, they made their way to Canterbury, and thence to London and Oxford, begging their bread along the highway and preaching to the poor. Their diocese was the lazar-house door, the stews, the stinking hovels along the stagnant ditches outside the town walls; their pulpit the dung-hill and garbage-pit, the pot-house and brothel. They made their habitations in the strongholds of poverty, vice and misery; their names—the Greyfriars in Stinking Lane, Sheer Hog and Scalding Lane—testify to the character of their work. Here they built their huts of mud and sticks, and "when it was time to drink at collation, they put a little pot on the fire with dregs of ale, and dipped a cup into the pot and drank in turn, each speaking some word of edification."

The all-embracing charity, cheerfulness and courtesy[15]—virtues prescribed by their founder—and the heroic example of these evangelists made a profound impression on Englishmen. They revived memories of Aidan and the Celtic saints. Despite

[15] "Courtesy is one of the qualities of God himself, ... and courtesy is the sister of charity and keepeth love alive." *Rule of St. Francis.*

the haunts of wretchedness they chose, they were so merry that they were known as God's jesters. They seemed to take a special joy in saving outcasts and sinners. They washed the feet of the unclean and kissed their sores. To the rich monks of the conventual houses, they seemed only vulgar sensationalists and interlopers, "utterly shameless and forgetful of their profession and Order." To the neglected masses of the city slums, they seemed like heavenly messengers. They were received with an enthusiasm which took the Christian world by surprise. Their sermons, racy, eloquent, charged with fervent emotion and illustrated by lively, colloquial tales that the simplest could understand, went straight to the hearts of uneducated men and women whose knowledge of the Christian story had been hitherto derived from services conducted in a tongue intelligible only to the learned. They introduced into the vernacular English speech words of faith like mercy, pity, patience, comfort, conscience and salvation. "With what devotion and humility," wrote the great theologian, Grosseteste, "the people run to hear from them the word of life. They illuminate all our land with the brilliant light of their preaching and teaching. Their most holy lives vehemently excite to contempt of the world and voluntary poverty, ... to maintaining humility even in dignity and power, to showing all obedience to prelates and the Head of the Church, to patience in tribulation, to abstinence in the midst of plenty."

The coming of the friars gave an immense stimulus to works of charity. Till now these had tended to be somewhat spasmodic, like the annual distribution of flour—still made after eight centuries—to the Hampshire villagers of Tichborne.[16] But London's two greatest hospitals—St. Bartholomew's founded by Rufus's courtier, Rahere, in the Smithfield marshes, and the even older St. Thomas' in Southwark for sick and needy travellers—had been established by Augustinian canons in the twelfth century. Such spitals were very small: St. Thomas's, rebuilt after the fire of 1207, had rush beds for forty patients, and a staff of four canons, three nursing sisters and a warden.

About a sixth of the hospitals in the country were for lepers, for those, that is, with incurable scabrous diseases which were generically classed with that terrible scourge. King John had a

---

16 A similar survival from the twelfth century is the distribution on Easter Monday of cake, bread and cheese to the villagers of Biddenden, Kent.

tender spot for lepers—perhaps because his excesses made him fear the disease—and bestowed several donations on the poor, shunned creatures, including permission to those in Shrewsbury to help themselves from the sacks of corn exposed for sale in the market-place. The Franciscans, following the example of their founder, made a cult of lazar houses, often establishing their friaries beside them and making their novices undergo a period of training in them. By reminding men that Christ was poor and lived among the poor, they started to deflect Christian alms and legacies from the over-endowed monasteries to institutions that relieved want, sickness and suffering. They were enthusiastic practitioners of medicine—a science recently revived by contact with the Moorish and Jewish scholars of southern Spain[17]—and administered it free to the poor among whom they worked. It was a ministration desperately needed, for the slums of medieval cities, situated mostly by the swampy side of streams outside the walls, were dreadful haunts of disease and wretchedness.

Above all the friars, both Dominicans and Franciscans, were teachers, and played a leading part in the universities which had grown during the previous century out of the cathedral schools. Their eloquence made them the natural leaders of the young students, as penniless and ragged as themselves, who, living in crowded garrets and taverns, flocked to the lectures of the learned doctors of theology, law and grammar in their hired rooms or schools and endeavoured to earn from the chancellor or bishop's representative the Church's licence to teach. These turbulent communities, for all their poverty, were intensely alive—gay, ardent and speculative. Though little accounted by the rich and powerful, it was with them, rather than with the sedentary and devotional monks of the Benedictine and Cistercian houses, that the future of Christendom and European learning lay. The friars, in touch with common humanity, had the perception to see this and, through their work in the universities, to mould that future. The famous Dominican house in the Jacobin convent at Paris was for the next half century the inspiration of Europe's greatest university. It gave her the two most eminent schoolmen of the age—Albert the Great, the Swabian Regent Master who made Aristotle, rediscovered by

[17] Arabic symbols are still used today by doctors for prescriptions.

Arab commentators, the basis of western scholasticism; and Thomas of Aquinas, "the big dumb ox of Sicily" who, seeing natural law as "the mind and will of God," sought to harmonise Christian faith with reason. His vision of the universe was one in which everything was ordered and balanced by the will of God; "they are called wise," he wrote, "who put things in their right order." His elaborate exposition, through the argumentative method of question and answer, antetype and antithesis, sought to carry men's minds, by a series of stages, to the comprehension of Heaven itself, just as the Gothic cathedral-builders, with their balanced trust and counter-thrust of soaring buttress and arch, sought to reach the sky. In the disputations in which they maintained their theses against all comers, these Dominican schoolmen tried to prove God by logic—a heroic feat of mind that in the end proved almost as dangerous to faith as to intellectual freedom.

In no land in Europe was the impact of the friars' teaching greater than in England. It gave a new and European importance to the schools of Oxford—founded in a small stone building in the churchyard of St. Mary's after Henry II, during his dispute with Becket, had recalled the English scholars from Paris. Both Dominicans and Franciscans established missions there, and at the East Anglian university which had arisen at Cambridge, on the site of a "little waste chester," following a murderous affray in 1208 between town and gown at Oxford. For a time, too, there were nascent universities at Stamford, Northampton and Reading. The exposure to vice and possible heresy of the indisciplined youths who herded together in such places was a challenge to the mendicant friars. The school which the Franciscans built in their friary at Oxford formed the model for the university's earliest halls and colleges. William of Durham's charitable foundation for theological students that grew into University College, Sir John de Balliol's slightly later one that became Balliol, and Merton, founded between 1264 and 1274 by one of Henry III's chancellors "for the perpetual sustenance of twenty scholars living in the schools," were all inspired by the discipline and communal industry of the friars' house. The lectures and disputations held there drew such crowds that the secular masters were left, we are told, at their desks "like sparrows alone upon the housetops."

One of the earliest triumphs of the Franciscans was to persuade the Master of the Oxford Schools, the great Robert Grosseteste, to become their Lector. Until his election in 1235 as bishop of Lincoln—the diocese in which the university lay— he was the inspirer of a group of young Franciscan scholars, whose experimental approach to the problems of the universe constituted the first serious Christian challenge to the authoritarian cosmology of the Middle Ages. Grosseteste, a Suffolk farmer's son, was a mathematician and physicist, as well as a theologian and grammarian, and was famous for experiments with lenses. His methods, unlike those of most medieval philosophers, were experimental and inductive. The greatest of his pupils, Roger Bacon—"the marvellous doctor"—a Franciscan from Ilchester in Somerset, carried his practice even further, making an investigation of natural science that brought him at times into conflict with the ecclesiastical authorities for unorthodoxy and even suspected heresy. He was a man consumed with wonder at the mechanism of the universe. His mind, reinforced by his study of Arabic scientific writers, was for ever voyaging into the unknown, dreaming of boats without oars, self-propelled carts, and bridges which hung suspended over space. His *Opus Majus*, written and secretly published at the request of the pope, is the greatest scientific work of the thirteenth century and possibly of the entire Middle Ages.

Yet it was neither the philosopher's cell nor the writer's desk that afforded the supreme expression of medieval faith. It came from the "engineers" or "architects" in monastic cloister and cathedral chapter who sketched on deal boards the designs of the huge edifices that arose at abbot's or bishop's command; from the master-masons, with their squares and compasses, who carried out their conceptions with teams of travelling craftsmen—hewers trimming the stone with axes and dressing it with chisels; setters laying the walls and making mortar-matrixes; turners with stone-lathes shaping columns and shafts; wrights and joiners, carvers and sculptors, slaters, smiths, plumbers and glaziers, fashioning the timber supports from the heart of the tree, graving statues, making ironwork fittings for doors, raising with primitive cranes and pulley-wheels the baskets of stone and rolls of lead to the soaring walls and roofs, filling the windows with intricately patterned and brilliantly coloured glass. The thirteenth century was above everything else an age of church-building. During it and the second half of the previous century nearly every great cathedral and abbey in the French-speaking lands on either side of the Channel was partly rebuilt or enlarged in the style which later became known as Gothic. The plain rounded vaulting, small windows and heavy columns of the Romanesque or Norman past were superseded by delicately pointed arches, clusters of slender pillars, and tiers of long lancet-windows that flooded the vast buildings with light —the crying need of the cloudy north—and lit the jewelled shrines, painted walls and stained glass within in radiant hues. The transformation was the result, partly of revolutionary advances in engineering technique, and partly of new ideas introduced into northern Europe from the Saracen and Byzantine East. The overwhelming impression was one of height, light and energy. With their soaring pinnacles and flying buttresses —built to take the outward thrust of the immense arches and fenestrated walls—these great new buildings, glittering in white stone, looked from a distance like giants on the march, resplendent with spears and streaming banners.

Inside they were filled with delicate carving, with sculptured shrines, tombs and statues, and with colour and ornamentation that humanised their immense size and made them resemble gigantic jewelled boxes. In England this tendency to fine internal decoration was ultimately carried farther than in almost any other land. Forests of airy shafts of Purbeck marble, exquisitely moulded trefoil arches, flowing leaves and flowers naturalistically carved in stone on capital and arch, elaborate and deeply carved roof-bosses were distinguishing marks of the English school. So were the compound piers that the Anglian masons, stubbornly persisting in an ancient native tradition, evolved to carry the intricate ribbed vaulting—itself partly an English invention[18]—and which reached perfection in the nave of Wells, where dynamics and pure poetry blend and become indistinguishable. So, too, as the century developed, were the vast traceried windows and the immense timber trusses and posts of native oak—the hardest in Europe—which, bearing the laminated stone roofs, gave a sense of illimitable height and mystery to the worshippers in choir and aisle below.

[18] First introduced on a major scale in the rebuilding of Durham, completed in 1133, and adopted and perfected by the great French architects of the twelfth century.

The first English essays in Gothic were made towards the end of the twelfth century. They were stimulated, as in France —the home *par excellence* of early Gothic—by the crusades and the influence of the pointed Armenian and Saracen arches: an interesting example can be seen in the ruins of Furness abbey in Lancashire. But their starting-point was the fire which, four years after Becket's death, destroyed the choir of Christ's Church, Canterbury, England's metropolitan church. Rebuilding was begun in 1175 under a French mason, William of Sens, who, though starting in the familiar Norman idiom, imported many revolutionary features from the great new cathedrals of northern France. Three years later, following his fall from a scaffold, the work was taken over by "William the Englishman," a man small in body but "in all kinds of workmanship most acute and honest." It was possibly he who adopted the use of Purbeck marble, brought by sea from the cliff quarries of Dorset, and he who made the beautiful crypt of the Trinity chapel to house St. Thomas' bones.

Canterbury illustrates the transitional stage from Norman to Gothic. The first example in both England and Europe of pure Gothic, without any Romanesque intermixture whatever, was the choir of Lincoln cathedral, raised by Geoffrey de Noiers for the saintly Burgundian, Hugh of Avalon, during Coeur de Lion's reign. The good bishop, who once refused to pay an unjust tax and bearded the furious king in his own camp, carried, we are told, the hods of stone and building-lime with his own hands. With its vaulting like some great bird's wings, its trefoil arches, carved foliage and lancet-shaped windows, St. Hugh's choir was the signal for an outburst of English Gothic. It was closely followed by the galilees or porches at Durham and Ely—the former a chapel built to enable women to hear the services without breaking the monastic rule—the retrochoir and lay chapel at Winchester, the choirs of Wells, Rochester, Lichfield, Worcester, Fountains, Southwell and the Temple church, the greater part of St. David's cathedral and St. Saviour's, Southwark, the west front of Peterborough, and the transepts, nave and chapter-house of Lincoln. And in the heart of London, towering above its two-storied houses, arose the immense cathedral—first begun after the fire of 1135—that for four hundred years dominated the city until its destruction in a still greater fire. Its wooden and lead steeple, raised in 1221 and later rebuilt in stone, was one of the wonders of Europe.

These tremendous buildings, so far transcending the apparent economic and technical resources of the time, were not raised like the architectural monuments of the East by slave-labour.[19] They were made by craftsmen able to bargain and of the same faith as those who ordered their making. In addition to wages they occasionally received—as a special reward or spur—the much sought-after ecclesiastical indulgences, or remission of penance for sins, which the Church at a price conferred on the rich and powerful. Though behind them lay the quarrymen and burners of the limestone-hills, the seamen and drovers who brought the materials to the building-sites, and the labour-services and carrying-dues of the local manorial tenants, the main work of building was done by bands of travelling masons who, under their contracting-masters, moved from one great church to another. The name of the lean-to "lodges" which they erected against the rising walls for shelter still survive in the nomenclature of the modern freemasons.

Their services were eagerly competed for by prelates whose desire to outbuild one another was as much a stimulus to the craft of building as the later rivalry of eighteenth-century country gentlemen and twentieth-century bureaucrats. So were the new fashions of Christian worship that necessitated the erection at the eastern end of great churches—sometimes, as at Canterbury and Lincoln, round a semi-circular walk or ambulatory, more often in England in rectangular transepts—of chapels to house the shrines of saints and the tombs of benefactors. Particularly popular were the Lady Chapels, where men and, still more, women, prayed to the Virgin Mother, whose worship afforded an outlet at this time for a kind of sublimated chivalry and adoration of the womanly virtues of pity, tenderness and compassion.

More utilitarian were the chapter-houses which provided meeting-places for the wealthy and aristocratic prebendaries and monks who controlled these great churches. In England, following the example of Worcester, built in the Norman style

[19] Ibn Jubayr of Granada, visiting Egypt at the time when the new Christ's Church, Canterbury, was being built in England, saw the citadel at Cairo being raised by Christian prisoners, "whose numbers were beyond computation." *The Travels of Ibn Jubayr*, 43.

in the twelfth century, these were often polygonal in shape, the lofty vault of the roof being supported by a single, deli-cately-moulded central-column and the windowed walls cut with niches to accommodate the brethren. All this brought about during the first half of the thirteenth century an enlarge-ment of the eastern ends or presbyteries of cathedrals and ab-beys, which was later balanced by the addition of preaching-naves to provide for the congregations that flocked to hear the friars' sermons. This made English churches—generally inferior to those of France in height—exceptionally long.

The most complete example extant of the architecture of Henry III's reign is the church which rose in the Avon water-meadows at Salisbury. Here, following quarrels between the cathedral clergy and the garrison of Old Sarum castle, Bishop Richard Poore—formerly dean—embarked in 1220 on the pro-digious task of re-building the cathedral on a new site. Its designer was one of the canons, Elias of Derham—a distin-guished connoisseur who, as Archbishop Langton's steward, has been the joint-creator of Becket's shrine at Canterbury. He was assisted by a master-mason named Nicholas of Ely. Built of freestone from the Chilmark quarries twelve miles away and taking half a century to complete, Salisbury cathedral still stands—save for its spire and upper tower, added a century later—as its builders designed it, the only medieval cathedral in England which is all of a piece. Inside, save for its main outlines, it has been transformed by restoration; like all great contemporary churches, it was originally brilliantly coloured, with scarlet and black scrollwork walls, white-painted vaulting and gilded capitals, across which jewels of ruby and blue in the windows cast glittering reflections with every change of sun and shadow. But, outside, in the close, and in the cloisters— the largest in England—with their arches looking on to the quiet garth, we can still feel the faith that prompted men to raise such monuments to their belief in the unity of earth and heaven.

The first stones of Salisbury were laid in the spring of 1220 by Bishop Poore, and William Longespée or Longsword, earl of Salisbury, the hero of England's first naval victory and one of the witnesses of Magna Carta.[20] Six years later the earl, who

[20] His copy of it can still be seen in the cathedral library.

had been defending Gascony against the French, returned to England to die and was buried in the cathedral he had helped to found. That autumn its first completed building, the Lady Chapel, was dedicated by Cardinal Stephen Langton, who preached to the crowds outside before celebrating mass. Among those who watched its rising walls was the young king from his hunting palace of Clarendon a few miles away. They may have helped to make him the greatest patron of ecclesiastical architecture this country has ever known.[21] No English sovereign has presided over the birth of so many magnificent buildings or entered so fully into the artistic aspirations of his people. The glorious Cistercian abbeys of Yorkshire and South Wales, the re-building of Malmesbury and Glastonbury, the presbytery at Ely, the transepts at York and Beverley, the choirs of Christ Church, Oxford and Carlisle, the great abbey of Hayles —built by the king's brother, Richard, earl of Cornwall, to house a phial of the Precious Blood[22]—all date from this germinative reign. So do the wonderful chapel of the Nine Altars at Durham and the great west front of Wells, begun in 1239, with its hundreds of life-size statues of saints and missionaries, bishops and kings, telling the story of Christian England from the earliest times and rivalling the finest contemporary sculpture in Europe.

One national possession above all others England owes to Henry. From his earliest days he had been brought up to venerate the Anglo-Saxon saints. In 1244, four years after the consecration of St. Paul's, he started to rebuild the abbey church of Westminster in honour of its founder, Edward the Confessor, in whose name he had christened his eldest son. In doing so he drew his inspiration from the wonderful new cathedrals which, under his cousin, Louis IX of France, were being raised on the other side of the Channel. From Amiens and Rheims—the crowning-place of the French kings—and, above all, from the exquisite Sainte Chapelle in Paris,[23] which the devout Louis was

[21] He employed the architect of Salisbury to supervise the re-building of his palace at Winchester, ordering the sheriff of Hampshire in 1236 to carry out the work "according to what Master Elias de Derham, to whom the king has fully explained his wishes, tells him." L. F. Salzman, *Building in England*, 9–10.

[22] Hence the old saying, "God's in Gloucestershire."

[23] Henry loved and admired the Sainte Chapelle so much that it was said that he wanted to carry it away to England in a cart.

building to house the reputed crown of thorns and other relics
of the Crucifixion—he borrowed the lofty eastern chevet and
the mosaic-paved ambulatory with its semicircle of radiating
chapels, and to the west of them and St. Edward's shrine made
a raised theatre where the coronation of England's kings could
be solemnised. Yet though the abbey's eastern outline was taken
from Rheims and the soaring pointed arches, flying buttresses
and great circular rose-windows from Amiens, its general plan
with its bold transepts and the exquisite craftsmanship that
made its interior so lovely—"outshining all the churches in the
world for costliness and splendour"—was mainly English. The
master mason who supervised its building was an Englishman,
Henry of Reyns, and so were his successors—for the work took
a quarter of a century to complete[24]—John of Gloucester and
Robert of Beverley. At one time eight hundred workmen were
employed on it. From the Abbey muniments we know the names
of many of these craftsmen, who were settled by the chapter
in houses in Westminster: Alexander the carpenter, Odo the
goldsmith and Edward his son, Henry the glazier, John of St.
Albans, the great master-sculptor whose twin angels, once brilliantly coloured, still swing their censers under the vast rose-
window of the south transept. The work of another wonderful
English artist—Walter of Durham, the king's painter—is represented by the huge figures of St. Christopher and St. Thomas
touching the side of the risen Christ, which were discovered a
few years ago, hidden by monuments and buried in dirt, on
the wall of the south transept. The rest of his painting, like the
original coloured glass of which only a few panels now remain,
and the marble and mosaic-work of the Confessor's jewelled
shrine, were destroyed by the iconoclasts of later ages.

Such a work, which absorbed Henry as much as the abbey's
original building the Confessor, cost a great deal of money.
Yet it was the kind of expenditure that men of the time approved and which in their eyes made their country rich and
blessed. To lavish treasure on Christ's Church and maintain the
glory of the royal state was what a thirteenth-century king was

---

[24] Henry was often impatient at the slowness of the work compared with that
of the French cathedrals. He tried to get the workmen to work on feast-days,
but had to accept a compromise by which they worked every other feast-day.
F. M. Powicke, *King Henry III and the Lord Edward*, 572.

expected to do. Henry loved pageantry and brightly painted pavilions, splendid robes and ritual and the outward show of religion. The chronicles of his reign are full of the festivals he kept, his accounts of the treasures—golden statues, precious stones, relics—bought for his palaces and favourite shrines. He kept a school of artists at work building, decorating and improving his residences, and was for ever urging them on through his Clerk of the Works:—"as they value themselves and their goods" "though it cost £100!" He put glass into the windows of his palaces instead of wooden shutters, wainscotted their stone passages and covered their walls with paintings, like the map of the world he ordered for his hall at Winchester or the pictures "in good colours of God's Majesty and the four Evangelists and the figures of St. Edmund and St. Edward" which the keeper of his houses at Woodstock was instructed to have made in the chapel.

In 1236, when he was twenty-eight, Henry married Eleanor of Provence, the fourteen-year-old daughter of the troubadour count, Raymond Berenger—a great beauty whose sister was the wife of the French king. It was a happy marriage, for the rather childlike pair shared the same tastes. They delighted in ceremonies and feasts, religious services and pilgrimages, magnificent jewels, clothes and buildings. In the Liberate Rolls[25] of orders to the sheriffs and exchequer officers we can read of the provision Henry made for these tastes—of the rose of Provence painted on the walls of the queen's chamber and the stars stencilled on a background of vert and azure; of the cherry trees planted in her garden and the trellised way to her *herbarium;* of the "house of fir" he had built for her, "running on six wheels. . . . . . roofed with lead"; of the figure of Winter, "made the more like winter by its sad countenance and other miserable attitudes of the body," that Edward the son of Odo, keeper of the works at Westminster, was directed to have painted over her fireplace. We read, too, of the clasps and nails of silver for the royal book of romances; of the money paid to the clerks of the Chapel Royal for singing "Christus vincat"; of the fifteen lasts of "the best and most exquisite herrings" that the sheriff of Norfolk had to buy from Yarmouth and the lampreys which his brother officer of Gloucester had

[25] So called the Latin opening *"liberate"* or "deliver to."

to place in bread and jelly and send to Westminster[26]; of the dates and figs, pressed grapes and ginger salmon pasties, and mulberry and raspberry-flavoured wine, that figure so strangely in the records of State.

In all this Henry and his queen—a princess from the luxurious South—were children of their age. The thirteenth century was the high summer of the society that had grown out of the institution of knighthood and the Cluniac reforms. It was the age of St. Louis, the great crusading king of France whose passion for justice set the moral standards of the western world for half a century. It was the age of the brilliant Hohenstaufen emperor, Frederick II, who founded a university at Naples, spoke six languages and, blending the civilisations of the Latin, Saracen and Byzantine worlds, made his brilliant Sicilian court a bridge between East and West. It was the age of the great merchant cities of Venice, Genoa and Pisa, whose fleets, exploiting the crusades, opened the doors of Europe to the luxury and learning of the Orient, and, whose traders penetrated, in Marco Polo's fabulous mission, to the remote court of the Mongol conquerors of China. Through their adventuring, and that of the crusaders themselves, there flowed into the West a stream of germinating ideas and arts—some preserved from the Greek and Roman past by the Byzantines, others wholly new to Europe. It was a time when Frankish princes and churchmen, whose grandfathers had been content with bare walls and unpaved floors strewn with filthy rushes, built themselves palaces and chapels with marble pillars and gilded vaults and furnished them with oriental carpets and curtains, cushions and embroideries, Greek enamels and Cordovan leatherwork; when Venetian artists studied captured Byzantine masterpieces, and scholars sat at the feet of doctors who had absorbed the medical, scientific and philosophical learning of the Moors of Andalusia and Arabia; when Persian carpets and Chinese and Indian silks, sugar and pepper, lemons and apricots, muslin, damasks and tapestries were borne in Arab dhows and on camels to the quays of the crusading ports of Outremer; in which the windmill and the mariner's compass became part of the equipment of European civilisation.

[26] " . . . . . . Since after lampreys all fish seem insipid to both the king and queen." *Close Rolls, 1234–37,* 420 cit. Hennings 262.

Judged by the standards of that age Henry was a good and worthy Christian king—not a saint and moral leader like his brother-in-law, Louis IX of France, and certainly not as clever and versatile as the Emperor Frederick who, in the eyes of most of his contemporaries, was too clever by half and, for all his genius, died a suspected heretic under the ban of the Church. He shared the eager, curious tastes of his time; he even possessed an elephant—given him by King Louis[27]—and a lion which he kept in the Tower. He was a faithful husband—an uncommon virtue in a medieval king—a devoted father, and a generous employer who was always making gifts to his servants. His accounts are full of directions for feeding the poor in the great hall at Westminster—"as many as can get in"—and for distributing clothing and shoes to them. On one occasion he ordered his treasurer to feed fifteen-hundred people in St. Paul's churchyard: on another to feast a thousand poor scholars at Oxford. He had his children publicly weighed and their weight in silver given to the destitute.

Yet Henry had little capacity for understanding and ruling those who thought differently to himself. He had the narrow-mindedness of a boy and could never see a problem from anyone's point of view but his own. In dealing with opponents he was quite unscrupulous; feeling that, as an anointed king, his intentions justified every subterfuge, he never even tried to keep faith with them. But as he was seldom strong enough to pursue a consistent policy, he inspired more contempt than fear. He had a noble head, a long determined nose and fine regular features, save for a drooping left eyelid; they can be seen, with his curling Plantagenet locks and long delicate hands, in William Torel's exquisite effigy in the Abbey. Yet about his eyes and little mouth there was a fretful, shifty look and an unmistakable hint of petulance. He had none of his father's vice or satanic genius, yet had inherited his restlessness, his lack of steady purpose and, where his family was not concerned, his deeply suspicious nature.

Unlike his father and grandfather, Henry was without business sense. He was full of splendid projects, but was seldom able to relate them to reality. Outside the realm of architecture —his one consistent passion—he never completed anything. In financial matters he was a child, and a dangerous one, for he

---

[27] The people, Matthew Paris relates, "flocked together to see this novel sight."

had no idea of adapting ends to means. He was wildly optimistic and extravagant, and always in need of money. This, however, was partly due to circumstances beyond his control; in the thirteenth century the price of every commodity was rising: the hire of a professional knight, cost three times as much as in Henry II's day. And many sources of royal revenue had been closed by Magna Carta. Not only was the king unable to take additional aids from his feudal tenants without their consent—a grave disability since their wealth was all the time increasing with the price of commodities—but since the Conqueror's time the Crown's demesne lands had been progressively diminished by royal grants. By now their annual value was only about a third of those of the Church.

Yet none of these factors prevented Henry from exceeding his income. He embarked on projects without a thought of their cost and, when his normal revenue proved inadequate, borrowed recklessly from the Florentine and Sienese moneylenders who, with the rise of the mercantile cities of northern Italy, were supplanting the Jews as the chief providers of credit. Actually the nation was growing richer, and an understanding of how to equate its credit to its expanding capacity to produce might have solved many of the financial and constitutional problems of the reign. At no time was the Crown's debt more than the equivalent of a couple of years' revenue. Yet, with a primitive fiscal machinery and the exorbitant rates of interest charged by moneylenders—who had to run the gauntlet of the canon law to lend at all—even such a modest degree of anticipation spelt bankruptcy. After four decades of hand-to-mouth living and constant borrowing, Henry was financially incapable of governing at all.

Three factors hastened his decline: his generosity to his mother's and wife's relations, his European adventures and his loyalty to the papacy. His predatory Lusignan kinsmen were an early embarrassment. After his marriage his wife's needy Savoyard uncles proved a worse one. One of them became a leading member of his council, another earl of Richmond,[28] and a third, archbishop of Canterbury. All three were intensely unpopular, especially the last, for Boniface of Savoy—a first-rate man of business, who found his diocese in debt and set about in a rather downright way enforcing his rights—seemed to the

---

[28] The Savoy in the Strand, where he built a palace, is still named after him.

English, though unjustly, not only a foreigner but a greedy and violent extortioner. His attempt to enforce a visitation in the diocese of London led to a pitched battle with the mob, during which, wearing armour under his episcopal robes, he was forced to take refuge on the river. What was most resented was the feeling that these favoured aliens were draining the country of revenues in order to feather their nests elsewhere. Again and again the barons, as the natural leaders of English society, protested in Council that offices of trust, royal castles and native heiresses were being given "to men not of the realm of England." Matthew Paris in his St. Albans scriptorium was expressing more than a personal prejudice when he wrote of the king's "indiscreet invitations to aliens to whom he foolishly, incredibly and extravagantly scattered the good things of the kingdom."

Yet the toll exacted by the king's foreign relations was nothing to the drain of what the St. Albans chronicler called "the yawning gulf of papal need." As Rome's control on the western Churches grew, so did the army of administrators, clerks and lawyers it employed. On every diocese and abbey in the West there descended a growing torrent of demands, framed by hard-headed lawyers, for subsidies to the papal exchequer and for "provisions" or benefices for Roman officials and nominees. Made in the name of the "plenitude of power" which the pope enjoyed as Christ's vicar, they were almost impossible to resist. Least of all could they be refused in the land John had surrendered to Rome in return for Rome's protection. His son, who was bound by that surrender, had especial reason to be grateful to the papacy.[29] Yet even he was driven to protest at its intolerable claims of his country's ecclesiastical revenues. The pages of contemporary chroniclers are full of complaints about foreign extortioners, armed with papal powers, asking for benefices and grants from English chapters under threats of suspension and excommunication. They also record—with undisguised delight—the occasional terror of such Italian interlopers when the English rounded on them.[30] In a single year the

[29] It had raised him, he wrote in his earliest extant letter, "from weeping to laughter, from darkness to light and from the narrowness of the cradle to the spaciousness of kingdoms." Hennings 12.

[30] "Martin immediately set out on his journey keeping close to the side of his guide, and whenever he happened to see any horseman or passers-by, he was

bishops of Lincoln and Salisbury were asked to provide livings for three hundred papal nominees, many of them pluralists and nearly all foreigners. The primate, Edmund Rich, was so harried that in 1240 he left the country in despair, to die as a simple monk in exile.

With the archbishop's place taken by the queen's uncle, the moral leadership of the English Church passed to the bishop of Lincoln, Robert Grosseteste. The greatest ecclesiastic of the age and the lifelong foe of clerical corruption, absenteeism and neglect of pastoral duty, he had an almost mystical veneration for the pope's plenitude of power and right to obedience. Yet when in the last year of his long, noble life he was presented with a demand for a benefice for one of the pope's nephews, he passionately refused. "No faithful subject of the Holy See," he wrote, "can submit to mandates of this kind, no, not even if the author were the most high body of angels. . . . . Because of the obedience by which I am bound, and of my love of my union with the Holy See in the body of Christ, as an obedient son I disobey, I contradict, I rebel." He was thinking of parishioners deprived of their pastors, of the poor robbed of endowments, of the discipline of the Church disregarded and turned to mockery. On another occasion, in one of his fearless, yet deeply respectful letters, he warned the Holy Father that even a pope might be in danger of Hell.

Yet by the middle of the thirteenth century no pope was in a position to heed such protests. With the papacy's claim to give law to kings and its growing ambition to rule Italy, it had entered on a new phase in its history. In the days of Hildebrand it had aimed at the restraint of lawless power. Later, in its struggle with secular rulers, it had gone further and sought the restraint of lawful but unhallowed power. Now, impelled by the urge to dominate for righteousness' sake, it was demanding power uncontrolled. In doing so it descended from the heights of spiritual supremacy over men's hearts and entered the dusty arena of competing claims in which the workaday world is governed. Just as, in its establishment of the Holy Office of the Inquisition to root out heresy it employed,

seized with such fear and trembling that if the earth had opened he would have hidden himself under the turf. . . . He did not spare his horse's flanks, but, chiding his guide for delay, hastened to the sea." Matthew Paris, *Chron. Maj.* IV 420, cit. Hennings 62.

out of the highest motives, spies, forced confessions, the tor-
ture-chamber and stake, so in pursuit of its political aims it
used force, bribery and deception. It was compelled to employ
armies and mobs, financiers and lawyers, extortioners and usurers, and pay the price for their services.

For the fatal flaw in the popes' bid, not merely to minister to
Christendom but to rule it, lay in the impossibility of doing
both. Seeking, not out of vulgar ambition but for righteousness'
sake, to control the world, they lost sight of their real mission,
the salvation of souls. In trying to render unto God the things
that were Caesar's, they ceased to be able to render unto God
the things that were God's. They abandoned the substance for
a shadow. The power they sought was never within their reach,
for, though for a time they might outmanoeuvre secular rulers,
they were playing a game against men better experienced and
equipped than themselves. And they precipitated a conflict
which, by unloosing violence, weakened the very virtues on
which Christendom depended.

During the second quarter of the thirteenth century Pope
Gregory IX and his successor, Innocent IV, waged unrelenting
war against the Emperor Frederick II's attempt to restore the
imperial dominion over the Lombard cities and rule all Italy
from his Sicilian capital. To destroy that red-headed, fat, witty
and brilliant man they were prepared to wreck the unity of
the Church in Germany, excommunicate every imperial supporter, and unloose anarchy and civil war on half Europe. At
the start of that fratricidal strife, in 1228, Gregory demanded a
tenth of the revenues of the English Church, for a crusade, not
against the infidel but against the one European ruler who
proved able to regain Jerusalem. More than twenty years later,
after a horde of savage Tartars from the Mongolian steppes
had overrun Russia and Poland and all but conquered Germany, and after Jerusalem had again been lost to the infidels,
Bishop Grosseteste stood before Pope Innocent and drew the
picture of a world in which Christ's Church was hemmed into
a little corner, while its leader neglected his charge to war
against those who should have been its defenders and brought
shame and disillusionment to the faithful by his scandalous
trade in benefices.

Even after Frederick's death the papacy continued to fight

his illegitimate son, Manfred. In 1254, in order to enlist the wealth of England in the struggle, it offered the Sicilian throne to Henry's nine-year-old son, Edmund. Four years before, fired by the noble example of King Louis, who faced death and captivity in Egypt in an attempt to recover Jerusalem, the irresolute English king had taken the cross. From this expensive and perilous vow Alexander IV now offered to release him in return for his underwriting the papacy's debts and financing the war in Sicily.

The pope knew his man. The most stay-at-home king of England since the Confessor, Henry had never been able to forget that his forbears had ruled a continental empire. He was always trying to win prestige abroad by ambitious family alliances, and twice had engaged in inglorious campaigns—for he was as lacking in military as financial talent—to recover his father's lost fiefs. He had merely been left with an empty treasury and a load of debt. Only the French king's scrupulous regard for the rights of others had saved him from losing his last continental possessions in Aquitaine.

Henry, therefore, accepted the pope's flattering offer with alacrity. Armed with the papal grant of the crusader's right to levy taxes on his country's clerical revenues—so much greater than his own—he felt himself at last the king he wished to be. No longer need he go, as in the past, to the assembled barons at the Christmas or Pentecost Feast and beg them for an additional aid to meet his pressing debts or the charges of some fruitless campaign against the French or turbulent Welsh, only to be met with an indifferent *non possumus* or, worse, a demand for some impossible condition like their appointment of his own chief officers, or the even more unacceptable proposal they had made a dozen years before to elect four "conservers of liberty" to supervise his government. On that occasion, in his dire financial straits, he had at first offered to give it his consideration, but later had returned what the chronicler called "an unmannerly reply." "You have wanted," he said, "all you leading men of England, and not particularly politely either, to bend your lord the king to your will. Every head of a household may place in office who he chooses of his household, but yet you have boldly presumed to deny this to your lord king. And he would not be your king but as a servant if he were to bend thus."[31] After which the barons had curtly replied that, if the king could not "live on his own," that is on the revenues of his own demesne and royal rights, he must not expect their aid. What these conservative, bucolic and unhelpful lords wanted was a form of government in which he consulted them in all important matters of state and ruled with the "counsel of the faithful men of his realm." Henry wanted one based on the royal will alone. There had therefore been a complete deadlock, and the king had been forced to sell his plate to the city merchants.

And now, when with the pope's delegated authority the king imposed taxes on clerical incomes, the very clergy—and not merely the greater prelates who sat with the barons in the great Council—demanded that before any tax was paid their formal assent should be obtained. True, that in the face of the pope's "plenitude of power" over the Church's property—no longer tempered by any royal protection—these assemblies of monks, canons and parish clergy could do no more than protest, yet the very fact that the alliance of pope and king caused them to combine in such a way seemed an affront to the royal dignity. And Henry quickly discovered that every penny of the crusader's taxes on the Church's revenues granted him was mortgaged to finance a war over whose conduct he had no control and to pay the interest on the papal debts he had underwritten. A horde of Roman tax-collectors and usurers' agents descended on the country and fastened on the Church's wealth. The king had merely lent them his authority by his injudicious bargain and gained nothing for himself in doing so.

And the *curia* and its ruthless financial agents were quite pitiless in their demands. They even mortgaged, without the chapters' consent or knowledge, the property of English monasteries to the Italian merchant houses which were financing the Sicilian war. When Henry, who found himself ever deeper in debt, pleaded his inability to meet the papal demands, he was threatened with excommunication and an Interdict for failing to fulfil his crusader's vow.

When he turned to his barons for help they were equally

[31] "Therefore he will neither remove nor find substitutes for chancellor, justiciar or treasurer, as you have proposed. . . . But he demands from you pecuniary aid to gain beyond seas his rights." Matthew Paris, *Chron. Maj.* V. 20. cit. Hennings 69.

unsympathetic. In their hour of testing, magnates and prelates stood side by side. In vain did the king parade the youthful Edmund before them in the gorgeous costume of Apulia and appeal for their aid to enable him to win his kingdom. They merely replied that the business of Sicily reduced them to despair: it was too far away, occupied by superior forces, the cost was ruinous and efforts to meet it might expose Gascony to the French and England to the Welsh and tempt the king to "fall away from the law of the realm." They could do nothing.

A year later, penniless, threatened with imminent excommunication and interdict for his inability to meet the *curia's* bottomless debts, and, with the English clergy protesting furiously at the never-ceasing demands made on them by Roman tax collectors, Henry stood before the assembled magnates at the Easter feast at Oxford and made a clean breast of his embarrassments and inescapable need. The barons' leaders debated together what they should do. Their spokesman was Roger Bigod, earl of Norfolk, the earl marshal. They took an oath to aid one another in the cause of right, saving the duty they owed to the Crown. Then at the end of April they came to the Council armed. They left their swords at the door—a custom still enshrined in the ritual of Parliament—but made the king and his reluctant eldest son, the young Lord Edward, swear to abide by their advice. It was agreed that a committee of twenty-four, half chosen by the barons and half by Henry, should draft proposals for a plan of reform to redress the nation's grievances and restore the ancient co-operation between Crown and magnates.

That summer, at a meeting at Oxford of the great Council which was now beginning to be called Parliament, the reforming committee's provisions were announced. They were accepted by the king who saw in them his only hope to obtaining the aid he needed. They were of the most drastic kind. A Council of Fifteen, nominated by four members of the reforming committee, was to "have the power of advising the king in good faith concerning the government of the kingdom . . . in order to amend and redress everything that they shall consider in need of amendment or redress." If its members failed to agree or were not all present, a decision of the majority was to bind all—a principle of immense significance. It was to have authority over the justiciar or chief justice—now reappointed —and over the other officers of state, including the treasurer and chancellor. It was laid down that the royal household should be reformed, that its foreign members should leave the realm, and that the chancellor should seal nothing by the king's will alone but only with the Council's knowledge. The castles were to be placed in the hands of native-born custodians, and the sheriffs appointed annually from men of the counties they administered.

Yet of these measures by far the most important was that which regulated the meetings of the great Council of the realm or Parliament—the enduring embodiment of the ancient English custom that a king should take counsel of his chief men and have "deep speech" with them. Parliament was a French word for such deep speech, for talking things over. Magna Carta had indicated the means by which the magnates—earls, barons, bishops and greater abbots—were to be summoned to meetings of this body. It was now enacted that Parliament should meet regularly three times a year, at Michaelmas, Candlemas and in June. "To these three Parliaments," it was declared, "the chosen councillors of the king shall come, even if they are not summoned, in order to examine the state of the kingdom and consider its common needs and those of the king." And to them were to come twelve representatives of the general "community"—that is the general body of barons. Their approval of whatever the Council decided was thereafter to bind the community.

The reforming Fifteen acted quickly. They repudiated Henry's Sicilian commitments, dismissed his foreign advisers, and forced him to negotiate a treaty with the French king under which he renounced his father's lost provinces. Then, while Parliament received and investigated hundreds of judicial petitions, it began with furious energy to reform the kingdom's internal wrongs, appointing four representative knights in every shire to draw up for the consideration of the royal judges lists of grievances and unjust administrative practices. For, with all their limitations, the barons had learnt the lesson that Langton had taught them at the beginning of the century. Their attitude was now not feudal but national; their business, as they saw it, not only to defend their interests, but to champion those of the community as a whole. "We wish," their spokesmen had declared in the Council as far back as 1234, "to keep in mind the common welfare of the realm and not to burden the poor." They had made provision in their periodic meetings for relieving poor suitors from a ruinous attendance on the royal courts by permitting them to plead by attorney, and sought to protect merchants from royal purveyors, and widows and minors from grasping overlords. Now, at a time of widespread hardship and discontent, when a succession of bad harvests, with famine and pestilence, had brought many to the verge of ruin, they proclaimed their intention of investigating the complaints of the lesser freeholders, even the poorest and most obscure.

Yet in doing so, their movement lost its unity. The zeal of the more ardent reformers outran the disinterestedness of the more conservative. The barons had been united in their resolve to check the king's extravagant foreign adventures, to rid the government of aliens and to take their rightful place in the control of the realm. But when it was proposed that, having reformed the abuses of the royal administration, the Council of Fifteen should investigate those of the baronial courts—in other words, the grievances of their own tenants—many barons, led by the great Marcher earl of Gloucester, Richard de Clare, felt that it was time to call a halt.

Yet, as much as the magnates, the lesser landowners of the shires had been politically awakened by the growing efficiency and extortionate power of the royal officials. They too, had to unite to control them or lose their self-respect. And the very use the barons were making of them and the part they already played in the kingdom's administration rendered them a force to be reckoned with. They had been called upon in the past year to elect four of their members in every shire to ensure that the sheriff observed the law and to report his misdemeanours to the justiciar. They had now been given the duty of electing in the county courts four men from the shire from whom the exchequer was to choose the sheriff of the year. And they were accustomed, in a humble and attendant capacity, to send representatives or "knights of the shire" to the king's courts at Westminster, and had occasionally been summoned to meetings of the great Council or Parliament to answer questions on oath on local matters of taxation or justice.

Had king, barons and prelates—the privileged ruling Orders of the realm—been united, these rustic knights, or bachelors as they were called, would have counted for little. But in the revolutionary situation that now existed they were able to make their voice heard. They did so—in no uncertain fashion—for the first time in English history in the autumn of 1259, when at the royal feast of St. Edward held at Westminster before the meeting of Parliament they addressed a corporate protest to the Lord Edward, the king's son and heir. In this document, known as the "protest of the Community of Bachelors of England," they complained that, while "the lord king had performed and fulfilled all and singular that the barons had ordained . . . the barons themselves had done nothing of what they had promised for the good of the realm; but only for their own good and to the harm of the king elsewhere."

The twenty-year-old prince, whose ardent, noble head as a youth can be seen carved in stone above a capital in the north transept of Westminster Abbey, responded to this tactfully phrased appeal with characteristic frankness. Though devoted to his father, he was in his directness his complete opposite. He had sworn, he declared, a solemn oath at Oxford and, though he had made it reluctantly, "he was not on this account less prepared to stand by it and to expose himself to death for the community of England and for the advantage of the State."[32] He, therefore, informed the barons that, unless they fulfilled their oath, he would support the "community" of bachelors and help to enforce it.

As a result, further reforms entitled the Provisions of Westminster—the complement of the earlier Provisions of Oxford—were enacted in Parliament. These provided among other things that no-one except the king and his ministers should levy distraints outside his fief, that no-one without a royal writ should compel his free tenants to respond in his court to any matter concerning their free tenements, that none but the king should hear appeals of false judgments, and that no charter of exemption from assize or jury service should exempt a man, however great, from the obligation to testify on oath in the royal courts if his doing so was essential to justice.

The reforms for which the Council of Fifteen had been set up were now complete. A wilful, vain monarch had been taught the lesson that England could only be ruled with the assent of her leading men. And unlike his father, he had learnt it without bloodshed. Moderate and informed opinion, therefore, began to veer towards the Crown, feeling that the nation should return to the form of government to which it was used.

Yet England had a further lesson to learn and a harsher. Her sovereign's obstinacy had awoken feelings that could not be easily resolved. There was a strange ferment in the air: of vague, vehement talk of justice and treason, not to the king but to the community; of friars preaching apocalyptic sermons in streets and on village greens; of cities arming their men and watching their gates; of war in the Marches where the great prince of Gwynedd, Llywelyn ap Gruffydd, enraged by the encroachments of English officials, was making a new nation of the Welsh and burning the lands and castles of the Marchers.

All this might have come to nothing in that politically immature age but for one circumstance. That circumstance was a great man. Simon de Montfort had come to England from France thirty years earlier to claim the earldom of Leicester and marry the king's sister. When in 1257 that shrewd man of business, Richard, earl of Cornwall, had accepted the elective crown of Germany,[33] de Montfort had been one of the magnates who succeeded to his place at the head of the reform party. Now, with the earl of Gloucester and the Bigods seceding to the king, he had been left virtually alone. He had never forgiven Henry for his weak betrayal when the nobles of Gascony, whom he had been sent to govern as viceroy of Aquitaine, had falsely accused him in the royal court. Henceforth he had despised his brother-in-law, a contempt he made no attempt to disguise. In his turn the king feared Simon. Once, when caught by a storm on the river and driven to shelter in his house, he had told his attendants that he was more afraid of him than all the thunder and lightning in the world.

---

[33] He was elected king of the Romans—the title by which the titular ruler of Germany was known—but was never crowned Emperor by the pope or accepted by more than a fraction of the divided and warring German princes, whose only motive in inviting him had been to secure his money.

De Montfort had little liking for the English and never really understood them.[34] But he was obsessed with the belief that power should be exercised as a sacred trust and that it was a Christian noble's duty to enforce justice. It was this conviction, and his dynamic capacity to communicate it to others, that won him the devotion of all whose hopes of a more just society had been quickened by the baronial reforms. He appealed to the discontented, to the hothead young lords and bachelors, to the men outside the Constitution, to the merchants and apprentices of the eastern towns, particularly of London and the Cinque Ports, to the preaching friars who went among the poor, to the ragged scholars and simple craftsmen and artisans who wanted to see God's kingdom made on earth. The son of the crusader who had crushed the Albigensians and won Provence for the French Crown, he invested every policy he championed with a passionate religious earnestness. He was a man, it was said, who watched more often than he slept; "Sir Simon the Righteous," they called him. The Provisions of Oxford which he had helped to frame had become in his eyes divine commandments. "He stood firm like an immoveable pillar," wrote a monkish admirer, "and neither threats, promises, gifts nor flattery could avail to move him . . . to betray the oath which he had taken to reform the kingdom."

The trouble was that Simon did not attach the same meaning to that oath as either the king, who had subscribed to it, or the ordinary conservative-minded Englishman of his day. He maintained that the Council of Fifteen set up at Oxford was no mere temporary expedient to reform abuses and re-establish government by assent, but a permanent executive council to rule in the king's name. Yet the throne had always been the medium through which England had been governed, and it was hard for Englishmen to conceive of any other and still harder to devise a substitute for it. To constrain an English king to rule with the assent of his magnates was one thing, to exercise his functions for him another. De Montfort, in the name of reform, was advocating a form of government wholly foreign to English tradition.

Without this provocative challenge Henry, an ageing man

[34] That "coward" people, he once called them. "'An Englishman,' he said, 'would put you in a hole and then turn tail,' and when he said this he was thinking of the legend, of which Frenchmen made a favourite gibe, that the English had tails." F. M. Powicke, *Henry III and the Lord Edward*, 409.

who had learnt his lesson, would almost certainly have acquiesced in the baronial reforms. They had been demanded by the entire nation. But this oligarch, with his haughty claims to subject him to a council of nobles and summon Parliament in his absence, aroused all his obstinacy and petulance and his most treacherous, dangerous mood. And the jealousy and alarm which the proud, unbending Frenchman awoke in his associates, and in moderate and conservative men generally, created a party for the king which had not before existed. For Simon's violence and intransigence sooner or later alienated everyone who tried to work with him as an equal. He was incapable of sharing power: he could only give orders and be obeyed. Compromise—the breath of self-government—was alien to him. He wished to establish the rule of righteousness on earth and viewed everyone who opposed him as the agent of unrighteousness.

For the next three years the shadow of civil war lay over the land. No Englishman wanted it who could remember the last. Yet with two such opponents—a crusader who could not compromise and a king who could not keep faith—it was inevitable. Henry could only accept de Montfort's thesis by becoming a puppet, and de Montfort could not trust the king. While the latter secretly sought, as his father had done, papal absolution from his oaths and introduced foreign garrisons into the Tower and Dover castle, Simon and his supporters imperiously demanded confirmatory oaths from all who had sworn to the Provisions of Oxford and denounced as "capital enemies" those who refused. Henry's strength was in the conservative North and West and in the Marches where the only alternative to a strong throne was anarchy and a Welsh triumph. He was supported by most of the great lords, who could no longer stomach de Montfort's dictatorial ways. The latter's strength lay in London and the south-east, in the reforming party in the Church, in popular anti-foreign and anti-Jewish feeling, and in the young who all looked on him as a prophet—from the heirs of the great feudal estates to the eager, unruly scholars who, hanging on his words, passed from hand to mouth by balladmongers and friars, turned out with slings and bows to harry his foes.[35] He also enjoyed the rather uncertain and invidious sup-

[35] When they did so at Northampton the king threatened to hang every man of them.

port of Llywelyn ap Gruffydd, who was out, like a good Welshman, to take advantage of England's troubles.

For a time war was averted by the king's lack of money and
de Montfort's of military strength. But in the spring of 1263, following the death of Richard earl of Gloucester and the accession
of his eighteen-year-old son, the reformer gained the support
of the most powerful of all the Marchers. Thus strengthened, he
called a parliament of his supporters who denounced as traitors
all who would not accept his uncompromising interpretation of
the Provisions. Then, bearing the king's standard, they laid siege
to the royal castles in the west and plundered their opponents'
lands, while their sympathisers in London besieged the Tower
and mobbed the queen as she tried to make her way by river to
Windsor.

That winter a final attempt was made to avert disaster by
an appeal to the arbitration of Louis of France. But when his
award in the king's favour was published at Amiens early in
1264, de Montfort refused to accept it. "Though all should for-
sake me," he declared, "I will stand firm . . . in the just cause
to which my faith is pledged." On May 14th, to the amazement
of everyone, his army defeated the royal array on the Lewes
downs in Sussex. It was a triumph of youth over numbers, of the
towns over the country, of the green-clad archers of the weald—
prototypes of the yeoman infantry of England's future—over the
glittering but old-fashioned feudal chivalry of the court. Both
Henry[36] and his son were taken prisoners, and de Montfort became virtual dictator.

For a year he ruled England in the king's name, with the
help of a nominated council of oligarchs. He proved no more
capable than Henry of simultaneously founding the rule of
justice on earth and pleasing everyone. His dilemma was that
his only legal claim to authority in a land inherently monarchical
was either the captive king, in whose name he governed and
who could not be permanently constrained by force, or a conception wholly repugnant to a nation which liked law without
a sovereign as little as a sovereign without law. Yet, though his
triumph at Lewes was ephemeral and the civil war itself unnecessary—since the king had already accepted the principle of

[36] His brother, the king of the Romans, was captured in a windmill on the
edge of the town.

government with baronial counsel—the representative conception of Parliament was enlarged through de Montfort's need to obtain wider support for his rule. In January, 1265, he summoned to a Parliament, not only the greater barons and prelates by separate writ, and two knights elected in the shire court of every county, but two burgesses from each of the larger towns to represent the urban freemen and taxpayers. This was revolutionary, for at law no burgess had any right to refuse consent to a tallage demanded by the Crown. Only a few years earlier such a claim had caused Henry III to imprison some rash London citizens who made it. By this step de Montfort unconsciously placed what was to prove, in a precedent-loving nation, a barrier across an avenue of taxation that might, as commercial wealth grew, have made the Crown independent of a Parliament of land-owners.

The rule of the great champion of oligarchy lasted little more than a year. His difficulties and critics multiplied; the one made the other. In the spring of 1265 he fell out with his chief supporter, the young earl of Gloucester. At the end of May Prince Edward—whose political stature had been growing fast—escaped from his captors at Hereford and joined the Marcher lords with whom he had been secretly negotiating. Civil war broke out again at once. At the end of July Edward, with the Marchers, Gloucester and Mortimer, placed his forces between de Montfort, who was returning from south Wales, and his son who was hastening to his aid. Making a forced night-march from Worcester to Kenilworth, he surprised the latter's army asleep in its billets and destroyed part of it.[37] Then, hurrying back to Worcester, he found that de Montfort had crossed the Severn in the direction of Evesham. For the third time in four days he marched by night to place his army across the loop of the river north of Evesham, so cutting off de Montfort from any hope of succour. When on the morning of August 4th the old warrior saw the royal banners bearing down on the town, he is said to have exclaimed, "May God have mercy on our souls, for our bodies are theirs!"

It was a massacre, not a battle, for de Montfort's English

---

[37] "They were seized with fear and trembling . . . when they heard the noise of horns and armed men shouting horribly at them and saying, 'Get up, get up, rise, rise from your beds and come out, you traitors . . . . . for, by God's death, you are all dead men!'" *Chronicles of Melrose*, 198, cit. Hennings 128.

knights and half-armed Welsh infantry were no match for the fierce Marchers. The old king, helmeted in the midst of the doomed army, only escaped death by gasping out, "I am Henry of Winchester, your king!" De Montfort himself was struck down and dismembered. During the next year, while a remnant of his followers desperately held out in the isle of Axholm, Kenilworth castle and the Cinque Ports, revenge, proscription and confiscation were the order of the day.

Yet, though the royal party had triumphed, there was no going back on the principle for which so many had striven: that the government of England, though primarily and fundamentally monarchical, should be with the counsel and consent of the realm expressed through frequent meetings of its chief men in Parliament. The real victor in the war was the Lord Edward, who was a man of his word and understood England. Unlike his father he was a prince of dominant personality who wished to rule a strong and united people and instinctively saw that the only way to do so was through frequent counsel with their leading representatives. "That," he said, "which touches all should be approved by all." It was this knowledge, learnt from the tragic experience of his father's reign, that made him, when his time came, one of the greatest of English kings. And seeing how bitter and stubborn was the resistance of de Montfort's defeated followers, when the first feelings of triumph and bitterness were over he took a leading part in their reconciliation. In the "Dictum of Kenilworth" in 1266, he offered the right to the "disinherited" to buy back their estates at a judicially assessed rate. A year later he was the moving spirit in the great Statute of Marlborough, by which the king in Parliament, while subordinating once more and for all time the baronial franchises to the royal, formally confirmed the Provisions of Oxford and Westminster and made them part of the mainstream of English law.

Nor did de Montfort's influence end with his death. In a sense it became stronger when his over-powerful personality had been removed. Thousands of simple Englishmen sympathised with the disinherited; it was this that had made Edward offer them reconciliation. During this time there seems to have first arisen the popular legend of Robin Hood and his merry men, lurking in the green wood to war against the rich and proud and seize their wealth to help the poor. Sung as ballads and passed from mouth to mouth in hedgerow and ale-house, such tales constituted a new ideal of chivalry: a chivalry so far unknown in feudal Europe, for it glorified the lowly against the great. Simon's own memory was venerated by the poor as that of a saint and martyr. His ideal of the rights of the "universitas" or "commonalty," of an imaginary community of the whole realm to which even village craftsmen and petty traders and peasants could appeal in the name of justice, struck deep roots in the English heart.

In 1268 the revolutionary precedent by which burgesses from the chartered boroughs were asked to give their assent to their own taxation was employed in a royal Parliament. A year later the relics of Edward the Confessor were borne by the old king and his sons to their new resting place in the shrine Henry had made behind the Abbey's high altar. Afterwards Parliament was asked for an aid to enable the Lord Edward to join the crusade which Louis of France—Christendom's protector—was about to lead against the advancing flood of Islam. It was voted, in the shape of a twentieth of all personal property, on behalf of "all the free men of the realm of England, in townships, as also in cities, boroughs and elsewhere," by the largest assembly of barons and knights ever gathered for such a purpose. Then, like his great-uncle, Coeur-de-lion, Edward sailed in August 1270 to join King Louis at Tunis.

Two years later, while recovering from an assassin's wound at Acre, Edward learnt that the old king was dying. In November 1272 the longest English reign of the Middle Ages closed in a profound peace. There was no disputed succession, no outbreak of baronial anarchy, no plunder of the dead sovereign's effects by his attendants. "The governance of the realm," ran the letters which were sent out in the absent Edward's name, "has devolved on us by hereditary succession, by the will of our magnates and by the oath of fealty which they have taken to us. For this cause our magnates and faithful men, in our name, have ordered our peace to be proclaimed throughout the realm." The English nobility saw in the leadership of a strong prince, who trusted them and sought their counsel, the best guarantee of their privileges and just rights. So did a young and vigorous rustic knighthood and a nascent merchant community. Hereditary succession was acclaimed in place of the older expedient of election, while election itself was to be superseded by parliamentary counsel as the permanent expression of a monarchical nation's will.

Chapter Twelve

MERRY ENGLAND

England is a strong land and a sturdy, and the pleasantest
corner of the world . . . England is full of mirth and game,
free men of heart and with tongue, but the hand is better
and more free than the tongue.
Bartholomew Anglicus

The England to whose throne Edward I had succeeded
rested on the labour of some nine thousand scattered agricultural
communities. The basis of its polity and of all its artistry, fine
taste and craftsmanship was the native clearing—Anglo-Saxon,
Danish or Celtic—in the wild, and Piers Plowman in the "field
full of folk" raising food for all. The head of the village was its
French-speaking lord, resident or absentee, with his *manoir*
or manor court to which every villager owed suit. Its pastor was
the parish priest with his church, to which everyone repaired
for communal worship on sabbath and feast-days and for all
the important occasions of life. But its hard core, and that of
England's economy, was the husbandman. In Kent and the
Danelaw, and the pastoral west and north, he was more often
than not a free man, owning the land he tilled and able to sell it.
In the south and midlands a majority of cultivators were villeins:
men tied to the soil.[1] They went with it and could not leave it
without its lord's consent. They were not, legally speaking, slaves,
for they could not be bought or sold as individuals but only with
the land they cultivated. Nor, so long as they paid the feudal
dues and tithes with which it was charged, could they be de-

[1] According to Professor G. O. Sayles, in a proportion of about six to four.
Medieval Foundations of England, 433.

prived of its fruits. At a time when there was more land in England than labour to work it they were indispensable. They held it by hereditary tenure of "fork and flail."

Personal slavery, in the old Roman sense, existed in England by now only on a very small scale. Both the Church and the Norman kings had set their faces against it, and by Edward I's reign it was almost extinct. Yet a villein, or serf as he was called, was far from free. If he or his children left the manor they could be brought back to it in chains on proof of villeinage in the royal courts. Their service was "in the blood." The only legal escape was by public manumission, by entry into the church—for which the lord's agreement was necessary—or by residence for a year and a day in a chartered borough.

There were many types of villein. They ranged from substantial farmers, employing other men's services and commuting for their own by money payments, to humble cottars and bordars holding only a few acres and supplementing their yield by working three or four days a week on their neighbours' land for wages. The average villein-holding was a yardland or virgate of thirty acres. For this a man had to till the lord's land with his own implements, personally or by deputy, for two or three days a week, perform cartage or carrying duties, give additional "boon" services at the spring and autumn sowings, harvest-time, hay-making and sheep-shearing, and render on special days a seasonal tribute of farm-produce, like the Easter eggs which still appear on our children's plates. Thus in the Black Book of Peterborough forty villeins at Kettering, each holding around thirty acres, are shown as having to plough with their own plough-teams 88 acres for the abbey. Every man owed three days' work a week on the abbey's land and contributed to it 50 hens, 640 eggs and 2s. 1½d. a year in cash—a sum worth perhaps sixty or seventy times that amount in present-day values. As money became more generally used, services on the smaller estates—though seldom on the larger arable ones—were increasingly commuted for "fines" or cash payments. In a survey of Martham at the end of the thirteenth century Thomas Knight held twelve acres in villeinage, paid 16d for it and 14d in special aids. "He shall do," it was stated, "sixteen working days in August and for every day he shall have one repast—viz. bread and fish. He shall hoe ten days without the lord's food—price of a day ½d. He shall cart to Norwich six cartings or shall give 9d, and he shall have

for every carting one leaf and one lagena—or gallon—of ale. Also
for ditching 1d. He shall make for malt 3½ seams of barley or
shall give 6d. Also he shall flail for twelve days or give 12d. He
shall plough if he has his own plough, and for every ploughing
he shall have three loaves and nine herrings. . . . For carting
manure he shall give 2d." These arrangements, which varied
from manor to manor, were supervised by the lord's bailiff and
by an elected representative of the villeins called the reeve who
directed the common husbandry. The larger the holding, the
greater the services demanded of it. A poor cottar with four
or five acres might owe only a single day's labour a week.

Though, like all holders of land, a villein had to pay tallages
and aids to his lord, such as the *merchet* on his daughter's
marriage, he enjoyed the usual hereditary rights of feudal
tenure. On payment of a *heriot* of the best beast on his holding,
his heir was entitled to succeed to it. Nor were the "boons" he
proffered to his lord wholly one-way. Attached to his services
were certain customary privileges, like the haymakers' right at
Borley in Essex to receive for every load of hay three quarters
of wheat, a pat of butter and a piece of cheese of the second
sort from the lord's dairy, the morning milk from the cows,
salt and oatmeal for a stew, and as much hay as each man could
lift on the point of his scythe. A sower was usually entitled to
a basketful of any seed he sowed, a cowherd to the first seven
days' milk of every cow after calving, a shepherd to twelve nights'
dung from the folds at Christmas and a bowl of whey or butter-
milk during the summer.

What distinguished villein service from the higher feudal
tenures was that it was menial and "servile." To the extent
of the time for which his service was due, the serf was at the
disposal of the lord and his bailiff. He was not his own master
and, as Bracton wrote, legally speaking did not know in the
evening what he should do on the morrow. The stigma in his
status was that he was not, in the old English phrase, "law-
worthy." He could not defend his person or property in the
royal courts or claim a freeman's right to be tried by his equals,
though gradually, as the power of the Common Law grew, he
received from it protection of life and limb and of the tools of
his labour.

Yet the rule of the royal courts was comparatively new.
They were not the only source of protection from violence and

injustice. There were other and older courts to which a man could resort. The manor court or moot belonged to the lord; its jurisdiction and fines were among the most valuable of feudal rights. It was presided over by his seneschal or steward and met once a fortnight in his hall or outhouse,[2] or in summer under the village oak-tree. But it was open to the whole village, and the assessors or jurymen who stated the local customs on which its judgments were based, and which formed the law of the manor, were the tenants who owed it suit. Those customs were handed down from father to son and recorded on the court rolls. They expressed the common experience and conscience of the neighbourhood. Nor was it easy for even the most powerful lord to ignore the custom of those on whose labour and skill he depended. Like the Great Council of tenants-in-chief, who made a tyrant king promise to observe ancient law and govern with the consent of his chief men, the manor-court was the means by which, little by little, the English community, often in the teeth of tyrannical encroachment, preserved and extended its rights.

In such courts, in thousands of villages up and down England, justice was done between man and man; offences against manorial custom were punished, and the services and rights of the villein-tenant enforced and recorded. On its rolls were entered the exact terms of tenure under which he held his land. In time copies of these entries came to be regarded as title to his holding. It gradually became customary to claim possession of land by "copyhold" or hall meeting, a form of tenure which was later recognised, as the villein acquired full legal rights, by the king's judges.

Service in the manor-courts helped to train humble Englishmen for a free system of society. It taught them to weigh evidence and distinguish between personal feelings and public needs. "Richard Smith" ran the entry of a court leet in 1311, "beat Alice Hannes twice—Mercy, Order, Poor." The village jury, that is, found him guilty and recommended him to the mercy of the court, which ordered a fine but remitted part of it because he could not afford it. In his everyday task of helping to administer a little corner of the realm of which he was part, the English peasant learnt to blend legal precision with human

---

[2] It was often called a *halimote*.

give-and-take. The village halimote, which dealt with cases of trespass, neglect of manorial duties, and offences against the village peace, and which twice a year became a police-court to try crimes short of felony presented by a jury, had its formal pleadings like a royal court. A thirteenth century book, written to enable stewards and bailiffs to know their business, gives such typical examples as,

"Alice, widow of, ... , complaineth of . . . . , her neighbour, that on such a day his pigs entered her garden and rooted up her beans and cabbages, so that she would not willingly have had that damage for 2s nor that shame for 12d. and she demandeth that amends be made."[3]

In manorial court-rolls of Henry III's reign we find such entries as, from Ruislip, Middlesex—

"Hugh Tree is in mercy for cattle of his taken in the lord's garden. Pledges: Walter of Hull and William Slipper. Fine 6d.";

from Tooting, Surrey—

"Elias of Streatham is in default of autumn labour service. Fine 6d.";

from Ogbourne, Wiltshire—

"Adam Moses gives half a sester of wine to have an inquest as to whether Henry Ayulf imputed to him the crime of larceny and used vile and insulting words. Later they came to an agreement, and Henry gives security for amercement. Fine 12d."[4]

An English village was responsible to the king's sheriff for preserving the peace within its boundaries, and could be collectively fined for any crimes committed in it. It had its stocks, cucking-stool—for scolding wives—and pillory. Its priest, reeve and "four lawful men" represented it at the hundred court and at coroner's inquests, and presented to the royal authorities those suspected of felony. It had to find a nightly watch and ward from a rota of householders and apprehend all suspicious travellers

---

[3] F. W. Maitland, *The Court Baron* (Selden Society), 75.
[4] F. W. Maitland, *Select Pleas in Manorial Courts*, transl. from the Latin by C. Stephenson and F. G. Marcham, *Sources of English Constitutional History*, 187–9.

after nightfall. "If any such passing strangers do not allow themselves to be arrested," ran an ordinance of Henry III, "then the watch shall raise the hue upon them on all sides, and pursue them with the whole township and neighbouring township with hue and cry from township to township until they are taken!"

The manorial system of cultivation was communal, though ownership was individual. In the Celtic and pastoral west scattered homesteads and hamlets, small unified holdings and little stone-walled fields were the rule. But in the flat, clayey Midlands and the south, where corn-growing was the principal activity, the arable land around the village was grouped in two, or, in the better farmed manors, three fields, according as to whether a two or three year rotation of crops was followed. These open fields, fenced against the cattle in the summer, were often several hundred acres in extent and far larger than any to be seen today save in a few places like Laxton. They were divided, without hedges, into vast numbers of narrow, curving strips like elongated Ss, each a furlong or ox-plough-furrow's length. Between the strips were narrow ridges made by the ploughs. As the course of husbandry was the same for all and enforced by the manor court, every villager had so many strips in each field, according to the size of his holding. In some villages the lord's land, called the demesne, and sometimes the parson's glebe land, were enclosed; in others they were scattered about the open fields, where their cultivation, like everyone else's, had to conform to the common rule. The crops were wheat, rye—often used for the bread of the poor, though much less so in England than on the continent—barley, oats, vetches and peas. They were threshed on the barn floors by flails cut from holly or thorn, and winnowed by hand. The wooden ploughs were usually drawn by teams of eight oxen. As few could afford a whole plough-team, they were shared. The normal arrangement was a team to every four yardlands, the hide— approximately 120 acres—being the measure, though it varied widely, of what an eight-ox team could plough in a year.

In addition to the arable there was the meadow lying beside stream or river and tended by the village hayward. Here, too, every peasant had his strip or strips. When the hay had been

cut the village cattle were pastured on it, and after the harvest—
from Lammas to Candlemas—on the arable stubble, which they
helped to dung. They were very small and scraggy, for, under
such a communal system of grazing, selective breeding was
very difficult. As there was little winter-feed—for root crops
were unknown—they were mostly slaughtered and salted at
Michaelmas. A few stalled cows[5] and the breeding stock struggled through the winter till the spring.

Beyond the fields and meadow was the waste—forest, moorland, swamp and brackeny common—still covering more than
half the country and surrounding the lonely villages like the sea.
The lord of the manor might own the soil, but his tenants
enjoyed the common use of its rough grasses and herbage for
pasture and of its turf and brushwood for fuel. Every holding
carried a right or "stint" to feed so many cattle, horses, geese
and swine on the waste, and to take, "by hook or crook," sticks,
fallen timber and loose bracken for litter, sand and clay for
building, nuts and berries, rabbits and small birds for the pot.
The adjoining woods were full of the villagers' thin, half-wild
pigs feeding on beech-mast and acorns. They also abounded
in game and, in the wilder parts of the country, with robbers
and outlaws, and occasionally with wolves.[6]

The life which such a system supported was very simple.
There was little scope for initiative or progress, and the pace
was that of the slowest and least enterprising. The cottages
straggling along either side of the unpaved village street and
flanked by heaps of manure—the peasant's principal wealth—
were mere rectangular-shaped cabins of timber-framing, filled
in with wattle, turf and mud and thatched with straw or reeds.
They contained usually a single unfloored, hearthless room in
which the family slept with the oxen stalled at the bed's foot,
pigs roaming the floor and poultry perched on the beams. The
only household goods would be a straw mattress or sack, a few
cooking-pots, some home-made tools and, in the homes of the

[5] The winter milk-yield was less than a quarter that of the summer. A. L.
Poole, *Domesday Book to Magna Carta*, 52. In wooded districts ivy would sometimes be cut during the winter from the trees and the cattle summoned to it by
horn.

[6] These were dying out in the south. King John gave 15 shillings—a vast sum—
to a huntsman for killing two near Gillingham in Dorset in 1210. But in Wales
more than a century later a drowned royal messenger was presumed to have been
eaten by wolves.

richer villeins, a rude oak chest and perhaps a stool or two.[7] Behind the houses were little closes, growing cabbage, parsley, onions, leek, garlic, herbs, apples and quinces. Their owners' clothes were of coarse, greasy wool and leather, unwashed and unwashable, made from their own beasts. Their diet was of cheese, bacon and, in the summer, milk; bean and vegetable broth; oaten cakes and rough, black wholemeal bread; herrings or other salt-fish, honey from their own hives, and small ale or cider. Its staple was cereal; a thirteenth century English agricultural writer reckoned the labourer's average allowance of corn at 36 bushels a year. Butcher's meat was a rare luxury. In Lent everyone fasted, not only because the Church enjoined it, but because, with the harvest so far away, there was no alternative. "Fridays and fast-days," wrote a later poet, "a penny's worth of mussels were a feast for such folks."

Though the village, especially on the large monastic and baronial estates, by now exported much of what it grew for cash-sales to the towns or to feed and finance some distant lord, it still supplied nearly all its own wants except for salt and iron brought by travelling chapmen. It spun and wove wool for clothes from its own sheep, and linen from its own flax. It made shoes from its own wood or skins. It had a miller—a tenant of the lord and usually the richest man in the place, for every villein had to have his corn ground by him[8]—a smith, a wheelwright and a millwright, a tiler and thatcher, a shoemaker and tanner, a carpenter, wainwright and carter. Their callings, and those of the parish agricultural officers, survive in our names: Shepherd and Foster, Carter and Baker, Parker, Fowler and Hunter; Wolf and Forester; Smith, Cooper and Carpenter. So do the country places, buildings and beasts among which they spent their skilful, laborious lives: Field, Pitt and Fox, Lane, Bridge and Ford, Stone and Burn, Church and Hill, Brook and Green,

---

[7] The inventory of a peasant's tools taken in 1301 consisted of a hoe, spade, axe, billhook, two yokes for carrying buckets and a barrel. G. G. Coulton, *Medieval Village*, 101. A peasant Christ surrounded by his tools can be seen on a fourteenth century wall-painting in Hesset church, Suffolk, and another with a halo made of them at Ampney St. Mary, Gloucestershire.

[8] "Suit of mill" was a most jealously-guarded monopoly, as a passage in the life of Abbot Samson of Bury reveals. "Herbert the dean built a windmill at Haberdon. When the abbot heard this he was so wroth that he could hardly eat or speak a single word. 'By the face of God,' he said, 'I will never eat meat until that building is overturned . . . Nor is this without harm to my mills as you pretend, for the burghers go to your mill and grind their corn at your pleasure, and I cannot hinder them since they are free men.'" Jocelin of Brakelond, 75.

Lamb, Bull and Hogg, Sparrow, Crow and Swan. Other men
were called after the masters they served—King, Bishop, Abbot,
Dean, Prior, Knight, Squire—or after their own appearance—
Black, Brown and White, Short, Round and Long. To an English
ear there is poetry in these homely names, hallowed by history
and association, and in the Christian names which also became
transmitted from father to son: John, James, Robin, William,
Richard, Dick; Johnson, Jamieson, Robinson, Williamson, Rich-
ardson, Dickson.[9]

Book education for the husbandman there was none. Few
could read, nor was there opportunity for doing so. There were
no printed books—only the priceless, laboriously-copied, jealously-
hoarded manuscripts of the monastery libraries, larger parish
churches and the very rich. The peasant's hours of labour were
long, and when daylight failed wax candles were far beyond
his reach: his sole illumination was a feeble rushlight dipped in
fat. There was no travel for him, unless his cart was requisitioned for some baronial or royal service, for the vast majority
of villagers never left home.

Yet he was not a wholly uncultivated man. From his father
and the fields in which he worked he learnt a knowledge of
nature's laws. He learnt, too, from his earliest years to look
after animals and to take pride in his hereditary work as husbandman or craftsman. Nor did he live by plough or adze alone;
he was partaker in a Faith and a civilisation. If he would not
read, he could see and he could hear. The bold, brightly coloured
and beautifully fashioned images and paintings that covered
the walls and, later, the windows of his parish church; the moving
music and ritual which he enjoyed from childhood; the familiar
legends and parables of the Christian legend linked him with
the whole invisible, yet ever-present culture of Christendom.
Its festivals, which were his days of rejoicing, gave him, it was
reckoned, something like eight weeks' holiday in a year. Deeper
than the servile divisions of class, the harsh bonds of status, the
grinding poverty and squalor of the peasant's lot, the unity and
consolation of the Christian faith sustained him and gave his
life meaning.

The cold dark winters in the wild northern landscape must

[9] So, too, across the Welsh border, John ap Harri became John Parry.

often have seemed very lonely and comfortless. It is no wonder that men suffered from superstitious fears and were haunted by ghosts and witches and demons. They must often, too, have been hungry. When the harvest failed, famine followed, and, in its train, pestilence, haunting the noisome ditches and in-sanitary hovels. Yet at the darkest hour of the long northern night, rich and poor, old and young, celebrated the beginning of things and the mystery of Christmas. The interminable proces-sion of days in rain-sodden or frozen fields, with bare trees and grey, colourless skies, and the nights of shivering in draughty hovels, was broken by the sweet, wintry festival of Christ's birth, with its bright fires, lighted windows and good fare. It came just when it was most needed and broke the winter into two halves, each bearable for the hope of the Christian feast that ended the one and the coming of spring that ended the other. Soon after it the first lambs were born and the earliest primroses appeared in fields made rigid by bitter winds. When everything was at its bleakest, a light was lit in darkness.

To look down on England during the second half of the thirteenth century would have been to see a country in process of change. The wild woodlands of Allerdale, Sherwood and Lonsdale, Cannock and Dean, Rockingham and Salcey, Bern-wood, Epping and Windsor, Selwood and Alice Holt still covered an immense area. But they were shrinking fast. With the growth of population, both on the continent and in England, prices were rising and the nation's economy expanding. Despite the stubborn conservatism of the open-field peasants, the larger proprietors, including the monasteries, were nibbling into forest and fen, common and moor, and using the ground so gained to make new experiments in husbandry. In Henry III's reign an Englishman named Walter of Henley, who had been a bailiff,[10] wrote the most important agricultural treatise of the Middle Ages. Marling and composting, careful estate-management, ex-perimentation with seeds, a liberal use of manured straw, and improved breeding of livestock were the pillars of the new de-mesne farming. Corn, bought by travelling middlemen from the villages as well as the larger estates, was being regularly exported from south-eastern England to feed the cloth-towns of the

[10] We know this from a phrase in his book: "When I was bailiff the dairymaids had the geese and hens to farm, the geese at 12d and the hens at 3d."

Low Countries; so was bacon from East Anglia. And on the open downs from Dorset to Yorkshire and from Cambridgeshire to South Wales, the flocks of the gentry and yeomen and, above all, of the white-robed Cistercians, were giving the upland grass the vivid green that is the hall-mark of the folded sheep. Even Richard I's ransom had been paid mainly in woolsacks. In the middle of Henry III's reign the bishop of Winchester owned 29,000 sheep, while the humble villagers of South Domerton in Wiltshire alone kept nearly 4000. The average annual export of wool was reckoned at about seven million pounds a year.[11] The clothiers of Ghent, Arras, Ypres, Bruges and Mechlin could not have enough of England's fine fleeces. Their export was making her a richer land than she had ever been before. Everywhere in the plains and valleys, and even in the stony folds of the limestone and chalk hills, bright new stone churches, with belfries or spires, and great barns of stone and timber were rising to show that the villages and little market burghs of the Anglo-Saxon past were centres of a proud and conscious culture.

Linking them and bridging the uncultivated wild between, the winding green roads were trodden by ever-growing numbers of men and horses. Though still the basis of the country's road-system, the great metalled highways with which Rome had spanned southern Britain had by now become little more than a ghostly network. Their paved surfaces had vanished, their cause-ways been broken in innumerable places for quarrying, and their course deflected to serve local needs. The medieval road did not run straight from capital to capital. It meandered round field, park and pale, respecting a thousand local "liberties" and quirks of history, from one little market town and village to another. It was not surfaced for wheeled traffic or swift travel-ling. It was a mere grassy trackway for horses, light carts, cattle and sheep, with the brushwood cut back, by an ordinance of Edward I, for a couple of hundred feet on either side to prevent ambushes. It was not so much a road as a route over which travellers had a right to pass.

Where there was a national highway subject to the king's peace, the proprietors along its course were under an obliga-tion to keep it open. No one might raise fences across it or dung-heaps or use it for quarrying stone or gravel. Towns and vil-

[11] *Cambridge Economic History of Europe* II, 126.

lages which permitted such encroachments were constantly being fined. In winter, in the clay lowlands, these soft roads became quagmires; in summer a maze of hard-baked hoof-holes and ruts. But so much of the countryside was still waste that it was easy to make a detour across adjoining land. This, however, created a multiplicity of tracks and made it equally easy to lose the way. There are records of travellers on Watling Street finding themselves as far off as Buckingham to the west or Newport Pagnell to the east. Travel was still arduous and dangerous. The Church in its prayers grouped travellers with prisoners and captives, sick persons and women labouring with child. The repair of roads and bridges and the provision of hospitality for wayfarers were regarded as the concern of the Church and Christian charity even more than of the State. Crosses were erected by the wayside in lonely places, lanterns kept burning in church-towers at night, and bells sounded to guide benighted wayfarers. Rich men left sums to provide rest-houses and *maisons dieu,* and monasteries and incumbents of rectories were enjoined to entertain and relieve travellers.

The lords of the highway, as of everywhere else in that intensely aristocratic age, were the earls, barons and prelates, with their immense trains of followers, their armour, ceremonial furs and emblazoned mantles and banners,[12] making their way to Council or Parliament, or travelling from one estate to another. The greatest of all was the king and his Court. In a single half year Edward I moved his residence seventy-five times. In days when there were no regular posts or means of transmitting news, it was the only way in which a ruler could keep himself abreast with what was happening in his kingdom. The grander members of the Court travelled on horseback, the vast army of menials, scullions and poor suitors on foot. Its treasure, plate, pavilions, hangings, beds, cooking-utensils, wine, and legal and financial rolls were borne in panniers on pack-horses or in rough, box-like, two-wheeled carts, drawn by oxen, donkeys or dogs and requisitioned in vast numbers from the countryside. It was on a country dung-cart that William Rufus's body had been carried, dripping blood, from the New Forest to Winchester. A few great ladies—a queen or some royal invalid—might ride in a litter borne between horses or in a gilded waggon with an

---

[12] A main royal highway like Watling Street, Ermine Street or the Fosseway had to be wide enough for sixteen armed knights to ride abreast. Poole, 78.

arched roof hung with tapestry and suspended on carved, unsprung beams and huge nailed wheels. But the normal mode of transport was the cavalcade: the long procession of jingling, brightly-accoutred, splendidly-caparisoned horses, with riders chattering or singing as they wound their way across the fields. To journey in company and make music as one went was the mode of the time. Only the king's messengers, forerunners of the post, travelled alone, and lepers with their bells and clappers, sores and pallid, hooded faces, and adjured felons making their way from sanctuary to the nearest port with bare feet and loose white tunics and wooden crosses as signs of the Church's protection.

The chief interest of the age being religion, there were many clerical travellers. There were monastic officers visiting their estates and busy archdeacons nosing out moral offences punishable in Church courts, pardoners selling indulgences for sin, summoners with writs for breaches of ecclesiastical law, papal agents collecting money, and poor clerks on their way to the universities. These were the religious professionals; others were amateurs. Every spring companies of pilgrims set out, with wallet, staff and scallop shell, and bagpipe and jangling Canterbury bell, to visit some distant or local shrine and return afterwards with relics—for the rich a splinter from a saint's staff or a flask of holy-water, and, for ordinary folk, a souvenir pewter-badge to be worn on cap or breast. Many sought cures; more were holiday-makers, travelling partly in piety and partly in the mood that takes their successors to Blackpool or Stratford-on-Avon. A few exceptionally pious or wealthy did not confine themselves to England but crossed the seas to visit some famous international shrine like St. James's of Compostella in Spain, Rome itself or even the Holy Land.

The most celebrated English places of pilgrimage were St. Thomas's shrine at Canterbury—the word "canter" entered our speech through it—and Our Lady's statue at Walsingham in Norfolk, with its famous phial of the Virgin's milk, "the most holy name in England." Both were visited every summer by immense crowds. So were St. Joseph of Arimathaea's winter-blossoming thorn at Glastonbury, the philtre of Christ's blood at Richard of Cornwall's new abbey of Hayles in Gloucestershire, and the Confessor's glittering shrine in Westminster Abbey, where the hollows worn by the feet of kneeling pilgrims can still be seen. The routes to these were lined with chapels, inns, stables for hiring horses, cells where hermits besought alms, and hostels like the gild-house at Coventry where a poor woman was kept to wash the pilgrims' feet.

Hundreds of lesser places of pilgrimage were scattered about the island. Such was the holy well of Master John Schorne at North Marston in Buckinghamshire, a poor country parson who, being visited by the Devil, cunningly lured him beyond the altar-rails and conjured him into a boot. A mechanical replica of the miracle re-enacted it daily before the eyes of pilgrims, and small wooden reproductions, said to be good for gout, were sold by the shrine's custodians, becoming forerunners of the child's toy, the Jack-in-the-Box. It was symptomatic both of the simple credulity of the age and the isolation of one part of England from another that villages in Norfolk, Suffolk, Devonshire and even Northumberland all claimed and commemorated the same saint and incident.

The most cautious road-users were those who travelled with merchandise or money, for the woods and thickets were full of thieves. In the early Middle Ages the main roads, especially those to the southern and eastern ports, were much used by foreigners—Flemings and Italians buying Cotswold or York-shire wool, Spaniards with fine steel blades from Toledo, Lombards with silks and spices, Easterlings with furs and tar from the Baltic. But by the end of the thirteenth century their trade was beginning to pass to Englishmen. As there were no posts and few facilities for transferring money from one country to another, a merchant had constantly to be on the road attending his business. Like the poor man in Chaucer's tale who was deceived by his wife and the young monk, he was always off to Bruges or Bordeaux at break of day.

Humbler traders like pedlars, chapmen and charcoal-sellers went on foot, with their wares on a pack-horse or in a box or sack on their backs. So did a host of poor itinerants, travelling from one village to another: minstrels, buffoons and ballad-singers, some aiming high at the castles and others at gaping rustics on the village greens; bears and bearwards; men with performing monkeys; clowns, jugglers, girls who danced on their hands with swords in their mouths, and herbalists selling panaceas for every disease. There is a picture of one of these in a thirteenth century herbal-book, spreading his wares on his carpet or drugget and haranguing the villagers:

"My good friends, I am not one of those poor preachers, nor one of those poor herbalists who stand in front of the churches with their miserable ill-sewn cloak, who carry bags and boxes and spread out a carpet. Know that I am not one of those; but I belong to a lady who is named Madam Trote of Salerno . . . . the wisest lady in all the world. . . . . And because she made me swear by the saints when I parted from her, I will teach you the proper cure for worms if you will listen. Will you listen? Take off your caps, give ear, look at my herbs which my lady sends into this land and country. . . . These herbs, you will not eat them; for there is no ox in this country, no charger, be he never so strong, which, if he had a bit the size of a pea upon his tongue, would not die a hard death, they are so strong and bitter. . . . . . You will put them three days to steep in good white wine; if you have no white take red, if you have no red wine take fine clear water, for many a man has a well before his door who has not a cask of wine in his cellar. If you breakfast from it for thirteen mornings you will be cured of your various maladies."[13]

At certain times of the year the roads became crowded with travellers converging on a single spot. Fairs were occasions before villages had shops, when a rural neighbourhood did its shopping and caught a glimpse of the outer world. The greatest fair in England was Stourbridge near Cambridge. Here for three weeks every September a town of wooden booths offered for sale everything a rustic community needed. There were streets that sold soap, streets that sold garlic, streets that sold coal. Others vended fish, nails, grindstones, Sussex iron and Worcestershire salt, shovels, brushes and pails, oil and honey, pots and pans, horses and pack-saddles. The most important place in the fair was the duddery, where the "duds" or cloths of East Anglia were displayed. Among those who brought their wares were Spaniards and Moors with Damascus blades and armour, Venetians with gems and velvets, Flemings with linen, Dutchmen with cheeses, Greeks with almonds and spices, and Easterlings with tallow, fur, and pitch. A special court of *Pied Poudré* or "dusty foot"—called by the English Pie Powder—was held to

[13] Rutebeuf, cit. J. Jusserand, *English Wayfaring in the Middle Ages* (transl. L. Toulmin Smith), 178–9.

preserve order and enforce the regulations of the fair's owners about weights and measures and the quality of foodstuffs. In the jovial mode of England the fair also provided horse-races, wrestling-matches, tippling, gambling and music booths, rope-dancers and a maypole.

Other famous fairs were St. Bartholomew's in Smithfield and St. Giles's on the hillside at Winchester, St. Frideswide's at Oxford and St. Audrey's at Ely, whose tinselly wares gave the word tawdry to the language. They were a great source of revenue to their ecclesiastical proprietors. St. Botolph's at Boston, and St. Ives in Huntingdonshire, St. George's at Modbury, the Barnet horse and the Abingdon cattle fair were all famous far beyond their locality. So was Woodbury hill in Dorset, with its five days—Wholesale, Gentlefolks', Allfolks', Sheep Fair, and Pack-and-Penny. But the number of fairs was legion; in Somerset alone there were nearly a hundred.

What fairs were temporarily, towns were permanently. But, though in that age of expanding economy the door of opportunity was still open to the newcomer, they were much more exclusively regulated. Control of the hours of dealing, of prices, weights and measures, and of the quality of goods sold, was delegated by royal or baronial charter to their corporations and, often, to associations of their licensed traders. These merchant-gilds were empowered to fix wages and prices fair to both buyer and seller, to take advantage of any quit-tolls granted by the Crown in an age when countless private toll-barriers impeded the trader along every road and river,[14] to exclude non-members from trading in the town, and to fine and punish for breaches of their rules. They appointed the hours announced by bell, for the opening and closing of markets, and levied tolls on all goods brought for sale. They also made treaties, interchanging commercial privileges, with the traders of other towns. In a few of the larger cities, like London, Norwich and York, separate gilds, too, of craftsmen already existed—weavers, fullers, cordwainers, saddlers, loriners and goldsmiths.

Like the juries of the villages, these self-governing corporations trained Englishmen for political responsibility. They were administered by voluntary officers elected annually, whose duties were borne by the members in turn, and governed by rules

[14] Thanks to the power of her kings England, however, was by far the freest internal trading area in Europe.

reached after mutual and open discussion. A common code of
conduct was agreed, to which all were party and all responsible.
Members were punished for selling inferior goods, for sharp or
shoddy practices that lowered the name of their craft, for brawling and eavesdropping and breaches of social and professional
etiquette. A trader who sold food made from diseased carcasses,
who put sand in his bread or water in his wine or otherwise
tricked the public, was sentenced by his fellow craftsmen to be
drawn through the streets on a hurdle or to sit in penance in the
pillory with the offending goods hung round his neck and his
crime published on a placard. "The said John Penrose," ran the
order of a London court, "shall drink a draught of the same
wine which he sold to the common people, and the remainder
of such wine shall then be poured on the head of the same
John, and he shall forswear the calling of a vintner in the city of
London for ever unless he can obtain the favour of our lord the
king as to the same."[15]

Every English town with the possible exception of London,
had grown out of a village. Its institutions had a rustic origin:
the borough and ward officers with agricultural names, like the
pound-keeper at Canterbury, the moot that had begun as a
manorial jurisdiction, and the burghmote horn that summoned
the burghers to its meetings; the annual perambulation of the
bounds when the city fathers, like their village forbears, solemnly beat the young fry over the boundary-stones to make
them remember where they stood.

The sanitary arrangements of the borough also derived from
the village. Such drains as it had, ran down the unpaved or, at
best, cobbled roadways. The household refuse and ordure,
thrown out of the windows at nightfall, were scavenged by
pigs, dogs and kites. Even in London, where the poorer dwell-
ings were totally without privies, there was only one latrine for
every ward and a dozen dung-carts for the whole city. The
larger the towns grew, the more unwholesome they became,
though, after a time their corporations, alarmed at the rising
death-rate, began to issue regulations about street cleansing and
water supply.

[15] G. G. Coulton, *Medieval Panorama* 303, who also cites the case of John Rus-
sell of Billingsgate, "who was put in the pillory for exposing 37 pigeons for sale,
putrid, rotten, stinking, and abominable to the human race, to the scandal, contempt and disgrace of all the City."

Yet though the towns were dirty, they were also beautiful, with their church towers and spires, their stately gateways and wide market-places, the fine new stone and half-timbered houses of the well-to-do, and the trees and blossom of their gardens. Their encircling walls were designed more for preventing robberies and controlling suspicious travellers at night than for war. Except on the Welsh and Scottish borders they were seldom the elaborate affairs of the ever-warring continent, where even the smallest town was heavily fortified. Some of the later boroughs, like Cambridge, never even had walls, but only palisades and ditches crossed by gated bridges. Being in little danger of attack, they were free from the military restrictions that cramped life for European burghers. They did not need governors and garrisons.

For this reason, too, they spread outwards rather than upwards, running to leafy suburbs that, secure in England's immunity from invasion, nestled outside instead of inside the walls. Yet, as no English town save London had more than 10,000 inhabitants and few a third of this number, the fields were never far away. Most of the richer merchants had farms or orchards in the surrounding country-side, as well as gardens, stables and cow-stalls round their houses. English urban economy was as much rural as urban. Even the great city of Norwich, capital of the clothmaking industry of East Anglia and the second largest in England, suspended trade during the harvest and sent its weavers into the fields.

The first sight the traveller had of a medieval town was its towers and spires on the horizon, with, perhaps, a castle on higher ground. Boundary stones beside the highroad marked the beginning of its land—the arable strips of the "town field" with hired labourers working on them, and the great meadow along the river where the cattle grazed under the municipal cowherds. Entry was through a stone archway and a vast wooden gate, closed from sundown to sunrise by a porter who collected the corporation's tolls. The streets were narrow and winding, with upper stories overhanging the cobbled roadways till they almost touched. From them gilded signs swung and creaked in the wind,[16] while apprentices bawled out the wares set out on the benches before the open doors. Through these could be seen

---

[16] They had by law to be nine feet above the street level to enable a horseman to pass beneath.

journeymen working at their trade. The shouting was terrific, the hoofs and iron-rimmed wheels on the cobblestones made a perpetual hammering, and the bells of the churches and monasteries kept pealing and chiming. The stink, too, was overwhelming, especially in the streets occupied by tanners and butchers. For mutual protection and co-operation all the bakers and cook-shops tended to be in one street,[17] the mercers in another, the goldsmiths, shoemakers or saddlers in another. Leading out of them were narrow alleys giving on to stables and laystalls and the fetid, tumbledown hovels of the poorer artisans and labourers.

In the centre of the town were the fine stone houses of the richer citizens, the guildhall with its belfry-tower, and the market-place—a square or broad street, like modern Oxford's Cornmarket, with a cross where the town-crier made public announcements with bell or horn. Here, too, were the stocks, where offenders were pelted with filth and rotten fruit, and the ducking-stool for scandal-mongers. On market days the surrounding country-side poured in to sell its produce, doubling the population for a few noisy hours and filling the cookhouses and taverns.

One town in England stood by itself. London, with her "square mile" along the Thames between the Tower and Ludgate, was still much smaller than the great continental cities of Bruges, Milan and Florence, and only about a third the size of Paris. Yet it was by far the country's largest town, with by Edward I's reign, some 50,000 inhabitants. Newcomers were all the time being drawn to it by the commerce that flowed up its tidal river, and by the royal courts at Westminster two miles away. Already the Strand, the highway between the two places, was lined with nobles' and prelates' palaces whose gardens sloped down to the unembanked Thames. The king, unlike his cousin of France, had no palace in his capital—only the Tower on its eastern wall with a garrison of a few hundred men-at-arms.

For the City was a law to itself. "Come what may," ran an old saying, "the Londoners should have no king but their mayor." This functionary, who, though only a merchant, had taken his place at Runnymede among the twenty-five greatest magnates of the realm, ruled the capital with the help of two

[17] In Cambridge to this day one of the principal streets is called Petty Cury or little cookery.

sheriffs, elected annually like himself, and a court of aldermen representing its twenty-five wards. Behind this court's weekly hustings in the Guildhall lay the general body of the corporation —the old folkmoot of the citizens assembled thrice a year by bell in the open air outside St. Paul's. With the population growing so fast, there was a constant tendency on the part of the less privileged to try to gain control of the city's government and oust the older merchant families who monopolised it—a struggle which resulted in frequent faction-fights and rioting. In the course of Edward I's reign this antiquated and by now unmanageable public assembly was abandoned in favour of an elected Common Council. Through its officers the corporation collected the royal customs on foreign merchandise and levied its own tolls on all goods coming in from the country. It made bye-laws on such matters as building, public order, the use of fountains, and precautions against fire. It decided who should have the right to trade in particular districts, where swine should be allowed to wander, when taverns should close and slops and refuse be emptied from the windows. It also fixed the hour of curfew, after which none with swords were allowed in the streets, "unless some great lord or other substantial person of good reputation."

London could be a very turbulent city. Behind its bridge and seven portcullised gateways crowded the warlike rabble of apprentices and journeymen who, when roused, became a terrible, raging beast. Almost the last sound Henry III heard as he lay dying at Westminster was the London mob shouting for its new mayor. Any infringement or supposed infringement of its rights brought it swarming through the narrow streets like a torrent. On one occasion much later, when some Hoxton residents enclosed a meadow where the Londoners had long taken their Sunday walks, a turner in a fool's coat ran through the streets crying, "Shovels and spades! Shovels and spades!", upon which the whole town turned out to level the hedges and ditches. The German merchants of the Cologne steelyard and the rich Italians of Galley Quay and Mincing Lane barricaded their houses against their English neighbours like fortresses.

Yet the beauty of medieval London impressed travellers even more than its turbulence. It was bordered on the south by a wide, clear river, teeming with fish and with swans on its waters.

Beyond it, save for the disorderly little suburb of Southwark, lay unsullied meadows and the wooded Surrey hills. To the north of the walls cornfields and pastures diversified with streams and water-mills, stretched to the heights of Hampstead and Highgate. To the east lay the great hunting forests of Epping and Hainault. All round were thriving villages supplying the city's needs—Stepney, Bethnal Green, Islington, Hoxton, Holborn, Marylebone, and, farther afield, Bow and Bromley, Hackney, Highbury and Stoke Newington, Kilburn, Paddington and Knightsbridge. Though, save for its immense cathedral on the hill and its famous twenty-arch bridge, crowned with houses, it lacked imposing buildings, the towers and spires of its hundred and fifty churches and monasteries made a wonderful show as they crowded above the walls and river. The sound of their bells was almost continuous and—since English bellfounders were the finest in Europe—of incomparable sweetness. And between the brightly painted wooden houses and red-tiled roofs were countless little gardens or "herbers" and orchards of waving fruit-trees—mulberry, apple, plum, peach and cherry.

The Londoners were not alone in their pride in their city's fame and beauty. All over England men were becoming conscious of the excellence of their native place and of a new-found patriotism. Even a century earlier Gerald of Wales had written of Manorbier in his beloved Pembrokeshire that it was the fairest spot, of the fairest district, of the fairest shire, of the fairest country in the world. And twelfth-century Jordan Fantosme had sung of East Anglia:

> "Who can tell me or who can mention
> A country from here to Montpellier which is worth
> That of Norfolk, of which you hear me speak,
> More honoured knights, nor more liberal,
> Nor more merry dames to give freely,
> Except in the city of London whose peer no one knows."[18]

These had written in Latin, but by now even educated men were beginning to think and feel and, on occasion, to write in English. It was no longer the formal, over-inflected tongue of

[18] A. L. Poole, *Domesday to Magna Carta*, 38.

the old Anglo-Saxon court, but a vigorous and expanding vernacular, constantly enriched with new words from Latin and French. The earliest English songs that have come down to us date from the second half of the thirteenth century:

> "Summer is i'cumen in
> Lude sing cuckoo!
> Groweth seed and bloweth mead
> And springeth the wood new————"

sung on the Berkshire downs in Henry III's reign, and

> "Between Mershe and Averil
> When spray beginneth to spring,
> The little fowl hath her will
> On high loud to sing."

in the time of his son.

It must have been a very beautiful England to inspire poets, with its clear rivers and great forests and the song of its innumerable birds. Its people were famed for their love of outdoor sports, of running, swimming and wrestling, of boxing and cudgelling. Their obsession with sport was already noticed by foreigners. During the Crusades the grave Saracens had been much shocked at the levity of the young English knights who set the Syrian countrywomen running races for greased pigs. The king and nobility were no more addicted to hunting, hawking and tournaments than the common people to tilting, football, cockfighting, quoits, hammer-throwing, baseball, cudgelling and quarterstaff. They delighted, too, in church-ales and dancing, singing and miming. In their traditional dances, the performers joined hands and accompanied one another in interminable verses or "carols" whose narrative they enacted.[19] By what they and their poets sang about we can tell what the men of the time loved. They sang of youthful longing—of the rustic swains dancing in the Worcestershire churchyards as they serenaded the maidens with the refrain, "Sweetheart have pity"; of the transitoriness of earthly beauty—

---

[19] A thirteenth century poem on Hugh of Lincoln describes the graceful marble shafts round the stone pillars of the cathedral as a *carole:* "these slender columns which stand round the great piers even as a bevy of maidens stand marshalled for a dance." G. G. Coulton, *Social Life in Britain from the Conquest to the Reformation,* 472.

"Where is Paris and Heleyne
That were so bright and fair of blee?"

of

"Lenten is come with love to town
With blossom and with briddes' round,"

of freedom and the spring and the green wood. We can see them
with their big bones and red faces: yeomen walking behind the
plough or riding bareback to mill to grind their corn; shepherds
on the hills at lambing and sheep-shearing, or driving their
flocks at dusk into great stone sheepcotes; foresters in green
jerkins with bows and arrows; bell-ringers, with the sweat gleaming on their foreheads, at their rhythmical, companionable
art; "spinsters" turning their wheels at open doors on summer
evenings. As the men gathered in the village drinking-houses they
raised their beakers to one another and called out, before draining them, the traditional greeting of their race, "Je bi a vu!" "I
drink to you!" It was a symbol of their unity and nationhood.

INDEX